PARTIES

PARTIES
The Real Opportunity for Effective Citizen Politics

*by John S. Saloma III
and Frederick H. Sontag*

Vintage Books
A Division of Random House, New York

*To the men and women of America—potentially
the most gifted politicians of them all*

Contents

Foreword by M. J. Rossant ix

Introduction by James MacGregor Burns xi

Genesis xv

Prologue Citizen Parties: A Revolutionary Goal for the 1970's 3

I Party Reform: A Movement Comes to Life 13

II The National Conventions: Apexes of Party Power 50

III The National Committees: Shadows or Substance? 92

IV The Congressional Parties: The Insulation of Power 120

V The Untapped Potential of State Parties 153

VI A New Motivation for Politics: The Ability to Govern 183

VII Citizens and the Parties: Can the Amateurs Play Politics? 217

VIII The Media: Information Brokers for Politics 246

IX   Political Consultants and
the Technology of the "New Politics"   280

X   Alternative Futures
for American Politics   314

XI   Strategy for the Seventies:
Investing in Party Politics   353

Action Guide   375

Outlook: Parties in Practice   391

Index   follows page 411

Foreword

Although the nation's political parties are accorded a great deal of public attention, particularly at election time, they remain relatively unknown institutions. For the focus, understandably, is on open party developments—candidates, issues, campaigns, and that quadrennial party spectacular, the national convention. Yet the workings of our political parties, i.e., the means by which representative government is elected and organized, are insufficiently understood by most voters and even by most party members. In this timely and useful book, John Saloma and Frederick Sontag have gone beyond the overt to provide a detailed, informative, often fascinating, and frequently provocative picture of what goes on backstage in political parties—both in election years and between them. In doing so, they have performed a service to everyone concerned about the political process in the United States.

But the authors are not intent only on enlightening the reader about what they consider to be the unsatisfactory state of the major political parties. Even more, they want to bring about a rejuvenation and a reopening of the parties, which they now describe as closed and largely unresponsive institutions. As reformers who fervently favor much broader public participation and involvement in politics, they also present a series of recommendations to transform the parties so that they may be much more accountable and representative.

Unquestionably their recommendations amount to an indictment of the parties as they now exist. But if some such overhaul is not undertaken, the authors are not at all sanguine about the future of political parties. Far from taking the position that the parties are moribund, they offer a wealth of evidence on the growing influence of technology and increasing use of professional consultants which suggests to them that the parties may become even more closed than they have been. In their view, politics and political parties are too important to be left solely to professional politicians. Because they believe that representative government depends on a thriving and open system of political parties, the proposals they put forward are designed to broaden and strengthen public participation in the art and practice of politics.

Party reform has been a recurrent theme in the nation's political history. The authors, who take note of recent reform efforts, are committed optimists over the prospects for further action, pointing out that more people are more able—in terms of knowledge and skills—than ever before to get involved effectively in the reform of our political institutions. They will be even better equipped after reading this book.

Obviously, then, the future of political parties will in large measure be decided by what citizens are willing to do about them. Perhaps we have had the political parties we deserve. But citizens who read this book and its blueprint for action can no longer claim that they lack either power or alternatives.

M. J. ROSSANT,
Director
The Twentieth Century Fund

New York, N.Y.

Introduction

Once upon a time party politics nourished and quickened the very life blood of American democracy. Competition between the two major parties was keen not only in Washington and the state capitals but in counties and cities and towns. The local newspapers were proudly and blatantly partisan. Local party militants jousted with each other in debates, torchlight parades, occasional fisticuffs. It was the local party that ran excursion trips up the river, provided jobs and welfare, made welcome the immigrant at the dock, sponsored the fireworks on the Fourth of July.

It was a rowdy, raucous politics, and we are well rid of much of it. But today we sorely miss the vigor, the combativeness, and the pervasiveness of the populist party spirit that once animated our political processes at every level of government. Of all the major institutions of American society, the parties seem to be the most resistant to reform and modernization. Indeed, some observers contend that our parties as institutions have retrogressed in this century, during a period of tumultuous change in almost every other sector of national life. Perhaps all this is true because nobody has much cared what happened to the parties.

It seems unlikely, however, that the two parties can continue much longer as the anemic, anachronistic creatures they are. Too many changes are afoot: the rise in numbers of thoughtful, discriminating Independents; the millions of young people flooding into the political arena; the widespread boredom with conventional politics; third-party yearnings at both ends of the political spectrum; the politicization of the Negro and other mobilizing minorities; the ever increasing impact and versatility of the mass media. The great political question of this bicentennial decade is whether the parties will continue to stagnate organizationally or will be superseded—or transformed.

Dr. Saloma and Mr. Sontag are intimately familiar with the

obscure processes and mossy labyrinths of the parties, sensitive to the new currents pushing through the old party channels, principled and clearheaded in the standards of representation and responsibility they wish to establish for American parties. They have subjected our party organization and machinery to a most searching and ruthless examination. The great value of their study is that they clearly delineate their ends and their means and propose the most explicit set of recommendations for reform that I have seen. By exploring all the dimensions of our many-chambered party system they provide an illuminating portrait of both what our parties are and what they could be.

Their proposals are clearly laid out in the following pages and need no preview here. But a reader who becomes infected by the sweep of these proposals may be excused for hoping that the authors and their readers will press even harder in the directions recommended. I found especially important their suggestion that a major reason for the vast expansion of presidential power has been the atrophy of the political parties. By the same token, a stronger national party, with an authoritative, responsible top leadership that knows how to help govern while in power and to mount a vigorous opposition while out of power—such a leadership, perhaps directed and sustained by annual party conferences, could serve as a source of both support and restraint of Presidents tempted by either foreign or domestic adventurism.

If the presidency needs more purposeful institutional steadying and restraint, Congress needs to be rejuvenated as an affirmative, creative branch of government. Here again the authors propose some valuable specifics in the structure and processes of Congress and in its political base. They stress the possibilities of a new programmatic spirit and commitment, of mobilizing talent and initiative, of strengthening party organization in the congressional districts. Whether even all this will be enough to topple the power structure of the congressional parties, which have shown themselves so resistant to change, whether indeed the congressional parties can be overcome by anything except a sharp and direct confrontation, will be pressing questions in this decade.

Are the authors' sweeping proposals "practical"? If this book had appeared a year earlier their ideas might have seemed utopian if not quixotic. But events may be running ahead of conventional thinking. In early 1972, the Democratic party, prodded by the recommendations of the McGovern–Fraser and O'Hara Commissions, was being rejuvenated at its base as tens of thousands of "amateurs" flocked to party caucuses not simply to watch and cheer but to take direct part in the vital processes of choosing delegates to the national convention. In 1964, countless conservative Republicans had found that their party primaries were unexpectedly open to citizen participation. The key question for both parties was whether citizen participation amounted to a mere spasm or to a long-term commitment and adventure that could transform the structure of the entire party.

This is the question that is posed so rigorously and yet imaginatively in this volume. It is prophetic in the two best senses of the word. It forecasts the likely course of basic changes in the parties in this decade. And it spells out not only the democratic and humane ends of such change but the precise reforms that must be made in our archaic party processes. It is an invitation to rejuvenate the processes of democracy by working with them—and within them.

JAMES MACGREGOR BURNS

Williamstown, Mass.

Genesis

For some time we have been struck by the lack of a comprehensive analysis of the American political parties, how they actually functioned, and what could be done by concerned and politically active Americans to make them more responsive and effective institutions. No one seemed to be addressing in any consistent and realistic manner the absurdities of our political system and the utter chaos and charade of supposedly organized and competitive party organizations incapable of governing. Those people who from time to time grew indignant at "politics as usual" did not seem to know quite where to begin in constructing something better in its place.

Although the origins of this book extend back through more than a decade of discussion between the authors, earnest plans got under way during the turmoil of the primaries, national conventions and elections of 1968, when public dissatisfaction with the parties reached a new high. Our conclusion then and now was that among the most urgent political requirements for the 1970's was an overall examination of American party politics available to a wide public audience in the form of a book, candid in exposing the masquerade of the traditional political parties and expansive in stating the realistic possibilities for positive and constructive citizen action.

To accomplish this we saw the need for extensive original research on how the party system actually functioned and for time for creative thinking to develop extensive recommendations for effective citizen politics. We were acutely aware of important deficiencies in political information and projected an intensive schedule of interviews, coverage of major political meetings, and regular reporting "beats" of key political news sources. From the beginning, we sensed that lack of adequate political intelligence and analysis was one of the critical reasons why party politics did not function. A broad and informed perspective on the operations of the contemporary political system was lacking on the part of the parties, the media and concerned citizens. The most difficult part of the task we projected, however, was moving from description and analysis to prescription. We were proposing to chart new paths and ways of thinking that seemed to fly in the face of contemporary wisdom and despair about the decline of political parties in the United States.

The Twentieth Century Fund and its director, M. J. Rossant, a man of vision who has pioneered in the modernization of foundations and the advancement of social and politically relevant research on major institutions in American life, responded to our initial financial and sponsorship needs and made it possible for us to launch the project.

The completion of *Parties: The Real Opportunity for Effective Citizen Politics* prior to the 1972 national party conventions was made possible through the tireless work of a remarkable project team and the generous contributions of time and energy of more than 50 men and women who aided the authors throughout the study. A Cambridge, Massachusetts, office served as nerve center for the project and gradually developed into a comprehensive library and research facility on current party politics.

Of our project team, Miss Jessie R. Janjigian has been an invaluable member with unusual maturity and professional judgment. More than an editor or researcher, she assimilated a wealth of suggestions from project advisers and manuscript readers, and assisted in editing over 1,000 original manuscript pages to the final length. Mrs. Marjorie M. Shultz served as the project's principal "Washington representative" in the best sense of the word, an accurate and thorough rapporteur who combined personal charm and tact in a variety of difficult assignments. Mrs. Barbara S. Phillips managed the Cambridge office and a multitude of administrative details with maturity, discretion and a personable manner, in addition to assuming the heavy burden of manuscript typing and production. Sandy Harlow, Cathy Buckley and Robert Barr gave major help in office operations as well as substantive project research. Completing the Cambridge team were Elizabeth Bennett, Gail Bochenek, Richard Partridge, Marc Tipermas, Joseph Waddie and Wayne Wenger. Also participating in project research in Washington were Patricia Kiley and Kathleen Lyons. The most valued member of our group, however, who shared intimately in literally every phase of the study as a full partner, has been Edith Sontag. Throughout, she remained a great encouragement and source of strength to us both.

The authors were immeasurably aided by a core group of advisers to the study. Neal R. Peirce served as a respected senior consultant to the project from its very beginnings, going over every chapter in each draft, giving his candid editorial judgment and offering a constructive discipline for all of us based on his political editorship of *Congressional Quarterly* and *National Journal*. Charles F. Moore, Jr., among the most imaginative and innovative thinkers and implementers in politics and the private sector, with a special skill for training and bringing along younger associates, gave the project his enthusiastic encouragement from its inception. One of the high points of the study, a Cape Cod weekend conference in April 1970 involving more than 30 political activists, party organizers, political scientists, journalists, computer scientists and advertising executives, was graciously hosted by Mr. and Mrs. Moore at their Orleans, Massachusetts, farm.

Three individuals from the Cape conference also agreed to participate in a weekend editorial conference on the completed draft manuscript in New York City in May 1971, sponsored at The Twentieth Century Fund by M. J. Rossant. Roscoe Drummond, among the initial endorsers of the project, brought a genuine historical perspective and great wisdom and balance of judgment to our work. We are indebted to him for his continued enthusiasm and valued advice and assistance. Thomas B. Curtis tempered our scholarship with his detailed knowledge of party organization and procedures, and has taught us through his example the highest standards of personal integrity and political courage. Millard Cass, who has practiced the ability to govern through a long and distinguished career in the Federal civil service, gave our deliberations a unique and invaluable perspective on politics as the art and science of government. Also joining the New York editorial conference was Mrs. Lark Wallwork, who has from the earliest drafts contributed the enthusiasm, candor and hopes of a political activist genuinely concerned with the success of this book.

Our advisers also included Edwin J. Putzell, Jr., whose profound, farsighted and practical counsel on the role of political parties in the economic life of the nation and whose support of forward-looking ideas for many years have served as inspiration to us; Sam Krupnick, a participant in the Cape conference and a forceful and incisive man of wide-ranging talents and abiding faith in the ancient verities; and Len Burchman, whose competence and human qualities have been a source of continuing encouragement.

James MacGregor Burns read the draft manuscript as an independent outside reader selected by The Twentieth Century Fund and has been enthusiastic about the ideas it advances. Ashbel Green and Anthony M. Schulte put the full resources of Alfred A. Knopf, Inc., behind a timely publication of the manuscript.

Among those who gave graciously of their time in reviewing the project proposal, participating in our Cape weekend conference, reading the entire manuscript or selected chapters, and offering us valued counsel and encouragement were: John Quincy Adams, Samuel H. Beer, Nancy Ellen Brigham, Walter Dean Burnham, Bishop Albert A. Chambers, Robert J. Citrino, Roan Conrad, Joseph Cooper, Paul T. David, Edwin Diamond, Geoffrey Drummond, Ralph B. Earle, Jr., Bruce Felknor, Kevin George, Harold Graham, Herbert Hill, Terry A. Knopf, Esomor Krash, Shirley M. Kyle, David L. Lewis, John D. Little, Moya Connell-McDowell, Charles J. V. Murphy, Elaine (Cissy) Musselman, Jack Nelson, John F. Olson, Sidney Olson, Anne Peretz, Martin Peretz, Roy Pfautch, William G. Phillips, Anthony Podesta, Martin Rosen, David Rosenbloom, Rosalie Ruoff, John S. Saloma, Sr., Robert Schaeffer, Russell G. Simpson, Eugene B. Skolnikoff, Jeanne Smillie, Ronald P. Smillie, Dick Smith, Eric G. Snyder, Neil Staebler, Jack Steele, Chandler Harrison Stevens, George Sweeney, Jr., Robert D. Sweeney, Senator James H. Wallwork, Herbert Warburton, Joseph Weizenbaum, James Russell Wiggins and Robert C. Wood.

Among the New York and Washington staff of The Twentieth Century Fund who have assisted the authors have been John

Booth, Nicholas Danforth, Mrs. Frances Klafter, Frank Popper and Richard Rust.

The individuals who contributed directly to the study through interviews or who assisted our research in other ways would fill many pages if we could list them—from Walter Lippmann and Arthur F. Burns to representatives of the new generation of young activists coming of political age as we wrote. In an important sense this book is as much theirs as ours. We have learned much from their experience, interpretations, expectations and dreams of American politics.

JOHN S. SALOMA III
FREDERICK H. SONTAG

Cambridge, Mass.
Montclair, N.J.

PARTIES

Citizen Parties:
A Revolutionary Goal
for the 1970's

For a decade American politics has been gripped by a sense of frustration and helplessness. No political figure has been able to give personal leadership or expression to the real concerns of most citizens. Many have resigned from party politics for the time being and few effective avenues have been opened to motivate a new generation of activists to enter party politics. The presidential campaigns of 1964, 1968 and 1972 have been dominated by candidates identified with the traditional political order, many of whom were established national party leaders or presidential contenders even before the 1960's. For millions of Americans, party politics has taken on a painful character of *déjà vu*, its rhetoric ever more hollow and distant from political reality.

There is at the same time a mood of anticipation in the country, an expectancy, a restless searching, even a deep yearning for some issue, some leader, some catalyst that will effect a new synthesis, a new reality in political and governmental performance. There is a widespread sense that something fundamental has been happening to American politics but that the full impact of this change has yet to be felt.

Meanwhile, the diverse ranks of citizen volunteers in politics have continued to swell. The Americans from all walks of life who joined in civil-rights demonstrations and black political organization, in the Draft Goldwater movement, in the peace movement and McCarthy-Kennedy-McGovern campaigns of 1968, in George C. Wallace's American Independent Party, in women's liberation, in the successful drive to extend the voting age to 18 and in citizen causes of every ideological coloration share a common spirit and a desire to participate in shaping the American future.

This new citizen spirit in American politics has continued to mature rapidly. Its most advanced political expression has been in the public interest movement and its strategies to influence public and private bureaucracies in such areas as consumer affairs and environmental policy. Its philosophy is political realism: a uniquely American blend of tough pragmatism— a "no-nonsense" approach to problem solving—and of political idealism—an almost naïve faith in the civics-textbook statement of how the American system ought to work.

America thus approaches the commemoration of its bicentennial with a large but disorganized and leaderless army of citizen patriots ready to answer a call to political action—to participate in what could be the equivalent of a second American Revolution in basic political institutions, a new era of political development and institutional innovation. Perhaps for the first time in the history of any modern democracy, the United States today has the base of educated and socially motivated citizens as well as the sizable reform elites that could provide political entrepreneurial skills to make possible a major extension in the forms and realities of self-government.

It is for these Americans and for this purpose that we have written this book—for citizens who want to share in the exciting era of political change and development that lies ahead in the 1970's, from the young activist who is just beginning to learn about "the system" to the veteran party leader who has been unwilling to give up a lifelong fight to modernize his party.

What is most needed at this time of searching is a *rediscovery* of politics as the meeting place where Americans can resolve their differences and set their common course as well as a *rediscovery* of the political parties, which have been neglected or misused for decades.

The important political work of this decade is not to rebuild old party coalitions but to define new political means and instruments, within the parties or beyond them, that will allow the American people to express their deepest concerns and aspirations through popular government.

We have thus attempted to write an action-oriented book that combines a realistic assessment of American political institutions and their relatively low level of performance with detailed feasible proposals for citizen action. From one perspective the book provides a strategic overview of the American party system and how party institutions can be used more effectively by citizens for governmental policymaking. This book can also be viewed as a kind of political *Whole Earth Catalog* that introduces the reader to the almost unlimited possibilities for citizen initiative in the parties and provides information on political procedures and means to those of all political persuasions who want to make the political process function.[1]

The approach of this book is based on some general but important assumptions that should be stated clearly at the outset. First, we believe that American political parties, whatever their current limitations, offer the best potential means for achieving broad citizen participation in politics and continuing citizen influence in the direction of government. While the parties have been derelict in their failure to develop their resources for government and to encourage extensive citizen involvement in politics, they occupy too strategic a position in American politics to be bypassed or ignored. National nominating conventions, with their growing logistical complexity and physical security measures, are still firmly controlled by the party organizations. And the odds are heavy that any presidential candidate elected during the 1970's will be either a party-designated Democrat or Republican.

---

[1] The *Whole Earth Catalog* "functions as an evaluation and access device" whose stated purpose is to aid the individual to "conduct his own education, find his own inspiration, shape his own environment, and share his adventure with whoever is interested." (Portola Institute, Inc., *The Last Whole Earth Catalog: Access to Tools* [New York: Random House, 1971].)

Parties remain the instruments for organizing government—the formal means through which Presidents, governors, many mayors and their administrations are put into governmental office. They are also the formal means for organizing the leadership of Congress and its powerful system of standing committees as well as most state legislative bodies. At the state level they are frozen into complex election statutes that have evolved over more than a century. The major parties are built into the administrative and regulatory processes of government through statutory bipartisan boards and commissions. Contrary to some estimates that the party organizations are decaying, we have found party institutions, nationally and in many states and counties, better financed and more professionally staffed than they have ever been in modern times. Party organizations are extending their financial bases through self-sustaining direct-mail fund raising and are increasing their professional skills and services through the use of political consultants and new technologies.

The real issue is not whether the parties will survive, but what kind of political parties we will have in the 1970's. A critical assessment of the political parties is sorely needed, not as a justification for their abolition but as a basis for their reconstruction and revitalization.

The traditional parties are effectively closed political organizations whose operations frustrate broad citizen participation in politics. For the most part a handful of party notables, key officeholders and party professionals actually control the party organizations within the states and at the federal level. Insulated and inbred, these party elites exercise power without challenge over such functions as fund raising, national convention arrangements and party policy formulation. The closed party organizations ignore even the forms of participation. County chairmen, state chairmen and national chairmen, all of whom in theory are elected by and accountable to a representative party committee or broader party constituency, are usually named by other leaders in the organization or by a single man—the governor, the President, or the party's presidential candidate. Party committees formally charged with managing party affairs at all levels of organization are rarely

convened and even less frequently involved in any conse-
quential business. National committeemen and committeewomen, the elected party representatives from the states, have
essentially no role in developing or reviewing party strategy or
budgets. There are now no obvious effective means for members at any level of party organization to hold leaders accountable for their performance. Party conventions, the formal
representative governing bodies of the parties, have not been
structured to encourage delegate participation and decision
making.

The parties, which are supposed to provide all levels of government with political executives, have also exhibited a remarkable lack of concern with or ability to move the direction
of government nationally or in the states. Parties have no formal
means to screen the candidates they present to the voters in
terms of their ability to govern. They have not developed continuing talent-hunt programs for staffing municipal, state and
national governments. Parties have no training programs for developing political executives or party professional staff that can
assume political staff positions in the executive branch or legislature. They are generally poorly structured or staffed to contribute talent, ideas and political initiatives for government.
Party policy councils set up with great fanfare when a party is
in opposition are disbanded just at the time they could be of
most help—when a party takes office. Most governmental problems are discussed without any reference to Democratic and
Republican problem-solving initiatives.

These criticisms of the party system imply a second general
assumption, namely, that citizen parties represent the most
desirable direction for party modernization or reform and an
essential political goal for the 1970's. In contrast to the traditional closed parties, citizen parties would be structured and
enlarged to provide significantly increased opportunities for
greater citizen participation and to emphasize new problem-
solving and governing capabilities that would systematically
involve the talents of citizens in government.

The goal of citizen participation in government is as old as
the American parties themselves. The convention system of
local, state and national party organizations that developed

rapidly after the 1820's was based on the principle of popular nomination. Jacksonian democracy, however, expected too much of the citizen of the period. The average voter did not have the continuing political interest, sufficient political information or time to operate the complicated machinery of nominations or decide on each office to be filled at elections. Instead, he delegated this function to a specialized class of politicians who were all too eager to manage the organization and supply party tickets or lists of candidates.

Progressive reformers at the turn of the century sought to advance citizen participation through a direct attack on the power of the party "organization" or "machine." Political parties were subjected to detailed statutory regulation. The direct primary, functioning as a popular preliminary election, sought to correct the abuses that had become common under the unregulated convention system. But Progressive-era reforms offered no real or long-term solution to the problem of participation in the parties. They gave citizens a broad new kind of access to the parties through the direct primary but they provided no incentives for citizens to participate in the work of the party organizations themselves and in fact consciously undercut party functions and organizational effectiveness.

The goal of citizen participation has more recently become the central theme of the Democratic party reform movement. As valuable as procedural reform in itself may be, in order to transform the parties it must be coupled with a new conception of the governmental role of parties. Political parties *can* play a significantly expanded role in making government work, especially within the complicated system of American federalism. Modernized state parties and interstate party problem-solving teams could involve the creative talents of countless citizens in government during the 1970's. The political parties at all levels could become the vehicle for a fresh problem-solving approach to American politics.

Citizen parties offering a constructive partisan involvement in the real problems of government and a new capacity to deal with governmental responsibilities should attract substantially more Americans into their ranks at the national, state and local levels. Party organization performance would be improved through the increased qualitative participation of more party members. Parties with vital policy research and study groups, active committees to review party relations with the media or to evaluate party campaign strategy and long-term personnel recruiting and development programs, for example, could productively involve innumerable citizens not now participating actively in the parties. The closed hierarchical character of traditional party organizations could be gradually transformed through growing part-time citizen involvement and the use of new internal reporting and appeal procedures designed to ensure greater accountability of party professional staff charged with operating significantly expanded party budgets.

We believe that the goal of party modernization as outlined in subsequent chapters is entirely feasible within the 1970's. The resources available today for political innovation and development in America have never been greater—in citizen competence in politics, in a widespread affluence to sustain political activity, and in communications and transportation technologies to link geographically dispersed political activists. The parties are surrounded by opportunities. There is so much slack and room for improvement in American politics that it is possible for citizens to achieve whatever goals they set out to accomplish politically.

Missing, however, have been sustained strategies for action and a broad perspective for citizen initiatives in the parties. In our years of participating in, observing, reporting and teaching politics, we have found nothing available as a comprehensive guide to political action in the American system. "How to" action books and pamphlets deal with essential but elementary steps such as precinct organization and writing letters to Congressmen.[2] Wide-ranging proposals for party reform, such as

---

[2] Both major national parties and their women's and youth auxiliaries offer party workers and citizens a number of organization manuals and "how to" political guides of varying quality. Some of these are obtainable on request from the Democratic National Committee, 2600 Virginia Avenue, N.W., Washington, D.C. 20037; and the Republican National Committee, 301 First Street, S.E., Washington, D.C. 20003. Many citizen organizations from the League of Women Voters to the Liberty Lobby furnish

the 1950 report of the Committee on Political Parties of the American Political Science Association, "Toward a More Responsible Two-Party System," have been rare and when released have been quickly discounted by party leaders, political scientists and others for their lack of realism, usually for prescriptions that assume a degree of party cohesion and discipline on legislative programs that American parties would never accept.[3] Most of the formal literature of American political science has been descriptive or analytical, often in terms incomprehensible to the layman.

While the extensive recommendations advanced in this book are not a single blueprint for party modernization, they are an attempt to define the job that lies ahead. Within the broad goals of party modernization, all of the recommendations are desirable *and* practical. None is so radical as to require a constitutional change. None is frivolous. Any one of them can be achieved by a relatively small number of individuals inside and outside the parties who follow a well-thought-out strategy of reform. Individually their impact will be largely incremental. Collectively, they can effect a qualitative change of historic significance in the character of American politics.

No priority or ranking is assigned to individual recommendations. The process of reform cannot be that neatly structured, nor will party reform be achieved, realistically, through a carefully selected "ten-point program." Like a road map, this

---

members with action guides. Among the several published guides to citizen action are Lee and Anne Edwards, *You Can Make the Difference* (New Rochelle, N.Y.: Arlington House, 1968), and Sam Love (ed.), *Earth Tool Kit: A Field Manual for Citizen Activists Prepared by Environmental Action* (New York: Pocket Books, 1971).
[3] See, for example, Committee on Political Parties of the American Political Science Association, "Toward a More Responsible Two-Party System," *American Political Science Review*, September 1950 (Supplement); Stephen K. Bailey, *The Condition of Our National Parties*, An Occasional Paper on the Role of the Political Process in the Free Society (New York: The Fund for the Republic, 1959); and James MacGregor Burns, *The Deadlock of Democracy: Four-Party Politics in America* (Englewood Cliffs, N.J.: Prentice-Hall, 1963). For a critique of the academic contribution to party reform since the end of World War II, see Gerald M. Pomper, "Toward a More Responsible Two-Party System? What, Again?" *Journal of Politics*, November 1971, pp. 916–40.

book outlines critical features of the political parties and their environment that deserve the attention of citizens in the 1970's. The approach of extensive action recommendations has been purposefully chosen because of the complexity of the task ahead. Different citizens have different skills, interests and levels of competence in party politics, and they are likely to involve themselves in many different aspects of party reform. To make our analysis and recommendations more useful, we have added a concluding Action Guide that outlines many of the specific possibilities for action discussed. It is our hope that this book will serve as a reference and source of incentives and ideas to a continuing citizen movement for party reform.

The most basic assumption of the book is a faith that citizens have the interest and capacity to act in politics and that representative government can be strengthened through their greater involvement. What is new about the 1970's is the emergence of a qualitatively different demand for citizen participation and a citizen potential for action that the parties and governments at all levels have yet to grasp. Countless citizens are willing and able, we believe, to make a substantial contribution to politics in the decade ahead. Whether and how these talents and expectations are used, however, is the fundamental challenge. Americans could let the political parties, the historic means for popular control of government, become more ineffective and unresponsive through studied neglect and apathy. The alternatives to the revival and development of our political institutions are already all too clear—a steady increase of power exercised by politically unaccountable technocratic elites, the new mandarin class in America; a decline in political participation, growing voter apathy, and a "dropping out of politics"; a straining of traditional Democratic and Republican party coalitions beyond the breaking point, with resultant political fragmentation and chaos—or worse.

One response would be for Americans to undertake, as a national political goal for 1976 and beyond, the creation of citizen parties that will achieve new levels of self-government and citizen participation in politics. In commemorating the forthcoming American Revolution Bicentennial, citizens can refocus their attention on their political institutions per se and their importance to the Revolutionary period and to contemporary America.

In the 1770's, during the crisis of political independence, Americans had to construct national political institutions de novo—creating a network of Committees of Correspondence and a Continental Congress of delegates that resembled a primitive party convention of the Whig or Patriot parties in the colonies. The modern party system was another uniquely American invention—a response to the political crisis of the 1820's concerning how the American President was to be popularly nominated and elected. Between 1820 and 1848 the complicated two-tier system of American national and state politics was permanently linked by two broadly competitive political parties, the Democrats and Whigs, each "a federation of state machines or cliques led by state leaders either in the state or national capitols."[4] With the emergence of the Republican party in the presidential election of 1856 and the collapse of the Whig party, the modern two-party form of American politics had been established.

The 1970's are another critical decade of political challenge for Americans. The choices made in the next few years will shape American politics for decades to come. Americans can demand that party institutions and government become more relevant to the real concerns of their lives.

Our role is one of indicating what can be done constructively by citizens to reclaim the political parties and, even more important, the process of politics itself. Ultimately the test of democratic politics is the citizen himself. What happens to American politics during this decade is a responsibility that every citizen must answer. If Americans accept the necessity of party modernization and the challenge of developing citizen parties, they will face the most demanding test yet of the American political genius.

---

[4] Roy Nichols, *The Invention of the American Political Parties: A Study of Improvisation* (New York: Macmillan, 1967), p. 365.

I

Party Reform:
A Movement Comes to Life

Is party modernization a feasible goal for the 1970's? The cynics, skeptics and self-styled realists of American politics have long since abandoned hope that the political parties could ever be reformed. Like the Tammany philosopher George Washington Plunkitt, they have dismissed reform movements as "mornin' glories" that "looked lovely in the mornin' and withered up in a short time, while the regular machines went on flourishin' forever, like fine old oaks."[1]

Since 1968, however, something new has been happening in American party politics. There is little question that unprecedented changes have already occurred in the Democratic party. The real question is whether the beginnings of party reform will be broadened and extended beyond 1972 to accomplish wide-ranging party modernization.

Cautious observers of the Democratic party reform movement, like Senator Harold E. Hughes, are "amazed" at the progress state parties have made in complying with national standards for the selection of 1972 national convention delegates. "Two years ago I doubted that ten states would be in conformity," Hughes remarked in 1971. "Now I think that between forty-five and forty-eight states will be." "It's simply beyond my belief," stated Professor Samuel H. Beer of Harvard, former national chairman of Americans for Democratic Action and an active member of one of the party's reform commissions.

---

[1] *Plunkitt of Tammany Hall,* recorded by William L. Riordon (New York: E. P. Dutton, 1963), p. 17.

Events have moved so rapidly during the research and writing of this book that the discussion of the party reform movement has required extensive rewriting at several stages. This movement, which few observers of American politics have been able to keep adequately abreast of, is a heartening indication of the feasibility of extensive party reform. The 1972 Democratic and Republican conventions in Miami Beach may well be remembered as much for the changes they make in party representation and structure as for the presidential candidates they nominate.

The Democratic Party Reform Movement: A Continuing Mandate?

On the floor of the Chicago International Amphitheater late Tuesday evening, August 27, 1968, "We Want Kennedy" signs and chants from the New York and California delegations competed with the gavel of Permanent Chairman Carl Albert of Oklahoma, Democratic Majority Leader of the House of Representatives, for the attention of the delegates. The Democratic convention's leadership had been caught by surprise by the introduction of the minority report of the Committee on Rules and Order of Business. In order to give all Democratic voters "full and timely opportunity to participate" in nominating candidates, the report proposed that the 1972 convention require that the unit rule be eliminated from all stages of the delegate selection process and that "all feasible efforts be made to assure that delegates are selected through party primary, convention, or committee procedures open to public participation within the calendar year of the national convention."

Democratic National Chairman John M. Bailey hurried to his delegation, urging them to vote "no." Illinois Governor Samuel H. Shapiro, chairman of the Rules Committee, opposed the recommendation on the grounds that it should be referred for further study to a postconvention committee for consideration at the 1972 convention. Supporters of Hubert H. Humphrey had already accepted a compromise reform of the unit rule embodied in the majority report. But Senators Eugene J. McCarthy and Edward M. Kennedy, and a few Humphrey supporters like Minnesota Congressman Donald M. Fraser, had been working even harder in the state caucuses, and at 11:30 p.m. the McCarthy-Kennedy forces achieved their only clear convention victory by a roll-call vote of 1,350 to 1,206. New York, along with California and the other states holding primary elections, had voted overwhelmingly for the reform resolution. Illinois, Ohio, Pennsylvania, Connecticut and other strongholds of the party organization stood in opposition. Almost the full margin of victory was accounted for by the unexpected vote of the entire Missouri delegation, which was won over, according to some sources, by the direct appeal of Iowa Governor Harold Hughes (soon to become Senator) to Missouri Governor Warren E. Hearnes. Together with other reform provisions in the majority reports of the Credentials and Rules Committees, the minority report was to become the mandate for two Democratic party reform commissions and a major impetus for the Democratic party reform movement.

The origins of the minority report are worth recounting both as an introduction to the movement for party reform and as an example of the significant impact a small group of dedicated individuals, with a timely issue and well-designed strategy, can have on the course of American politics. In late June 1968, Geoffrey Cowan, a student at the Yale Law School and a McCarthy worker in Connecticut, seized upon the idea of a private citizen commission to research and dramatize the abuses that he and others working for Senator McCarthy in nonprimary states had encountered in the procedures for selecting convention delegates. During July, Cowan developed the idea with Eli J. Segal, a recent graduate of the Michigan Law School and also a McCarthy field worker, and Harold Ickes, Jr., of the New York McCarthy organization. William Johnson, another McCarthy supporter, contributed $10,000 to the project through his publishing brokerage house, which would retain the rights to publish the resulting research. Within a few days, the young lawyers had won the agreement of Governor Hughes and Congressman Fraser to serve as chairman and vice chairman, respectively, of the ad hoc Commission on the Democratic Selection of Presidential Nominees (Hughes Commission).

On August 1, a working staff team was established in New York. It included Thomas P. Alder (who had also been intimately involved in the credentials challenges in 1964) as staff director, Cowan as associate director, and Simon Lazarus, then legal assistant to Nicholas Johnson of the Federal Communications Commission, as editor. The commission and its staff immediately recognized the importance of having a published document to interest the media and delegates in their cause. Within two weeks, the staff had compiled data on delegate selection in the 50 states, attended a meeting with the commission in Chicago, completed revisions of its report and delivered 7,000 copies of the 85-page document *The Democratic Choice* to Chicago.

Accompanied by a drumbeat of favorable editorial comment, Governor Hughes presented the recommendations of the commission to the convention's Rules Committee on the afternoon of August 22. Among its most dramatic findings was the fact that more than 600 delegates—almost half the number needed to nominate a President—had been selected by "processes which have included no means (however indirect) of voter participation since 1966." The commission staff then joined forces with reform Democrats on the Rules Committee like Anne L. Wexler of Connecticut and Joseph F. Crangle of New York, and with McCarthy's Chicago staff, which included Eli Segal. When the minority report, drafted by Crangle, Lazarus, and a small committee, was defeated 44–40 in the Rules Committee, the reformers decided to go to their state caucuses and the floor. The stage had been set for eventual triumph.

Some six months later, as the Democratic reform commissions were getting under way, Senator George S. McGovern of South Dakota observed that "there has never been a political party which, when confronted with the choice of reform or death, has chosen reform." He hoped the Democratic party would break with that tradition. On January 7, 1971, when he resigned the chairmanship of the Commission on Party Structure and Delegate Selection (McGovern-Fraser Commission) to seek the party's nomination for President, Senator McGovern predicted that the 1972 Democratic National Convention would be "the least boss-ridden and most democratic in American history." In the course of two years, the party had undertaken a historic open process of self-examination and reform. Not since the Progressive era of the early 1900's had party structures and electoral procedures been the subject of such scrutiny. Together with the Commission on Rules (O'Hara Commission) and Democratic reform commissions in virtually every state, the McGovern-Fraser Commission engaged in the drafting of what was in effect a new constitution for the Democratic party.

Still, some prominent Democrats have questioned whether the party would accept basic reform. Former Senator McCarthy has suggested that the party has not moved much beyond what was obvious at the 1968 convention through the work of the Hughes Commission. If party reform fails, in his view "there may be a need to threaten from outside." The contest between Senator Hughes and Washington lawyer Mrs. Patricia Roberts Harris in October 1971 for the position of temporary chairman of the 1972 convention's Credentials Committee was widely interpreted as a test of strength between party reformers and regulars. Mrs. Harris's 72–31 victory, made possible by the active lobbying of organized labor's Alexander Barkan and National Chairman Lawrence F. O'Brien, revived party antagonisms in spite of O'Brien's personal pledge to enforce reform.

Acting on the resolutions and mandates adopted by the 1968 convention, in February 1969, Senator Fred R. Harris of Oklahoma, then Democratic National Chairman, appointed the 28-member Commission on Party Structure and Delegate Selection, to be headed by Senator McGovern as chairman and Senator Hughes as vice chairman, and a second 28-member Commission on Rules, with Congressman James G. O'Hara of Michigan as chairman. After a preliminary meeting in March, the McGovern Commission organized into five-member task forces and embarked on a series of regional hearings in 17 cities in which over 500 witnesses testified. At the same time, the commission's staff, headed by Staff Director Robert W. Nelson, Staff Counsel Eli Segal and Director of Research Kenneth A. Bode, and aided by a group of summer interns and a consultant committee, was analyzing the delegate selection systems of each state. The O'Hara Commission began its work by requesting more than 700 party leaders and political scientists to submit comments and suggestions for its consideration. In December 1969, the commission published "Issues and Alternatives," a document that outlined 48 proposals to modify national convention procedures. These suggestions were sent to potential witnesses and considered at nine regional hearings in 1970.

In September 1969, the McGovern Commission adopted a tentative set of guidelines for delegate selection, which was then circulated to 3,000 Democratic officials, reformers and academicians. On November 19 and 20, 1969, the commission reconvened in Washington and hammered out final agreement on 18 official guidelines in a marathon session in the Senate caucus room.[2] About one month later, copies of the guidelines

---

[2] In order to achieve nondiscrimination and grass-roots selection of delegates, the commission "required" the following action by state parties to meet the requirements of the "full, meaningful and timely opportunity" mandate of the 1968 convention and the call of the 1972 convention:
1. Adopt explicit written party rules governing delegate selection
2. Adopt procedural rules and safeguards for the delegate selection process that would:
   • forbid proxy voting
   • ban the use of the unit rule and related practices
   • require quorums of not less than 40 percent of all party committee meetings
   • remove all mandatory assessments of convention delegates
   • remove excessive fees (over $10)
   • remove delegate petition requirements in excess of one percent of the Democratic vote
   • ensure, except in rural areas, that party meetings are held on uniform dates, at uniform times and in public places
   • ensure adequate public notice of all party meetings concerned with the delegate selection process
3. Seek a broader base for the party in the following manner:
   • ensure that party rules specify no discrimination on the basis of race, color, creed, or national origin
   • take specific steps to encourage representation on the convention delegation of young people, women, and minority groups in reasonable relationship to their presence in the state's population
   • allow and encourage all persons 18 years of age or older to participate in all party affairs
4. Make the following changes in the delegate selection process:
   • select alternates in the same manner as delegates

were forwarded to all Democratic state party chairmen, national committeemen and national committeewomen. Then on February 27, 1970, 53 of the most important letters written in contemporary American party history were sent by Senator McGovern to the party chairmen of the 50 states, the Canal Zone, Guam and the Virgin Islands. Each so-called compliance letter included an analysis of the individual state's delegate selection process based on the extensive testimony taken by the commission and research compiled by its staff. States were informed point by point where laws, rules and practices in the state were inconsistent with the mandatory requirements of the commission guidelines.

Every Democratic state party organization was required to make some changes. More than 10 states with no party rules

---

- ban designation of ex-officio delegates
- conduct the entire delegate selection process within the calendar year of the convention
- select at least 75 percent of the delegation at a level no higher than the congressional district
- apportion each body selecting delegates at all levels on the basis of population and/or Democratic strength
- designate procedures by which delegate slates are prepared and may be challenged
- select no more than 10 percent of the delegation by the state committee.

The Commission considered the following steps desirable (but not mandatory before the 1972 convention) and accordingly "urged" their adoption by state parties:

1. Remove all costs and fees involved in the delegate selection process;
2. Explore ways of easing the financial burden on delegates and alternates;
3. Make all feasible efforts to remove or alleviate voter registration laws and practices such as residency requirements which prevent the effective participation in the delegate selection process;
4. Provide easy access for unaffiliated voters and non-Democrats to become Democrats;
5. End all selection systems which require or permit party committees to select any part of the state delegation;
6. Adopt procedures which will provide for fair representation of minority views on presidential candidates.

For the full report of the McGovern Commission see *Mandate for Reform: A Report of the Commission on Party Structure and Delegate Selection to the Democratic National Committee* (Washington, D.C.: The Commission on Party Structure and Delegate Selection, Democratic National Committee, 1970).

were required to adopt new party rules and make them readily available. More than 30 states were asked to change their procedures to ensure compliance with the guideline that all delegates should be chosen within the calendar year of the convention. Virtually every state was required to effect changes to allow or encourage any Democrat 18 years of age and over to participate in all party affairs.

Since the publication of the official guidelines and individual compliance letters, few party leaders have openly challenged the authority of the commission. Discussion has instead focused on what state actions would satisfy the guidelines, how many states had achieved full technical compliance and how credentials challenges would be resolved. Periodic progress reports were issued by the McGovern-Fraser Commission and subjected to a careful critique by party reformers.[3] The full final reports of both party reform commissions were subsequently accepted by the Democratic National Committee without debate.

The McGovern Commission was clearly aware that, while most of the required changes could be incorporated at the state and local level by amending party rules, some called for legislative action. In each letter, the commission clearly defined what it expected whenever a provision of state law or the state constitution differed from the guidelines. The state party was required to make "all feasible efforts" to accomplish the stated purposes of the guidelines. The state party, the commission declared, "will be obliged to show that it has held hearings, introduced bills, worked for their enactment, and amended its rules in every necessary way short of exposing the Party or its members to legal sanctions." The commission recommended that the Credentials Committee of the 1972 convention, in the event of any contest or challenge based on the guidelines, be guided by "the principle that the state parties must assume the

---

[3] Reformers maintained steady pressure on the commissions through open criticism of their work. See Andrew J. Glass and Jonathan Cottin, "Democratic Reform Drive Falters as Spotlight Shifts to Presidential Race," *National Journal*, June 19, 1971, pp. 1293–1304; see also Ken Bode, "Democratic Party Reform: Turning Sour," *New Republic*, July 10, 1971, pp. 19–23.

burden of ensuring opportunities for full, meaningful, and timely participation in the delegate selection process for all party members."

The detailed provisions of the guidelines, especially the large number of constraints they placed on the delegate selection process, raised additional problems of internal consistency and workability. For example, the commission reduced the number of delegates or alternates who could be selected by state committees at the same time that it asked that racial minorities, women, and youth be represented "in reasonable relationship to their presence in the population of the state" (the so-called Bayh amendment introduced by Indiana Senator Birch Bayh). Will D. Davis, former chairman of the Texas State Democratic Committee, pointed out during the commission's deliberations that this proposed wording was in effect a quota. "It's not possible to have such a provision and still maintain the mandate to elect more delegates," Davis noted. Even commission staff members later admitted privately that the Bayh amendment did present an inherent conflict between participation and the concept of representation it defined. The final interpretation was left to the Credentials Committee and the 1972 Miami Beach convention.

In spite of such legal and practical problems, the McGovern Commission guidelines constitute a remarkable statement of "national party authority." Whatever interpretation is given to the "flexible quotas" of the commission, for example, the principle of minority-group representation has been built into the Democratic party's nomination procedures. The 53 compliance letters represent a significant body of "party legislation"[4] and an unprecedented intervention by a national party body into the party organizations of the individual states. The McGovern guidelines, even if unevenly implemented, should introduce a

---

4 Eli Segal and Simon Lazarus, in a lengthy memorandum on party reform prepared in January 1969, discussed the new role of the party convention as "a law-making institution on a significant scale" and the "administrative process of a party statute," i.e., how a major political party could perform as a "law-administering and enforcing institution." ("Preliminary Outline: Should the People Pick the President?," memorandum dated January 22, 1969.)

measure of standardization in Democratic party operations that most observers of American politics would not have thought possible a few years earlier.

The success of the Democratic reform movement, of course, cannot be measured simply by the volume of party reform legislation or regulations produced by reform commissions. Although full evaluation must await the implementation (or rejection) of specific reforms, there have been several positive accomplishments of the Democratic reform movement that go well beyond the formal reports. First and foremost, the representative party commission mechanism has succeeded in opening a new means of evaluation, communication and participation to party leaders, party members and the general public. The public testimony at the regional hearings of both commissions exposed a range of grievances and aspirations that had not been adequately expressed through normal party channels and that might otherwise have been ignored until the 1972 conventions. Unfortunately, many of the grievances and recommendations presented went beyond the jurisdictions of the commissions, which chose not to involve themselves. Nevertheless, the continuing party commission, mandated by the party convention acting in its capacity as the supreme party lawmaking body, is a significant innovation in American party politics. The representative commission mechanism is a new participant party structure that has involved diverse people and ideas in historic decisions and precedents in party reform.

Another promising development has been the impact of the state commissions on party reform, the so-called Little McGovern-Fraser Commissions. The Democratic National Committee reported in October 1971 that every state Democratic party had named a reform commission or committee to study its delegate selection system and propose appropriate changes. Admittedly, some state reform commissions represented minimal efforts by reluctant state leaders. In Missouri, Governor Hearnes and State Chairman Delton Houtchens deferred state committee consideration of the party reform commission until after the call for the 1972 national convention had been issued, allowing themselves, in the view of the St. Louis *Post Dispatch*, "the luxury of avoiding democratization except to the extent that it is imposed by the national party." The Missouri New Democratic Coalition issued a scathing critique of subsequent state committee reform measures.[5]

While progress has been uneven, a network of state party reform units has been created, and a number of these commissions have been catalysts for significant change in state party structure and roles. The North Carolina Democratic party took steps to open the operations of its party structure to more voters and elect three vice-chairmen to represent blacks, women and young people. In Minnesota, a new party constitution was adopted that provided for proportional representation. Alabama reapportioned its state committee on a one-man, one-vote basis and revised its election procedures to ensure seats for up to 20 black members. The Michigan Democratic reform commission, headed by former University of Michigan Dean William Haber, approved well in advance of the national party a report calling for one-man, one-vote proportional representation in all party affairs; extension of voting rights to 18-year-olds, college students, and prisoners awaiting trial; elimination of voter residency and registration requirements; closer scrutiny of campaign financing, and establishment of an appeals committee to hear grievances about party operations. The work of the state reform commissions has also resulted in new presidential primary statutes in Arkansas, Florida, Michigan, New Mexico, North Carolina, Rhode Island and Tennessee and a revival of the Maryland primary law.

At both the state and national level, a new pool of party talent is being developed and trained. More than a thousand Democrats have been involved in the work of state reform units and many others in the reform activities of groups like the New Democratic Coalition. Young lawyers and law students have become familiar with the complex state statutes governing party organization and procedures and have initiated actions to correct abuses in the delegate selection and

---

[5] "Missouri Democrats' Retreat from Reality," St. Louis *Post Dispatch*, December 20, 1970; and New Democratic Coalition of Metropolitan St. Louis, "New Democratic Coalition Releases Study of [Missouri] State Democratic Constitution and Bylaws," press release dated June 22, 1971.

other party processes. These already seasoned veterans of the party reform movement, familiar with the intricacies of parliamentary procedure, party organization and convention operations, will afford the Democratic party an invaluable resource for the future.

The mandates of party reform commissions have also given the Democratic party an agenda and a built-in timetable of reform through the 1972 national convention. The issuance of official guidelines for delegate selection in late 1969 and the compliance letters to each state chairman that followed in early 1970 gave the state parties extended lead time to accomplish the necessary reforms. The Democratic National Committee set a precedent for one of the major parties by issuing a two-part call for the 1972 convention. The first part, issued on February 19, 1971, included both the McGovern Commission guidelines on delegate selection and the O'Hara Commission recommendations establishing detailed procedures for credentials challenges, thereby giving all state parties ample time to monitor the delegate selection process and to prepare challenges.

The work of the Democratic reform commissions had clearly demonstrated that political parties can meet and deliberate on important party issues in sessions open to the public and the press. Both the McGovern-Fraser and O'Hara Commissions held open sessions and frequent press briefings. The staff of the McGovern Commission has also made virtually all relevant background material and documents available to interested scholars. The O'Hara Commission wrote into its final recommendations a provision making "all convention, pre-convention, and post-convention records of business and correspondence of the Convention's committees, its officers, and of the Democratic National Committee relating to the Democratic National Convention open and available for public inspection at reasonable times and for copying without expense to the Democratic National Committee."

The party commission process has also had the observable effect of democratizing the organization and procedures of the Democratic party. Both reform commissions at times functioned as independent party legislatures, pressing the commission leadership and staff for broader reform objectives (a process that it was fortunately possible to observe, thanks to the policy of open deliberative sessions). The O'Hara Commission, on point after point in its deliberations on convention arrangements, redrafted suggested wording to reduce the discretionary powers of the Democratic National Chairman and to build in a formal review function for the Democratic National Committee.

The Democratic reform commissions deserve full credit for their significant accomplishments within limited mandates, with meager party financial resources and within a remarkably short period of time. (The Democratic National Committee reported expenditures of $310,000 on its reform commissions through October 1971.) However, some notable deficiencies and weaknesses which may limit the reform process should also be emphasized.

One of the most troubling aspects of the Democratic reform movement has been the poor public attendance at its hearings. The November 1969 deliberative sessions of the McGovern Commission held in Washington to draft the official guidelines were viewed by only a handful of people. Public hearings of the McGovern Commission in New York and Philadelphia, cities with a long history of reform activity, attracted well under 100 people each, and even the Chicago hearings, about the largest in the series, drew only about 150. Some of the O'Hara Commission hearings attracted so few witnesses and observers that it was difficult for the chairman to conduct effective proceedings. Something is awry when party groups committed in principle to participatory democracy conduct such important proceedings before such sparse audiences. Admittedly the commissions did operate with limited staff and financial resources, which hampered advance work and follow-up procedures. Nor could state party contacts always be relied on to make adequate preparations. Regardless of explanations, the effect has been to limit public involvement in the party reform process.

The actual membership of the reform commissions and the constituency they have activated have also been limited in certain respects. Although both panels included reformers, labor

leaders, blacks, and Mexican Americans, two groups were significantly underrepresented—women and young people under
the age of 30. (David Mixner and Dennis T. "Teddy" O'Toole,
campaign workers for McCarthy and Humphrey in 1968, referred to themselves half jokingly as the "token youth" on the
commissions.) Several who appeared before the commissions
also criticized the underrepresentation of blacks, Chicanos,
Indians and other minorities on the lists of witnesses as well
as in the audience.

There was some effort on the part of groups like organized
labor to boycott the reform hearings or to maintain a diplo-
matic silence until the strength of sentiment for party reform
could be determined. But the more general problems that reform leaders encountered in encouraging the participation of
important elements of the Democratic coalition suggest some
long-term difficulties in building a reform constituency.

The Democratic reform movement, despite its network of
state reform bodies and intense and vocal reform-oriented
minority, has apparently been unable to institutionalize itself
within the party structure as a permanent impetus to reform.
There is not even a simple mimeographed reform newsletter
with progress reports from the states. Nor has a national citizen
committee been established to back Democratic reform. Even
groups outside the formal party structure like the New Democratic Coalition, Americans for Democratic Action and the
Center for Political Reform have had little success in establishing a clearinghouse on party reform. Unless renewed, the
mandates of the reform commissions are scheduled to terminate in 1972, and reform Democrats will be left without an
organizational focus inside the party.

Party reformers, backed by sympathetic Democratic national chairmen, have in effect decided to use the Democratic
National Committee and formal organization resources as
the base for party reform. Whatever the advantages of this
approach, the failure of the reform movement to institutionalize
itself at minimal cost may well be one of the most serious
handicaps to Democratic party reform.

The lack of intensive media coverage and analysis has also
weakened the reform process. During the early phases of

Democratic party reform, Alan L. Otten of the *Wall Street Journal* observed that neither reform commission was being taken quite seriously: "Many party pros are aloof, and the press is paying surprisingly little attention."[6] The reports and open deliberative sessions of the national commissions have received periodic attention and enough national columns to make some Republican leaders envious of the press coverage given the Democrats. But no national news agency has followed the commissions in the field, and the Washington *Post* covered one of the major Washington meetings of the O'Hara Commission with a brief wire-service item. The *National Journal's* June 1971 state-by-state analysis of Democratic party reform was the first comprehensive evaluation of the reform effort to be published.[7] There has generally been a critical lack of information in the media on the status of party reform.

Part of the responsibility lies in the repeated failure of reformers to recognize the need to interest the news media in the work of party modernization. Neither Democratic reform commission retained a press or public relations director or consultant, although the McGovern staff did take an active role in encouraging press coverage of its activities. Part of the responsibility also lies with the reporters, who, according to Senator Hughes, are often "more interested in presidential politics than in political reform." Considering the resources the news media devote to the quadrennial national political conventions, it is surprising that such a significant development as the party reform movement has not received more interpretive analysis. NBC-TV's November 1971 program about the loyal opposition, entitled "A Democratic Reformation," was the first coverage by network television of the extensive changes occurring in the preconvention processes of the Democratic party.

The momentum and cohesiveness of the reform effort could be seriously damaged in 1972 by the individual various Demo-

---

6 Alan L. Otten, "Reform Movement," *Wall Street Journal*, September 17, 1969.
7 "Compliance with Major Reforms: A State-by-State Analysis," *National Journal*, June 19, 1971, pp. 1302–03.

cratic presidential hopefuls as they seek delegate support and bargaining advantages at the national convention. The resignation of Senator McGovern as chairman of the Commission on Party Structure and Delegate Selection in January 1971 formally signaled the beginning of a new phase in the reform effort. The decision of George Meany to enlist the resources of the AFL-CIO's Committee on Political Education in the fight for a record number of labor delegates means that all major candidates and interests within the party will be operating within the new guidelines.

Some observers, among them the columnist Joseph Alsop, have expressed fear that anticipated delegate challenges may be used to attempt to discredit the Democratic convention rather than to reform it. The credentials row, he believes, "will provide the ideal fuel for a fourth party movement."[8] Party reformers, in turn, who have watched Chairman O'Brien railroad party reform measures through the national committee without debate, question the spirit with which the party organization and labor leaders will play the game. The entry of George Wallace in a number of Democratic primaries adds yet more uncertainty to the convention outcome. Although the potential for a serious party split remains, there is an important change from 1968. The Democrats will all be fighting within generally well-understood ground rules under an unprecedented public spotlight.

The greatest obstacle to Democratic party reform, however, may lie in how the Democrats handle success. The commitment the Democrats made to reform at the 1968 Chicago convention has thus far been strong enough to more than outweigh actual and potential difficulties. But the Democratic reform movement has been limited to the major reform objectives of increased popular control over the nominating process and reestablishment of public confidence in the national convention. Accordingly, Democrats have focused their reform activities on one major function of the parties, the nomination of the party's presidential candidate, and have largely ignored other con-

---

[8] Joseph Alsop, "Perils of Fourth Party Hang over Democrats," Boston *Globe*, November 22, 1971.

tinuing or new functions for political parties in the four-year period between conventions: the recruitment and development of candidates, the staffing of state and national administrations, the continuing development of party programs, party regulation of political consultants, and the long-term financing of party modernization.

As significant as their initial efforts may be, the Democrats have no long-term program for party reform beyond a joint report of the two reform commissions to the 1972 national convention dealing with the future of the Democratic National Committee and other interim party bodies. No major Democratic party leader or presidential contender has outlined or called for such a program. The Democrats may congratulate themselves on their success and disband their reform efforts in 1972 after simply endorsing the work of the reform commissions without extending or expanding their mandates, and return to the pattern of party politics as usual. The attitude of the Democratic state committee of New York is a suitable warning. After voting extensive changes in the state party rules to satisfy the McGovern guidelines, the committee defeated a resolution commending the commission for its work by a 3–1 margin. The real test of the Democratic reform movement will be what happens at and after Miami Beach.

Where Is the Republican Reform Movement?

The Republican process of self-examination and reform, initiated in the relative tranquillity of Miami Beach in 1968, was entrusted to the Delegates and Organizations (DO) Committee. Appointed in June 1969 by Republican National Chairman Rogers C. B. Morton, the committee was authorized to review and study the rules of the convention; the relationship between the Republican National Committee (RNC), Republican state committees and other Republican organizations; and implementation of Rule No. 32, which provides that "in selecting delegates to convention at all levels, participation shall in no way be abridged for reasons of race, religion, color or national origin." Reporting to the national committee some 18 months later, DO Committee Chairman Mrs. M. Stanley

Ginn, national committeewoman from Missouri, summed up the committee's work of encouraging "natural reform": "One cannot tamper with so great an institution as the Republican Party without being grateful for what we have." The Democrats took the occasion to mock the "DO nothing" Committee and its deliberations: "The elephant labored—and brought forth a slick, 35-page souvenir that was a loud cry for the *status quo*."

In contrast to the diverse membership of the Democratic reform commissions, the DO Committee was composed of 18 members of the Republican National Committee (either national committeemen, national committeewomen or state chairmen), primarily from the West and Midwest. Mrs. Ginn noted that the members of her committee had a total of 430 years of Republican party experience and 96 years of service on the Republican National Committee. "We did this with much of our lives," she told the full RNC. Reflecting the representational limitations of the national committee, the DO Committee included no blacks, other racial minorities or young people. Of the ten most populous states, only Illinois was represented. Unlike the Democratic commissions, however, the committee did have a nearly equal number of men and women (ten to eight) and a woman as chairman. The DO Committee staff was closely identified with the party organization, in contrast to the McGovern staff, which was decidedly young and reform-oriented. The press was given little information on Republican reform and, except for two brief progress reports to the RNC in 1971,[9] the bulk of the committee's work has gone unreported in either party or general publications.

The procedures of the DO Committee also sharply contrasted with the McGovern and O'Hara Commissions. The committee, operating as a kind of Republican star chamber, held no open hearings and issued no invitations to the public to testify before

---

[9] Delegates and Organizations Committee, *Programming for the Future: Part I,* Progress Report of the DO Committee to the Republican National Committee, Washington, D.C., January 15–17, 1971 (Washington, D.C.: Republican National Committee, 1971); *The Delegate Selection Procedures for the Republican Party: Part II,* Progress Report of the DO Committee to the Republican National Committee, Denver, Colorado, July 23, 1971 (Washington, D.C.: Republican National Committee, 1971).

closed hearings or to submit written testimony or recommendations. Instead, the DO Committee relied on a series of ques-
tionnaires and a process of self-examination by the party
leadership. First, a memorandum was distributed to all members
of the Republican National Committee (which includes all state
chairmen), Republican members of both houses of Congress
and Republican governors, asking for their recommendations
on how to get maximum citizen participation in state parties
and for any comments on the conduct or processes of the
national convention. They were also requested to submit the
names of six "informed people" in each state, who were then
sent a detailed questionnaire on the delegate selection process.
Oral testimony was taken from members of Congress who
wished to appear before the committee, state leaders were
requested to forward any reports or reform recommendations
developed at the state level and a few outside experts were
invited to discuss specific topics. Then a second nine-page
questionnaire on citizen participation and the convention was
circulated, in which party leaders were asked to judge 42
specific reform suggestions either "acceptable" or "unaccept-
able." The questions appeared to be similar to those asked by
the McGovern Commission, e.g., "Does any step of the delegate
selection process occur before the presidential election year?";
"Is the unit rule imposed at any point in the selection of delegates in your state?" No binding recommendations to state
organizations, however, resulted from the survey. In a separate
action, Republican Counsel Fred G. Scribner wrote to the
state parties requesting information on the implementation of
Rule No. 32.

The recommendations incorporated in the committee's progress reports were put at the disposal of the national chairman
and the convention's Arrangements Committee without a
formal vote of either the DO Committee or the Republican
National Committee. Among the few controversial recommendations presented were a proposal that each state delegation name "one man and one woman, one Delegate under the
age of 25, and one Delegate who is a member of a minority
ethnic group" to each of the major convention committees and
proposals for "equal representation" of men and women on

state delegations and the inclusion of "delegates under 25 years of age in numerical equity to their voting strength within the states."

In view of the leisurely pace of the committee, the time required to implement reforms at the state level and the fact that the reform "recommendations" have no binding force until enacted by the Rules Committee at the national convention, it is questionable whether there will be substantial reforms in Republican state delegate-selection procedures until after 1972. The DO members consider the Democratic efforts to provide mandatory representation for blacks, women and youth ill-advised and unworkable. One Republican state chairman said: "You can't control that and have an elective process, too. Anyone who wants to influence the process has to be a delegate and anyone who wants to serve as a delegate should run for election as such. You can be thoughtful and conscious of the need to bring in more youth. You can use intern systems, hear youth testimony, but you can't *require* youth representation." Republican state organizations such as the one in California, however, are making serious efforts to recruit representative delegations, including delegates under 25. In Minnesota, Republican women have waged an active campaign in party caucuses for equitable delegate representation.

While the DO Committee may not have been the catalyst for Republican party reform that its Democratic counterparts were, the failure of a vital Republican reform movement to develop is puzzling for several reasons. Republicans, with less than 30 percent of the public willing to identify with the party, have long had practical political incentives to want reform. Republican liberals, moderates and conservatives may disagree on which group or groups should receive priority attention— blacks, young people, blue-collar workers, suburbanites or white Southerners—but they share an interest in broadening the party base through greater popular participation. A prospective reform constituency within the party can also be identified. Some four million Republicans are still willing to identify themselves as liberal Republicans, and issue polls on Vietnam, civil rights, welfare reform and other social problems reveal a persistent though reduced strain of progressive Republicanism. Nor is likely support for party reform limited to party liberals. Republicans from former National Chairman Leonard W. Hall to columnist Kevin Phillips have criticized their party for its social exclusivity and failure to appeal to broader social groupings. Former California Senator William F. Knowland's Oakland *Tribune* has editorially warned Republican party leaders not to take "a holier-than-thou attitude" toward the current studies of the Democrats. "There are logical, almost necessary improvements in procedures and rules being studied that would seem to be in the best interests of both parties."[10]

Nor is party modernization unfamiliar to Republicans. The 1948 and 1952 convention credentials fights tested and updated rules relating to credentials challenges. After the 1964 convention that nominated Arizona Senator Barry Goldwater divided the party and cost it the election, former President Eisenhower urged the national committee to reform the convention system. The result was an extensive study and report[11] whose recommendations were implemented by Chairman Ray C. Bliss in what many Republicans view as a model party convention in 1968. In taking office, President Nixon set his administration on the course of reform with comprehensive proposals for changes in government, taxation, the postal system and welfare. The President's long-standing reputation as a party leader and builder raised some hopes that his agenda might also include party reform. His first nominee as National Chairman, Rogers Morton, initiated several innovative long-range party programs, although few, including the ambitious Mission 70's program of revitalizing party organization, survived Morton's 21-month tenure in vigorous form.

What steps have been taken in the direction of party modernization illustrate a potential rather than an actual reform movement in the Republican party. No nationally prominent Republican leader has endorsed party reconstruction as a major objective, although Congressman Paul N. "Pete"

---

10 Editorial, Oakland *Tribune,* April 30, 1969.
11 *Report of the Committee on Convention Reforms,* report to the Republican National Committee, New Orleans, La., January 23, 1967 (Washington, D.C.: Republican National Committee, 1967).

McCloskey, Jr., listed it as one reason he decided to enter the 1972 presidential contest. Erwin D. Canham, editor in chief of the *Christian Science Monitor,* observed that "had Mr. Nixon been able to be a strongly partisan Republican leader, he might have forged a resurgent party. He could not do that in the face of the congressional majorities."[12] The President, when he assumed office, also lacked sufficient political strength within his own party, its congressional wings and Republican state organizations to press reform. Robert M. Coard, Executive Director of an antipoverty agency, Action for Boston Community Development (ABCD), may have pinpointed the guiding principle of the Nixon administration's approach to reform when he noted the President's preference for efficient management at the expense of neighborhood participation. Republican party modernization programs at both the national and state level have clearly reflected this emphasis on improved professional skills and management techniques. At some point, however, the Nixon administration, already sensitive to the power of the reform movement in consumer affairs and environmental protection, might also recognize the significance of party reform.

The Ripon Society, which speaks frequently on Republican party politics, has limited itself to a bystander's role, satisfied with publishing an article wondering "Where Is the Republican McGovern Commission?," outlining "a few principles and possible approaches" to party reform, and later urging "Republicans who want to reform American government and their party" to join John W. Gardner's "nonpartisan" Common Cause. In November 1971, the society initiated, with the legal assistance of New York attorney Robert M. Pennoyer, a last-minute court test of the formula for allocating delegates to the 1972 Republican National Convention.[13] Ripon quickly withdrew

---

[12] Erwin D. Canham, "The Shape of the Parties," *Christian Science Monitor,* August 25, 1969.

[13] The Ripon Society subsequently issued a statement setting forth the facts included in the complaint and its reasons for resorting to legal action. See "Delegates Discrimination and the Constitution," A Ripon Society Statement on the Malapportionment of Delegates to Republican National Conventions, n.d.

the challenge after meetings with party representatives. The society has not appointed task forces on party reform or otherwise lobbied the party organization to implement reform measures.

Republican reform efforts at the state level (often encouraged indirectly by the activity of Democratic state reform commissions) have remained isolated, lacking an active focus or institutional impetus comparable to the national Democratic reform commissions. In Missouri, five Republican task forces were formed in mid-1969 to study party organization and ways to broaden membership among young persons, the elderly, women's groups and the black community. In New Jersey, James H. Wallwork, a young reform Republican state senator, called for a revitalization of the Republican party and introduced legislation to establish a bipartisan commission to review state laws and update both the Democratic and Republican parties. Under the leadership of Chairman C. Montgomery Johnson, the Washington State Republican Committee approved the participation of 18-year-olds in all precinct, county, district and state conventions and granted college and university students direct representation through a 25-member voting delegation to the state convention. The Erie County (Buffalo) New York Republican County Committee initiated a series of reforms, among them a requirement that the party's ward and town committees submit periodic written reports including information on how many committeemen attended and what ideas or recommendations were advanced.

The leadership of the party, however, has voiced a generally complacent view of the current state of Republican party organization, delegate selection and convention operations. "Many of the things the Democrats are now trying to reform the Republicans took care of one hundred years ago," observed one Republican professional. "The Republicans have no fractional votes, abolished the unit rule many years ago, and always have new rules adopted four years in advance which govern the convention process and the formula for the number of delegates. Everyone knows the ground rules in advance."

Members of the DO Committee were struck by how many of the Democrats' problems "we don't have to worry about." The

Democrats "offer no counsel or inspiration for us," observed Mrs. Ginn. Only Senator Jacob K. Javits (R-N.Y.) sounded a warning that "the party would do well to guarantee that delegations represent in some reasonable measure the composition of the population of each state, so that we have some framework within the rules to challenge all-white delegations from those states which continue to practice racial discrimination in the selection of delegates." Nor do Republicans anticipate the credentials challenges that have plagued recent Democratic conventions. Quite the contrary, according to columnist Flora Lewis: "The Republicans are inclined to enjoy the Democrats' dilemma—insist on reform and infuriate the South or dawdle and infuriate the liberals." Republican leaders are confident that "Southern Democrats will rebel if the national Democratic party pushes through the reforms ordered at its Chicago convention."[14] Democratic party reformers, however, have announced plans to assist challenge delegations at the 1972 Republican convention. "It is time that the Republican Party came face to face with the substantive issues of open participation and anti-discrimination in the delegate selection process," reported one group.[15]

The slow response of Republican party leaders to the party reform issue and the relative complacency of the party membership may also be attributed in part to the relatively closed style and homogeneity of the party itself. The substantial black minority whose struggle for representation in the Democratic parties of Alabama, Georgia and Mississippi dramatized the need for reform has no counterpart in the Republican party. Instead, according to Marcus Raskin, a founder of the New Party, the GOP has maintained its narrow white, Protestant, middle-class base and its leaders have attempted to "inoculate" the public from government with the slogan "We will take care of your problems." "The Republican party never even gives up a piece of the action," Raskin asserted.

---

[14] Flora Lewis, "2-Party South?," *Citizen Register* (Ossining, N.Y.), March 13, 1969.
[15] Center for Political Reform, "Projected Activities," memorandum distributed in Washington, D.C., July 1971, p. 4.

The Republicans have failed to grasp the longer-term significance of the Democratic reform movement as a means for reinvigorating the party's base. Party reform is viewed by Republicans as a responsibility of the leadership and of insiders who understand and appreciate the needs of the party organization, i.e., people who can make "positive suggestions." DO Committee proceedings have been treated primarily as an in-house party operation, and virtually no demand has been voiced by the party's rank and file to participate in the committee's work. In consequence, the Republicans have missed an excellent opportunity to build a reform constituency, to raise significant new issues for party modernization, or to provide institutional or procedural means to encourage participation.

It is not possible to forecast what events or elements within the party will precipitate a Republican reform movement, but the potential is there. Assuming that the Democratic party is able to sustain a long-term reform movement that substantially restructures the organization, it is difficult to see how the closed style and narrow base of the Republican party can escape the demand for reform during the 1970's. The Democrats may be happy to "go it alone," but in the long run a vital Republican reform movement would broaden the scope of the party reform movement, encourage reform efforts at the state level, provide additional opportunities for experimentation, and open new avenues of participation in the political process.

The Public Interest Movement:
A New Impulse for Social and Political Reform

The movement for party reform could be strengthened significantly in the 1970's by the energies of the public interest movement represented in the myriad so-called public interest law firms and related institutions that have flourished in recent years. Young public interest lawyers were intimately involved in the early successes of Democratic party reform and they may play an even more significant role in the future restructuring of American political institutions.

Although the activities of public interest lawyers are not new—litigation, investigation, policy research, counseling, public relations, lobbying and community organization—"the programmatic use of various strategies and various forums by a single lawyer or law firm in behalf of broad social causes" has been novel in legal representation. The decision of these young lawyers to remain outside of government or corporate law practice distinguishes them from those lawyers who have contributed to the public good through government service, a channel opened in the New Deal administrations of the 1930's, or pro bono activities of commercial law firms that permit their staff to spend a certain percentage of their time on public interest cases. The new public interest lawyers "are committed ultimately to causes, not clients. . . . Their efforts take on added significance because the resources available to pursue causes of social justice are limited; thus these lawyers are not only advocates in particular causes, but also arbiters of social priorities."[16] They are "gadflies" and "catalysts" for what they hope will be a major reallocation of legal resources to unrepresented or unorganized constituencies.

Although the public interest movement has often been described as "above partisan politics" or as a new "professional citizen" movement, its experience is of vital importance to the political parties and the party reform movement for several reasons. First, public interest lawyers have successfully evolved political strategies to pressure corporations and major public institutions to make their decision-making processes more open and accessible to the public. At the same time, they have established a wide variety of viable institutions and programs to develop public consciousness of issues, to mobilize effective political coalitions, and to sustain the reform impetus. The techniques and institutions developed by lawyers representing the poor, political and cultural dissidents, and radical movements, and other public interest lawyers attempting to further more diffuse and general causes such as consumer and environmental affairs, can be transferred and adopted in numerous ways to party politics. A landmark Conference on the Vote,

---

[16] "The New Public Interest Lawyers," *Yale Law Journal*, May 1970, pp. 1146–47. Simon Lazarus is completing a critical historical and philosophical study of the new populist movement.

convened in Washington, D.C., in November 1971 by the Lawyers' Committee for Civil Rights Under Law and almost a score of cosponsoring organizations, sought, for example, to further legal strategies for removing or alleviating barriers to new voting rights. More than 200 public interest lawyers, party activists and interested citizens participated in workshops on such varied topics as eligibility to vote, the presidential nominating process, campaign finance, minority racial groups and the poor, and apportionment of legislative districts.

Second, public interest firms have been well in advance of the parties in evaluating governmental performance and in exploring the legal pressure points for reform in federal and state governments. As pointed out by Jean C. Cahn, director of the Urban Law Institute in Washington, D.C., "The crucial anti-democratic obstacles in the system often are in the administrative actions of the government—not in elections or legislation. Legislation gets undone or reinterpreted in executive departments or in rulings of administrative agencies." Like several other public interest units, the Washington Research Project, according to Director Marion Wright Edelman, functions as "a monitoring operation at the federal level" with a good internal information network in government and persistent surveillance of the second and third levels of the bureaucracy.

Third, if the parties are to be strengthened as agencies for citizen involvement in government, they will have to assume some of the problem-solving roles public interest groups have been performing in lieu of the parties. The group of Washington institutions created by Ralph Nader, including the Center for the Study of Responsive Law, the Public Interest Research Group and the Nader intern program (the well-known Nader's Raiders), have served as models for the mushrooming public interest movement. Nonprofit research corporations like the Center for Analysis of Public Issues in Princeton, New Jersey, have been started in various states. Individual national and state legislators have set up their own raider units, and one state governor, Republican William T. Cahill of New Jersey, has enlisted local law students in the state attorney general's office to aid in the fight against consumer fraud. Alumni of

Nader organizations have begun moving into appointive governmental positions such as the Maine Public Utilities Commission.

Of particular significance to the parties is Nader's attempt to organize college youth, a sector of the electorate where party identification is already weakest and still declining. The Oregon Student Public Interest Research Group, launched in November 1970 as a national model for other states and regions, is a Nader challenge to students "to organize their own professional action arm" by raising their college fees by one dollar a quarter. (Students opposed to the assessment could request a refund.) If successful, the plan's potential return of about $150,000 a year in Oregon would help to finance a staff of 10 to 15 full-time professionals, including lawyers, scientists, engineers and lobbyists. Students themselves would choose the issues they wanted to lobby for or against. The college financing plan, at an average assessment of $3.00 a year, if extended to all 8,000,000 students enrolled in over 2,000 colleges, could yield a $24,000,000 base for the student arm of the movement. The plan has received enthusiastic but scattered initial backing in more than a dozen key states.

Perhaps of most significance to the party reform movement in the long run will be the as yet largely untapped pool of talented manpower and organizational and strategic skills represented in the public interest law firms. Common Cause, which describes itself as a nonpartisan "public-interest lobby," has, for example, taken some initial steps in the direction of involving public interest lawyers more directly in political reform. A suit filed in January 1971 in the Federal District Court for the District of Columbia enjoined the Democratic and Republican National Committees and the Conservative party of New York from violating federal campaign spending laws, especially those provisions setting a limit of $5,000 on individual contributions to or on behalf of any candidate or any political committee. Common Cause for a time maintained a clearinghouse service for public interest lawyers involved in litigation of student residency requirements for voting and sought revision of state laws governing the methods of selecting delegates to the presidential nominating conventions. The Citizens' Research Foundation of Princeton, New Jersey, has retained a public interest lawyer, William A. Dobrovir, to explore possible courses of litigation as "alternative strategies" to legislation on campaign fund raising and expenditure. Organizations like these could easily expand their use of public interest lawyers to effect political reform.

The first attempt to coordinate the public interest approach and resources with the party reform movement has been the Center for Political Reform, a nonprofit (but not tax-exempt) corporation in Washington, D.C. The center was established in January 1971 by Kenneth Bode, former research director for the McGovern Commission, specifically to provide "ongoing manpower and technical assistance" to assure implementation of the McGovern Commission guidelines, to encourage adoption by the O'Hara Commission of rules which will provide for a more open, more responsive national convention, and to continue the democratization process within the Democratic party by encouraging the adoption of further organizational and procedural reforms at the 1972 convention. The center has attempted to exercise leverage on the reform process through massive research and information combined with technical and legal expertise in the complicated and expanding area of party law, rules and procedures. It has concentrated its efforts on the two Democratic party reform commissions and the 20 most populous states, which will dominate the national convention and its committees as a result of O'Hara Commission reapportionment reforms. Among its services the center has provided extensive research memoranda for members of the Democratic reform commissions, computer printouts on alternative apportionment formulas for the national convention, technical assistance in drafting new primary laws for states like Connecticut and Massachusetts, and aid to individual state parties in drafting new party rules and legislation and developing strategies of litigation. The center has coordinated challenges on delegate credentials among women's, blacks' and youth political caucuses with the support of an ad hoc funding mechanism, "People Politics," established in early 1972 with a $100,000 contribution from philanthropist and political activist Stewart Mott.

At present, the Democratic party stands to gain most directly from the resources of the public interest movement. There is no consensus, however, on the future political direction of the movement. Spokesmen for the New Party like Marcus Raskin and novelist-playwright Gore Vidal view Nader as an ideal presidential candidate. Journalist James Ridgeway expects "a serious drive to create a Populist wing within the Democratic party" through the stitching together of "a political apparatus that can embody and develop the politics of Ralph Nader."[17] Public interest lawyer Geoffrey Cowan, now with the Center for Law and Social Policy, feels that the Democratic party has responded to many of the demands that he and his associates advanced through the Hughes Commission and accordingly that he "owes the party something." At the same time, he thinks that the party reform and public interest movements may ultimately come together in a separate political party organized not to win elections but to find ways for citizens to intervene directly in decisions that affect their lives. "The party would have an office in Washington and maybe a couple of senators. It might not even run a candidate for President. Instead it would concentrate on developing operative constituencies for action."

While the public interest movement faces problems, including the development of a long-term financial base, it already overshadows the traditional political parties in output, reformist zeal and talented professional elites. If the energies of the movement flow into the political and governmental vacuum of the existing party structure, the American system could indeed be entering a new era of political reform.

Recommendations: Broadening the Movement for Party Reform

The requirements for party modernization and reform are much more extensive and urgent than either major party organization now envisages. If the longer-term goal of citizen parties is to be realized, the party reform movement needs a

---

[17] James Ridgeway, "Nader's Efforts May Become the Focus of 'New Populism,'" *American Report* (New York), May 7, 1971.

new and broader mandate, a higher degree of institutionalization, and a long-term strategy. A much bolder vision of the role that parties can play in influencing and leading government and in developing citizen competence through participation in political decision making must inspire party reformers.

The prospects for substantial party reform throughout the 1970's are good. A dedicated group of men and women with well-defined goals and remarkably little in the way of political resources can win general public and party support and make compelling demands for reform on party leaders. The successful reform strategies of the young lawyers of the ad hoc Hughes Commission on the Democratic Selection of Presidential Nominees and the Democratic party's official reform commissions have been followed by plans of the National Women's Political Caucus to ensure that women constitute at least half of the delegates to the presidential nominating conventions. A national black political convention will coordinate strategies for black participation in the major party conventions and local, state and national elections of 1972. The reform strategies and organizational skills of the public interest movement have yet to be extended in a substantial way to the political parties. If public interest lawyers and party reformers join forces, party reform could spread rapidly through systematic legal action in the states.

The party reform movement has barely tapped the political resources that we believe are available to it among the general public. As currently organized, the reform movement is still an elite operation involving a relatively small number of activists. Perhaps a measure of party reform can be achieved and sustained without a large, organized, active reform constituency. But fundamental changes in the directions suggested by this book require that the energies and creativity of massive numbers of individual citizens be enlisted in the work of party reform. In the following recommendations we suggest steps that can be taken to strengthen and sustain the party reform movement.

Recommendation 1. Both parties should make more frequent use of representative party commissions to resolve the wide

range of issues facing them in the 1970's. The Democratic
and Republican National Conventions should establish permanent commissions on party reform. Each national committee should appoint a full-time deputy chairman for party
reform.

The experience of the Democratic reform commissions has
clearly demonstrated the potential of the representative party
commission mechanism in opening new means of evaluation,
communication and participation to party leaders, party members and the public. To improve the effectiveness of future commissions, the parties should evaluate their current reform
commissions and consider the expanded use of professional and
academic consultants and public interest lawyers to supplement
party commission staff.

As the highest formal authority in the American political
system, the Democratic and Republican National Conventions
should reaffirm their long-term commitment to party modernization and establish permanent commissions on party reform
responsible for implementing convention mandates and for coordinating activities of state reform commissions. The 1972 national conventions should also authorize interim national party
conventions to meet prior to 1976 (and at regular intervals
thereafter) and, among other tasks, to review the work of party
reform commissions and to initiate reform measures as appropriate. Such interim conventions would periodically refocus
public and party attention on crucial reform questions and further legitimize the ongoing process of party reform.

In consultation with the national chairman and reform elements within the party, the Democratic and Republican
National Committees should each elect a full-time deputy
chairman for party reform responsible for the modernization
of party functions and organization. The deputy chairman
would maintain liaison between the national party reform
commissions and other party and citizen reform groups at the
national, state and local levels. He could also seek the advice
and services of the legal staff of the office of the party's general counsel, public interest lawyers and consultants knowledgeable in party reform, party organization and political

campaign operations and technology. His staff could offer communications, fund raising, polling and public relations services to party reform groups and coordinate such activities as the public education campaign and party reform newsletter suggested below.

Recommendation 2. Reform-oriented leaders and members of both parties should develop and implement comprehensive strategies for promoting party reform through the national conventions, the congressional parties, other party forums, and the presidential nomination process.

Since fundamental party reform is a long-term process that will extend over several national party conventions, reformers in both parties should develop a comprehensive strategy for the 1972 national conventions to produce new mandates for party reform in the 1970's. Working through existing party reform units, special or ad hoc reform commissions, or reform caucuses, they should define priority objectives such as a major restructuring of the party national committees and state party organizations, the permanent establishment of representative party reform commissions, the call for interim party conventions and an evaluation of national party–congressional party relationships. Such planks could be incorporated in majority or minority reports of convention committees and resolutions of the Platform, Rules and Credentials Committees for action on the convention floor. Party reformers should also establish planning and evaluation units to study the 1972 convention process and to develop strategy for the 1976 conventions.

The resources of the congressional parties could complement party reform efforts in numerous ways. Senate and House party caucuses could press for congressional action on such questions as electoral reform, public service broadcasting, broadening the base of political fund raising and regulation of the political consulting and polling industry. Congressional committees or groups of Congressmen could sponsor public hearings, mail and telephone surveys and field investigations on a wide range of political reform subjects. A bipartisan ad hoc Senate-House committee could develop a legislative program of party reform and recommend coordinated action by Congress and the political parties to further specific reforms. This committee could also issue regular reports on pending bills, required legislation and committee and congressional action bearing on party reform and function as a clearinghouse for the activities of similar committees in the 50 state legislatures.

The Democratic and Republican Governors' Conferences could evaluate the potential role in party reform for governors and adopt a program for action at state, regional and national levels. Individual governors could either appoint representative citizen or legislative task forces or urge the state parties themselves to undertake the comprehensive examination and modernization of their organization and operations.

Reform-oriented Democratic leaders and party members should work to extend and strengthen the movement beyond the 1972 convention, encouraging state party reform commissions to broaden their mandates and to organize regional conferences of various state reform commissions.

Reform-oriented Republican leaders and party members could initiate a distinctive program of Republican party modernization that would build upon Democratic accomplishments as well as define new areas for party reform, such as allocation of party funds and services, the role of corporations and trade unions in the parties, and codes of ethics for elected officials, party spokesmen and endorsed candidates. A reform Republican organization could also call upon the Republican National Committee's Delegates and Organizations Committee to encourage full participation of party members in its work, to open its proceedings to the public, and to broaden the scope of its report to the 1972 national convention. Such a group could also advance its own program through a well-planned strategy of testing the fairness of delegate selection procedures in the states; testifying before the regional and national hearings of the convention's Platform, Rules and Credentials Committees; issuing minority committee reports where appropriate; and introducing reform resolutions on the convention floor.

Reform members of both parties could call on all presidential contenders, as prospective titular heads of their parties, to present their views on the need for party modernization together with recommendations to the party reform commissions, the appropriate convention committees and the voting public. Each candidate could also designate a staff member to serve as liaison with the reform commissions and pledge his aid in the implementation of reform guidelines and recommendations.

Few systematic efforts have been made to preserve records of party proceedings, files, records of votes and other documentation, with the result that most of this reference material has been lost for future party or public use. The recommendation of the O'Hara Commission that all Democratic convention records be collected and maintained at the headquarters of the Democratic National Committee and made available for public inspection is to be highly commended. Both parties should institute similar procedures for all records of the various party bodies and adopt as soon as possible a policy of publishing all proceedings, findings and recommendations of national and state reform commissions and making relevant background documents available to the public.

Independent publishers could be approached on the feasibility of issuing either the entire proceedings or key excerpts from the work of the various reform commissions, or a volume highlighting Democratic and Republican party reform efforts (along the lines of the *Congressional Quarterly*'s excellent summary of the 1968 national party conventions). Selected reform documents could also be included on a regular basis in the *Congressional Record*.

To further accountability for party reform, reform members of both parties could also work to ensure that votes on party reform in legislative and party bodies and statements on reform by party or elected officials or candidates are recorded and made available on request.

Recommendation 3. National and state parties and all party reform groups should encourage citizen participation in all aspects of the party reform movement and launch an educational campaign to build a reform constituency among the general public.

Citizen participation in party reform can be advanced by ensuring representative membership on all party reform bodies, publicizing and regularly scheduling open hearings and sessions around the country and making all relevant party records widely available to the public.

An educational campaign should be launched to dramatize the citizen's stakes in politics and the critical need for greater citizen participation and modernization of party functions. National parties and their reform commissions could adopt many of the techniques successfully used by the public interest movement in activating a consumer constituency. Reports on specific practices in the states out of compliance with national party standards could be issued, a series of documentaries on reform issues like the *Nader Report* could be prepared for public television, and a series of well-publicized preconvention hearings on party reform could be held in various parts of the country.

The party reform leadership should regularly brief the press on reform activities, encourage periodic news reports on the status and prospects for party modernization, and make themselves and key staff readily available for interview and talk-show programs. Reporters, commentators, and investigatory teams could be encouraged to use the occasion of the preconvention campaign and national conventions to explore party reform issues and objectives in background interviews and analyses. Reform-oriented groups could examine the opportunities for public education and political participation that technological advances such as cable television may present.

A party reform newsletter could be prepared at modest expense and circulated as widely as possible to party leaders, members of state party reform commissions, witnesses before reform hearings, contributors to reform activities, leaders of citizen groups, interested individuals and the press. Such a newsletter could include succinct status and background reports on relevant reform issues, summary proceedings, recommendations and reports of the various reform commissions; a timetable of current hearings, meetings, conventions and law cases dealing with party reform, and suggested action readers could take. All party and reform publications could include coupons or return postcards inviting readers to support party reform by submitting ideas and recommendations, by subscribing at a nominal charge to the party reform newsletter and by contributing to the party reform group or activity of their choice.

Recommendation 4. Individual citizens and citizen groups should actively encourage and participate in party reform through the various electoral and lobbying means at their disposal.

Citizens can encourage party reform through such means as electing convention delegates pledged to reform; testifying at regional convention platform hearings; lobbying for reform of state party statutes and rules; calling for and attending open sessions of party reform bodies; running reform slates in primaries; supporting congressional, gubernatorial, and presidential candidates committed to party reform; asking the media to cover reform hearings and activities on a regular basis; and contributing money to reform groups of their choice.

In order to reinforce the reform impetus of the national parties and to ensure essential coordination, evaluation and documentation, an independent reform unit should be established and funded on a long-term basis by a consortium of citizen organizations or by a political institute. Such a unit would monitor party reform activity, develop extensive information files and issue regular reports on the status of party reform. It could also coordinate the reform efforts of Independents and other concerned citizens and provide technical and information services to reform groups. Through educational programs, workshops and reports it could broaden public awareness of the need for reform and exert pressure for the implementation of specific reforms.

II

The National Conventions: Apexes of Party Power

The national party conventions of 1972 offer dramatic evidence of the ferment in American party politics and represent an extraordinary potential for party development.

A record number of women, blacks, Spanish Americans, and young delegates selected by new party guidelines, together with new convention rules requiring full debate and votes on all resolutions and reports, mark the progress of Democratic reform at Miami Beach. The tightly controlled, efficiently programmed convention of the Republicans presents a study in contrasts. At no point in recent party history have the widening differences between the two major parties been so evident. Underlining the importance of the national convention as a political institution, the American Independent Party, the New Party or People's Party, blacks, women, youth and other national groups have scheduled their own national conclaves to influence the Democrats and Republicans or to develop independent strategies.

Yet the major national party conventions are still largely lifeless shells of the traditional parties, controlled, planned and managed by a relatively small number of party officials. For a few short days they are given life. From every corner of the continent the great names of American politics, the local party notables, the candidate cadres, the politically curious, the political analysts and seers literally descend from the skies, transform the life of a city and capture the attention of the nation and the world. Then, as suddenly as they have been constructed, the conventions are dismantled, to be put together again in another four years. In the interim, only literary crafts-men of the caliber of Theodore H. White and Norman Mailer, joined by British observers Lewis Chester, Godfrey Hodgson and Bruce Page, have reawakened the overwhelming sense of mystery and majesty that is a national convention.

As the President has become the apex of power in American politics, so too have the national nominating conventions be-come apexes of party power. But conventions have taken their chief responsibility—the nomination of the President and his constitutional successor—in a shockingly casual manner. The preconvention campaign, media coverage, and candidate meet-ings with state delegations provide most of the screening—such as it is—of presidential candidates. The national convention itself is not structured to exercise its most critical function, deliberative choice of the party's and, more importantly, the nation's leaders. Nor have the national conventions functioned as governing bodies for the parties. They assemble vast pools of talented politicians, then fail to utilize their time and unique resources. In spite of the elaborate and detailed coverage by network television and radio and published accounts that have taken millions of Americans inside the convention hall, the inner workings of the convention, especially the critical ad-vance functions of the convention Arrangements Committees, remain the province of the party elite. As pointed out by Profes-sor Alexander M. Bickel of Yale, "No American political institu-tion is more visible than the convention, or more often visibly shoddy, and none is less visibly constituted and managed."[1]

Any long-term revitalization of the political parties as instruments for popular control of government will require modernization of such central party institutions as the con-ventions and their interim executive bodies, the national com-mittees. The direction of party reform suggested in this book—toward activist, participant-based party government—requires a new conception of the national convention and its functions.

Fortunately, few American political institutions are more

---

[1] Alexander M. Bickel, *The New Age of Political Reform: The Electoral College, the Convention, and the Party System,* Harper Colophon Books (New York: Harper & Row, 1968), p. 23.

susceptible of fundamental restructuring and modernization within the system. Since national conventions are constructed on party rules and precedents, unfettered by federal statutory regulation, with advance planning and proper structuring they can become active party congresses and working conventions—vital components of citizen parties in the future.

The Convention Game: Trends in the Convention Process

The current significance of conventions derives from one principal fact: they are the gatekeepers to the presidency. A unique institutional invention of the oldest extant democratic party system,[2] the national party conventions, with delegates apportioned by states, has evolved from the 1830's as an instrument for democratic succession to leadership. Yet what is striking about the American national party conventions is their continuity of form and failure to develop new functions over the years.

The major functions of party conventions—nominating, platform drafting, campaign rallying and acting as a governing body—were already substantially developed by 1860 and have survived essentially intact. The second national convention of the Republican party at the huge wooden Wigwam in Chicago in 1860 already had many of the elements associated with modern political conventions. Some 40,000 visitors, 500 delegates and 900 reporters jammed the facilities of the new first city of the great Northwest, whose population by the just completed census had reached 109,260. Lincoln publicists had staged a clever dramatization of Lincoln the Rail Splitter at the Illinois state Republican convention the week before the opening of the Chicago convention. Straw votes of delegations were taken on railroad trains converging on the city. A high-powered staff of "Lincoln hustlers, evangelists, sales-

---

[2] For an analysis of the historical origins of the national convention system see Roy Nichols, *The Invention of the American Political Parties: A Study of Improvisation* (New York: Macmillan, 1967); also, for a briefer account, see Paul T. David, Ralph M. Goldman, and Richard C. Bain, *The Politics of National Party Conventions* (rev. ed.; New York: Vintage Books, 1964), Ch. 3, "Origins of the National Convention System."

men, pleaders, exhorters, schemers,"[3] and, one might add, skilled politicians, fanned out from the headquarters hotel, bargaining hard with the important Indiana and Pennsylvania delegations and collecting political debts from delegates who were political and business associates throughout the Midwest. Inside the Wigwam, Lincoln's Chicago managers exploited every advantage, postponing the first ballot until tally sheets had been prepared and surprising the forces of New York Senator William H. Seward by counterfeiting seat tickets on the third day of the convention.

The only significant modifications of the convention system —the addition of popular presidential primaries—resulted from the demand for popular participation in the nominating function during the Progressive period.[4] When former President Theodore Roosevelt decided to challenge Republican incumbent William Howard Taft in 1912, the most dramatic way to demonstrate his popular support within the party was through the new presidential primaries in several states. Although Roosevelt bested Taft in nine out of ten races, including a stunning victory over the President in his home state of Ohio and decisive triumphs in the key states of California, Illinois, Oregon, Pennsylvania and New Jersey, Taft controlled the Republican party machinery, including the rotten-borough Southern delegations Roosevelt himself had used to consolidate his leadership of the party in 1904 and 1908. While ruthless in his exercise of power, Taft broke few party rules or precedents and saw nothing illegitimate in his nomination. Roosevelt, charging a steal of contested seats, ordered a bolt of his delegates and established a new national Progressive party. The Progressive presidential line failed but Progressive forces were able to enact presidential primary laws in 26 states by 1916.

As Progressive enthusiasm waned and President Woodrow Wilson chose not to press his call for a national presidential

---

[3] Carl Sandburg, *Abraham Lincoln: The Prairie Years and The War Years* (New York: Harcourt, Brace, 1954), p. 170.
[4] James W. Davis, *Presidential Primaries: Road to the White House* (New York: Thomas Y. Crowell, 1967), pp. 24–37.

primary law, it became clear that the convention system had survived its most serious test. Party leaders maintained ultimate control of the nominating function through the convention mechanism, although the new hybrid system of popular and party selection of convention delegates in the states gave candidates arenas where they could demonstrate their popular support before the convention. The defenses of the convention against replacement by a national primary remain strong.

Other changes in the nominating process have occurred, however. Several maturing trends are clearly visible within the convention framework broadly defined.

First, preconvention campaigning has accelerated and intensified. The name of the convention game is delegates, and every serious presidential candidate has encountered the problem of constructing a preconvention mechanism to search out, identify and influence a faceless mass of convention delegates. The style of presidential nominating politics, however, has changed substantially over the years. Although active preconvention campaigns were undertaken as early as 1844 by Martin Van Buren and Henry Clay, tradition usually dictated that "the office seeks the man." The aspirant's managers bargained for delegate support at state conventions and the national conclave while he waited at home for an official delegation of the party to notify him, often weeks later, of the convention choice.

As the presidency grew in stature and power during the twentieth century and as ambition accordingly followed power, many traditions of the convention system fell by the wayside. In 1932, Franklin D. Roosevelt broke precedent by flying to Chicago to deliver his acceptance speech in person. In 1940, Wendell L. Willkie became the first candidate in modern times to campaign personally in the convention city. In 1948, Harold E. Stassen of Minnesota forced a major presidential contender, Governor Thomas E. Dewey of New York, to campaign actively in the Oregon primary, and by 1952, when the Eisenhower-Taft contest raged within the Republican party, primary campaigning had become an essential feature of the preconvention period. Since then, the art of preconvention delegate operations has been progressively refined by John F. Kennedy in 1960, the Draft Goldwater organization of F. Clifton White in 1964, and Richard M. Nixon in 1968 and 1972.

The most vivid and detailed published account of preconvention strategy is White's memoir and manual of the Draft Goldwater movement.[5] After Senator Goldwater's dramatic speech to the 1960 Republican National Convention in Chicago withdrawing his name from nomination and challenging his supporters to recapture the Republican party through hard work, White and others began a four-year campaign for the 1964 nomination. White assembled a core group of 22 young men, many of whom had been associates in Young Republican politics, to plan strategy in Chicago in early October 1961. A two-room suite of offices was set up in New York (the so-called Suite 3505) and covert planning meetings continued until December 1962, when security on the well-advanced national network of Goldwater organizers was broken. Delegate operations were formally assumed in April 1963 by a National Draft Goldwater Committee directed by White. By late August 1963, full state organizations were rapidly being formed and many of White's associates believed that the Arizona Senator already had the Republican presidential nomination neatly wrapped up. From then until White received the final delegate tally in his huge electronic trailer command post outside the San Francisco Cow Palace, the Goldwater strategists skillfully outmaneuvered New York Governor Nelson A. Rockefeller, Ambassador Henry Cabot Lodge, Pennsylvania Governor William W. Scranton, former Vice President Richard Nixon, and a field of Republican hopefuls.

Second, the conventions have steadily become more national and centralized political institutions, reflecting in part the nationalizing trend also seen in the increased prominence of the President, of national officeholders, especially Senators, and of foreign and national domestic policy issues. In this regard the communications and transportation revolutions have exerted a powerful impact on the convention process.

---

[5] F. Clifton White, *Suite 3505: The Story of the Draft Goldwater Movement* (New Rochelle, N.Y.: Arlington House, 1967).

National conventions were first nationally broadcast by radio in 1924, and by 1952 network television convention teams had become a feature of the convention landscape. Between the conventions of 1956 and 1960, the jet airplane cut travel time in half. In January 1961, the American Telephone and Telegraph Company instituted its multiband Wide Area Telephone Service (WATS) lines, opening the possibility of effectively unlimited telephone service for preset monthly charges. Such technological advances made both the pre-convention primaries and state conventions and the national conventions themselves more accessible to the politicians and the public than they had ever been.

Other factors have served to erode the control of state political bosses, further increasing the national authority of the convention—the decline of patronage as the basis for state and urban party machines, the rise of nationwide interest groups like organized labor, and more recently, national Democratic party guidelines for state delegate selection procedures and apportionment of representation on convention committees on the basis of population.

A third trend has been toward increased public involvement in the convention process. Preconvention campaigns, presidential preference primaries, television and public opinion polls have dramatically opened what was previously a party affair for the party faithful to a new audience with quite different perspectives on politics and presidential selection. Television alone has created a vast second gallery at the national conventions. In 1960, an estimated 35 million Americans watched John Kennedy's acceptance speech in Los Angeles and some 100 million witnessed all or part of both national conventions.

As more announced and unannounced contenders are covered by the news media and as the use of public opinion polls by parties and aspirants increases, the public is becoming directly involved in the nomination process months before the convention actually meets. Democratic party reforms in the delegate selection process and challenges to state delegations in 1972 have also served to focus unprecedented news coverage on the preconvention campaigns within the parties.

The growing expectations and demands of the citizen audience have introduced a new and as yet unresolved tension in convention politics. Party delegates have the difficult task of selecting a nominee representative of the party and satisfying public preference at the same time. In 1964, for example, Republican delegates selected Goldwater, although several moderate Republican candidates had run well ahead of him in some critical primaries and although Governor Scranton held a 3–1 lead over the Arizona Senator among Republican voters in a Harris poll taken on the eve of the convention. The task may become even more difficult with the continued growth in Independent voter identification and the weakening of party ties in the electorate.

Fourth, the media have gained a pervasive new role in preconvention and convention politics. In one important regard the media have at least partially replaced the conventions, namely as "gatekeepers" to the presidential nomination. Public response to the national media has given the elite Washington press corps of national political writers and columnists, in particular, an indirect power through "exposure" to create, enhance or destroy candidacies apart from the actions of the conventions. Like a Greek chorus, these men of the highest caliber in their trade unobtrusively accompany announced and potential contenders, carefully screening and testing them in press conferences and network news programs, at major party conclaves and on the primary trail.

Political correspondent David S. Broder has acknowledged the "talent scout" role of political reporters and the formidable powers this "screening committee" possesses. Broder himself is concerned about the unrepresentative character of such a committee, which is predominantly white, male, middle-aged, middle-class, and Eastern by residence if not by birth: "Whether their standards are good or bad, whether they are characteristic or eccentric so far as the society is concerned, they make their standards stick."[6]

Recent campaigns provide numerous examples, real and

6 David S. Broder, "Political Reporters in Presidential Politics," *Washington Monthly*, February 1969, pp. 26–29.

alleged, of the power of media and their impact on public opinion polls and presidential elections. Governor Scranton's rise from a one-term Pennsylvania Congressman in 1962 to a serious presidential contender in early 1964 depended heavily on national media exposure. Early in 1971, almost a year and a half ahead of the 1972 Democratic National Convention, a small group of five reporters, one magazine writer and a photographer joined Senator Edmund S. Muskie and his staff on a two-week tour of Israel, Egypt, the Soviet Union and West Germany. "We were for Muskie, a constant reminder," Jules Witcover of the Los Angeles *Times* later observed, "of what has come to be known among national political writers as 'the George Romney syndrome'—that phenomenon of 1967 which saw Romney's front-running status for the 1968 Republican nomination demolished by a pursuing national press corps."[7]

In addition to a preconvention role in screening candidates, the media play a critical convention role in transmitting images of the parties "in convention" to the American voters, who tend to review their party and candidate preferences at that time. The Republican candidate in 1964, Senator Barry Goldwater, and the Democratic candidate in 1968, Vice President Hubert H. Humphrey, both blamed the media, especially television news coverage of the conventions, for their later campaign difficulties. In *The Making of the President 1968*, Theodore H. White has given us a vivid account of Humphrey's anger and hurt at the televised juxtaposition of his nomination and the rioting outside Chicago's Conrad Hilton Hotel on August 28.[8]

Fifth, there has been a trend toward reduced discretion in convention choice. Gone are the days when party conventions could run 103 ballots like the Democratic National Convention of 1924 or produce authentic dark-horse nominees like James

---

[7] Jules Witcover, "Muskie's Tightrope Trip," *Progressive* (Madison, Wis.), March 1971, p. 31.

[8] See Lionel Lokos, *Hysteria 1964: The Fear Campaign Against Barry Goldwater* (New Rochelle, N.Y.: Arlington House, 1967); and Theodore H. White, *The Making of the President 1968* (New York: Atheneum, 1969), pp. 301–03.

K. Polk, who came into the Democratic convention of 1844 with no initial delegate support. The trend has been distinctly toward fewer ballots and well-identified major hopefuls.

Among the reasons for this trend, the most important was simply the elimination by the 1936 Democratic National Convention of the century-old rule requiring a two-thirds convention vote for presidential and vice-presidential nominations. Another has been the growth of preconvention campaigning. Primaries and public opinion polls have tested the popular support of various candidates in much the same way as early ballots at previous conventions. Similarly, preconvention screening by media has served to identify serious potential candidates well in advance of the convention and to eliminate others altogether. At the same time that delegates and the public are much better informed about alternative candidates, the candidates and public also know much more about delegate commitments and intentions before the convention meets. The major radio-television networks, weekly news magazines and national wire services have set up their own elaborate delegate-counting operations in parallel to the contenders' delegate intelligence units and have issued frequent projections of delegate totals.

It would be a mistake, however, to point to the string of first-ballot nominations during the 1960's as evidence that national conventions are becoming ratifying bodies with no real choice. As noted by Gerald Pomper of Rutgers University in his study of convention choices throughout American party history, the percentage of conventions meeting only to ratify the nomination of an obvious leader on the first ballot (just over half) has increased little since 1928.[9] It would also be misleading to draw an analogy between one-ballot conventions and the Electoral College as vote-counting devices. Arthur Schlesinger, Jr., has similarly suggested that "the revival of the direct primary may soon bring us to the point, as more states adopt presidential primary laws, of a *de facto* national

---

[9] Gerald Pomper, *Nominating the President: The Politics of Convention Choice* (New York: W. W. Norton, 1966), p. 196.

primary." The convention would become "a forum, not for decision but for ratification."[10] The convention, however, continues to function as a decision-making process extending over time and involving individuals with discretionary choice.

Sixth, individual delegates have gained increased importance in convention politics. In a 1960 study of national party conventions for the Brookings Institution, Paul David and his associates concluded that "since 1948 the delegates have been measurably better educated, less boss-ridden, better adjusted to the requirements of an open political system, and generally more trustworthy in all respects than the delegates of 1900."[11] The Goldwater and McCarthy movements of 1964 and 1968 brought their own style of "new politics" delegates to the convention process. In Miami Beach, 80 percent of the delegates had been to college; at Chicago, college professors and clergymen outnumbered farmers and labor leaders.

Changes that have reduced the intermediary power of state party bosses and delegation leaders have at the same time enhanced the power of the individual delegate and produced a long-term decline in delegation unity. The Democratic National Convention of 1968 formally abolished the unit rule at the convention, a tradition permitting states to bind all their delegates to vote as a unit, thereby increasing state delegation leverage in the convention, and barred the use of the unit rule at any level of party organization in the 1972 delegate selection process. The Democratic Commission on Party Structure and Delegate Selection (McGovern-Fraser Commission) has required a number of changes that are likely to disperse convention votes among a number of candidates and to work against a single candidate's building an insurmountable delegate lead before the convention convenes. If reforms are implemented, the convention delegate game could be substantially transformed, with greater independence

---

[10] Arthur Schlesinger, Jr., "Scammon and Wattenberg vs. Lubell," *New York*, December 7, 1970, p. 12.
[11] David, Goldman, and Bain, *The Politics of National Party Conventions*, p. 245.

for individual delegates and more bargaining during more ballots in the convention city.

A final trend in convention politics has been the development of significant new forms of convention organizational power. While public and media attention has been riveted on the preconvention campaign and the delegate game, surprisingly little concern has been expressed about the growing organizational requirements and accompanying power of convention arrangements and security. In the period between 1940 and 1968, the costs of national conventions burgeoned from some $150,000 to almost $796,263 for the Republicans and from about $94,000 to $1,746,301 for the Democrats.[12] The gargantuan size of Democratic conventions in recent years (reaching 2,622 delegate votes alone in 1968, many of them half votes, compared to the Republican delegate total of 1,333) accounts in part for the skyrocketing costs for the Democrats. As the conventions have grown in size and costs, the authority as well as responsibilities of the convention committees and their staffs, i.e., the convention bureaucracy, have steadily expanded. Neither party in the past has made detailed information available on this aspect of party organization, although the reforms of the O'Hara Democratic Rules Commission have begun to open the process to the public.

At least two new factors have created major new organizational requirements for conventions apart from standard convention arrangements: the demands of television programming and the increased need for convention security forces.

Because of the importance of the convention period in influencing voter attitudes, party leaders have taken a serious interest in projecting the best party image possible. The Committee on Convention Reforms of 1966–67 stressed "the necessity of doing everything possible to make the Republican

---

[12] John F. Bibby and Herbert E. Alexander, *The Politics of National Convention Finances and Arrangements,* Study No. 14 (Princeton, N.J.: Citizens' Research Foundation, 1968), p. 7; and Herbert E. Alexander, *Financing the 1968 Election* (Lexington, Mass.: D. C. Heath, 1971), p. 73.

National Convention attractive to the eye, interesting in content and appealing to the ear and mind." Representatives of the Democratic National Committee have discussed with a political consulting firm the possibility of media simulation of the 1972 convention to aid in programming.

Party leaders have also tried to reduce or obscure conflict at the conventions. The historic Republican platform fight of 1964 in San Francisco was delayed until most of the East Coast television audience had gone to bed, by the tactic of reading the full text of the party platform before amendments were considered. Democratic peace delegates in Chicago rebelled against what they considered a similar leadership strategy to bury debate on the Vietnam peace plank in the early hours of the morning, successfully shouting down the no-adjournment ruling of Convention Chairman Carl Albert.

During the 1968 conventions, the public began to realize the growing significance of security forces in the convention process. Chicago dramatized conflict but Miami Beach was equally prepared for assault. Both major party conventions were characterized by a fortress mentality, facilities ringed by so many different kinds of uniformed and plainclothes police and security agents that convention reporters could well have used a directory to identify them. The ability of party leaders to control state and local security forces, including the National Guard, was a key factor in the Democrats' choice of Chicago, where the party controlled both the mayoralty and the governorship. Republicans in 1968 and Democrats in 1972 also took note of the ease with which Miami Beach could be "defended" by closing the causeways to the mainland. Security forces directly under contract to the party national committees or operating within the jurisdiction of the convention now constitute important new layers of convention personnel and convention machinery that are accountable to no one but the top party leadership.

Unresolved Problems

Party reformers have only begun to examine the deficiencies of the national conventions and their potential for development. Several current problems in the operation of the convention system deserve attention.

The first is the extensive control exercised by party organization leaders without formal accountability. The conventions remain one of the most closed and tightly run operations in politics. Time and again one is reminded how "inside" both party conventions are. On television, senior leaders of the congressional parties familiar with the uses of power and accorded deference within the party dominate the convention proceedings, often gaveling down dissent and refusing to recognize delegation representatives on the floor. Conventions and their committees, again deferring to congressional leaders and their parliamentary knowledge, have often invoked the rules of the House of Representatives with their complicated precedents, another advantage to the insider. Press accreditation, an increasingly important form of access to overcrowded conventions, is handled by representatives of the House and Senate press galleries, which operate on rules that exclude almost everyone but the Washington-accredited establishment media and which issue no reports of their activities.

It is understandable that the party organization should seek to manage and keep under reasonable control such elaborate and complex mechanisms as national conventions. In fact, the need for continuity and preparation for party conventions provided the initial impetus for the establishment of party national committees. The problem is not the need for management and control of conventions but who exercises such control and through what means.

The powers of convention arrangements and management have devolved on a small circle of party leaders and staff who are rarely visible to the general public or for that matter to most delegates. As Joseph F. Crangle, Jr., a prominent organization Democrat in his own right, pointed out during O'Hara Commission deliberations: "No one in 1968 knew who the convention manager was or how to find him or how to get anything done. . . . He's more than a technician—he's the one full-time man working on the convention to whom you can turn to ask questions. In '68 that one man was very hard to get a hold of and no one knew to whom he was responsible."

Even when abuses of organization power were flagrant, as in Chicago in 1968, the public was satisfied with the exposure of such "villains" as President Johnson's man for convention arrangements, John Criswell, or Mayor Richard J. Daley of the Host Committee.

The problem of party organization control was more quietly but vividly illustrated in the "model convention" that Republican National Chairman Bliss staged in Miami Beach in 1968. Virtually unnoticed by anyone but party insiders, Bliss skillfully tightened his personal control over all aspects of convention operations. Bliss himself served as chairman of the Committee on Arrangements. For his executive assistant on convention operations, Bliss recruited William Warner, an Indiana Republican with a party reputation as a tough operator and a former top deputy of Republican National Chairman William E. Miller of New York and Congressional Campaign Chairman Robert C. "Bob" Wilson of California. As vice chairman of the Committee on Arrangements, Bliss named a close associate, Donald R. Ross, national committeeman from Nebraska, who was later to be appointed to a federal judgeship by President Nixon. For chief of security for the Miami Beach convention, Bliss selected Jack Sherwood, who had served as a secret service agent with Richard Nixon when he was Vice President and who was still a close friend of the Nixons. Sherwood and Wisconsin State Senator Robert P. Knowles, executive secretary of the Committee on Arrangements, had access to all convention plans, copies of which were also made available to the Senate Minority Leader Everett M. Dirksen, who chaired the Platform Committee, and the House Minority Leader Gerald R. Ford, who served as permanent chairman of the convention. The Nixon staff, which enjoyed close working relationships with most of the principals involved, kept itself fully informed on convention arrangements.

Bliss made special efforts to avoid a repetition of the party-splitting platform fight in 1964. Soon after taking office in 1965, he established a top-level Republican Coordinating Committee to achieve a unified party position on issues. In appointing a former top aide, Dr. Arthur Peterson, to be staff director of the convention's Platform Committee, Bliss stressed that the position papers of the Coordinating Committee would serve as the basic working papers for drafting the 1968 platform. To ensure that the Republican governors did not upstage the RNC, Bliss appointed Dr. William Prendergast, a former research director for the national committee and for House Republican Conference Chairman Melvin R. Laird, to cover the regional platform hearings and preplatform preparations of the Republican governors. The only hitch in platform arrangements arose when Congressman Glenard P. Lipscomb of California, chairman of the Platform Committee's foreign policy and national security subcommittee, presented a strongly hawkish Vietnam plank to the committee. Forces favoring Governor Nelson A. Rockefeller, aided by Rockefeller's foreign-policy expert, Henry A. Kissinger of Harvard, successfully pressed the Nixon camp for a moderately worded Vietnam peace plank.

The firmest evidence of Bliss's control was the rigid system of floor passes, convention tickets and credentials instituted months in advance of the convention under his personal direction. Even the smallest details were strictly enforced, such as requiring individual tickets to afternoon subcommittee sessions of the Platform Committee, a practice that effectively barred observers from moving from one subcommittee to another and reduced public attendance drastically at most sessions. Convention staff were bedecked with engraved medals and insignia that resembled some mystical order and gained them free access to the inner sanctums of the party. Any exceptions or waivers required a personally signed letter from the national chairman.

While television commentators marveled at the smoothness of floor operations at the convention, the unprepared Rockefeller staff and state delegations spent precious time getting the credentials and passes to convention functions they had neglected to apply for well in advance of the convention. In spite of their major platform victory, Rockefeller aides never really penetrated the inner operations of the convention and its committees and never fully realized how much their own lack of access handicapped them.

Some basic questions are raised by this experience. Can any "outside" candidate who does not already have extensive personal connections inside the party apparatus ever breach the barricades the parties have erected around the conventions? Or is the convention game to remain strictly a party game, run by and for the benefit of the incumbent President and/or party organization? How open are conventions to be in the long process of planning and arrangements, and to whom are convention staff to be accountable? How will greater public participation be ensured in the convention? Simply televising convention floor sessions does not answer the question satisfactorily.

The Democrats have taken a number of steps to open their Miami Beach 1972 convention and make convention officials accountable.[13] Rules changes now provide for the election by the full national committee of the Arrangements Committee, the Site Selection Committee (which has been given specific criteria to consider in recommending a convention city), and the convention manager. Rules, Credentials and Platform (but not Arrangements) Committee meetings are open to the public. All convention, preconvention and postconvention records and correspondence are to be open and available for public inspection at reasonable times. Requests for recognition to speak from the convention floor are to be electronically registered in a manner visible to the chairman, the delegates and the news media. A journal of proceedings covering actions taken each day by the convention is to be printed and made available to all delegates and alternates the morning of the following day.

In marked contrast, the 1972 Republican National Convention was without question even more tightly orchestrated than the "model" convention of 1968. Originally, official preference was for the selection of San Diego, overriding such considerations as inadequate hotel space for visitors and working

---

[13] "Determinations of the Commission on Rules with Respect to the National Nominating Convention," the report of the Commission on Rules reprinted under Extension of Remarks of James G. O'Hara (D-Mich.) in *Congressional Record—Extensions of Remarks*, 92nd Congress, 1st Session, October 21, 1971, pp. E 11182–87.

space for broadcast media. The convention was to situate there with an impressive pledge, reportedly of $400,000, from the Sheraton Corporation of America, a subsidiary of the International Telephone & Telegraph Corporation.[14] On-site technical preparations were begun with the participation of White House aides more than a year in advance and the party requisitioned exclusive use of the San Diego Sports Arena three weeks in advance of the convention—all for a shortened three-day convention in which, according to White House Director of Communications Herbert G. Klein, "We don't expect much of a contest for the nomination." San Diegans complained that the host-city convention planning was in the hands of a small, powerful group of influential, business-oriented, conservative Republicans. Gus Chavez, the leader of the Chicano Federation, contended that "Chicano Republicans" were being excluded from the planning. Second thought subsequently brought the convention to Miami.

A related problem facing both parties is the continuing tension between the need for party organization control and the requirements of the media and their access to convention proceedings. The survey questionnaire of the Republican Delegates and Organizations (DO) Committee found the proposal that "the news media should be denied access to the floor during actual business sessions" was acceptable to respondents by a small margin. The proposed rules for the 1972 Democratic National Convention initially barred all "press, radio and television equipment" from the floor of the convention hall during official business except for direct coverage of proceedings from the podium.

The O'Hara Commission subsequently amended this prohibition, after a sharp debate, to bar only floor television cameras. "If we allow roving floor interviews," argued Pro-

---

[14] See Robert Walters, "Convention Pledge for GOP Questioned," Washington *Star*, November 29, 1971. The story was subsequently denied by Host Committee chairman Leon · Parma, an aerospace executive and former aide to Congressman Bob Wilson. "We're not going to use any funds other than those raised in San Diego," asserted Parma. The pledge did not become a major political issue, however, until columnist Jack Anderson revived the story in February 1972.

fessor of Law Carl Auerbach of the University of Minnesota, "we are encouraging media to decide whether to cover the podium or to hunt for action on the floor. They do this to compete, to jazz up the proceedings, but they are abridging the privilege of the American people to see what's going on at the convention." Donald Peterson, who gained national prominence as the chairman of the McCarthy Wisconsin delegation in Chicago and co-chairman of the New Democratic Coalition, spoke for the commission majority on the issue: "We on this commission are here today because in 1968 the public saw a large political institution dramatically unresponsive to the needs of the people. . . . The problems we had in 1968 were not the fault of TV—they were simply covered by TV." The commission, however, reached no definitive policy on rules to cover media at the convention, deferring the matter to Richard J. Murphy, the Miami Beach convention director. In the meantime, members of the Arrangements Committee, meeting in closed session, continued to press for limitations on newsmen on the convention floor.

Another major problem of the convention system is that of misplaced priorities in the presidential selection process. Liberals and conservatives alike share the assumption that the prize of the presidential nomination should go to the player who cares enough to strive for it early and long and is resourceful enough to construct a winning delegate strategy. By perfecting the game of delegate politics, John Kennedy and F. Clifton White captured the imagination of party professionals and the public but at the same time further distorted priorities in the presidential selection process.

The current priorities of presidential selection are: 1) who can win the nomination, i.e., play the best delegate game, a game at which party insiders have distinct advantages; 2) who can win the election, surprisingly a secondary consideration in several conventions of the 1960's; and 3) who can best govern the country, a subject rarely discussed in the convention process and insufficiently developed in the presidential election campaign. The system tests only the political support of a candidate within a party and his popular support in the electorate. It does not even weigh his commitment to the future welfare of the party, since a President can easily sidestep responsibilities of party leadership, as did Lyndon Johnson before 1968, or even pursue a political strategy that undercuts his own party, as did Richard Nixon in several states like New York, Virginia, Washington, and Wyoming, during the 1970 campaign.

Perhaps the greatest deficiency in the presidential selection process, however, lies in the selection of the vice-presidential candidate, who only rarely is chosen through the convention process. But if, as Paul David has concluded and as both 1960 and 1968 suggest, "the Vice Presidency is rapidly achieving a status in which a typical incumbent will be the most likely presidential nominee of the party in power whenever the President himself is unavailable,"[15] much closer attention should be given to the initial selection of vice-presidential nominees. The traditional assumption that such a choice is the prerogative of one person, the presidential nominee, is open to serious question. "Why shouldn't a man who wants it have to run for vice president as hard as they do for presidential nomination?" asks Democratic National Chairman Lawrence F. O'Brien. The Democratic party has responded in part with a rules change requiring both presidential and vice-presidential candidates to circulate nominating petitions for at least 50 delegate signatures. In September 1971, Governor George Wallace of Alabama began polling more than a million followers of the Wallace movement on their preference for a Vice President in 1972.

Still another area deserving attention is the stewardship function of the convention delegate in the presidential selection process and in party deliberations. Considering the enormous power they exercise, national convention delegates as a group are among the least visible and least formally accountable representatives in the entire American political process. Few people know the identity of national convention delegates from their state or congressional district. Even fewer know how they voted at the convention, yet a high percentage of delegates keep returning to party conventions. Moods of general confusion, of low expectations of performance and of boredom alter-

---

[15] Paul T. David, "The Vice Presidency: Its Institutional Evolution and Contemporary Status," *Journal of Politics*, November 1967, pp. 721–22.

nate with the excitement of presidential personalities and the occasional platform fight; but unless a delegate is named to a convention committee or enlisted in a candidate's campaign, he has little to do in the convention city except to cast his vote infrequently. Often even that is not his own choice, since many delegates still owe their allegiance to party bosses. New York reform Democrat Edward N. Costikyan warns that the first thing presidential candidates should realize is that "delegates are not free agents, nor are they subject to persuasion. The delegate is the property of his leader."[16]

Finally, one of the most serious problems of the existing system is the failure of party leaders to develop the convention as a governing body. In their 1960 study of party conventions, Paul David and his associates rated the parties most poorly on the governing-body function, i.e., ensuring the continuity and effectiveness of the party organization and contributing to its adaptation to new functions. Although they cited the lack of preparation of most delegates, they attributed the shortcomings they observed as due much more to failures in leadership than to the capacity of the delegates themselves. The party governing function, the team concluded, was that aspect of the conventions which "offers the greatest opportunity for further development, precisely because it has so far been least developed."[17] Little has changed during the intervening years.

The national parties make incredibly poor use of the time and space of the convention periods. They provide party members and leaders few if any structured opportunities to review the progress of the party and discuss its long-term challenges. National convention delegations often represent the top party leadership and talent of the state parties, but they are not

---

[16] Martin and Susan Tolchin, *To the Victor . . . Political Patronage from the Clubhouse to the White House* (New York: Random House, 1971), p. 4.

[17] David, Goldman, and Bain, *The Politics of National Party Conventions*, pp. 247, 345–47. Brookings is undertaking a new study of national party conventions as part of its Presidential Selection Studies program funded by the Ford Foundation and directed by Senior Fellow Donald R. Matthews.

called upon to share their knowledge and experience with other state parties in any systematic way. Collectively the delegates and alternates and visitors at a national convention are the largest pool of talent ever assembled at one place within the national party, yet no effort is made by the national parties to provide workshops or other training opportunities.

One explanation for the continued underdevelopment of the American conventions is that there is little perceived self-interest in developing the conventions, no incentive within the parties for creativity. Self-interest leads in the direction of either delegate politics to capture the presidential nomination or the least possible convention activity so as not to disturb the dominance of the party elites. The party reform movement has only begun to overcome this failure in imagination and motivation.

Alternatives to the Conventions

Critics of the existing two-party convention system of presidential nomination have advanced various alternatives: 1) the national primary; 2) third-party presidential nomination; and 3) the use of multiple party lines to endorse candidates. Beyond reform of the delegate selection process and limited rules change, there has been little consideration of the alternative proposed here—modernization of the convention system itself.

In our view, none of the first three alternatives stands a significant chance of replacing the major party conventions as the principal institution for presidential selection. More important, none offers the long-term potential for political and governmental modernization that the conventions do. The real choice for the future is between an unreconstructed and entrenched or a restructured and expansive convention system.

Almost all serious students of the nomination process have reached strongly negative conclusions about the national primary, and the idea has drawn little enthusiastic support during the hearings of the Democratic reform commissions. David and his associates stressed that "the most critical aspects of the nominating process arise from the fact that the alternatives of choice must be discovered as part of the process. . . . A primary election is an especially poor instrument for choice when the alternative candidates number three or more."[18]

Besides the elimination of deliberative choice in the selection process, the arguments advanced against the national primary include the tremendous costs that such a campaign would entail to establish the national identification of contenders; the confinement of choice to well-established political personalities; the narrowing of alternatives by the elimination of the possibilities of a draft or nomination of a minor candidate; a tendency toward factional division of the parties, with reduced chances for the moderating effect of a compromise candidate; and the relative inflexibility of a national primary law once it is enacted. Particularly lacking in a national primary, Gerald Pomper concludes, would be "the ease with which conventions accomplish the non-nominating functions" of platform writing, engendering campaign enthusiasm, and governing the party.[19]

The third-party alternative would attempt an end run of the major party conventions but would leave them essentially intact. It would not challenge their authority to nominate candidates but would simply broaden the choice available to voters. If third and fourth parties developed at the conservative and liberal-radical ends of the party spectrum, their effect might even be to reinforce the major-party conventions by reducing the ideological breadth of the parties, narrowing their membership bases and making them more homogeneous. Third parties would thus be escape valves for pressures that might otherwise open the convention process. They would also represent an admission of defeat, an admission that the major parties could not be reformed from within. In addition, third-party strategy is dependent to a large degree on the availability of an attractive national candidate and is highly vulnerable to action by the two major parties in selecting candidates and programs that seriously undercut minor-party appeal.

A variant of the third-party challenge that might attract citizen and cause organizations that are not inclined to work

---

[18] *Ibid.*, pp. 333–34.
[19] Pomper, *Nominating the President*, p. 222. See also Pomper's critique of several proposed forms of the national primary, *ibid.*, pp. 216–30.

within one or both of the major parties would be the extra-line ballot type of endorsement. New York State has pioneered in this form of ballot, which has allowed a candidate to accumulate popular votes on additional party lines. At the presidential level, the New York Democratic party has permitted the Liberal party to run the same presidential electors as an "add-on" vote. The New York Republican party in 1964 and 1968, concerned by the threat of the New York Conservative party, barred the listing of its presidential electors on the Conservative line. By the 1970 state elections, however, candidates of both major New York parties were seeking to add extra-line endorsements.

A memorandum circulated among reform Democrats after the 1970 elections, suggesting a supplemental line strategy in 1972, created a top-level controversy at the Democratic National Committee. "The supplemental line is merely an insurance policy for liberal Democrats," the memo stated. By having a supplemental line on the 1972 presidential ballots of all states (beginning with "a thorough research job on the Wallace effort in 1968," which was given due credit) liberals could "keep one option open for post-convention judgment." If the party fulfilled its commitment to reform, the supplemental line could be dropped or, in states where that was not legally possible, the Democratic ticket would be put on that line.[20]

If the Electoral College is replaced by the direct election of the President, there might be a tendency for a number of special cause groups to use additional ballot lines for bargaining purposes with the major-party candidates. Blacks, a women's liberation front, ecology groups and others might organize separate lines. The direct-election amendment, however, states that "the times, places, and manner of holding such elections and entitlement to inclusion on the ballot shall be prescribed in each state by the legislature thereof; but the Congress may at any time by law make or alter such regulations." Both the state legislatures and the Congress, which are

---

[20] "Supplemental Line Memo," *New Democrat* (New York), January 1971, p. 4.

predominantly two-party institutions, could be expected to make the qualification of new party lines on the ballot fairly difficult. Even more important, the national conventions could attempt to bar their endorsed candidates from accepting the nomination and designation of any other party, a tactic that if successful would eliminate the possibility of cumulative votes.

Major changes in the nominating process, and even more particularly, new functions for political parties, can best be achieved through a strategy of reform from within the parties. Alternatives that do not confront the convention system itself ignore a major part of the problem as well as a key to its solution.

Recommendations: Developing the National Convention as a Party Governing Body

National party conventions should assume major new responsibilities within modernized citizen parties for

- establishing new criteria and priorities for the selection of presidential and vice-presidential candidates
- overseeing the long-term government and health of the party organization
- achieving increased accountability in the management of party affairs
- strengthening itself as a deliberating and decision-making governing body in the party
- building a partywide capacity or ability to govern and lead
- evaluating party performance in elections
- training party cadres and citizens
- opening the entire convention process to greater citizen understanding and participation.

In turn, these expanded responsibilities for party conventions require new definitions for the role of the individual convention delegate and new expectations of performance.

The following recommendations suggest a feasible blueprint for party conventions of the future that could be substantially implemented by 1976. Indeed, it would be hard to plan a more suitable commemoration of the American Bicentennial than the holding of truly popularly governed party conventions.

Recommendation 1. The most important single function of the convention, the nomination of the President and Vice President, should be developed with emphasis on the ability to govern. The number and kinds of candidates considered by the nominating conventions should be expanded.

Several steps could be taken to encourage the conventions to give more formal attention to the governmental qualifications of the candidates they endorse. Qualifications for party leadership and vote-getting ability will continue to be tested informally by the convention process. Criteria applied for presidential selection should also be applied to the selection of the vice-presidential candidate.

The opportunity for announced and prospective presidential candidates to present testimony before party policy commissions and for party representatives to interrogate them should be formally built into the preconvention period and the convention structure itself. The major permanent party commissions dealing with substantive issues should subject all candidates to intensive public cross-examination in areas such as foreign and national security policy, economic policy, civil rights and civil liberties, welfare administration and housing and urban development. Candidates would be expected to demonstrate a reasonable grasp of major governmental and political issues and the potential for executive leadership. The parties should assume responsibility for the candidates they endorse to the public by insisting on such a review. No candidate for presidential or vice-presidential office should normally be able to receive a major party nomination without such a screening.

It may be objected that party leaders will be unwilling to expose the weaknesses of major candidates in public or that such party interrogation would interfere unduly with the policymaking prerogatives of elected officials and the government. The parties have a greater responsibility, however, to select and train candidates with the requisite qualifications for the offices they seek. If parties are to have more responsibility for the performance of government, it is essential that they begin to assume a more formal role in screening party candidates.

Selection of the Vice President in an open convention contest would provide the party in convention further opportunity to screen candidates for national office. The importance of the vice-presidential candidate as a deputy leader of the party and increasingly as the heir to the presidential nomination now outweighs traditional arguments that this choice should be the prerogative of the presidential nominee exercised in consultation with an inner circle of party leaders. Considerations such as ticket balancing, compatibility of the national ticket and intraparty compromise seem to pale against the criterion of the ability of the Vice President to govern the country and lead the party. Earlier optimism that the convention could defer this choice to its presidential nominee and the party leadership without undue concern has not been supported by events of the 1960's.

The national party conventions could assume a significant new role by insisting on an open selection process for the party's vice-presidential candidate. Aspirants to the office could enter separate vice-presidential primaries and compete for vice-presidential delegate support at state conventions. (One recent study of state primary laws concluded that candidates for Vice President were able to enter primaries in three states in 1972: New Hampshire, New Mexico, and Ohio.[21]) They could undergo the same process of convention review given the presidential contenders. Competition for the vice presidency would not preclude consideration for presidential nomination; in fact, it might be a far more credible and feasible preconvention strategy for minor hopefuls who might otherwise be eliminated from presidential competition. Conversely, unsuccessful presidential aspirants should be considered potential vice-presidential contenders.

---

[21] Michael F. Brewer, "Survey of State Primary Laws" (unpublished survey, Harvard Law School, 1971). Former Governor Endicott Peabody of Massachusetts campaigned for the Democratic vice-presidential nomination in several additional states, urging state legislatures in Michigan, Tennessee, and Rhode Island, for example, to provide for a vice-presidential primary in 1972

Convention selection of the Vice President could be by open ballot following the designation of the presidential nominee. The presidential candidate could be encouraged not to express a preference openly or at most to indicate several individuals he would find acceptable. The presumption would be that the convention should reach its own decision. The need for loyalty of the Vice President to the program of the President is not a sufficient argument for continuation of the present system. Party loyalty itself and the option of the presidential nominee himself to suggest that some contenders not be selected, by pointedly omitting their names from a list offered the convention, should be sufficient safeguards against a divided administration. In any event, the qualifications of the individual are a more relevant criterion for selection.

A representative citizen commission on presidential recruitment could attempt to define the necessary qualifications for presidential (and vice-presidential) office and broaden the number and kinds of prominent Americans given serious consideration for the presidency. Under the traditional form of convention nomination, little effort is made by the parties or party leaders to search for people qualified for national executive leadership. A limited initial field of governors, United States Senators and incumbent and former Vice Presidents for the most part enters the preconvention picture. Public dissatisfaction with the quality and range of candidates considered by the conventions suggests the need for a review of this selection process. As conservative columnist Holmes Alexander commented sharply on 1971–72 preconvention politics: "Instead of monkeying with the electoral college, the voting age and campaign expenditures, we could spend the next 12 months looking for better presidential candidates than those who have surfaced for 1972."[22]

An important first step would be to attempt a definition, in at least approximate terms, of the job specifications of the future presidency and the essential personal qualities that

[22] Holmes Alexander, "A Time of National Trouble Is Not the Time to Malign the President," Bangor (Me.) *News,* April 6, 1971.

should characterize a presidential candidate. In undertaking this task, the citizen commission could draw on the perspectives of former Presidents and Vice Presidents as well as historians, political scientists, psychologists and government officials who have studied the presidency. The commission could also attempt to set out both minimal and optimal qualifications over a broad range of categories. The admitted difficulty in developing a consensus of job specifications for the modern President is no excuse for the absence of any serious attempt by political leaders to consider the problem. National discussion and a debate on the subject in themselves could contribute to a reordering of priorities in the presidential selection process. Few Americans seriously subscribe to the proposition that "any" man can or should occupy the presidency and make final decisions on the use of the nation's nuclear arsenal or direction of foreign and domestic economic policy.

The findings of the commission, including full opportunity for the development of minority views, could serve as the basis for an open national talent hunt for potential candidates of presidential caliber. The study might reveal, for instance, that certain occupational career lines, such as those of major university presidents or some corporate executive development programs, should be added to the strictly political routes to the presidency. As a first step, parties could be encouraged to recruit such promising talent for major Senate or gubernatorial races or for the vice presidency, thereby providing new candidates some experience in the electoral process while broadening entry to the presidency through these traditional routes. Another step would be to introduce a wider range of expert opinion into the preconvention period, including surveys of party professionals and political consultants, political scientists, economists, educators, newspaper editors and a wide variety of professional groups. (At present only party elites—previous convention delegates, party county chairmen, Congressmen and state party leaders—are polled separately.)

The parties and/or an independent citizen commission could also initiate studies and recommendations to upgrade the vice presidency as a governmental and party office, in order both to attract more qualified candidates for the office and to prepare the Vice President better for the contingency of presidential succession.

Recommendation 2. The national parties should empower commissions on convention modernization to study the several hundred national conventions held by private organizations and develop a convention modernization program.

To begin the process of convention modernization, the national parties should empower commissions on convention modernization specifically to make a thorough study of the national convention institution as it has developed in the United States. The elaborate convention study and review committees of the two major parties have proceeded for years with virtually no formal consideration of the experience of the several hundred other national organizations such as veterans' groups, labor unions, religious bodies and professional and trade associations which hold national conventions and which could stimulate numerous ideas for upgrading national party conventions. An example of an innovative national convention deserving the attention of the parties was the First General Assembly of the World Future Society, held in Washington, D.C., May 12–15, 1971.

The commissions on convention modernization could research and prepare summary profiles outlining key aspects of major conventions, select and attend a representative number of conventions and take testimony from convention managers, other key convention personnel and various participants. On the basis of the findings of such comparative study, the commissions could recommend comprehensive convention-modernization programs for the parties in the 1970's, including new job specifications for party personnel and specific recommendations and models for county, state, regional and national party conventions.

The importance of convention modernization should not be underestimated. The task of completing this study should not just be added to a list of topics assigned to an omnibus party reform commission. It is a subject requiring the full, sustained and dedicated attention of some of the most talented men and women the party can assemble. The conventions of the future should be designed to accomplish the serious business of the party. If the parties are to merit the respect and participation of the American people, they should convey through their conventions a businesslike and professional spirit toward politics and government.

Recommendation 3. The national party convention should assert its prerogatives as the single governing body of the party and equip itself to exercise policymaking and enforcement powers.

Most observers have underestimated the potential of the national conventions as governing bodies for the parties. In 1968, however, the Democratic National Convention took "a thoroughly original and possibly epochal initiative: a resolution which is, in effect, a national statute requiring that all state parties meet modest but not insignificant minimum democratic standards in the design of their delegate selection machinery."[23] The Democratic reform movement has suggested the model of the national convention as a truly national party institution enforcing its own law. Such a model could be greatly strengthened by the following steps:

A series of longer-term actions to strengthen national party organization could be taken by the convention. The convention could upgrade the national committee and emphasize the committee's role as the executive agency of the convention. The complicated and separate systems for electing delegates to the national convention, national committeemen and committeewomen and state and local party officials could be studied in a major effort to rationalize overlapping systems of party representation. The convention could also study the relationship between national party organs and various congressional party bodies. A day of the convention might be set aside to consider resolutions for "the good of the party." The convention could implement such actions through the national committee and/or through expanded use of the representative

---

[23] "Preliminary Outline: Should the People Pick the President?," memorandum by Eli Segal and Simon Lazarus dated January 22, 1969.

party commission mechanism. Where appropriate, the convention could use its authority to mandate major reforms in national party machinery.

In order to function as a governing body, the convention should adopt the basic procedures of any formal representative assembly. In particular, convention procedures should incorporate formal recorded and visually displayed roll calls for daily attendance and all convention votes, including votes of convention committees. A formal reporting process could be built into the national party convention such that all party leaders and national and state party organizations would submit periodic written reports on past activities and future plans to the membership of the party. Written reports could be incorporated in the permanent files and/or in the published proceedings of the convention, providing a permanent record for party members and the public.

Floor Teletype units could also be provided for state delegations to increase the speed, accuracy and volume of convention communications. The current system of telephones, microphones and pages is clearly inadequate if the convention is to function as a deliberative body. A convention Teletype system of new-model quiet tickers could transmit to all delegations official updated convention schedules and meeting locations, texts of resolutions and amendments and official vote tabulations.

Continuing convention committees on platform implementation would be another means for building the authority of the national convention. Greater public and party attention to the platform after the convention and election might increase the appeal of the parties to issue-oriented groups as well as reduce general cynicism about the efficacy of party platforms. Platform implementation committees could hold periodic hearings, receiving testimony from national, congressional, state and local party leaders, as well as individual party members and representatives of citizen groups. The committees could then make continuing recommendations for platform implementation to appropriate party leaders and compile status reports for the national committees and the succeeding national conventions.

If the national convention is to be developed as the governing body of the party, a strong case can be made for more frequent meetings of the convention during the 1970's. The needs for party reform and the strengthening of internal party government are so extensive that biennial interim national conventions at a minimum are essential. Reformed national committees can meet some of these needs, but the convention is unique in its potential to serve as a national representative assembly of the parties. Interim conventions composed of delegates from the states, selected in roughly the same manner as delegates to national nominating conventions, could exercise the full functions of the expanded national convention except for the nomination of the party's presidential and vice-presidential candidates. If 1976 is set as a target date for convention modernization, a biennial convention in 1974 might be used to test experimentally many new procedures and organizational innovations. Supporters of the concept could press the 1972 party conventions to authorize interim party conclaves and initiate the process of soliciting bids from host cities.

Recommendation 4. The convention delegate should assume a more important role in the national party as the party conventions are modernized. State delegations should work as a functional team.

Closely related to the concept of the convention as the governing body of the party is the need to upgrade the representative role and effectiveness of the individual delegate and the state delegation within the convention. The following steps can be taken to enhance the delegate's role:

In the selection of delegates, a new set of guidelines should be developed that emphasize qualitative criteria, such as individual background skills, motivation to take an active role in the party and potential contribution to the convention. As the duties of a convention delegate become more explicit and strenuous, delegates who have served in an almost honorary capacity could be encouraged to retire, making way for younger delegates with higher levels of motivation and commitment to a working party convention. In addition to the efforts of the parties, citizen organizations could enter or endorse candidates for national convention delegations as part of a nation-wide search for new delegate talent in the states.

Convention delegates should be active, involved and accountable in the entire convention process. To emphasize the continuing stewardship and accountability of the convention delegate, all convention delegates could agree in advance to serve both as delegates and as active representatives. Their duties should extend from the preconvention through the postconvention period.

Before the convention they could travel extensively around their state, appearing at party meetings and public functions, sounding out party and public opinion, and answering questions about their positions on candidates and issues. Lists of each state's delegates with addresses and telephone numbers could be distributed by state party organizations and candidates. Local radio and television stations and papers could also publicize the names of convention delegates as a public service.

Delegates could meet in their home states shortly after their selection to elect their chairman and officers and to participate in a weekend working conference. The party national committees and candidates could provide field men to help train convention delegations to work together at both the state and regional level and to provide liaison on convention arrangements. What services and information the delegates need to function effectively could be determined by a survey of all present and past national convention delegates. The national parties, for example, could compile relevant biographical information and publish an indexed book of delegates. National party staff could encourage state parties to develop expertise among their delegations by appointing well-informed assignments officers to work with interested delegates.

During the convention, delegates could participate in state delegation meetings and take an active role in convention committee work, caucuses and floor sessions. The effectiveness of state delegations could be further enhanced by the appointment of knowledgeable individuals to serve as consultants authorized to sit with the delegation on the convention floor and attend executive sessions of convention committee meetings.

After the convention, delegates could file written delegate reports to their home constituencies, giving their votes on key convention decisions and their reasons for so voting as well as an account of their work in the various committees and caucuses. The parties could also develop formal postconvention programs in the states, including a report from the full delegation so as to provide continuing education for party workers and more formal accountability for each delegation.

Recommendation 5. Increased party participation and accountability as well as maximum public information in convention arrangements, management and security should be furthered through party rules and procedures.

The party convention is too important a meeting to remain the undisputed property of the President or any closed circle of party leaders, no matter what their formal credentials. As a general principle, all major decisions on convention arrangements, management and security should be made by responsible party bodies such as the national committees or by party officials who are responsible for their actions to these party bodies. Party rules and procedures should provide for substantial party participation and maximum public information regarding preconvention planning.

The party national committees and more broadly representative party commissions and advisory committees should have an integral role in an open convention planning and arrangements process. Key convention positions should be filled through open partywide competition and recruitment, subject to confirmation by the national committee. The permanent chairmanship, for example, instead of going automatically to the Speaker or Majority or Minority Leader of the House, could be rotated during the convention. The national committees could institute long-term programs for development of convention personnel so as to increase the number of individuals within the party familiar with the complicated logistics of a national convention. All convention committees could fully publicize their schedules of meetings and their personnel requirements, with a view to encouraging party members to observe and participate in the process.

Codification and publication of convention rules and precedents well in advance of the convention could be undertaken by the parties. Instead of relying primarily on members of Congress to serve as convention parliamentarians, the parties could call on state legislators and other informed party members to serve as advisers on parliamentary procedure. The conventions could also follow the example of some professional societies, such as the American Political Science Association, which have retained impartial advice from outside authorities like the American Arbitration Association.

The parties could adopt broadened criteria and assume party responsibility for press accreditation to the national conventions. The parties have relied on press committees from the several news galleries of Congress (daily press, radio and television, and periodicals) to accredit news representatives at the convention and thus have delegated one of the most important arrangement functions to a nonparty group that publishes no report on its activities. Because the rigorous and detailed criteria used to limit press access to the news galleries of Congress are not at all appropriate to the political conventions as party institutions, the parties could establish and staff their own committees for press accreditation to the conventions. Criteria should be broadened to include publications of citizen and private organizations, the student press and the underground or people's press. The parties should also make and publicize well in advance adequate provisions for accrediting scholars and official observers who wish to study the convention process.

As one of the most effective ways to open the convention process and ensure greater accountability, the parties could pledge themselves to a "freedom of information" policy, including open sessions, the right to public inspection of convention records and prompt publication of the official proceedings of the convention and its committees. Guidelines could be established for the national, state and local parties to ensure that, whenever possible, especially in meetings with candidates, convention committees and caucuses meet in open session.

Improved convention rules and procedures distributed in advance of the convention should reduce the number of instances of arbitrary exercise of power. The parties should also establish adequate internal appeals procedures to handle any alleged abuses in the convention process, including delegate and gallery seating arrangements. The offices of general counsel of both parties could make legal assistance available to any delegate or party member wishing to make such an appeal. Citizen and/or party reform groups could supplement party efforts by operating an independent convention abuse-and-complaint desk with legal staff assistance at the convention, perhaps including the services of a public interest law unit.

The growing security requirements of national conventions have fundamental implications for the integrity of the convention process and can no longer be left to the discretion of a national party chairman or appointed convention official. The parties should establish committees on convention security to study the following problems and make appropriate recommendations: preconvention security for presidential candidates; convention security forces to be required and the authority under which they should operate; personal (Secret Service or other) protection required by candidates and key convention officials; procedures for safeguarding the privacy of headquarters and candidate suites (including prohibitions and stiff penalties against the use of electronic surveillance equipment); and the role of governmental security forces in the convention.[24]

Recommendation 6. Increased citizen participation and public education throughout the convention process should be encouraged by the parties in cooperation with candidates, citizen groups and the media.

The entire convention process, from preconvention primary campaigns, precinct caucuses and state conventions involved in selecting delegates to preconvention committees, state dele-

---

[24] "The political parties should be prepared for the full range of confrontation tactics that protest groups have used at annual meetings of major corporations," states Edwin J. Putzell, Jr., general counsel of Monsanto, and former president of the American Society of Corporate Secretaries, which has published a guide for the conduct of annual meetings and security and admission guidelines for stockholder meetings.

gation meetings and convention-city activities, provides the single most visible and important chain of political events through which citizens can participate in state and national parties. In addition to giving citizens access to party power— presidential nominations, party platforms and internal party government—the convention process through the coverage it receives by the mass media is one of the best vehicles for public education in party politics.

National party conventions are so deeply ingrained in the American party system that to some degree they will always remain the property of the party faithful. Still, the convention process can be opened to substantially greater citizen participation at every stage.

To increase participation in the preconvention campaign, states holding presidential primaries could sponsor round tables and campaign workshops to acquaint actual or potential candidates with the state's political background, including state laws and party rules, demographic characteristics and trends, voting and poll data and effective campaign techniques. Such programs could be initiated and coordinated by political science departments of state universities or by citizen groups or other committees within the state and would be open to all actual or potential candidates, their campaign organizations, citizen and cause groups and interested individuals.

In view of the complexity of and frequent changes in state statutes that govern the delegate selection process, presidential preference primaries, third-party access to the ballot and the use of supplemental lines, a central information service on state primary and election laws could be established. An election-law reporting service could provide party reform units and citizen organizations with technical assistance in drafting model statutes to increase the citizen voice in delegate selection.

State and national party information for citizens on delegate selection in the states should be readily available as a matter of party policy. Any citizen should be able to write state party headquarters, a state party official, his Congressman or national party headquarters to obtain an accurate description of the state laws, party rules, procedures and customs that govern the selection of national convention delegates in his state, including an updated calendar of filing dates, party meetings and elections.

The weeks preceding the sessions of the full national conventions afford an excellent opportunity for the parties to develop an open curriculum of workshops and training and political education programs for key party workers and interested citizens planning to attend the conventions. The parties could draw on the resources of the state party organizations and other experts at the convention for staffing, and convention facilities and hotel space already reserved for convention use could be adapted for•party educational purposes at modest expense. In time, party convention political seminars could become a valuable addition to the normal convention program.

Citizen and cause organizations should monitor the preconvention campaign and establish convention-city operations in an effort to influence the convention's deliberative process. Organizations could sponsor open caucuses of interested delegates and develop their own committee and convention-floor strategies. They could also endorse individual candidates and resolutions favorable to their organization's position.

Since the conventions are unique experiences and practical training grounds that should be made available to as many citizens as want to observe them, the parties should take steps to encourage and facilitate public attendance at the conventions. As the critical problems of controlling convention size on the floor, providing working space to the delegates and media and ensuring basic convention security are solved, subcommittees of the convention Arrangements Committee could study imaginative ways to encourage public attendance and involvement in the convention. Site selection for the convention could give greater emphasis to the criterion of public access. (Washington, D.C., should be added to the cities now considered as hosts for national conventions through the construction of adequate convention facilities in the nation's capital.) Actual attendance in the convention hall could be increased through the use of rotating galleries, a long-standing practice in Congress. Auxiliary halls could be equipped with large closed-circuit color television screens to accommodate overflow crowds, and visitors could be given passes to other less crowded convention facilities and functions.

A significant new dimension of party and public participation in the convention could be provided by a major exhibition hall as part of enlarged convention facilities. State and local party organizations, party auxiliaries, political consulting firms and vendors of campaign supplies, citizen and cause organizations, publishers and news services catering to political audiences and virtually any interested group should be encouraged to staff convention booths and displays. Within the hectic and confused setting of the convention city, an exhibition hall could be a focal point of information and communications for party and citizen activists.

Under current communications arrangements in the convention city, it is virtually impossible for state and local party members or the general public to communicate with delegates at the convention. The parties should develop new means for home-state and local participation while the convention is in session. State parties could maintain home-desk officers to monitor state newspapers and radio and television stations for public response to the convention, to poll party members on convention issues, and to maintain a 24-hour open telephone line to receive local comments and suggestions. Special television and radio reports from state delegations could be regularly broadcast from the convention city and made available to local broadcast stations within the home state. The format of the televised report to the state could include a summary of actions taken by the delegation in major convention decisions and a question-and-answer period with questions phoned in by viewers to the local station and relayed to the convention. A convention arrangements subcommittee could work with the networks and broadcast programming consultants in advance to prepare such a home-state reporting service. The parties could also arrange for a network of telephone tie lines from the states to a delegate telephone message center at the convention, which would permit citizens to place station calls to convention delegates at local telephone rates through a pre-announced local number in each of the states.

The importance of a daily report at the convention—akin

to the *Congressional Record* although in digest form—cannot
be overestimated. Daily convention newspapers and a 24-hour
convention news service would permit delegates, press and observers to keep abreast of what is happening in committees
with which they would normally have no contact, as well as to
keep track of scattered convention developments on a daily
chronological basis and in much broader detail than the local
convention-city press ever presents.[25] The parties could commission a convention news service through competitive bidding. Such a project might be undertaken by a consortium of
journalism schools or pools of experienced newsmen. Independent citizen or news organizations could print convention
newspapers in competition with the party establishment's press,
a practice that has already been developed successfully at conventions of other national organizations. More adequate literature on recent conventions would also enhance public understanding and participation in the party conventions. A privately
sponsored task force should monitor both major-party conventions and publish a descriptive and analytical study of each
convention.

Convention coverage in the 1970's will place new demands
on the media. The various media should take immediate steps
to improve the quality of their convention news coverage
through more selective and imaginative programming, wider
use of guest commentators and pretaped interviews and documentaries on such topics as preconvention primary campaigns,
the delegate selection process and the party reform movement. The television networks might experiment, as did ABC
in 1968, with formats other than live continuous coverage of
floor proceedings. The Public Broadcasting Service or a cable

---

[25] A private news organization, *Congressional Quarterly,* maintained a
daily convention news service in Miami Beach and Chicago in 1968 and
succeeded in publishing within a month of the conclusion of the Democratic convention an excellent digest, *The Presidential Nominating Conventions: 1968* (Washington, D.C.: Congressional Quarterly Service,
1968). *CQ* will not continue the service in 1972, although its former director, Neal R. Peirce, now public affairs consultant with the *National
Journal,* estimates the costs of such a service to the parties would be
modest, perhaps $20,000 at each convention.

TV network might attempt continuous in-depth coverage of preconvention and convention committee deliberations directed to a more limited but highly interested audience of political activists. Adequate coverage of black, women's and youth caucuses, the technicalities of party reform fights or aspects of convention security will require advance preparation and expertise on the part of news agencies. Open reporting of the convention process will depend in good measure on the adaptability of the media in many instances.

The parties themselves should also assume a positive role in upgrading the quality of convention news and analysis. In addition to establishing convention newspapers and news services, the parties should name convention committees on the media to evaluate preconvention and convention reporting. These committees could issue postconvention reports noting examples of excellent convention programming, offering suggestions for improved political reporting at future conventions and itemizing instances of party dissatisfaction with media coverage. The parties could make key convention and party personnel available for frequent interviews and briefings on convention developments, and prepare audiovisual materials that could be used for presentation to delegates and home audiences.

III

The National Committees: Shadows or Substance?

In the vast underdeveloped terrain of American party institutions, the national committees, with their national party chairmen, modern headquarters, professional staffs, multi-million-dollar operating budgets and extensive programs, give the appearance of national power and national presence. In fact, they are shadow committees that have little contact with the real world of issues and politics. Less charitably, they are referred to by leaders in both parties as deadwood, an anachronism, or a gigantic political fraud perpetrated on the voter and the citizen. Political scientists have described their activities as "politics without power," and many political professionals like former Johnson White House aide Jack Valenti have argued that they should be abolished outright. These are admittedly harsh comments, but their performance in the several months before and after the critical 1970 elections did much to confirm these judgments.

The Republican National Committee (RNC) did not meet from the late summer of 1970 until mid-January 1971, when party leaders convened to dedicate the new Eisenhower headquarters building and rush through pro forma business. National committee members sat silently without questions while the first report of the Republican reform unit, the Delegates and Organizations Committee, was delivered. In a rare moment of candor, Mrs. Gladys O'Donnell, president of the National Federation of Republican Women, challenged the leadership before Acting Chairman and former National Chairman Bliss gaveled the meeting to a close one hour ahead of schedule. "I wish there had been the opportunity for this group of realists to explore the last election and to do post mortems on the techniques used in the campaign," Mrs. O'Donnell observed. "It is amazing how we can disregard the lessons of history politically. The Democrats don't defeat us, we defeat ourselves."

The Democratic National Committee (DNC) meeting a month later was a far more lively party function but similar to the RNC in several aspects. National committee and reform commission members like Mrs. Carmen Warschaw of California and Joseph F. Crangle, Jr., the Erie County, New York, Democratic chairman, openly challenged reports and actions of DNC Treasurer Robert S. Strauss and Democratic National Chairman Lawrence O'Brien. "Rather than telling us what's already accomplished on things like the National Finance Committee, I wish you'd inform us on the national committee before the press," Mrs. Warschaw rebuked Strauss. "We could help you out and you could help us." Chairman O'Brien pointedly ignored the California national committeewoman. Resorting to "a few tricks of the old politics," according to one observer, such as substituting his own interpretation of procedures for Robert's Rules of Order and simply gaveling down procedural points of order, O'Brien, with party General Counsel Joseph A. Califano, Jr., at his side, steered the revolutionary set of party reforms on the selection of convention delegates and procedures for challenging credentials, incorporated in the preliminary call to the 1972 convention, through the committee without discussion. Their work done, the two national committees then adjourned for another six months.

The nonperformance of the national committees would be a farce were it not for the serious issues of party leadership and participation involved. The national committees are responsible for overseeing the dispersed American party system in the years between national conventions. The Democratic National Committee normally employs a full-time staff of between 75 and 100, the Republican National Committee between 150 and 200—and these numbers may double or triple during a presidential campaign year. The DNC reported annual receipts and expenditures of $1.6 million in 1970, the

RNC $3 million. Separate funding put the overall national committee budgets even higher, with $4.2 million for the Republicans.[1]

What do the national committees do with these resources? What kind of stewardship of the party's future do party leaders and national committee members exercise? Can the national committees be modernized to develop new means of active citizen participation in politics and government and to serve as prototypes for broad-ranging reform in the hundreds of party central committees in the states and counties?

Inside the National Committees

The party national committees have not changed significantly since they were instituted by the Democratic National Convention in 1848 and by the Republican party at its first presidential nominating convention in 1856 as standing committees of the national parties to link one national convention to the next and to coordinate intraparty campaign activity.[2] The national committees are in theory creatures of the national party conventions, subject to the rules and resolutions of the convention. Members are nominated by the states and territories but must be formally confirmed by the convention before they commence their four-year terms extending to the next convention.

Essentially four methods of electing national committee members are used. Initially, members were elected directly by their state delegations to the national convention or by the same state conventions that elected national convention delegates, the two most common methods still used. The Progressive era at the turn of the century introduced a third

---

[1] "1970 Reports of Political Committees," *National Journal*, February 13, 1971, pp. 366–67; and "Campaign Spending: Record $42.4 Million in 1970," *Congressional Quarterly*, July 23, 1971, pp. 1570–73.

[2] For a history of the development of the national committees see Cornelius P. Cotter and Bernard C. Hennessy, *Politics Without Power: The National Party Committees* (New York: Atherton Press, 1964); and Hugh A. Bone, *Party Committees and National Politics* (Seattle: University of Washington Press, 1958).

method, direct election of national committee members in statewide primaries, used today by only four states and the District of Columbia. A fourth method, election by the state central committee, was gradually adopted by one or both parties in more than a dozen states.

Originally the composition of the national committees was based on the principle of equal state representation, with one representative from each state, territory, and the District of Columbia. A national committeewoman from each state was added after the passage of universal woman suffrage. After 1952, the Republicans added state chairmen from states that elected Republican presidential electors or major officeholders and in 1968 membership was extended to all state chairmen. The Democrats have not followed suit, although in 1969 Democratic National Chairman Fred Harris instituted informal joint meetings of the Democratic National Committee and the Democratic state chairmen. For the first time in modern party history, the Democratic National Convention of 1972 may give serious consideration to restructuring the Democratic National Committee on an equal-population basis.

Although the national committees have retained essentially the same form and purpose for well over a century, there is a striking contrast between their stated objectives and functions and their actual performance.[3] The national committees claim to be representative continuation committees for the parties. National party headquarters boast of professional communications operations, including the most advanced radio and television news services, available to candidates and party organizations. Party publications are spewed out in a variety of sizes, shapes and colors for computer-addressed mailing to the membership. Campaign divisions target field men and national funds for critical state and local races. Ambitious

---

[3] An extensive discussion of national committee functions is provided by Bone, *Party Committees*, pp. 36–125. Ray Bliss's 1968 report to the Republican National Committee lists 19 separate RNC activities. (See *The Chairman's Report—1968*, report to the Republican National Committee, Washington, D.C., January 16–17, 1969 [Washington, D.C.: Republican National Committee, 1969].)

programs of party organization and training are planned. New techniques of computer analysis mark advances in party research operations. Party policy councils publish volumes of position papers. The latest direct-mail operations are applied to party fund raising. Special divisions or staff devote years of preparation to staging the massive national conventions. Party patronage officers seek to screen potential governmental appointments. A party bureaucracy of women's and youth auxiliaries, special program offices for blacks, Spanish Americans, other nationality groups, older Americans and party task forces reaches out to virtually every major voting bloc in the country. Special party services are provided for state chairmen, governors and state legislators.

The responsibility for all these operations—from convening a national committee meeting to preparing the party's way to the White House—has been vested in one man, the party's national chairman, usually assisted by a deputy chairman who is a full-time administrator. Given such a wide jurisdiction for party affairs, it is not surprising that national committee performance is spotty and uneven. "My biggest problem," Lawrence O'Brien has noted, "is the leadership I must provide. . . . I'm spread thin as hell." The shortcomings of the committees, however, underline far more basic failures in participation and political and governmental effectiveness.

National committee members and state parties spend tens of thousands of dollars to travel to national committee meetings only to find that chairmen and staff have little for them to do. Hours of meeting time are consumed with lengthy introductions of new members and pronouncements and perfunctory reports by national party and congressional leaders. One RNC leader privately described its meetings as the most depressing aspect of his work. "The press voted among themselves that we close one of our recent sessions," he observed. "It was like slow death."

The only formal financial reports made by either national committee are those required by law to be filed with the Clerk of the House of Representatives. No financial statements or budgets are made available to national committee members, party members or contributors, nor are party finances the subject of open party discussion. Democratic Treasurer Richard Maguire managed DNC finances in the mid-1960's so secretively that no other responsible official of the committee, the DNC membership or the press had an accurate picture of the party's financial condition. Maguire somehow succeeded in concealing the party's $4.1-million 1964 election debt until 1966.

National committee members have no role in planning or evaluating party strategy for elections. In 1970, for example, in spite of the critical importance of the control of state legislatures for redistricting following the 1970 census, the membership of neither national committee was involved in party planning for the elections. Party headquarters made all the decisions, including providing the states with professional staff advice on such subjects as computer redistricting proposals. When the Republican party lost control of several key legislatures, including California, the former director of state services at the RNC, F. Bradford Hays, wryly observed, "All our sweetheart [redistricting] packages went out the damn window on election day." The key decisions concerning which campaigns will receive what kinds and amounts of campaign services are kept within inner party circles. After the elections, no party committee reviews expenditures or assesses election results and national committee performance except in the limited sense that a national chairman may occasionally be forced to resign. Neither the national committee membership nor the party rank and file has insisted on such elementary forms of leadership accountability.

Party publications exemplify the closed nonparticipatory character of national committee operations. Neither party produces or distributes an informative, high-quality newsletter or periodical to a broad cross section of party leaders and members. Publications tend to be glossy and propagandistic, containing relatively little information on internal party affairs. They are written from Washington in a "top down" style with no real encouragement to the reader to participate in party affairs or share experiences of constituent organizations.

National committee members and the public cannot even get a usable current directory of services provided by their party headquarters. The Republicans publish a chairman's report with a brief and not very helpful summary of national committee divisions and programs. The Democrats have not published a comparable annual report for more than a decade, and only a six-page leaflet summarizing national headquarters operations is available from the DNC.

In other national committee operations as well, impressive organization charts are often composed of hollow boxes. Although blacks constitute more than 10 percent of the electorate and by some estimates 20 percent of the national Democratic party vote, they have had to fight to maintain black programs in both national committee headquarters. Since Louis Martin completed a long and influential career as the head of the DNC's Minorities Division, the position of minority-group programs has been tenuous. In 1969, the RNC under Rogers Morton abolished the Minorities Division that had built up a staff of 35 under Ray Bliss. Perhaps reflecting a middle-class white bias that permeates both parties, the RNC bluntly stated that it had "no separate 'Black' operation, as such, but successfully uses Special Assistants to the Chairman in this area who work with the Political Division." (The Republicans reinstituted a separate Black Political Division under Morton's successor, Senator Robert J. Dole of Kansas.) The DNC under Lawrence O'Brien attempted a similar consolidation but resistance was sufficiently strong to force the retention of a separate black Minorities Division within the Office of the National Chairman. The top black aides at both national committees, John Dean at the DNC and Clarence L. Townes, Jr., at the RNC, resigned prior to the 1970 elections and their positions remained vacant for several months with scarcely any public comment.

In another critical area, reaching and involving young voters, national chairmen have found the youth auxiliaries of the parties too ideologically one-sided or too involved in their own internal politics to be effective instruments and have had to improvise their own youth operations. After a series of confrontations with the Young Republican National Federation, Ray Bliss organized the Opportunities Unlimited Program, an independent, well-financed, campus-oriented program within the national committee's Arts and Sciences Division. Fred Harris bypassed the Young Democrats in appointing a Youth Participation Commission of the Democratic National Committee in December 1969. His successor, O'Brien, chose other vehicles, a predominantly student-oriented Campaign '70 Clearing House and a National Action Council, to serve as forums for the coordination of Democratic party youth activities. Neither national committee, however, has been able to arrest or reverse the decline in party identification among younger voters.

In these and other ways, national chairmen and party headquarters staff repeatedly miss the most obvious opportunities to involve party members in timely and important political questions. Throughout the congressional debate on campaign finances, neither party's finance committee met to develop and present a party policy statement. In spite of the criticisms of the media by leaders of both parties and the growing importance of the media in electoral politics, neither party bothered to recruit a working commission of members with relevant experience in this area.

Even the elaborate party policy councils of recent years—the Republican Coordinating Committee established in 1965, followed by the Democratic Policy Council in 1969—have missed the mark. A fundamental limitation has been their almost automatic suspension when the party regains the executive branch. One observer reported that "the Democratic Advisory Council died of uselessness at the Democratic National Convention in July of 1960."[4] Another noted in February 1969 that "although the obituary has not yet been written, it appears to be Nixon's desire that the Republican Coordinating Committee . . . be allowed to die."[5] Thus at the very time the party assumes responsibility for government, the party organization dismantles the formal mechanisms through which it could contribute ideas and talent to government.

On perhaps the major issue of the past few years, the state

---

[4] Cotter and Hennessy, *Politics Without Power*, p. 222.

[5] Jules Witcover, "Nixon Moving to Cement Republican Party Strength," St. Louis *Globe-Democrat*, February 3, 1969.

of the American economy, neither party has involved its members in a broad-based assessment of the economy, the effectiveness of current economic policy, possible policy initiatives, and, most directly, likely political consequences. The Democratic Policy Council has called on a few party stalwarts in the academic community; the Republican party organization has done nothing. House Minority Leader Gerald Ford, perhaps sensing the political stakes involved, urged at the spring 1971 meeting of the Republican governors that the Republican Coordinating Committee be reactivated. The proposal won the unanimous endorsement of the governors but no action from National Chairman Dole or the White House.

Even in the traditional area of party patronage, the national committees seem to have lost their touch. During the early months of the Nixon administration, one senior member of the RNC, Tom Stagg of Louisiana, was turned away by a White House staff member who handled patronage with the curt message that he did not see visitors. A near revolt of the RNC gained only a small patronage office located in a remote corner of a separate floor of the party headquarters building and a request that national committee members submit 10 names for positions on ceremonial boards and advisory committees. A wall of politically inexperienced White House aides effectively screened the national committee from the critical function of recruiting and training political talent for government.

The failure of national party leaders and national committee members themselves to open the national committees to broader participation and to make them a more effective force in national party politics stems from several factors.

First, effective power within the national committees has traditionally been wielded by the national party chairman and a coterie of party leaders. But these national party leaders have tended to define their political self-interest in narrow terms and to ignore the long-term interests of the party organization. Presidents, congressional leaders and even national party chairmen have preferred weak national committees that will not challenge their individual authority and prerogatives of office. More often than not, the national committees are leaderless. The President has been increasingly unable or unwilling to devote detailed attention to party matters. National chairmen, in theory elected by and responsible to the national committee, are recruited by and serve at the pleasure and direction of the President or the titular leaders of the out party. In accepting the Republican chairmanship in 1971, Senator Dole told the RNC that "as your chairman, loyalty to the President will be my primary concern." Only in the exceptional case, like Paul Butler of the Democrats, has a party chairman broken the traces and actively worked to build the stature of the national committees.

Second, the current procedures for electing national committee members have not produced an activist constituency committed to modernizing the national parties. Many members are still elected in recognition of previous party or governmental contributions, while others are chosen merely because they have the time and money to serve. Although most are considered influential in their state parties, their influence does not necessarily mean a working familiarity with state or national party operations. Studies of internal party government have devoted limited attention to the problem of the quality of national committee membership and have advanced few proposals for reform.

Third, the national committees have been able to sustain their power and legitimacy, such as it is, because of the general ignorance and low expectations of most party members and citizens about party operations. Despite the plethora of party publications, only a limited amount of meaningful information on party programs, budgets and performance is made available to the public, even to active party members. The national party elites that run the central party committees in Washington have little motivation to inform and involve a broader base of party members. Most national committee meetings provide limited seating at best to the public and the press. Sessions of the RNC are often closed and minutes are not made public. The DNC in 1971 even instituted a ten-dollar admission fee for observers. DNC minutes are published once every four years as part of the party's volume on convention proceedings, which itself is usually not available until three years or more after the convention. The news media concentrate on individuals and insurgent party organizations in the public spotlight, overestimating their power and long-term impact on the political parties, while ignoring the nameless men who shun notoriety and controversy and exercise real and continuing power in party politics. Thus national committee operations are effectively closed except to the select few, and no institutional means for holding the party elites responsible to their party constituency is developed. Those who might really object to "shadow politics as usual" are rarely given a chance to be heard.

Contemporary Change in the National Committees

At the same time, several important contemporary changes are expanding the resources at the disposal of the national committees and giving them an important potential for encouraging party modernization in the 1970's. To date, however, their impact has been a continued increase in the discretionary power of the national chairman and his headquarters staff and a steady decline in the effective role of the national committee member.

Their approaches differ, but both parties appear strongly committed to the professionalization of party organization and procedures and to the building of a strong professional staff structure within what has traditionally been a weak and decentralized network of state and national parties. During the 1960's, the Republicans made extensive use of political consultants to build party organization, especially the campaign service capabilities of national and state central committees, a highly significant development examined later in this book. Political consultants have become a quasi-staff arm or extension of the parties, enabling them to reach into new areas of political organization and campaigning. A managerial and marketing attitude toward politics has made Republicans more receptive to the party organization's use of paid professional staff and consultants, survey research and computer applications. Simultaneously Republicans have placed a higher priority on unified, systematic fund raising and have developed a financial base that enables the leadership to invest steadily increasing amounts of money in the party structure.

The development of Democratic party organization during the 1960's lagged considerably behind the Republicans', although Democrats have made effective use of other organizational resources. In the late 1950's, the Democratic National Committee under Paul Butler had set the stage for a well-financed professional national committee operation easily the equal of the Republicans', only to have it dismantled by the administrations of Kennedy and Johnson. Neil Staebler, chairman of Butler's Advisory Committee on Political Organization, tried unsuccessfully to convince President Kennedy of the need for continuing development of party organization. In Staebler's view, by developing its sustaining membership program the DNC could have stayed ahead of the RNC as "a practical source of research and development for political methods and as a prod to the state and especially the county organizations in training and party operations." Strict economy measures under the Johnson staff in late 1965 eliminated the entire DNC registration section as well as a number of senior staff positions.

Although Democratic party organization was allowed to stagnate, other groups generally aligned with the party or its liberal wing assumed important organization roles. By 1970, for example, the AFL-CIO's Committee on Political Education (COPE), a leading political arm of organized labor, could claim that no party could match its political organization and full-time staff at the state level. The top 20 members of COPE's Washington staff alone were paid more than $440,000 in salaries and expenses during 1970.[6] Organized labor's three major political objectives prior to the 1972 elections were gaining maximum delegate strength within the Democratic convention, raising a record campaign fund to defeat the Nixon administration and maintaining Democratic party unity through the preconvention primaries.

---

[6] Senator Paul J. Fannin (R-Ariz.), "AFL-CIO Committee on Political Education—Salaries over $10,000," in *Congressional Record—Senate*, 92nd Congress, 1st Session, November 9, 1971, p. S 17932.

The Democratic party organization has also been able to draw for many years on the fund-raising and campaign assistance of liberal organizations like the National Committee for an Effective Congress, cause groups and party activists in the academic community. The party was able to supplement party headquarters resources with congressional staff and the personnel and program resources of the federal bureaucracy under Presidents Kennedy and Johnson.

Since August 1968, when Democratic presidential candidate Humphrey found virtually no national party organization, staff or facilities available for his campaign, Democrats have tried to make up for organizational lost ground with a handicap of a $9.3-million carry-over debt. At the same time, Democrats have been developing innovations in the process of party politics designed to promote broader participation. In the long run, these distinctive Democratic reforms in party organization and procedure may prove to be as significant as Republican advances in the maintenance and efficiency of party organization, in the broadening of the popular base of party finances and in the technology of managing information.

Although both party headquarters are still subject to the rapid turnover of national chairmen and top-level staff, there has been a conscious effort to expand professional capabilities and staff. The Republicans have revamped salaries and scaled fringe benefits to match those of other professional organizations and proudly claim "the best employee compensation program of any political organization." In May 1970, Lawrence O'Brien announced a complete reorganization of the DNC staff, the first such major overhaul in 20 years, to "take advantage of the most up-to-date campaign and communications technology" in the 1970's.

The national committees have increasingly served to coordinate, centralize or consolidate previously uncoordinated activities (including research, fund raising and electronic data processing) performed by state parties and other national party bodies such as the congressional campaign committees. The RNC has recently begun holding national Professional Staff Conferences to give personnel in state parties the opportunity to exchange ideas and participate in workshops with national committee staff.

Although the practice of appointing sitting members of Congress as party national chairmen continues, as seen in the case of Republican Robert Dole, the responsibilities of both the national chairman and many state party chairmen in campaign planning, fund raising and party administration are now generally recognized as requiring highly competent, full-time salaried political managers and spokesmen. The national chairman has also gained visibility, mobility and influence in national politics through advances in transportation, communications and information technology. O'Brien, for example, campaigned in 26 states between Labor Day and Election Day 1970. Ray Bliss, who appeared in public less frequently, had the reputation of regularly tying up one of the RNC's WATS lines with calls around the country. Television, direct-mail and polling techniques enable national chairmen and party policy councils to present and test party positions rapidly and effectively.

Perhaps the most important change in the national committees has been the gradual construction of a self-sustaining financial base of small contributors through direct-mail solicitation and political advertisements. The Republicans took the lead in the development of party fund-raising capabilities in the 1960's. In contrast to the loose organization, informality and confusion traditionally typifying Democratic fund-raising efforts, the Republicans began with a tested structure of closely coordinated finance committees at the national, state and local levels.[7] The Republican National Finance Committee, an independent organization not formally within the RNC structure, coordinates the party's national fund-raising operations. The party's National Finance Chairman, a volunteer selected by the National Chairman, works through a network of regional vice-chairmen and state chairmen and is assisted by some 220 members who are proven Republican money raisers.

---

[7] Alexander Heard, *The Costs of Democracy: Financing American Political Campaigns,* Anchor Book (Garden City, N.Y.: Doubleday, 1962), especially p. 196.

By 1964, 80 percent of national Republican money was raised through small contributions of less than $100, although the amount had dropped to between 65 and 70 percent by 1970. The combined number of direct-mail contributors to the RNC and Republican congressional committees had reached an estimated 650,000 to 750,000 by the end of the decade, with the RNC claiming a base of more than 225,000 Republicans in its Sustaining Membership Program donating a minimum of $15 annually to the party (for a minimum total of $3.4 million per year). This steady flow of funds has made it possible for the RNC to codify, update, systematically expand and distribute to state, county and other party organizations and workers an impressive volume of campaign and organizational manuals such as the party's research and electronic-data-processing manuals and its Mission 70's organization program, which cost the party $250,000 in its initial year and a half. The RNC has also been able to develop over several years an information-retrieval system (the Miracode automated microfilm system) containing more than 150,000 documents on the Nixon administration and more than 30,000 articles on the Democratic opposition, and information on the RNC itself, such as the party's comprehensive manual and checklist for convention planning.

As an indication of the substantial discretionary budget of Republican national chairmen, Ray Bliss was also in a position to invest $600,000 in an election simulation project in 1968, although the RNC ultimately decided not to undertake the project. Bliss banked a minimum cash reserve of $100,000 in 1968 so that the national committee could continue to operate its sustaining programs regardless of the 1968 outcome.

In 1960, the Democratic National Committee created a Democratic National Finance Committee patterned somewhat on its Republican counterpart. Its origin lay in jurisdictional and personality conflicts among top Democratic finance managers, and its purpose was to strengthen the financial bonds between the national committee and the state committees so as to provide a more stable party fund-raising quota system. These attempts at centralized finance came to nothing.

President Kennedy chose to create the $1,000 President's Club instead of developing Paul Butler's Dollars for Democrats and Sustaining Membership programs ($10 annual dues), which had provided the DNC with more than $1 million from 1957 through 1960. The President's Club, the effective finance arm of the Democratic party, turned the focus of the Democratic finances to sizable gifts from a smaller group of individuals. The clubs raised enormous amounts for the party in the mid-1960's. In 1966, for example, the President's Club for Johnson Committee reported receipts of $2,732,577, the largest single addition to the party's coffers that year. The Dollars for Democrats and Sustaining Membership programs and the National Finance Committee were allowed to languish and deteriorate.

The inattention to long-term finances proved disastrous for the Democrats. Without control of the White House, the party had little success in reducing its debt from the 1968 elections and actually ran a deficit in DNC operations during 1969. In August 1971, the DNC declared a moratorium on repaying its $9.3-million debt until after the 1972 election, hoping that such creditors as American Telephone and Telegraph would not insist on payment during the convention and election period. With the postponement until at least 1976 of a controversial federal tax-checkoff system to finance the 1972 elections, the state of Democratic party finances remained unchanged.

The Democrats have belatedly made efforts to build a sustaining financial base for the party. In 1970, Treasurer Robert Strauss initiated a $100-a-month club to meet DNC operating expenses and enrolled 650 Democrats (for a base of $780,000). Small direct-mail contributions under a program directed by Olga Gechas, formerly a fund raiser with UNICEF, rose from 10,000 to 50,000 in 1970, and a $100,000 revolving fund was set aside to expand the program. With the committee operating on a pay-as-you-go basis, Chairman O'Brien claimed "a year of significant financial progress." By mid-1972, the DNC had invited 10 million people to contribute to the party by direct-mail alone.

Emerging Challenges

The professionalization of various party central committee functions has proceeded without any substantial involvement of the elected national committees, themselves a potentially significant although as yet inactive party resource. Party leadership elites that control the growing resources of national committee operations will face challenges, however, on several fronts during the 1970's. The first demands for greater party participation have come through the Democratic reform movement. In urging a new 500-member Democratic National Council to supplement the national convention and national committee, Samuel H. Beer placed a good measure of the responsibility for the present fragmentation of American and especially Democratic party politics on the failure of the party to provide adequate channels for the growing number of issue-oriented voters.

Specific demands for significant party change have already come from blacks and women. Richard G. Hatcher, the Democratic mayor of Gary, Indiana, who has encouraged the formation of black political organizations like the Black Caucus in the House of Representatives, sees the need for blacks to develop new strategies within "the existing racist two-party framework." Hatcher and a group of other black leaders won a pledge from National Chairman O'Brien in October 1971 to appoint blacks to 20 percent of the Democratic National Committee and convention staff positions and announced their intention to meet with the Republican National Chairman as well.

"Women as a majority group will have a much greater impact on the organization of the political parties than the blacks or other minorities have had," predicts Vera Glaser, a nationally syndicated columnist with the Knight newspapers, and former public relations director of the Women's Division of the RNC. "The women's rights movement will have as far-reaching political consequences for the 1970's as the civil rights movement had in the 1960's."

Well before the 1972 national party conventions, the National Women's Political Caucus had demanded that half of the delegates be women, and the National Organization of Women was pressing for the elimination of all separate women's divisions in the political parties, devices designed "to keep women working, but in their places," according to former Democratic National Vice-Chairwoman Geraldine M. "Geri" Joseph.

One of the first signs of the women's revolt in the parties came at a meeting of the Democratic Policy Council on March 24, 1971. When its chairman, Senator Humphrey, announced a list of new nominations to the council, Gloria Steinem of New York, a leader in the women's liberation movement, rose to point out that no women had been included on the list. Humphrey, embarrassed by the oversight, withdrew the list pending the addition of other names. Ms. Steinem then introduced a lengthy resolution on the status of women in the Democratic party, calling for "equal representation of women on all committees and in all positions of influence in the party," including chairmanships of convention committees and convention officers. The resolution was passed unanimously.

Women are adopting some of the legal strategies of the public interest movement to effect changes in party structures. Young lawyers like Phyllis N. Segal of the Georgetown University Law Center have researched the legal dimension of discrimination and proposed several remedies in state legislatures, courts and party reform commissions. "The traditional party role of women is confined to dealing with other women and to physical work," observes Mrs. Segal. "We can begin . . . by creating a legal climate in which inequality is no longer sanctioned. Then and only then can we determine if women will ever be able to play a meaningful role in our major political parties."[8]

Women activists in the party organizations are optimistic concerning the prospects of the women's rights movement. "I see changes coming in the political parties," says Flora Crater,

---

[8] Phyllis N. Segal, "Women and Political Parties: The Legal Dimension of Discrimination," reprinted in Remarks of Martha W. Griffiths (D-Mich.), *Congressional Record—Extensions of Remarks,* 92nd Congress, 1st Session, March 17, 1971, pp. E 2773, E 2776.

a leader of the Virginia Women's Political Caucus and member of the Virginia Democratic state central committee. "The political process needs jacking up, and the women's caucuses are just the ones to do it." "The Republican Party," asserts St. Louis Republican alderman Doris Bass, "is ripe for a takeover by women."

Recommendations: Developing the Potential of the National Committees

Next to the national party conventions, the national committees are potentially the most important representative party institutions in American politics. Rather than their eclipse or abolition, we recommend their development as active party governing bodies and as significant points of citizen access and pressure to modernize the parties. The national committees can elect or remove the national party chairman. They can exercise control over the national party's multimillion-dollar budget and operations. Backed by mandates of the national convention, they can enact model reforms and guidelines for state party organizations and operations. They can stimulate innovation in the party through their own programs and services and through the interchange of ideas and personnel among the state parties.

The following recommendations are directed toward the development of effective, representative national committees. Many can be implemented at the discretion of the national chairman. The backing of an incumbent President could give a powerful assist. Others can be achieved only by resolution of the national party convention and active involvement and support of national committee members. All are feasible reforms that are within the power of the political parties and that citizens can urge through a broadened party reform movement. Collectively they represent a fundamental restructuring and new concept of active party central committees for the 1970's.

Recommendation 1. Parties should encourage the election of competent, active national committee members, including a new category of national at-large members.

If national committees are to exercise an important representative party governing role between conventions, it is essential that they be composed of the most capable party representatives possible and that they be more broadly representative of the party and of the population in general. National committee members of the 1970's should be party activists, conversant with the programs of both national and state parties, involved in major commissions and working groups of the national committee, and committed to the goal of party modernization.

The national conventions should establish representative party commissions on national committee modernization (or extend the mandate of current reform commissions) to study the various methods by which states elect national committee members, set national party guidelines for election consistent with the responsibilities of the office and maximum citizen participation in the process (similar to guidelines implemented by the Democratic party with regard to the selection of national convention delegates), and recommend apportionment formulas for composition of the national committees on a more nearly equal population basis. One approach might be to increase the size of the national committees with greater reliance on party executive committees. Adequate representation of youth, blacks, Mexican Americans and the poor, however, will probably not be solved through reapportionment or even through greater intraparty democracy. To ensure adequate involvement of these groups in party deliberations, the commission could recommend that party bylaws be amended to create a new category of national at-large members of the national committee with full voting rights. Such members could be recruited on an open basis, nominated by the chairman, by any committee member or by petition, and elected by the full committee.

In the meantime, steps can be taken to upgrade the membership and functioning of the party national committees. They could reimburse members for travel and essential expenses so that membership is no longer limited to those who can pay their own way. The national chairmen could ask for active involvement of committee members or for their resignation. Less active members of the national committees could be challenged for election by reform-oriented party members. The national committees could also set up an active program for training new or prospective members.

Recommendation 2. The national committees should promote party and citizen participation in the governing of national political parties through the creation of new participatory party mechanisms such as an open budget committee and permanent party policy and study commissions and through open or extended national committee meetings.

The national committees will gain significance only insofar as their members assume or insist upon full participation in important party policy and decision making. In many instances, participation in the national committee and in broader party activity will require new mechanisms within the national committee framework. For example, the budget-allocation process in the political parties now exercised by the national chairman, party campaign chairmen in Congress and a limited number of advisers could become the focus for a partywide review of all programs funded at the national level.

An open budget committee could be appointed by the national chairman and authorized by the national committee to hold hearings and take testimony on the annual and projected budgets of national party organs. In reviewing requests from party bodies for program or campaign funds, the committee could hold open hearings and invite testimony from individuals and groups of party members seeking to initiate new party programs or comment on existing ones as well as from party officials who could use the opportunity to explain their programs to the party and the public. Such an open budget-making process and hearings mechanism could serve as a central instrument for policy planning, a forum for major intraparty debates on political strategy, and an important pressure point for innovation and party reform.

Building on their experience with policy committees or task forces such as those of the Democratic Policy Council and the Republican Coordinating Committee, the national committees should establish permanent, representative party policy com-

missions to study major public policy issues and political subjects that have been largely ignored by the parties. These
commissions should be broadly representative, with membership open to any party member through a petition process.
The parties can draw on a virtually untapped reservoir of
issue-oriented politically skilled members to fill a wide range of
productive party commissions that could measurably increase
the creativity and influence of the national committees, build
the party's capabilities to assume governmental responsibility,
help staff new administrations through special efforts to identify talent in their areas of concern, give party leaders in
government continuing support and assistance, and provide the
parties with a continuing base of experienced personnel and
policy competence.

In carrying out their responsibilities, the commissions could
hold well-publicized and well-prepared regional hearings and
issue periodic reports on the implementation of their recommendations by party leadership. They could also encourage
the creation of similar policy commissions where appropriate
at the state level and establish procedures to enable party
members to recommend the establishment of party commissions in new subject areas by presenting a written prospectus
and supporting testimony.

The national committees could also develop procedures for
extended open meetings to increase the involvement and participation of state party leaders, party rank and file, and citizens,
and to ensure that their views are made known at the highest
level of the parties. As a rule, the committees should hold at
least four full several-day meetings a year scheduled in different regions of the country on a rotating basis and at times
and places that will enable a maximum number of interested
citizens to attend and participate. At least 30 days before
meetings, notice-questionnaire forms and return envelopes
could be mailed to computerized lists of major officeholders,
party officials, contributors and interested citizens within each
state. Recipients would be invited to attend, suggest agenda
items and evaluate the effect of specific national party programs and policies at the state and local level. Such action
could both encourage more active involvement of party leaders

and citizens and increase the substantive content and relevance of national committee deliberations.

The national committees could also install toll-free telephone lines at national party headquarters (the "800" area code listings used by federal and state governments and major business corporations) so that citizens can call in suggestions or ask questions on any party program of interest to them.

Recommendation 3. The national committees should establish the principle of accountability in the government of the party through adopting rules and procedures, providing an internal impartial party appeals mechanism, requiring reports and audits of all party bodies, and guaranteeing public access to information.

To promote party accountability and encourage public confidence and participation in the parties, the national committees should enforce a partywide freedom-of-information policy, including open party sessions, equal access to party facilities and services and open party records. The national committees should adopt guidelines to ensure that, whenever possible, they and other party bodies meet in open session and that all such meetings be publicized well in advance. It is also essential that all groups within the party as well as all candidates—incumbents and primary challengers—enjoy equitable access to party facilities and services offered by party bodies. As the budgets, resources, facilities and services of party central committees continue to grow, all parts of the party should have some voice in staffing national committee headquarters to ensure that they are not controlled by a dominant faction.

Although the national chairmen presently enjoy wide discretionary power that could be used to facilitate reform, the national committees should, in the longer-term interest of citizen parties, adopt and publish formal rules of procedure and document, publish, and regularly update the body of authoritative party precedents governing the decisions of the national chairmen and national committees. National committee procedures could specify formal recorded roll-call votes on all agenda items and decisions. A specified number of members, perhaps 10 percent, could be authorized to request a mail poll of the full committee to determine members' views on important topics concerning the party. The national committees could also adopt adequate internal appeals procedures or appoint a party ombudsman to handle alleged abuses of power and to ensure the full rights and equal access of all party members.

The national committees should endorse and implement the principle of full public reporting and auditing of all party operating and campaign funds at all levels of party organization. The committees themselves could set an example by developing easily understood procedures for financial reporting, by publishing complete audits and reports on all their own funds, by encouraging state and local parties to follow suit, and by opening party financial records to party members, interested citizens and the press.

The national committees could also prepare and publish summaries of their meetings and decisions, and members could regularly report back to their respective state party organizations. The committees could assume the function of serving as the repository for all reports and records of all party bodies and ensure public access to pertinent material.

The growing public concern with standards of official conduct in government at all levels requires an appropriate response from political parties as well. Party responsibility in this area includes both 1) party-endorsed candidates, elected public officials and government appointees; and 2) all party officers (including national committee members), professional staff and consultants. The national committees could establish standing committees on party ethics to define and widely publicize standards of party conduct, to determine public or private disclosure requirements for candidates' and officials' finances, to issue advisory opinions to candidates and party officials and staff on possible conflict-of-interest situations, to investigate complaints of unethical behavior and to recommend appropriate corrective action.

Recommendation 4. The national parties should be headed by full-time paid national chairmen recruited through a nationwide talent search and elected by the party national committees for a set term.

The national committees could take effective steps toward party modernization by redefining the role and responsibilities of the party chairman and by actively participating in his recruitment and election. In order to perform effectively and to minimize potential conflicts of interest in loyalty and commitment, the national chairmanship should specifically be a full-time salaried position directly responsible to the national committee. In contrast to the closed selection process of the past, each national committee should appoint an open recruitment committee to prepare a job description of critical skills required in such a party chairman and undertake a nationwide talent search, soliciting nominations from the state parties, party leaders, party members and the public at large. The recruitment committee could then recommend several candidates who in turn would discuss their qualifications and present their programs for party leadership and development to the full national committee, which after appropriate review would elect its own chairman.

Recommendation 5. The national committees should strengthen the capabilities of national party headquarters by expanding the number of top-level appointive positions, by establishing new functional offices or divisions, and by adding regional party offices. The national committees should function both as central command and communications facilities and as clearinghouses to encourage local initiatives.

Major areas of national committee responsibility—party reform, governmental staffing and assistance, relations with citizen organizations, women's participation, youth and minorities representation—require the full-time attention of top-level national committee officials. The national chairman should be given the authority to appoint a number of full-time paid vice chairmen or deputy chairmen to assume these and other responsibilities. The expansion of the party's top ranks of political executives would provide openings for women, blacks, young people and other groups not currently represented or underrepresented in the national party leadership and develop the limited pool of trained party personnel capable of running a modern national committee. Some deputy chairmanships could be filled on a rotating basis by state chairmen or vice-chairmen or prominent party members willing to assume a leadership role.

The capabilities of the national committees at the division or office level should also be increased, with special attention to important new functions the political parties can perform in the 1970's. A new office for personnel development could replace traditional patronage operations of the parties. In cooperation with permanent party policy commissions and state party organizations, the national committees could develop a long-term program for the systematic identification, training and placement of governmental talent. (Suggestions for further development of the party's ability to govern are considered in Chapter VI.)

Just as public interest lawyers have become a major force for reform in the governmental bureaucracy and private industry, the party office of the General Counsel can be developed into a major pressure point for innovation within the parties. The General Counsel's office could be staffed by a team of lawyers who could work with state party counsel and public interest lawyers to represent, in court or in party proceedings, members challenging any party rules or practices that discourage citizen participation. Party reform, campaign finance, voter registration and election statutes, and party access to mass media are all areas where party legal talent can be used to effect basic reform.

Although the parties do hold periodic regional meetings, retain regional field staff and dispatch occasional party task forces from Washington, they have not systematically developed regional political and governmental capabilities or promoted regional cooperation among state parties. In addition to central party headquarters in Washington, the national committees could establish and staff permanent party regional offices in New York, the Midwest, the West and the South.

These regional offices could become a vital operational link between the national committees, congressional party district offices and the state and local parties.

In view of the central position they occupy in the American parties, the national committees should also develop their communications and information service capabilities. National headquarters command and communications facilities and a party operations center could be established and staffed with a duty officer 24 hours a day seven days a week on the model of some government offices and businesses. The operations center could maintain a constant monitoring service on political news and developments using a network of Telex and WATS lines to link state parties, major campaign headquarters and national headquarters, to receive and disseminate political news and to alert party leaders to news developments bearing on their localities. National committees could use these facilities to develop party intelligence capabilities through telephone polls run from party headquarters, a technique used by other national organizations like the AFL-CIO's COPE.

In order to provide the party and the public basic information on party personnel and services, national committees could publish and update at least quarterly a citizen guide to party organization and services and encourage state supplements.

Recommendation 6. The national committees should develop new public information and education programs to increase citizen interest and participation in party politics.

The national committees have a major responsibility in developing communications with the party rank and file and the general public. The parties have been particularly lax in encouraging public interest in politics on a year-round basis. They must make politics come alive if they expect media coverage or the public's attentiveness. The parties could make much more effective use of upcoming conventions, the delegate selection process, the election of party leaders, platform preparation and other opportunities for educating and involving the public, as well as their membership in the ongoing process of party politics.

The national committees could each schedule a series of monthly reports to the American people, including an annual report on state-of-the-party politics and reports on selected timely issues for radio and television broadcast and distribution to the print media. The parties could also develop less formal and more frequent means for keeping politics before the media and the public, such as regular and special topic press conferences by national and state party chairmen, national committee members and other party officials. Party chairmen could also join Congressmen and other prominent political figures who write columns or give broadcast commentaries on politics. The effect would be heightened if the chairmen of both parties addressed the same topic each week. Parties could also place newspaper advertisements, as do many citizen organizations, to communicate directly with the public.

The national committees should use internal party media, including party newspapers and a variety of newsletters, to involve more party members in party programs. The DNC experiment in September 1970 with a three-hour closed-circuit, color-telecast campaign caucus hooking up party celebrities, Democratic candidates and campaign workers in 18 cities across the country suggests the potential for parties to develop their own alternative media channels. Audio and video-tape cassettes also provide parties with an exciting new potential for political education and training. Cassettes could be made readily available on a wide variety of topics, along with tapes covering meetings that members were unable to attend.

IV

The Congressional Parties:
The Insulation of Power

Renewed citizen interest in and concern about Congress as a representative institution vividly marked the beginning of the 1970's. Ralph Nader, with 80 student interns in Washington and hundreds of field researchers in Congressmen's home districts, initiated a broad citizen surveillance of Congress. John W. Gardner's citizen lobby, Common Cause, opened a continuing letter, telegram and telephone campaign to try to influence specific Congressmen on key legislative votes. The Cambodian incursion in the spring of 1970 brought countless groups of students, faculty, college administrators, lawyers and citizens to Washington to lobby Congressmen directly on the Vietnam war. New citizen-oriented fund-raising groups like the Universities Antiwar Fund and the Congressional Action Fund were set up to influence the outcome of the 1970 congressional elections. Common Cause and other groups took steps to effect changes in the congressional seniority system, and the National Committee for an Effective Congress (NCEC) sought the defeat of selected ranking members of Congress in primaries and general elections.

To date, however, the real structure of power in Congress —the congressional party leadership and committee leadership of both ' parties, the so-called congressional establishment—remains essentially untouched.[1] Probably no other

---

[1] *The Almanac of American Politics,* for example, a thousand-page compendium which provides informative profiles of members and districts and lists of standing committees "to help the interested citizen make sense of the flux and confusion of Capitol Hill politics," contains no information

segment of the American parties as they are currently structured has provided less opportunity for citizen involvement in
party affairs and continues to be effectively insulated from
political change in the country at large. While important
decisions on weapons systems, education and welfare appropriations and other budget priorities are made in the give-
and-take of the legislative process, the congressional parties
stay securely cloistered in a privileged sanctuary. Many
members of Congress regard their party committees as purely
internal party organs set up to serve the needs of members
only. For their part, the citizen activists who diligently lobby
Congressmen and testify before congressional committees seem
strangely unaware of the power and potential of the party
organizations in Congress.

The conventional analysis of the parties in Congress has
emphasized their weakness and lack of coherence. This view,
with its assumption that power is dispersed and will inevitably
remain so within the Congress, ignores two important points
—the degree to which power is coherently exercised by a
congressional establishment and the potential that exists for
Congressmen to develop formal and informal party organizations as part of a broad effort toward party modernization.

In some important aspects, the congressional parties possess
tremendous power as the complex, informal, largely hidden
system of leadership that actually governs Congress, that
schedules legislation, assigns members to committees, allocates professional and party staff and office space and funds
congressional operations.[2] More than a score of formal party

---

on party committees in Congress. (Michael Barone, Grant Ujifusa, and
Douglas Matthews, *The Almanac of American Politics: The Senators, the
Representatives—Their records, States and Districts, 1972* [Boston: Gam-
bit, 1971].)

[2] For a discussion of the historical development of party leadership and
campaign committees in Congress see Randall B. Ripley, *Party Leaders
in the House of Representatives* (Washington, D.C.: The Brookings Institution, 1967); Randall B. Ripley, *Power in the Senate* (New York:
St. Martin's Press, 1969), Ch. 2, "Competitors for Power: The Development of Party Leadership and Standing Committees"; and Hugh A. Bone,
Party Committees and National Politics (Seattle: University of Washington Press, 1958).

leadership offices and institutions are scattered throughout the Capitol and its office complex. Each party in each house has leadership offices (party floor leaders, party whip, etc.), a caucus or conference composed of the party's full membership in that house, a committee on committees or its equivalent charged with recommending (and in effect making) committee assignments, committees for legislative scheduling or strategy and for policy research, and a campaign committee that provides a range of services and fund-raising support for party incumbents and candidates. In addition to formal party committees, there are informal party groups not part of the official party structure, such as the Democratic Study Group, an organization of about 125 House moderates and liberals, and the Wednesday Group, a body of about 20 House Republicans.

For the citizen interested in influencing the course of government, the Congress with its relatively undeveloped party organizations is potentially the most tangible instrument available. Congressmen themselves are the most important party leaders readily accessible to the public, with established offices in their districts and in Washington. They are the most visible groups of party officials in continuing contact with one another capable of exercising national party leadership. They enjoy resources that few national or state party leaders can afford—sizable staffs, the franking privilege, telecommunications and a variety of services provided by congressional and party staffs. Compared with the national committeeman or committeewoman, a member of Congress is an easily reached party leader with the power to respond to a wide range of requests from constituents.

Congressmen are at the same time both a key part of the existing power structure and a major potential instrument for modernizing it. With the political resources available to them by virtue of their office and their relatively permanent presence, Congressmen individually and in groups can exercise considerable leverage in national party affairs. They can exercise their own prerogative to participate in and review national party operations and they can take steps to open the parties to broader participation. They can make the parties, and through them the Congress, more responsive to citizen needs.

The Entrenchment of Congressional Party Organizations

How have the congressional parties become so entrenched, and how has this affected the functioning of American party politics and government? At least half a dozen factors have operated to insulate the congressional parties and to undermine the efforts of activists and reformers to make the parties more responsive and useful.

One effective screen has been the sheer complexity and inscrutability of political organization within the Congress. The various party committees are a separate, less formal and less visible layer of congressional organization superimposed on and infused throughout the working structure of the hundreds of formal standing, select and joint congressional committees. While the membership, duties and deliberations of the formal House and Senate committees can readily be followed in the *Congressional Record*, the *Congressional Quarterly* and the press, even senior members of Congress and lobbyists with years of experience on Capitol Hill are at times confused on significant aspects of congressional party organization. With the lack of information about and the secrecy surrounding their operations, it is little wonder that so few people have even an elementary understanding of the parties in Congress or how Congress functions.

A systematic survey we conducted revealed that many congressional party offices were unmarked or located in obscure parts of the Capitol buildings to discourage outside visitors. The Capitol office of the House Republican Whip, for example, was both unmarked and virtually abandoned. Staff found it "impossible to get any work done there" and had retreated to the congressional office of Whip Leslie C. Arends (R-Ill.) in the Rayburn House Office Building. Most party offices distributed no annual report on leadership activities or other descriptive literature about their work for interested members of Congress or citizens. Neither the Majority Leader nor the Minority Leader of either house issued a comprehensive and informative report on party programs or accomplishments. In office after office, staff members admitted that no current literature on important aspects of the congressional power structure was available. A few offices offered term papers that had been written by student interns, while a staff member of a House leader's office pointedly observed that researchers were "always interrupting real work and sticking their noses into things where they didn't belong."

Not one of the four party leadership groups—House Democrats or Republicans or Senate Democrats or Republicans—provided its congressional members, the public or the press with centralized information services on current legislation and congressional party activities. With the exception of the Democratic Study Group's research and information service, including its weekly legislative report and staff bulletin, one could not find a single party staff member on the Hill exercising any publicly visible information clearinghouse function within the congressional parties.

Compounding this lack of information is a screen of secrecy that almost matches the security classification system of the federal bureaucracy in blacking out many congressional party operations from the public. Several party bodies like the conferences and policy committees keep detailed minutes and records that are "absolutely confidential." Minutes of the Democratic Conference in the Senate, for example, are opened only to scholars for the period before any living Senator was serving in the Senate—namely, 1937! The House Democratic Committee on Committees, which makes the crucial decisions as to which Democratic Congressmen sit on such House standing committees as Appropriations, Armed Services and Judiciary, operates in almost total secrecy. No printed information of any kind is available from the committee except for mimeographed sheets showing each member's final committee assignments. The committee refuses to release to the public the list of geographical zones and zone members through which it operates, although the same information can be obtained from individual members or from the liberal Democratic Study Group. The moderate Republican Wednesday Group is so secretive that it neither identifies its members nor itself in any public statements or releases or financial reports, using front groups like the Committee for Republican Research or the Institute for Republican Studies when necessary. Neither party has a system for declassifying party documents, in spite of all the furor Congressmen make about the overclassification of executive documents.

Secondly, congressional party leaders have preferred to rely on personal and informal techniques of legislative leadership, deliberately not developing leadership positions, party governing bodies or party staff. An institution like the office of the Speaker of the House, for example, has remained an essentially pre-twentieth-century leadership office unaffected by television, jet transportation and professional staff assistance; it is only now beginning to be developed under Speaker Carl Albert. Democratic party leaders in both chambers have resisted use of the party caucus, and Lyndon Johnson, as Senate Majority Leader in the 1950's, centralized virtually all party leadership positions and staff under his personal control. Ranking Republican leaders adequately provided for by the Democratic majority leadership during the 1960's have been among the most effective opponents of minority-party staffing available to all minority-party members on committees.

Many party bodies meet infrequently, leaving effective control in the hands of the leadership and/or staff. The National Republican Senatorial Campaign Committee, which allocated more than $1.2 million of reported campaign funds in 1970 and which became the subject of considerable controversy when party moderates charged funding discrimination against New York Senator Charles E. Goodell and other moderate Republican Senate candidates, meets "once or twice" a year. The Democratic Steering Committee in the House meets only twice a year, leaving strategy and scheduling to the leadership. The Republican Congressional Campaign Committee meets once every two years and an executive committee appointed by the chairman meets about once every three months. Most operational decisions, including the allocation of more than $3 million in campaign funds, are left to the chairman and his staff.

An informal but complex spoils system guided by few discernible principles allocates funds, office space and personnel slots among the majority and minority parties and among the various party units in each house. Public funding and party funding, government and private office space, and party staff and committee staff and members' office staff are all intermixed with the formal blessing or the tacit approval of the leadership. The Republican Congressional Campaign Committee, the largest single party unit on the Hill, with a permanent staff of 30 to 35, chose to locate itself in the Congressional Hotel and the new Republican National Committee headquarters building, yielding its quota of government office space to the House Republican Conference, the House Republican Research Committee and the House Republican Policy Committee. The Conference receives a direct legislative appropriation of $10,000, which is supplemented by funds from the Campaign Committee. The Minority Whip's office uses its payroll to fund two staff members of the House Republican Policy Committee and three or four under the Conference. On the Democratic side, space is divided between the Democratic National Congressional Committee and the informal Democratic Study Group, formerly housed in the basement of a private Capitol Hill townhouse. Members assign staff from their office allowances to the DSG and the Republican Wednesday Group. The two party policy committees in the Senate, authorized by statute, receive annual appropriations of $250,000 each.

Third, the folkways of the Senate and House as transmitted by senior members have institutionalized the virtues of compromise and minimal partisanship. Members are encased, as the late Congressman Clem Miller (D-Cal.) once put it, in "a cocoon of good will." The norm or myth of nonpartisanship pervades important committees and the operations of both houses. Professional staff are reputedly nonpartisan, although they are effectively controlled by committee chairmen. Committee reports are frequently printed without minority views and committee members offer a united front on the floor during debate. In 1970, 59 Democratic and five Republican members of the House of Representatives, one-seventh of the total membership, were reelected without a challenge in the general election, in many cases with the tacit agreement of leaders of the opposite party. Such nonpartisanship mutes competition between the parties and depreciates the contribution of the partisan activist to the legislative process.

There is also a strong tendency in the congressional system, especially the Senate, for activist members to be loners or to operate in essentially closed groups. Some groups like the Republican Wednesday Group in the House stress the exclusivity of their membership, strictly limiting their size. Activist Congressmen have generally not been willing to invest the necessary time and resources or to learn to work together effectively within their parties, on a bipartisan congressional basis, or in alliance with governors, state legislators, or supporting citizen organizations. By consciously or unconsciously accepting all these norms of "the club" and maintaining the separation of the congressional sphere from the outside world of politics, activists have helped to perpetuate closed congressional parties.

Fourth, the congressional parties operate with little if any formal internal discipline. Members occupying congressional party posts and staff positions have advanced on the basis of seniority rather than performance. As with the party national committees, neither officers nor staff are formally accountable to the full party membership in Congress, let alone to a broader party constituency. Congressmen, lobbyists and auxiliary groups have found little gain in challenging the party establishment.

Most party bodies operate without formal written rules, relying instead on precedents as interpreted by senior members of Congress and senior staff. The party conferences or caucuses tend to be the exceptions. But even here, for example, only one copy of the rules of the House Republican Conference was available and it could be read by Congressmen or staff only in the office of the Secretary of the Conference.

Overall financial reports for congressional party groups are unavailable. Interested citizens are usually referred to the mass of raw data filed with the Clerk of the House or to the government's quarterly record of public disbursements. Since personnel of the Clerk's office are patronage employees beholden to the establishment for their positions, they make it as difficult as possible within the law for the public to get information. Typewriters may not be used nor may any of the records kept in the Clerk's office be duplicated; everything must be copied by hand. This unusual procedure is not specified by law but is merely the interpretation of those managing the records that "examination" means eye view plus handwritten notes. The Clerk's office makes little attempt to enforce reporting procedures in the law, to check the records filed or to contact people on even the most obvious errors. (The Justice Department has stated that its policy is not to prosecute in the absence of a report of violation from the Clerk of the House or the Secretary of the Senate, but when Clerk William "Pat" Jennings did file a list of violations, the Department still refused to act.) Many top-level party staff reported that they knew nothing about the methods of financing their offices or the levels of their operating budgets and that only the chairman concerned could answer questions. One staff member of the National Republican Senatorial Campaign Committee insisted that the committee did not even file financial records with the Clerk of the House or the Secretary of the Senate (which of course it must do under the law).

Fifth, the assumption that the Democrats would continue to control both the Senate and House of Representatives has reinforced the party establishments since the mid-1950's. While the Republican party has won three out of six presidential elections from the end of World War II through 1968, it has controlled only the 80th (1947–48) and 83rd (1953–54) Congresses during the same period. Clearly, the incentive of vigorous party competition has been lacking. Instead, majority- and minority-party roles have been allowed to stabilize around a politics of influence, with the Democrats controlling Congress and the Republicans settling for a share of the influence. The Republican "influentials," to use David Broder's term, have established a cozy relationship with the interest groups and campaign contributors that surround the legislature.[3] They have lost the will to win and resigned themselves to being a minority in the Congress during their lifetime. The Democrats in turn, without the discipline of an effective opposition party, have become lax and arrogant in their operation of the congressional committee system.

Finally, there has been no effective, continuing outside pressure point for either the reform of Congress or the congressional parties. None of the myriad citizen and private organizations that have attempted to influence legislation has seen the value of structural and procedural reform. Occasionally a citizen group will tackle an issue like seniority, but none has had a continuing program. A group like the National Committee for an Effective Congress has paid little attention to the internal operations of Congress itself, concentrating instead on the election of members to Congress. A sporadic reform movement has existed within Congress, but it has operated without the support of a parallel citizen organization or information clearinghouse. Both the Democratic and Republican party reform movements in the national and state parties have proceeded almost as though congressional parties did not exist. How effective the public interest surveillance of Congress by Ralph Nader and his associates will be remains to be seen.

Closed, inbred congressional parties have had several consequences for party politics and government in general. The failure to develop a systematic open process of recruiting candidates is one of the greatest costs of closed congressional parties. Party campaign committees influence the quality of members recruited to the Congress. They dispense or channel campaign funds and professional staff resources selectively. They encourage candidates who will go along with the system and actively undercut candidates and even incumbent members who have shown independence. They even do not enter their own candidates against powerful members of the opposing party.

---

[3] David S. Broder, "The Struggle for Power," *Atlantic*, April 1966, pp. 64–70.

Also, the lack of effective responsible partisanship enervates the entire legislative process. If parties are ineffective organizations of "influentials" merely dispensing the spoils of congressional politics to private interests and party contributors, then the whole tone and viability of the legislature is called into question. Without the competition of ideas and thoroughly considered legislative proposals, the quality of legislation and administrative review suffers. Congressional leadership, the committee system and the effectiveness of the individual legislator continue to stagnate. Instead of an advocacy system of defined majority- and minority-party roles built on competition and initiative, the nonpartisan working arrangements of the closed congressional parties serve to eliminate one of the most important driving forces of competitive politics. Bipartisanship, observes Professor James MacGregor Burns of Williams, is a form of gradualism that "easily leads to paralysis of politics and policy."[4] The performance and capacity of the legislature and its members are never tested or fully developed.

The failure to develop internal party responsibility and accountability leaves activist members of Congress and citizens generally without the means to evaluate the performance of congressional party leaders or to exert leverage for party reform. The leadership of the parties perpetuates itself without fear of being limited or checked. Informal, minimally staffed congressional party leadership is easily controlled by senior party members at the same time that it denies younger activists scarce party resources and effective instruments. The real cleavage in Congress today is not between Democrats and Republicans or liberals and conservatives but between activist, legislatively oriented, working members in both parties and the congressional establishment. The long struggle for the Legislative Reorganization Act of 1970, for example, pitted younger congressional activists like former Congressman Donald Rumsfeld's (R-Ill.) Raiders and the Democratic Study

---

[4] James MacGregor Burns, "The Presidency as LBJ Saw It" (a review of *The Vantage Point* by Lyndon Baines Johnson), Washington *Post*, October 28, 1971.

Group against a bipartisan coalition of committee chairmen and ranking minority members.[5]

Congressional parties closed at three levels—recruiting membership, initiative in legislation and internal party operations—thus deny citizens access to government. While congressional parties can be bypassed at times, closed parties only add to the distance, the sense of unresponsiveness, and the hopelessness of effecting change that separates citizens from government.

The entrenched congressional parties enjoy a disproportionate influence in the direction of the decentralized American party system. A clear majority of major party nominees for the presidency and vice presidency have been members and former members of the Senate and House. The congressional parties have a continuing base of office facilities, professional and clerical staff and communications services (a considerable part of which is provided directly or indirectly by public funds), often volunteered for party use, that the national committees have to struggle to maintain. They have an independent fund-raising base through financial contributions of major private interest groups. Their permanent presence in Washington means that members and congressional staff will be disproportionately represented in actual attendance on formal party bodies like policy councils and reform commissions which normally meet there. They constitute a significant if not dominant part of the inner party leadership that actually runs the national party machinery.

Their strategic location confers other advantages on the congressional parties. Direct access to the legislative and administrative processes of government normally enables congressional party leaders to participate in early drafts and reviews of party policy statements and the party's platform and to occupy key leadership posts at party conventions. The chairmen of the Democratic and Republican Platform Com-

---

[5] See Andrew J. Glass, "Congressional Report: Legislative Reform Effort Builds New Alliances Among House Members," *National Journal*, July 25, 1970, pp. 1607–14.

mittees in 1968, for example, were House Democratic Whip Hale Boggs (D-La.) and Senate Minority Leader Everett McKinley Dirksen (R-Ill.). Party legislative leaders have actually written platforms or statements of principles interpreted to be the equivalent of a campaign platform for off-year congressional elections. The Rules of the House of Representatives have governed Republican National Conventions and Democratic party bodies such as the O'Hara Rules Commission, and a member or former member of the House normally serves as parliamentarian at the national convention. The national networks' news broadcasts and interview panels draw mainly on congressional party members as opposition-party spokesmen.

Because the congressional parties are largely self-sufficient, it is in their interest to keep the national parties weak and decentralized. Electoral swings may cut one way or another into the marginal seats of either party, but the power structure of Congress, with its safe seats and seniority, is almost untouched from election to election. Weak national parties leave the congressional parties relatively free from challenge by strong rivals. A new President elected by a small margin may not feel that he can afford to challenge the prerogatives of the congressional parties. Governors, without effective national leadership, are no match for the congressional hierarchy, and it is no surprise that congressional leaders have attempted to discourage or control party organizational moves by the governors. Nor can weak national parties develop alternative national leadership, especially in broadening the range of potential candidates for the presidency and the vice presidency.

Developments in the Congressional Parties

Congressional party institutions were established well after the national conventions and party national committees, and in many instances have responded more slowly to political currents in the country. Democratic and Republican congressional campaign committees date back to the 1866 elections when Democratic Congressmen organized to protect themselves against an expected purge of pro-Andrew Johnson Congressmen by Radical Republicans. Thereafter, Congressmen looked primarily to their own committees to provide national assistance for congressional candidates.

In the intervening years, congressional institutions and the congressional parties themselves have undergone considerable change, especially since the mid-1940's. As a result of the first Legislative Reorganization Act of 1946, the resources available to congressional parties have increased significantly without, however, comparable modernization of party leadership and operations. Several other recent trends may be discerned that have a bearing on national party development. As discussed below, a certain degree of party development has occurred, notably in fund raising and in the determination of national party strategy. The congressional parties have also had to reach a working accommodation with the party national committees, and the possibility remains that further party professionalization will impose new disciplines on them.

In order to serve the needs of their constituents adequately, in the last two decades Congressmen have provided themselves with extensive personnel, committee and institutional staff as well as communications facilities and other supporting services. Besides Washington and district offices and staff, members can make use of the congressional franking privilege; Federal Telephone Service; Telex lines to their home-state offices; Postal Service assistance in correcting mailing lists; bulk folding and mailing services; a book bank of government publications such as agriculture yearbooks, infant-care handbooks, packets for brides and bound copies of the *Congressional Record*; and the services of committee staffs, the Library of Congress and its Congressional Research Service, the General Accounting Office and liaison offices of the executive branch. Some of the costs of such services are reflected in the increases in the number of congressional employees, which rose from 7,091 to 11,815 between 1960 and 1970, a 67 percent increase. Operating costs of Congress, excluding the cost of buildings and the services of the General Accounting Office, rose from $70 million to $179 million, or to

about an average of $335,000 for each of the 535 members of
the House and Senate.[6]

There are few effective restraints on which of these services
a Congressman may use for campaign purposes, and their
skillful use has enabled many incumbents to build a constituency base that is relatively invulnerable to primary or opposition-party challenge. This no doubt accounts in part for
the fact that in 3,200 House and 224 Senate primary or general
election contests since 1954, incumbents have won 92 percent
and 85 percent respectively.[7] Further extensions of the constituency service function with computer-based information
systems and specialized mailing lists will give the incumbent
Congressman an even greater advantage over challengers.
Recent legislation limiting campaign expenditures further
favors incumbents by restricting the amount of funds challengers can spend without providing any equivalent compensation for services incumbents enjoy at government expense.
To tip the balance a little, Congressman Leslie Aspin (D-Wis.)
has sought to amend the 1971 campaign-spending legislation
to allow a challenger to spend 15 cents per voter or $90,000,
whichever is higher, compared to 10 cents per voter or $60,000
for incumbents.

The professional staff of the various congressional committees authorized by the Legislative Reorganization Acts of
1946 and 1970, together with the expanded staff of Congressmen's offices, have provided the congressional parties with a
pool of relatively competent experienced staff. The congressional parties, however, have given far less attention than the
national committees to the professionalization of party staff

---

[6] For an extended discussion of services available to incumbent members
see Donald G. Tacheron and Morris K. Udall, *The Job of the Congress-
man: An Introduction to Service in the U.S. House of Representatives*
(Indianapolis, Ind.: Bobbs-Merrill, 1966); and Robert J. Huckshorn and
Robert C. Spencer, *The Politics of Defeat: Campaigning for Congress*
(Amherst: University of Massachusetts Press, 1971), Ch. 6, "Auxiliary
Candidate Services."
[7] See *Electing Congress: The Financial Dilemma*, Report of the Twentieth
Century Fund Task Force on Financing Congressional Campaigns (New
York: The Twentieth Century Fund, 1970), pp. 3–10.

under their control as an increasingly important resource for party and government personnel. Specifically designated or earmarked majority and minority party staff on committees have, for example, been accepted only reluctantly and on a limited basis by congressional leaders of both parties. As a result, the "nonpartisan" staffs of congressional committees are largely controlled by the committee chairmen of the majority party. A 1970 survey, for example, found that 89.2 percent of the 706 committee staff positions in the House of Representatives were controlled by the majority and only 10.8 percent by the minority party although the ratio of Democratic to Republican members in the House was 56.5 to 43.5 percent.[8]

In spite of public discussions of the need for minority-party staff in the 1960's, the leadership of both parties and cause groups affected by the imbalance failed to correct the situation. A provision of the Legislative Reorganization Act of 1970 authorizing a division of committee staff on a 60–40 basis was voided by an unprecedented move by the House Democratic leadership under Speaker Albert in January 1971, which bound all House Democrats through caucus vote to repeal the agreement that had been written into the law.

In contrast to staffing, the congressional parties, especially the Republican campaign committees, have made serious efforts to professionalize party fund raising. After the major 1964 Republican congressional losses, the Republican Congressional Campaign Committee under chairman Bob Wilson established the Republican Congressional Boosters Club, a major fund-raising innovation to solicit funds exclusively for Republican House candidates running in Democratic-held districts. In 1968, the committee was broadened to assist Senate candidates as well. Memberships at either $3,000 or $1,000 apiece are solicited primarily through invitation-only luncheons in some 25 to 30 cities. Headed by professional Boosters staff and a lay structure of citizen chairmen and luncheon hosts, the Boosters in 1970 had a membership of 1,600 to 1,800 and an announced annual target of $1.5 million.

---

[8] Glass, *National Journal*, July 25, 1970, p. 1614.

Allocation of funds (two-thirds to House candidates and one-third to Senate candidates) is tightly controlled by an executive committee comprised entirely of ex officio members from the party leadership (House and Senate Minority Leaders, campaign committee chairmen, the chairman of the Republican National Finance Committee, and the professional staff director of the Boosters). The Republican Congressional Campaign Committee, in contrast, used direct-mail solicitation to raise almost all of its $3 million public budget in 1970. The National Republican Senatorial Committee receives most of the proceeds from the annual Senate-House Republican dinner in Washington.

The Democratic Capitol Hill campaign committees have continued to rely on the annual congressional dinner and direct solicitation by top campaign staff, leaving major fund-raising efforts to groups other than the formal party campaign committees. The Democratic Study Group, which as one of its functions has raised funds for liberal Democrats; the National Committee for an Effective Congress, which has endorsed and contributed predominantly to liberal Democratic candidates; and the Committee for the Democratic Process, the letterhead direct-mail committee organized by George Agree, the former executive director of NCEC who also organized the 1970 and 1972 Campaign Funds for Democratic congressional candidates, are three such fund-raising instruments that have reduced the dependence of Democrats on the party campaign committees. In 1970, for example, the Democratic Congressional Campaign Committee reported receipts of some $442,-000; the Democratic Senatorial Campaign Committee, $482,700; the Democratic Study Group, $182,800; the National Committee for an Effective Congress, $669,000; and the 1970 Campaign Fund, $874,000.

At the same time that the constituency base of many incumbents has become relatively invulnerable, national campaign planning efforts and financial and consultant resources are being focused on preselected target districts where the party feels it has the best chance to gain seats. The death, primary-election defeat, or retirement of incumbents; redistricting, especially after the 1970 census; and party realignment in such areas as the South and West, for example, present opportunities for shifts in party control of House seats.

Although the Hill campaign committees still allot more funds to incumbents than to new candidates, the Democratic Congressional Campaign Committee has begun to concentrate some of its funds in marginal districts (won by the Democratic party or the Republicans by less than 55 percent of the vote), partly in response to pressure from the Democratic Study Group. The Republican Boosters mechanism continues to channel funds exclusively to Republican challengers, while Democratic-oriented groups allocate funds to selected strategic races.

The congressional and national party committees, like the other campaign-financing groups, have considerably extended their influence through the extensive use of professional managers and consultants. Republican party units in particular have used consultants both at the planning level (for extensive polling and the development of election and polling data banks, task-force visits to states, and political intelligence estimates) and in individual campaigns (through recommending campaign managers and personnel and by making national party contributions contingent on the use of specific consultant services). The Republican Congressional Campaign Committee, for example, distributes its funds in the form of credits to an account, not in cash. Freshmen members and marginal incumbents in 1970 received a $5,000 public relations subsidy and a $7,000 organization and education subsidy. All other incumbents received credits of $3,000 and $4,000 for these activities. The Campaign Committee claims to regulate only the type of expenditure charged to each category and not the particular company or consultant with whom it is spent, but the leverage the committee exercises through its credits is important in either event.

Democrats have tended to pool the use of consultants in congressional races as elsewhere. The Democratic Senatorial Campaign Committee, for example, retained Lester Goldsmith of Los Angeles to produce a series of campaign films for Democratic Senators and worked with Oliver Quayle and the United Steelworkers in developing polling data and state profiles in key Senate races. The most impressive effort of a Democratic

organization to pool consultant resources was the Democratic
Study Group's Campaign Seminar for Nonincumbent Candidates run twice in the spring of 1970. The seminars involved
consultants like Joseph Napolitan, Matthew Reese and Robert
Squier, the political directors of the International Association
of Machinists, the United Automobile Workers, and the Steelworkers respectively; representatives of peace action groups
and other citizen organizations; and top DNC and Democratic
congressional staff.

It is important to note, however, that none of the party
campaign committees has written rules or procedures governing
the allocation of campaign funds, that meetings of the committees are in executive session with no public records, and
that no appeals procedure exists for a member or candidate to
question decisions made. Similarly, while steps have been taken
to achieve more rational allocation of resources, no procedures
exist to review the strategic assumptions and objectives of
party leaders. Neither party has developed a means for reviewing and evaluating its national campaign performance.

Another noticeable development has been the growth of
party policy committees and caucuses. One of the objectives
of the reformers who drafted the Legislative Reorganization
Act of 1946 was the creation of vigorous party policy committees in both the House and the Senate. Although only
Senate policy committees were funded at the time and the
Legislative Reorganization Act of 1970 took no further actions,
several related developments have moved the congressional
parties in this direction.

During the 1960's, the House Republican Conference established a number of committees, including the House Republican Policy Committee and the Committee on Research or House
Republican Research. The Policy Committee deals with party
policy and legislative strategy on bills before the Congress.
A long-term policy-research arm, House Republican Research
coordinates the activities of about 10 separate task forces on
different subject areas. Some, like the Task Force on Education
and Training, have made field trips, invited testimony from
experts and drafted legislation. House Democrats have relied
mainly on the Democratic Study Group for their party re-

search. The DSG issues several major research documents a year known as DSG Fact Books. The House Democratic caucus has also mandated a Special Research Committee under the Democratic Congressional Campaign Committee to do research projects on specific issues.

Both parties have activated their House party conference or caucus and used them to adopt party positions on issues and intraparty affairs. The House Republican Conference under former chairmen Gerald R. Ford and Melvin R. Laird became an important party institution in the mid-1960's. The Democrats changed their caucus rules in January 1969 to require monthly meetings of the House Democratic Caucus while Congress is in session.

Several problems remain, however. Neither the House Republican Conference nor the House Democratic Caucus is adequately staffed, funded or structured. In the Republican case, the Republican Congressional Campaign Committee funds much of the House Republican apparatus, extending its influence into noncampaign areas and giving its chairman and staff an undue voice in party policy and research. The House Democratic Caucus has no separate office or staff. Its business is simply transacted from the congressional office of its chairman. When the caucus discovered in December 1970 that it had no rules for conducting caucus elections, it improvised its own, prohibiting candidates from entering the contest after nominations were closed. Neither party has yet developed the potential of open party caucuses.

The congressional parties still present an overall picture of entrenched power. Even their policy functions remain largely undiscovered by the citizen and party activists who attempt to lobby individual Congressmen on national priorities. However, restructured and modernized congressional parties could expand their already impressive resources to improve the quality of party politics and government in the 1970's.

Recommendations: Making the Congressional Parties Responsive and Effective

A number of reformers have argued that congressional modernization should be based on a new emphasis on national party programs.[9] In their view responsible, disciplined parties in Congress would be achieved through binding party caucuses. Members who disregarded caucus decisions would be subject to punishment in the assignment of committee posts and the apportionment of patronage; senior members who opposed the commitments in their party's platform would be barred from committee chairmanships.

The plan for development and modernization of the congressional parties recommended here is based on somewhat different assumptions and conceptions of party accountability and responsibility. The congressional parties should be open to public scrutiny and participation. They should be activist parties, evaluated in terms of their initiative, partisan political effectiveness and governmental performance. Such congressional parties could strengthen the capabilities of Congress for problem solving, investigation, and policy research and development, both seeking and involving new ideas and people in the governmental process whenever possible.

This emphasis on openness, problem solving and political flexibility assumes a more tolerant, pluralistic, participant base than that suggested by proposals for more disciplined parties. Party unity and cohesiveness would be found in a new party *esprit* and commitment rather than through sanctions. Congressional parties built on constructive partisanship and party competition and designed to bring outside ideas and talent to bear on the legislative process at every point could introduce a new dynamic to congressional politics.

Within this activist conception, accountability and responsibility take on different meanings. Party leaders and staff would be evaluated less in terms of their support or loyalty to a written party program than in terms of actual political performance and party due process. What programs did the leadership

---

[9] See Committee on Political Parties of the American Political Science Association, "Toward a More Responsible Two-Party System," *American Political Science Review*, September 1950 (Supplement), pp. 56–65; Joseph S. Clark, *Congress: The Sapless Branch* (New York: Harper & Row, 1964); and Richard Bolling, *House Out of Order* (New York: E. P. Dutton, 1965).

initiate? How effectively did they involve the talent on the party's back benches? What legislation or amendments were enacted? How effectively did the party monitor and test the administration? the opposition? Did the party contest every congressional seat with qualified candidates? Did leaders allocate campaign funds effectively and fairly? Each of these questions assumes that the leadership is accountable to a broader party constituency for its stewardship of the party's electoral fortunes and its capacity to govern. Each also assumes that adequate mechanisms or procedures exist within the party to hold leaders and party staff responsible for their actions. The following recommendations outline practical steps that can be taken to modernize congressional parties to achieve these objectives.

Recommendation 1. The caucuses or conferences of the congressional parties should be developed as one of the principal organizations of a modernized party system for the 1970's. Party caucuses should further the development of open congressional parties through the publication of party rules, the requirement of semiannual reports from all party bodies, and public information programs.

In a congressional system based on seniority and the specialized expertise of standing and select committees, the party caucus or conference affords a forum where each member's vote has equal weight and where topics can be discussed with considerable freedom. Properly developed, the caucus can be used effectively to open the closed power structure of Congress and develop a modern congressional party organization.

The caucuses can take a number of steps to open congressional party operations to greater party and public understanding and participation:

They should meet regularly on a preannounced schedule and their actions should be clearly reported to the news media and through appropriate party publications. Just as some faculty meetings have been opened up in response to student demands for participation in university governance, party caucuses could experiment with open caucus sessions where press and public could be seated on a space-available basis. The caucuses could welcome the contribution of party leaders and activists outside Congress and institute formal means for citizens to place items on the agenda of the conference, perhaps through congressional sponsors or by appropriate petition. Task forces, commissions and investigating teams could be employed by the caucuses in an imaginative way to undertake special party studies.

Party caucuses should require that all party bodies in Congress publish and abide by written rules and procedures and that relevant party precedents are compiled and published. Bipartisan efforts could be undertaken to ensure that rules and precedents of both houses and their standing committees are updated and published. The precedents of the House of Representatives, for example, have not been updated since 1936.

All formal party bodies within the Congress should be required by House and Senate resolution to file with a designated congressional agent semiannual public reports on their programs and activities, staff and budgets. At a minimum, the party caucuses could require the submission of written reports. Precedents for reporting within Congress have been established for some time: committees of the House must list all staff and salaries with the House Administration Committee; congressional campaign committees must file limited financial reports with the Clerk of the House and the Secretary of the Senate; and lobbyists attempting to influence legislation before Congress are required to register with the House Clerk and Senate Secretary.

Party caucuses should establish procedures for the declassification of party records and the curtailment of party secrecy. The open information policy practiced by the Democratic Study Group in recent years is an example that could be followed by both formal and informal party bodies.

Most important, the caucuses should sponsor vigorous programs of public information to educate party members and the public on the congressional party role in government and party politics. The individual caucuses or joint House-Senate party leadership committees should provide current information clearinghouse services on the party's legislative program and the activities of all party units.

Finally, the caucuses should adopt internal appeals procedures as a further safeguard against the unauthorized or arbitrary use of any party facilities or resources by congressional leaders or by a party faction. All party members in Congress should enjoy equal access to all party facilities and services offered by official party bodies.

Recommendation 2. Citizens should be given opportunities to participate in the congressional parties through strengthened party organization within congressional districts, extensive use of citizen advisory committees, and the establishment of guesthouses and meeting facilities for party use on Capitol Hill.

At the same time that the congressional parties are being opened to greater public visibility and understanding, a conscious attempt should be made to involve party members outside Congress in the work of the congressional parties. Citizens could be encouraged to participate through active party organizations within each congressional district.

Each party could establish permanent party offices at the congressional-district level to provide an effective link between the constituency party and congressional and national party leaders. The Congressman's office only partially meets this objective since it serves primarily the incumbent member and indirectly only one party. District party offices would service all candidates in party primary contests and would be of special value in helping opposition party challengers overcome the built-in advantages enjoyed by incumbents. Party agents or field representatives could work through the district offices and assist local party leaders in building district parties.

Representative congressional-district party committees with elected chairmen could assist in recruiting congressional candidates, in advising candidates and national leaders on party strategy, and in the financing of congressional campaigns. On a broader scale, a congressional-district chairmen's association could be a valuable resource to the national parties.

A wide range of citizen advisory committees could be established to enable Congressmen to meet and work with national and state party officials, state legislators and citizens at regular intervals within a party context. The congressional campaign committees, party caucuses or conferences and policy committees all afford excellent opportunities for independent outside contributions and review by such advisory committees. The majority and minority members of each standing committee of Congress and/or policy research task forces set up under the party conference could also name advisory committees. These citizen groups could, for example, make postelection analyses and reports on the effectiveness of the party's campaign planning and operations or provide a sounding board for the opposition party's proposed policy statements. Besides exposing members of Congress to points of view and representatives of groups not adequately represented within the congressional parties themselves, the advisory-committee system could be used to train party members for future governmental responsibilities. Membership on such advisory groups, which should be broadly representative, could be patterned after the permanent party commissions recommended for the national committees and could include, among others, national committeemen and committeewomen, state party leaders, state legislators and leaders of citizens and cause organizations.

Both parties could establish guesthouse and meeting facilities located near the Congress to serve a wide variety of party social and special program needs and to provide greater citizen access to the party's congressional leadership. Such facilities are particularly essential to the party out of power in the executive branch as a means to counteract the political benefits of occupying the White House—the full White House social schedule, including luncheons and dinners, the visits of heads of state and foreign dignitaries, and the use of Blair House. A John F. Kennedy memorial house, for example, could have been a major center of operations for the Democratic party after the Republican victory in 1968.

To ensure that these facilities serve the broadest possible party use, they should be supervised by a representative board of party leaders and members that would report regularly to the party caucuses and the public. A director could be appointed to carry out a vigorous program of party functions such as receptions, luncheons and formal dinners to introduce national leaders in all fields, journalists, party workers, community representatives, interested citizens, and visiting foreign delegations to the party's leadership and congressional talent.

Citizens can take the initiative in opening the congressional parties to greater public participation by establishing an independent monitoring and reporting service. Just as the Congressional Quarterly Service monitors the entire legislative process and the Government Research Company's (formerly the Center for Political Research) *National Journal* covers the executive branch, a citizen monitoring and reporting service could provide current information on the congressional parties such as the membership, meeting schedules, agendas, summary proceedings and decisions of the various party units (such as caucuses, policy committees and committees on committees). Such a citizen unit could educate the public and the activist-reform constituency within Congress to the potentialities for working through the congressional parties.

Recommendation 3. The congressional parties in coordination with the party national committees should develop their resources in party leadership and operations.

The congressional parties have numerous opportunities to assume a more active role in national party politics in coordination with strengthened national committees. While professionalization of the parties should encourage greater intraparty coordination, more formal party coordinating units involving the national party chairman and congressional leaders would also be desirable.

Both congressional parties should institute joint congressional leadership committees and staff them on a permanent basis. These committees could assist in the formulation, implementation and evaluation of national party policy and programs. National party chairmen might be invited to chair meetings of the leadership, a practice developed in the mid-1960's by Ray Bliss, while his party was in opposition, on the basis of his earlier experience with Republican legislative leaders in Ohio. Congressional leaders or their representatives should also participate in meetings of all national party units convened periodically by the national chairman. The national committees might each assign a full-time professional as liaison with the party committees on Capitol Hill.

The office of the Speaker of the House should be developed as the second most important party office in the federal government after the President. The Speaker of the House is next in line of succession to the presidency after the Vice President, yet the speakership remains a largely undeveloped power base in the decentralized American party system. Recent Speakers have rarely ventured out of Washington and only Carl Albert has begun to use television and modern communications media. Albert's Far East visit of August 1971 was a significant example of the expanded role the Speaker can play in the 1970's.

The modern Speaker, chosen by and responsive to an active party caucus, could use his office and party resources to build a dynamic, issue-oriented, problem-solving party in the House of Representatives. The Speaker as a national party spokesman could be advised by a policy staff drawn in part from party staff on congressional committees and in part from the various party bodies on Capitol Hill. He could initiate congressional task forces for special fact-finding missions and convene national congressional conferences, comparable to White House conferences organized by the President. He could hold regular televised news conferences and deliver major addresses at public and party functions around the country. As the office of the Speaker gains in national stature, younger members of Congress might seek election to the post as they do for the presidency, and prominent Americans might even seek election to Congress as prospective candidates for the speakership. Congressional elections as a result could gain new national party significance. The modernization of the speakership could also be complemented by expanding the party responsibilities of the House and Senate Majority and Minority Leaders.

In order to facilitate coordination of congressional party activity, each party should establish a congressional operations center with unified command and communications facilities. Properly staffed and operated party command and communications centers could infuse new energy, excitement and initiative in the relatively lifeless congressional parties, giving them the capacity to move rapidly on a much broader political front and with more consistent actions.

The party operations centers could maintain schedules of all congressional committee hearings and executive sessions and ensure that all important committee deliberations were covered by party members and staff and that public policy questions of concern to the American voter were fully discussed. The centers could also monitor political news and developments, help in the prompt national and local release of statements by congressional party leaders, and assist in advancing on-the-spot field investigations by party task forces.

Each party operations center should include a centrally located party press office headed by a professional director of communications. The director could schedule regular press briefings, especially during the legislative session, experiment with various formats for press conferences, such as presenting some of the party's younger committee members, and set up a reference library for press use with updated party policy positions and statements on specific pieces of legislation.

The parties could also make a determined effort to publish party reports, policy positions, majority and minority views in committee prints and reports, activities of party bodies, and documents to inform the public of the party's record. The *Congressional Record* especially could be used more imaginatively for the presentation of party views and useful political information.

The congressional operations centers could establish liaison with state legislative parties and facilitate through a congressional clearinghouse service the exchange of information and technical and staff assistance. Congressional party representatives and staff could attend national meetings of state legislative leaders, the National Legislative Conference and the Citizens Conference on State Legislatures. Congressmen could draw on the experience and skills of state legislators and staff in such areas as legislative data processing, thus benefiting directly from the experimentation and innovation taking place in state legislative bodies. In turn, the congressional parties could encourage state legislative party modernization by using congressional party field teams to encourage development of concepts like the Republican Research Committee or the unofficial Democratic Study Group mechanism.

Recommendation 4. The congressional parties can contribute to the governmental capabilities of the national parties through improved procedures for recruiting congressional candidates and making committee assignments, through training and development of partisan congressional staff, and through the establishment of specialized party policy units.

The congressional parties have special responsibilities in building the capabilities of the national parties to assume leadership of government. Congressmen themselves participate in government through the legislative authorization and appropriation of funds. Congressmen and congressional committees exercise legislative oversight or review of executive agencies and their programs. The congressional party provides a continuing governmental base for the party whether or not it controls the White House.

Congressional parties could build their governmental competence through the open recruitment of more qualified candidates for Congress. Congressional parties could develop, through public party hearings in the states, enforceable model procedures or guidelines for the open recruitment and screening of congressional candidates, with special emphasis on their qualifications.

As a matter of principle, every seat in Congress should be contested by a competitively screened candidate. If local party organizations cannot produce qualified candidates, the congressional parties could send special task forces of recruiting experts into the districts concerned to assist in the search for a suitable candidate. To encourage more candidates to seek office, the congressional parties could guarantee a minimal campaign budget (through technical assistance in fund raising or direct contribution) for any party nominee running in the general election. Parties should be willing to invest in and develop talent in congressional districts over several elections to increase the likelihood of defeating incumbents of the opposite party or of winning a special election or newly created district. A continuing program could also be developed to involve unsuccessful candidates (and incumbents) in local and national party affairs and to keep them from becoming discouraged and drifting away from party politics. The governmental capabilities of the congressional parties could also be enhanced by more effective use of retired members of Congress who have recently organized a former members' association.

Both local and national party officials should be held accountable for their performance in meeting recruitment objectives. The chairmen of all congressional campaign committees could hold public hearings and file written reports on the successes and failures of candidate recruitment, explaining, among other things, how each seat was contested and how recruitment guidelines had been followed.

Within Congress, the parties could give greater attention to governmental competence in the assignment of members to standing committees. The committee assignment process through the party committees on committees, which is now cloaked in secrecy and subject to undue influence by private interests, should be more open to public view and participation. Members could make a formal statement, in writing or in person, which would include the reasons they seek a particular committee assignment, their background experience and qualifications, and the work they hope to accomplish as committee members. Private organizations and individuals could have an opportunity to file supporting statements or testimony.

To strengthen the party role in the legislative process, all congressional committees and operating units should provide for adequate majority and minority party staff. Effective congressional parties require adequate party staffing at the heart of the legislative process—the committee system. Party staff attached to the conference or policy committee meet only part of the need. Professional and clerical staff assigned to and familiar with the day-to-day business of specific committees are essential to developing legislation, preparing for hearings, initiating field investigations, drafting committee reports and minority views, monitoring the opposition and communicating with the public. Instead of the current system of staffing congressional committees, which gives undue control to committee chairmen and the majority party, members of the respective parties on each committee should be empowered to designate, hire and control majority and minority party staff on their request.[10]

The partisan professional staffs of Congress could be developed as a major source of political executives and governmental personnel for future national, state and municipal administrations. Although many congressional employees have moved into positions of executive responsibility, there are no congressional programs for recruiting and training competent professional and clerical staff, including representatives of minority groups in the population. Parties could expand the informal staff meetings and social groups that now exist on the Hill to more formal party-sponsored training programs. In cooperation with the personnel offices of the national committees, the congressional parties could provide short-term in-service training for state legislators, party leaders and other recruits to the party's executive reserve. For the party that does not control the White House, congressional staff are a critical resource both in developing and implementing opposition party programs and later in staffing an administration. The failure of the Republican party to develop minority-party staffing during the Kennedy and Johnson years may have compounded the problems of recruiting top-level officials in the Nixon administration.

Modernized congressional parties should assume a positive definition of partisanship in the legislative process. Vigorous party roles built on advocacy and competition can raise both the quality of legislation and the governmental performance

---

[10] The Committee for Increased Minority Staffing of the House Republican Conference and its staff under the chairmanship of Congressman Fred Schwengel (R-Iowa) documented and publicized the need for minority staffing in the early 1960's. For a statement of the case see Congressman James C. Cleveland (R-N.H.), "The Need for Increased Minority Staffing," in Mary McInnis (ed.), *We Propose: A Modern Congress, Selected Proposals by the House Republican Task Force on Congressional Reform and Minority Staffing* (New York: McGraw-Hill, 1966), pp. 5–19.

of the parties and open up the static pattern of closed politics.

Through the expertise of its members and the resources of its professional staff and facilities, the congressional party can also assist national administrations and national party headquarters, when the party does not control the White House, in the development of party policy. The congressional parties could supplement the work of the permanent party policy commissions of the national committee through their own policy and conference committees and through the establishment of specialized party policy units. A minority economic council, modeled after the President's Council of Economic Advisers,[11] could, for example, fill the need for a continuing, professionally staffed, opposition party watchdog at the government level to counterbalance the near monopoly on professional advice enjoyed by the executive branch. When one party controls both the White House and the Congress, the disproportion in staff and consulting resources between majority and minority parties under current arrangements makes serious party dialogue almost impossible. Other councils could further constructive partisanship in such areas as national security affairs.

Recommendation 5. Groups of Senators and/or Congressmen should pool their resources to establish new congressional action groups to encourage innovation and reform in the political parties.

Members of Congress enjoy a unique opportunity in American party politics. The Congress provides an excellent base for a new form of party organization that lies somewhere between the formal party bureaucracy and ad hoc citizen organizations. Like-minded groups of Congressmen could pool some of their staff and other resources to establish new congressional action groups. Properly developed, these intermediate party organizations could represent one of the most significant means currently available to encourage innovation and reform in American political parties.

---

[11] The concept of a minority economic council was first developed by former Congressman Thomas B. Curtis and his staff on the twentieth anniversary of the Employment Act of 1946.

•

The Democratic Study Group and the Congressional Black Caucus are prototypes of this kind of intermediate party organization. The DSG constitutes a caucus within a caucus, a parallel fund-raising and campaign unit, a separate base of research and intelligence, a private whip system and communications network. The Black Caucus has provided a national focus for black political action inside and outside of the Congress. Smaller groups like the McGovern-Hatfield "end the war" amendment group have been formed for more limited purposes. But the significant potential for intermediate organization remains largely untapped. Examples of initiatives that congressional action groups could take are also provided by the joint store-front office opened in Harlem by Congressman Herman Badillo (D-N.Y.) and two New York state legislators; by the "National Constituents" newsletter circulated by Congresswoman Bella Abzug (D-N.Y.) to thousands of citizens outside her district, especially women active in politics; and by six Tennessee state legislators who formed a private organization to conduct issue research including statewide polls. On his own, Congressman David Pryor (D-Ark.), set up and operated an ad hoc committee on the aging from a trailer at the Capitol when congressional leaders refused to move on the issue of substandard nursing homes for the aged.

Congressional action groups could work within their respective parties to implement many of the recommendations suggested above. Besides pooling their own staff and office resources, these groups could buy computer time, recruit specialized staff and retain consultants.

Congressmen and/or congressional action groups could encourage the extension of party reform commission mandates to subjects concerning the congressional parties, such as questions relating to the financing of congressional campaigns. The representative party commission approach could be a significant additional means for introducing reform in the congressional parties.

V

The Untapped Potential
of State Parties

If the American voter is indeed frustrated with unresponsive government and party institutions and is searching for political means to cope with local and state problems, then state and local politics will become a major political battleground of the 1970's and the setting for extensive political innovation and party modernization—a 50-state revolution. The states offer many of the essential ingredients for effective citizen participation in politics that are lacking at other levels. The impressive state-by-state accounts of American life by a John Gunther or a Neal Peirce only begin to reveal the rich diversity of resources that are available for political development within the states,[1] each with a distinctive historical past, economic and cultural base, political tradition and potential.

Over the past decade, the states have become increasingly important political and governmental units. The modernization of state and local governments during the 1960's has reinforced the position of the states in the American federal system. State constitutional reforms have increased the executive authority of governors. Legislative staffing and reorganization have enhanced state legislatures. Court-ordered reapportionment and redistricting have made access to state legislatures more equitable. State attorneys general, crime commis-

---

[1] John Gunther, *Inside U.S.A.* (rev. ed.; New York: Harper & Row, 1951); and Neal R. Peirce, *The Megastates of America: People, Politics, and Power in the Ten Great States* (New York: W. W. Norton, 1972), which is to be followed by a series of regional volumes covering all 50 states.

sions and citizen groups—supported by public opinion—have helped to raise the standards of performance of state government. The revenue-sharing proposals of President Nixon's "new American revolution" have signaled a new emphasis on state and local government. The states, by virtue of their constitutional position, are also the key to the establishment of regional authorities and the reorganization and consolidation of local governments.

The states remain the building blocks of American politics. The President and the Congress are elected through the states (even the proposed elimination of the Electoral College would leave the states the authority to specify how presidential candidates could get on the ballot). Politicians have long recognized their significance. George C. Wallace's 1968 campaign was based almost completely on individual state organizations without a sizable Washington headquarters operation. In 1971, Wilbur D. Mills (D-Ark.), the powerful chairman of the House Ways and Means Committee, chose to initiate his bid for national office with an unprecedented series of addresses before joint sessions of state legislatures. By late 1971, President Nixon had fulfilled a campaign pledge to visit all 50 states during his term of office.

Similarly, organized labor's highly touted political machine relies on state political action committees, statewide computer registration programs, and political endorsements and campaign contributions by state labor organizations. Public interest law firms are turning their attention toward state politics, as demonstrated by the Nader report on California land-use policy and DuPont influence in Delaware state politics. A nationwide litigation campaign by public interest lawyers to strike down student residency requirements for voting was carefully planned in the state courts. A favorable decision in the California Supreme Court served as the basis for a series of opinions by state attorneys general who, observed public interest lawyer William Dobrovir, "turned the law around." The move toward statewide black political conventions by groups like the Congress of African Peoples and the organization of more than a score of state caucuses in target states by the recently formed National Women's Political Caucus also suggest that citizen and special-interest groups will devote much greater attention to the states during the 1970's.

As the stakes of state politics continue to rise, the state parties could, because of their particular advantages, provide the means for broader citizen participation and party modernization. State parties, for example, afford the advantage of access. In all but a very few of the largest states, party conventions and meetings are within commuting distance for most residents. Citizens can attend hearings and debates in the state legislature more readily than they can come to Washington. State party officials can be visited in person. State party headquarters with statewide WATS lines can be only a local telephone call away. Live coverage of state and county committee meetings and conventions will be possible as cable television systems are expanded. Broad-band two-way cable communication will afford many more opportunities for local initiative and new approaches to participatory forms of party organization.

State parties also are manageable units. Experienced party professionals may become frustrated in trying to influence unwieldy national party organizations, while the interested citizen may despair that he can ever learn enough about the political system to become an active participant. But state parties are neither unwieldy nor incomprehensible. The state delegation to a national party convention can usually be identified and located in the convention city. State party chairmen can have a much higher success rate in projects they initiate than do national chairmen. Citizens can follow and influence party actions at the state level much more easily than at the national party level.

State party operations are relatively inexpensive. A permanent party headquarters can be opened and staffed with some paid aides and party volunteers at a cost of only a few thousand dollars. Annual state conventions can be run for a small fraction of the cost of national party conventions. Travel and overnight expenses and some operating expenses like telephone service and local media rates are greatly reduced within states. Party reforms can be tried experimentally with modest funding. In the same manner that national party campaign committees and private organizations discovered the so-called "cheapies"—United States Senate seats in the less populated states like Idaho, Nevada, Utah and Wyoming that could be won for a small fraction of the investment required in one of the major industrial states—astute political leaders and citizens will undoubtedly soon discover the investment potential in many state parties. Federal spending limits on campaigns for national office could also result in a shift of political money to the states.

For those seeking change, state parties have the advantage of a rapid turnover in personnel. Governors, state legislators and state party officials have no tenure approaching the seniority system of the congressional parties. Nelson A. Rockefeller of New York, the dean of the nation's governors, would have ranked only 121st in seniority in the House of Representatives and 34th in the Senate when he was inaugurated for his fourth term in January 1971. A high rate of turnover in state party leaders means a loss of continuity in state parties but it also means that new groups can advance their own representatives and objectives rapidly, even to the point of taking over existing state party organizations. Instead of investing energy and funds trying to dislodge senior members of Congress, political activists may turn to the greater opportunities available at the state and local level.

The states, in short, offer perhaps the most exciting potential as well as the critical test for citizen use of modernized political parties. Talented people can be easily assembled, operations can be designed on a feasible scale, start-up costs for new organizations and projects are relatively low, and targets such as party or elective offices, legislative programs, or court tests are abundant and often within immediate reach. Innovation and reform in state politics, however, have not begun to reach the scale of citizen use of state parties that we believe is attainable. At few points is the bankruptcy of the traditional party structures more evident than in the lack of imagination and initiative in developing the political resources of the states. Most state parties have not modernized and remain effectively closed to citizen participation. Few have developed problem-solving capabilities. While some have developed professional staffs and adapted new-politics campaign techniques, the potential for state parties is largely untapped and has not been developed in any systematic manner.

By emphasizing problem solving and issues, state parties can give citizens fresh incentives to participate in state and local politics and increase the effectiveness of their action. State parties can be used for improved candidate selection and for the evaluation of the performance of elected officials. They can also encourage greater party policy initiatives in state legislatures, a new long-term approach to the staffing of state administrations and program direction of state civil-service bureaucracies, and wider availability of citizen talent to government.

Unrealized Potential

State and local party organizations, which antedate national party organizations, have evolved since the colonial period within several broad political traditions and in countless variations.[2] Despite this diversity, it is useful to examine what appear to be some common problems which have contributed to the unrealized potential of state and local party organizations and which still present formidable obstacles to party modernization.

Since the political managers of the Jacksonian era linked together state party organizations in the framework of the national nominating conventions, the two-tiered American party system has remained strangely compartmentalized and immobilized. By linking state and national politics in broad coalitional structures, such institutions as the national party conventions, party national committees and congressional parties made the complicated American federal system operable. State parties, however, which formed the essential

---

[2] See Roy Nichols, *The Invention of the American Political Parties: A Study of Improvisation* (New York: Macmillan, 1967); and Daniel J. Elazar, *American Federalism: A View from the States* (New York: Thomas Y. Crowell, 1966), especially Ch. 4, "The States and the Political Setting."

base to the party system, were steadily weakened. The movement to impose statutory regulation in the 1880's and 1890's left formal state party organizations in "disarray and disuse."[3] The rigid party structures specified in many state laws gave state parties the "counterfeit participation" of members who could participate in choosing party officials through party primaries or precinct caucuses but who exercised no other role or influence.

At the same time, the incentives for citizen participation in party politics decreased as the traditional functions of state parties narrowed. The policymaking function of state parties was seriously hampered by detailed state constitutions which circumscribed executive powers by the "long ballot" and made possible a divided party control of state government, and by the failure of many state legislatures to reapportion themselves, which through gerrymanders led to more or less permanent party control and rural domination of one or both houses. The introduction of the direct primary challenged the principal function of state parties—the electoral function—as candidate organizations began to appeal directly to the voting public and score dramatic victories over party organization candidates. The rise of the civil service and federal policy initiatives such as welfare gradually undercut the economic and social incentives of patronage politics and further decreased the stakes of state politics.

Relatively low participation of rank-and-file party members in the activities of state party organizations has been one of the lasting results. In a comprehensive study of state parties for the National Municipal League, Richard S. Childs pointed out that although millions of people turn out in support of parties on election day, less than three percent of those voting for the party actually take part in the functioning of the party organization.[4] Most voters in effect have no voice in party operations except to choose precinct committeemen and women

---

[3] Frank J. Sorauf, *Political Parties in the American System* (Boston: Little, Brown, 1964), p. 47.
[4] Richard S. Childs, *Inside 100 State Parties* (New York: National Municipal League, 1969), p. 5.

once every two years at a precinct caucus or primary. As a result, according to another survey,[5] one in five precinct positions is left vacant while party posts of importance, such as county or state chairmanships, are sheltered behind indirect and obscure election procedures.

The 1968 Party Precinct Participation project of the League of Women Voters confirmed these findings. A Kansas state party chairman noted: "You will find on the primary ballots in 50 percent of the precincts no candidates at all for precinct committeemen. There may be contests and a choice in 3 percent of them. In the remainder there will be one uncontested candidate for each post. . . . I was once elected by a landslide of one write-in vote. On another occasion I was defeated 3 votes to 2." The Seattle *Times* reported that in one caucus "a precinct committeeman and his wife had held a caucus and elected each other to the district and county conventions." Summarizing such experiences, Childs observed that "voters found their way into the vestibule of the party of their choice but not into any real influence. . . . Unless they joined the 3 percent of activists, assuming obligations to provide extensive personal service, they were out of the party activities for another two years."[6]

Insulated and ineffectual state party committees and leadership also survived. Although the comprehensive statutes enacted during the nineteenth century created what appears to be a hierarchy of legally regulated town, city, state legislative district, county, or congressional district committees and/or conventions with the state party chairman and state central committee at the apex, a bewildering variety of state and local party organizational patterns contributed to the lack of central party authority. In almost a fourth of the 100 state parties, for example, the state committee is composed of members elected at state conventions by delegates from the counties, in some 30 parties by local conventions; in 10 by county committees, and in 30 at primaries.

---

[5] Frank J. Sorauf, *Party Politics in America* (Boston: Little, Brown, 1968), p. 70.
[6] Childs, *Inside 100 State Parties*, p. 31.

In no state, moreover, are the legal party units organized as true hierarchies with the lower levels accountable to the upper. As a result, authority has not been concentrated in any single statewide party agency. One observer's description of an Ohio state party in the 1960's could well apply to many other states: "There was, in fact, no statewide Democratic party in Ohio. The state's Democratic party was an aggregation of city machines which had little or no interest in statewide elections unless the candidate was from their city. Ray Miller, the Cuyahoga County [Cleveland] Democratic boss, explicitly maintained that his organization was an independent entity with neither legal nor moral ties with a state Democratic party."[7] In his classic study of state politics, V. O. Key was more succinct in summing up the performance of state committees themselves. Although state committees have broad responsibilities—for calling and organizing party conventions, drafting party platforms, supervising party campaign funds and selecting the party's presidential electors, national committeemen and national convention delegates and alternates —he observed that "the general impression that most of them are virtually dead is probably not far wrong."

Much the same evaluation has been extended to state party leadership. According to Key, "The most apparent, and perhaps the fundamental, incapacity of state parties lies in the frequency with which the leadership corps is fractionalized and lacking in both capacity and organization for action. . . . [Party] organizations prepared to cope responsibly with statewide matters with a statewide view are the exception." Because of the system of indirect elections to party posts and low voter participation, moreover, few state party leaders have a popular constituency or following, and state committees are, as Key concluded, "virtually self-designated."[8]

It is from such leadership, however, that state party chairmen are usually drawn whether they are elected by the state

---

[7] John H. Fenton, *Midwest Politics* (New York: Holt, Rinehart & Winston, 1966), p. 137.
[8] V. O. Key, Jr., *American State Politics: An Introduction* (New York: Knopf, 1956), pp. 287, 271, 287.

committee or, as is more often the case, designated by the titular head of the party in the state. Just as the national chairman exercises the main responsibilities of the national committees, state chairmen are entrusted with such responsibilities as recruitment of secondary leadership and rank-and-file workers, nomination of candidates for both public and party office, patronage and party appointments, formulation of issues and public education, news coverage, conduct of election campaigns, fund raising, and implementation of the party's program.[9] Contrary to the traditional "party hack" conception of the party leader, however, most state chairmen are "middle-aged, well-educated, successful Americans who are well integrated into their communities and have entered party politics in order to satisfy philosophical and impersonal needs." But few consider their positions full-time jobs, according to one recent survey, and still fewer receive salaries.[10]

The degree of weakness and fragmentation of party organization varies considerably from state to state. A number of political scientists and scholars have generalized that state parties facing the closest competition are likely to have the most centralized control of nominations, the highest cohesion in state legislatures and in gubernatorial-legislative relations, and consequently the most effective and responsible governing agencies.[11] The general conclusion has been that relatively even competition seems to be a necessary but not sufficient condition in order for state parties to operate as unified governing agencies. In studying six Midwestern states, John H. Fenton

[9] Neil Staebler and Douglas Ross, "The Management of State Political Parties," in Cornelius P. Cotter (ed.), *Practical Politics in the United States* (Boston: Allyn and Bacon, 1969), pp. 54–69.
[10] Charles W. Wiggins and William L. Turk, "State Party Chairmen: A Profile," *Western Political Quarterly*, June 1970, pp. 321–32.
[11] Austin Ranney and Willmoore Kendall, *Democracy and the American Party System* (New York: Harcourt, Brace & World, 1956), pp. 190–91; Austin Ranney, "Parties in State Politics," in Herbert Jacob and Kenneth N. Vines (eds.), *Politics in the American States: A Comparative Analysis* (Boston: Little, Brown, 1965), pp. 63–70; Fred I. Greenstein, *The American Party System and the American People* (2nd ed.; Englewood Cliffs, N.J.: Prentice-Hall, 1970), Ch. 5, "State Politics: The Varieties of American Party Systems."

found that other variables affected the responsiveness of state government. "Specifically," he concluded, "the competitive two-party states that were in the vanguard in their expenditures for welfare and education tended also to be states with a reputation for issue-oriented two-party politics as opposed to the more traditional job-oriented two-party politics."[12] Ohio, Indiana and Illinois can be cited as the archetypes of traditional job-oriented state parties. Minnesota with its Farmer-Labor party tradition, Wisconsin with its La Follette Progressives, and Michigan with the United Automobile Workers union, as well as the present parties in Maine, Michigan and Oregon, can be considered programmatic or issue-oriented. Others have suggested that Fenton's analysis be extended to measure the degree of sharing of power or rank-and-file participation as well as the principal motivation of the party. They posit "a spectrum bounded by 'bossism' and manipulation on one end and participatory politics on the other."[13] (The modernized state parties projected in this chapter are both issue-oriented and participatory by this classification.)

Despite their direct interest in making the component units of the federal system function effectively, the national chairmen, national committees and headquarters staff have compiled a dismal record and they continue to operate almost as though the state parties did not exist. There is no evidence that anyone has advanced a continuing program to develop the potential of state politics. A permanent national field staff and program for state parties was proposed by Neil Staebler, chairman of the Democratic National Advisory Committee on Political Organization, but his plan was not implemented by national party leaders. Ray Bliss, as Republican National Chairman, was unable to gain the cooperation of several Republican state parties when he made the first serious attempt to collect basic data on the state parties. Although the McGovern-Fraser Democratic reform commission established in 1969 represented the first systematic effort by a national party

---

[12] Fenton, *Midwest Politics*, p. 3.
[13] Staebler and Ross in Cotter, *Practical Politics*, p. 48.

to study state party rules and procedures, the work of the commission with state parties was limited mostly to the process of selecting convention delegates. The Mission 70's program of internal party management developed by the Republican National Committee under Chairman Rogers Morton, although tailor-made for individual states, paid only nominal attention to the important differences in state party history and operations. Morton's successor, Senator Robert Dole, cut back on much of the program when he took control of the committee in early 1971.

More significant than the failure of the national parties to take their constituent state parties seriously, however, is the inability of state parties and state political leaders to define their political interests in terms broader than their individual states. Nowhere have potential state party resources for cooperative political and governmental projects been systematically developed. State political leaders and state parties seem virtually unable to cooperate and help themselves even on the basis of fairly well-defined common interests such as regional ties or urban problems. The national committees have served as an umbrella (and means for controlling) a few partisan bodies like the Republican and Democratic Governors' Associations, associations of state party chairmen, and the Republican State Legislators Association providing limited funding, office facilities and staff. But party officials at the state level have not yet succeeded in developing, funding and staffing their own cooperative program for state politics. As John H. Chafee, former governor of Rhode Island and chairman of the Republican Governors Association, once described the situation, "The problem is that no one will pick up the telephone."

Sensing the limitations of their national committees, various groups of state party leaders have attempted alternative organizations, but none of these has developed into an effective force for interstate action. Republican state chairmen in the 1960's under the leadership of Bliss of Ohio, Dr. Gaylord Parkinson of California and John Andrews of Ohio formed a continuing association, with national and regional chairmen, and got some staff support from national headquarters. But only the Southern Republican chairmen, many of whom were recruited through Operation Dixie, the Republican organizational effort in the South during the 1960's, still confer regularly. Democratic state chairmen took roughly 10 years to catch up; now, under the leadership of young state chairmen like Severin Belliveau of Maine, Richard Moe of Minnesota and Jon Moyle of Florida, they have pressed for full representation on the national committee and have obtained an office and executive director at the national headquarters.

The most ambitious interstate party organization is the Republican Governors Association, which evolved in the early 1960's from the informal caucuses of Republican governors at the various functions of the National Governors' Conference.[14] Idaho Governor Robert E. Smylie, chosen the first chairman of the association at its founding in Miami in July 1963, described the event as a "real breakthrough" and predicted that the governors would emerge as a "third major force" in the party alongside the national committee and congressional party. Congressman Fred Schwengel of Iowa, then chairman of the Committee on Increased Minority Staffing of the House Republican Conference, was invited to Miami to present suggestions for continuing cooperation between Republican governors and Congressmen. But critical organizational problems were left unsolved: funding, staffing, Washington facilities and details of national committee and congressional liaison.

The organizational modus vivendi eventually worked out between the Republican National Committee and the Governors Association seriously limited the latter's potential effectiveness. Under National Chairmen Miller and Bliss, the association gained staff, office space at the RNC headquarters and a sizable budget subsidy. However, the national committee effectively controlled operations. Staff were usually recruited or assigned by the national chairman rather than by the governors; funding was arranged through the national

---

[14] *The Republican Governors' Association: The Case for a Third Force,* A Ripon Society Report with Recommendations to the Republican Governors meeting in Denver, December 4–5, 1964 (Cambridge, Mass.: Ripon Society, n.d.).

chairman; and liaison with congressional leaders was handled personally through Miller and later through the formal apparatus of Bliss's Republican Coordinating Committee. The association organized a policy committee which produced some impressive policy research papers under the chairmanship of Nelson Rockefeller and a campaign committee which sponsored a series of professional campaign seminars for governors, gubernatorial candidates and their staffs. Yet with almost a decade's experience under a number of chairmen, both liberal and conservative, each in his own right a distinguished state party leader, the association has not developed a definite role as either a clearinghouse or an initiator and coordinator of team projects. The more recent Democratic governors' organization has not learned much from the Republican experience. In 1972, both were more concerned with winning a convention and election role than in long-term plans to develop a functioning interstate association.

With so much action occurring in the states, the governors of both parties should be among the most influential members in the national parties. Yet even in 1971 they were described as "the faceless men" of American politics by the NBC-TV news team covering the 1971 National Governors' Conference in Puerto Rico. Nor was a single governor a serious contender in a field crowded with contenders for the 1972 Democratic nomination.

There are a number of reasons for the failure of governors and other state party officials to capture attention and for the ineffective nature of their interparty organizations. For one thing, state party leaders are scattered geographically, while the national party committees and party elites are conveniently concentrated in Washington. National party figures such as congressional leaders can assert their prerogatives in matters like convention arrangements and policy formulation more easily and frequently than individual governors. For another, party organizations like the Republican Governors Association are unlikely to be effective so long as they are run from national party headquarters. The most progressive national chairmen do not have the perspective or operating responsibilities of the governors, and they and their staffs cannot be expected to plan and operate successful programs *for* the governors or to build up viable organizations that could conceivably threaten their position in the party. Weak, ineffective and divided governors (or state chairmen) appear to some national chairmen to be less of a problem than a strong and active group.

Even more important, there is a tendency of both state and national party leaders to think in terms of either the nation or the individual states' efforts rather than of the "states" as such or in combination. The media also compartmentalize the two, treating national and state political news as isolated, almost autonomous spheres. If something cannot be handled by an individual state, the assumption is that it must be a national problem to be dealt with by existing national institutions. The fact is that there is almost no public attention given to regional or interstate political organizations. The press, state and national party leaders and citizen organizations keep informed about the national and party governors' meetings as part of the preconvention presidential campaign and almost totally ignore other important bodies like the National Legislative Conference. Unlike the delegate counts in presidential campaigns and the legislative box scores in Congress, there are no continuing measures of the organizational progress of party governors, legislative leaders, state chairmen, or other state party leaders.

Governors and other state party leaders are also limited, to a degree at least, by the weaknesses of their individual state party organizations. Unreformed state parties do not attract citizen activists who might serve on interstate team projects although governors and state chairmen can usually set up advisory panels or special committees to give such people a role in the party.

Another handicap to cooperative state action has been the failure of national and state party organizations to develop current files and reference materials on state politics. Neither major party or for that matter any political group or private reporting service maintains updated files on the 50 Democratic and 50 Republican parties or a library on the states assembling books, articles, and state-government documents on the 50 states and their parties. The only way that one can get a summary of current political news from the states is to retain a national press intelligence clipping service of key state newspapers. As a result, a political information gap exists within the parties, which means that party leaders, staff and activists have no convenient way to become acquainted with the politics of other states.

The problems of state party organization, however, are not insurmountable. Individual state parties have been successfully rejuvenated, and a number of factors ranging from constitutional and state legislative reform to reapportionment and revenue sharing are creating a more favorable environment for further reform.

The potential of state parties has been illustrated by some recent party-related reforms. Democrats in South Carolina, encouraged by the Democratic reform movement at the national level, have been working to bring blacks into the party framework, and a successful coalition of moderate whites and blacks now controls the state government. A Black Democratic Caucus was formed in January 1971 to provide a unified political voice for black Democrats in the state. Plans for the caucus include a statewide organization with from one to four blacks in each county to serve as "eyes and ears" for the black community, to function as lobbyists on issues of special interest to blacks, and to channel local complaints and problems to the three black state legislators. Congressional-district coordinators and a steering committee are expected to work closely with the governor on matters of interest to the black community and to recommend blacks to serve on state boards and commissions. In Wisconsin, Colorado, Florida, Delaware and Massachusetts, Republican governors have undertaken complete reorganizations of the executive branch of government. They encouraged the formation in 1967 of a State Urban Action Center, a privately financed, nonpartisan agency of experts in state government. Governor Linwood Holton of Virginia has used his position to chart a party strategy based on racial accommodation, which some view as an alternative to the so-called Southern strategy.

Party members within several state legislatures have formed

study groups, often modeled after the Democratic Study Group in Congress, as a forum to develop legislative ideas. In Illinois, one member of the legislature's Democratic study group observed, "We want to see the party more issue-oriented. . . . Many of the guys involved in this study group are hardly rebels. They want a voice, but they believe in working within the party. After all, it's the only crap game in town."[15] In Massachusetts, 13 liberal young Democrats in the legislature formed an alliance, assigning each member primary areas of concern (taxes, automobile insurance, civil-service reform, conservation, structural and procedural changes within the legislature); the controversial 1970 no-fault automobile-insurance legislation was one result of the effort to develop new ideas and to define new Democratic positions. In California, Jesse M. Unruh started to build a staff of competent aides as far back as 1961; today it supplies the Assembly with a full array of services. Assemblymen are given an administrative assistant, a secretary and a district office allotment; college and university graduates interested in public affairs are recruited to provide professional staffing for Assembly committees. Unruh also made extensive use of outside consultants and added staff assistants, research specialists and other subsidiary services. According to one observer, Unruh's attempt to provide the California legislature with decision-making capability of its own must be rated one of the most significant experiments in modern government.[16]

The new emphasis on professionalized state party organizations, especially on the Republican side, has already demonstrated the feasibility of centralizing certain party management and service functions under greatly strengthened state party headquarters staff. Political consultants working for both parties feel that the technology of the new politics will further enhance state party organizations. California Republicans, with the aid of political consultants, built a

[15] Jerome Watson, "Springfield's Big Four Take On the Fiscal Crises," Chicago *Sun-Times*, February 9, 1969.
[16] Lou Cannon, *Ronnie and Jesse: A Political Odyssey* (Garden City, N.Y.: Doubleday, 1969), p. 209.

$600,000-a-year state central committee operation virtually from scratch during the 1960's, despite state laws designed to prevent hierarchical party organization. Democrats have lagged behind Republicans in building state organizations, although the Minnesota Democratic-Farmer-Labor party retained political consultants to prepare a comprehensive package of research, technical assistance and finances for 117 legislative candidates during the 1968 state elections. Features of the program included computerized electoral data analysis to help determine priority seats, recruit candidates and develop campaign strategy and tactics, and pooled legislative funds for redistribution to candidates on a priority basis.

In the course of his interviews with state party chairmen, Robert J. Huckshorn found convincing evidence of growth in state party organizations.[17] "There is a strong movement underway," he concludes, "toward fulltime paid state chairmen or part-time chairmen with a fulltime executive director or both." State parties in California, Colorado and New York have developed the equivalent of a party civil service. Most state parties are now leasing office space on a long-term basis and a few are planning to buy their own buildings. Huckshorn also notes a trend toward locating party headquarters in the state capitol as a means of improving relations with party members in the legislature. The development in state parties that impressed him most was "the number of state headquarters of both parties that are moving into computer operations."

Informal clublike party organizations offer another way to get around statutory bars to party organization. Both the Republican and Democratic parties in Wisconsin have made use of extralegal organizations like the Republican Voluntary Committee and the Democratic Organizing Committee to circumvent legislation enacted by the La Follette Progressives to weaken state party organizations. Californians have re-

[17] Dr. Huckshorn, chairman of the Political Science Department at Florida Atlantic University, is completing a study, *The State Party Chairman: His Role in American Politics,* under a grant from the National Science Foundation.

sorted to a variety of club movements within the state's weakened party structures—the California Republican Assembly, its conservative rival United Republicans of California, the California Democratic Clubs, and the Democratic Volunteers Committee among them. In states like New York and Illinois, the Democratic club movement of the Stevenson era and the more recent New Democratic Coalition have served as vehicles for new issue-oriented, upper-middle-class amateur party activists.

These signs of new life in state party organizations, however, have stopped short of a major effort to reform the state statutes that have handicapped state parties. The work of the McGovern-Fraser Democratic reform commission on state laws bearing on the selection of national convention delegates merely represents the first stage if there is to be a complete overhaul and updating of state laws regulating the parties. The steps toward broader interstate party programs have been tentative at best. But none of the factors discussed is a fundamental barrier to the development of the potential effectiveness of the state parties.

States as an Effective Force for Party Modernization

The rediscovery of state politics in the 1970's may well begin with the modernization of political parties at the county level. In the same way that the convention system and the direct primary began with local party units and then spread through the states during the nineteenth century, a new era of party reform, emphasizing opportunities for citizen participation and the ability of parties to govern massive and often unresponsive public bureaucracies, may find its first expression in the counties.

The counties remain viable political units in many states— the effective layer of party organization between the local precinct and the state central committee. Party county chairmen are regarded as the key men in many state party organizations. They are among the select number of political leaders in the country regularly polled concerning their preferences for party presidential nominees. The trend toward profes-sionalized state party organizations has already extended down to the county level in some states. The Ohio Republican party is well on the way to developing staffed offices at the county level, according to political consultant Robert Teeter of Market Opinion Research Corporation. Some major county organizations like the Bergen County (New Jersey) and Harris County (Houston, Texas), Republican organizations have retained their own political consultants directly.

County organizations afford some of the best targets for citizen reform groups as illustrated by the successes of groups like the Kansas City (Missouri) Democratic reform move-ment and the Essex County (New Jersey) Reform Republi-cans. But, like interstate activity, the potential for cooperative action among reform groups at the county level has remained undeveloped. The initiative of a progressive county organiza-tion like the Wayne County (Detroit) Democratic organiza-tion, which sponsored a party conference with nationally prominent guest experts on municipal law enforcement, is rarely shared with other local party units that might easily adapt such projects for their own use.

Other factors may also lead to the revitalization of party organization at the county level. The modernization of county government has produced a new breed of strong elected county executives or suburban mayors to replace the weak multicommissioner form of county government. The potential of cable television for politics may be most rapidly developed at the level of local and county party organization. Popula-tion growth in the suburbs and the "one man, one vote" re-apportionment rulings have increased the political significance of suburban counties which are now as critical in determining the electoral outcome in urban swing states as the heavy big-city vote once was. Ralph G. Caso, the Republican County Executive of Nassau County, Long Island, observes that dur-ing the 1970's more than 80 percent of the anticipated national population growth of 23 million will occur in the suburbs. If the counties continue to modernize their politics, in Caso's view they will become "the political unit of the future" representing the balance of political power within national affairs.[18]

One of the most exciting possibilities of state politics in the 1970's—cooperative action by state party leaders—faces few of the difficulties that have frustrated effective state party organizations. What can be called the "team concept" of interstate planning and action can be applied with relatively little effort or expense to a wide range of political and governmental problems. A few early experiments suggest the potential that is open to imaginative party leaders.

At the National Legislative Conference held in St. Louis in August 1969, state legislators from the "Big Ten States" organized a caucus to discuss common problems. The caucus did not function at the following year's conference but a precedent had been established. Neal Peirce outlined some of the common political interests of these states in an extensive study, *The Megastates of America,* observing that the nation is "dividing into two new sections, 10 states versus 40. The 10—and especially the great metropolitan areas within them—dominate every aspect of American life. Fifty-five percent of the American people—111,422,366 in the 1970 census—live in these 10 states. Scattered from one seacoast to the other, they are nonetheless tied together by bonds of economics, culture and attitude as strong as any geographic area."[19] The decision of Democratic party reformers to concentrate on these large states is a recognition of their potential leverage in the national parties.

In a memorandum to black politicians, Georgia state legislator Julian Bond has suggested another grouping of states—those states where "black votes have traditionally made the difference between victory and defeat for statewide candidates, usually Democrats, and Democratic presidential hopefuls." This group includes Arkansas, Florida, North Carolina, Illinois, Pennsylvania, Maryland, Indiana, Ohio, California and

---

[18] "Counties: New Suburban Power and Influence," A report on suburban growth and proposals for coordinated action by the nation's major suburban jurisdictions, presented by Ralph G. Caso, County Executive, Nassau County, New York, July 19, 1971.
[19] Peirce, *The Megastates of America,* p. 7.

New Jersey, plus the District of Columbia. Bond urged blacks to enter favorite sons in presidential primaries and to work for the selection of independent black convention delegates to build bargaining strength for blacks. The Episcopal Church, as another example, has tackled a variety of problems and opportunities in new regional groupings of its dioceses organized along geographical lines and/or by subject matter.

The team concept of planning and action by party representatives from groups of states has many possibilities. In electoral politics, state parties with common interests can share field workers and technical experience—Republicans interested in developing programs to involve minority groups and organized labor, Democrats trying to unite black and white ethnic-group support, state parties developing computerized direct-mail fund-raising and campaign services, states that must plan for presidential primaries. In policymaking for government, state parties can pool the experience of the party's governors, state legislators, mayors and other elected officials. Party governors with similar problems in industrial pollution, party mayors faced with a crisis in financing municipal services, state legislators concerned with improving the delivery of health services, and countless other groupings of party leaders and citizens can be formed to improve governmental performance within individual states and localities.

There are few regulatory or legal barriers to such cooperative action. Apart from campaign financing and corrupt practices, neither state nor federal laws regulate interstate party groups. Technological advances in communication—telephone conference calls, WATS lines, closed-circuit television, leased wires, time-shared computer terminals, and in the future two-way broad-band cable television—can link geographically scattered party members for specific purposes. Many clearinghouse functions of interstate party groups can be handled inexpensively with a mimeograph and the mails.

There is an abundance of talented and skilled individuals who would join state party work teams if invited to do so. The distribution of skills may vary among the states, but in a nation of more than 200,000,000 with 100 state party jurisdictions it should be possible to assemble a party team from several states on just about any important issue or problem.

Incentives for such an approach exist for both state and national party organizations. What one state cannot accomplish by itself may be feasible through a pooling of resources by several state parties. This method of strengthening constituent state parties also expands national party resources for presidential and congressional campaigns and for the staffing, administration and review of the federal bureaucracy. Both state and federal levels of party organization should realize substantial benefits in performance and at the polls from investing in interstate programs. Bipartisan or nonpartisan intergovernmental committees as well as citizen organizations lack such a clear electoral incentive.

The real failure in cooperative state party action, however, has been a failure of imagination. The clearest parallel in party history to the situation today was the problem of popular nomination of the President. Between the 1820's and the 1840's, a new type of party manager emerged who succeeded in linking together the separate state party constituencies through the ingenious solution that still survives as the national convention system of nomination.

The political and governmental crisis of America in the 1970's differs substantially from that of the 1820's, but it does share an important common element—the need to make the federal system function. The first party managers were concerned with power—how to organize the fragmented pieces of power in state party organizations and popular followings so as to win control of the presidency. The power motive is still a driving force in American politics, but it has been challenged by a new conception of politics that demands political and governmental competence and performance. The party manager of the future must accordingly be more than a power broker. Like the party leaders of the Jacksonian period, he must meet the demands for popular participation and devise new institutions that will make the federal system work.

A major element not present in the early nineteenth century is the existence of huge and entrenched governmental bureaucracies—federal, state, and local—relatively impervious to popular control or direction through elected officials. Thus the problem for party leaders today is one of making both party and governmental institutions responsive to the public.

American party politics today critically needs a new type of party manager or entrepreneur who combines practical political skills with a tough, pragmatic, problem-solving interest in government. He must know how to "work" state and national politics to achieve hard political results in the same way that the old convention managers had to master the politics of the federal system. He must be a broker of ideas—ideas generated within the states under vigorous party administrations and developed and spread to other state parties through the team concept of special-purpose organizations. Above all, he must understand the creative possibilities of state politics. As Supreme Court Justice Louis D. Brandeis wrote in 1932, "It is one of the happy incidents of the Federal system that a single courageous state may . . . serve as a laboratory and try novel social and economic experiments without risk to the rest of the country."

All of the elements necessary for this next stage in the development of the parties are present. What has been missing has been a catalyst—some agent that could demonstrate the potential for cooperative state party action. Reformed national committees or caucuses within the national committees might fill that role. Alternatively, as in the first era of experimentation with federal party structures, the initiative may come from and through the states.

Recommendations: A Program for Developing State Parties

Virtually everything in this book on the national political parties can be applied to state parties and, to a different degree, to county and other local party organizations. Proposals for reform of the national committees generally apply to state and county committees; of congressional parties, to state legislatures; of national conventions, to state and county conventions. There are several approaches to the modernization of state and local parties, however, that require separate emphasis.

Recommendation 1. Citizens, both individually and in ad hoc and other citizen groups, should encourage state and local party modernization by actively participating in the party jurisdictions in which they live.

As the soft underbelly of American politics, state and local party organizations in particular provide citizens countless opportunities to have a direct impact on the political process. The citizen interested in participating effectively in state and local politics should first learn the basic political information about his state and community to determine where his skills and resources can best be applied. He could, for example, obtain a description and rules of the state and local party organizations either from the parties themselves or private groups like the League of Women Voters. The citizen could also identify the major elected and appointed party officials responsible for party operations and programs at various levels in his state, including his county chairman, state committeeman and committeewoman, state chairman, state executive director, and chairman of his state party reform commission. He could also brief himself on the history of party politics in his state by checking various library reference works, attending lectures or discussions on the subject, or requesting community radio and television stations to schedule such programs.[20]

To increase the responsiveness of county and state party organizations to local political needs, citizens can work to raise general expectations of party services and demands for performance. They should register to vote and, if they so decide, to become active members of the party of their choice.

---

[20] A useful current bibliography of sources on state politics and state parties is unfortunately not available. The forthcoming regional volumes of Neal Peirce to complement his *Megastates of America* will include references on individual states. Other works of general (but often dated) interest are John Fenton, *Midwest Politics* (1966); Fenton, *Politics in the Border States* (New Orleans: Hauser Press, 1957); Frank Jonas (ed.), *Politics in the American West* (Salt Lake City: University of Utah Press, 1969); Duane Lockard, *New England State Politics* (Princeton, N.J.: Princeton University Press, 1959); and V. O. Key, Jr., *Southern Politics in State and Nation* (New York: Vintage Books, 1949).

Citizens should also specifically inquire about opportunities for participation at all levels of the state party organization, such as opportunities to run for precinct committeeman or committeewoman, for delegate to county and state party conventions, or for any higher state party office; opportunities to serve on state party platform and policy committees, state party reform commissions, and special committees charged with such party programs as registering new voters or recruiting candidates for elective state offices; and opportunities to attend various party functions as observers. Where information on party opportunities is not readily available, citizens can encourage party leaders to collect and publish such information; if the party is unresponsive, they can undertake the task themselves as part of a party reform effort. Experienced citizen and party activists can also invite and encourage less experienced but interested citizens to attend public party and governmental meetings and activities.

Citizens should regularly submit written recommendations and suggestions for improved party programs and operations to responsible party officials. Party leaders will in many instances carefully weigh and accept ideas from party rank-and-file members. Where party officials are hostile or unresponsive to such citizen initiatives, citizens should gain a minority position inside the party organization, file minority reports, and build a case for party reform by documenting inadequacies and abuses of party leadership and making copies of communications with party leaders available to higher party officials and state and national party reform commissions.

As a last resort, citizens can organize reform groups to take over unreconstructed county and state party organizations. Reform groups drawing on the experience of party activists in other states can devise model county party organizations with such features as active county committees, regular reports from the county chairman, a county party office and staff, a county newsletter, county-level party study and policy groups, and an annual county convention. The chairmen of reformed county organizations could form a continuing association to encourage statewide party reform to share ideas, and to reinforce reforms achieved in their own counties.

Recommendation 2. Modernized state parties should be structured to function as effective political units that encourage
citizen participation in state politics and a new problem-
solving party orientation in state government. State laws
regulating the parties should be revised to reflect these
objectives.

Party reformers at the state and local level do not need
to wait for national party reform commissions and guidelines,
helpful as these may be, to begin substantial party modernization in the states. The comprehensive reform of individual
state party organizations can be initiated, to mention some
possibilities, by a dedicated state chairman, a governor who
chooses to exercise state party leadership, a prominent party
member (such as a national committeeman), a party reform
commission, a reform caucus in the state legislature, or reform
county organizations.

Broader citizen participation in and use of state parties can
be furthered through such means as the establishment of permanent state party headquarters accessible at local telephone
rates from any point in the state; expanded and active state
and county committees; statewide party policy committees,
task forces and action groups; and annual state and county
party conventions with special programs and workshops.

The policymaking and governing function of state parties
can be furthered by new state party programs to recruit and
train political executive talent for state government; to recruit
capable party candidates to contest every state legislative
seat and elected office; to develop party caucuses, professional
staff, and legislative services in state legislatures; and to involve and train citizens in government through party advisory
committees. State parties can experiment at the state level with
such innovations as partywide issue referenda included in the
party's primary ballot and state party councils composed of
the governor and/or the state chairman, party organization
leaders, state legislative leaders, other state constitutional
officers, mayors and county executives, former governors, and
representative citizen leaders.

State and local party organizations could actively promote the service-bureau concept, encouraging citizens to list the services and information that they need to be effective in local party activities such as elections to the state legislature and county government, voter registration and fund raising. State and local party organizations could compile, update and distribute lists of key governmental party members and their responsibilities to interested citizens.

State party reform commissions cooperating on a bipartisan basis could make an intensive study of state statutes regulating the parties and develop omnibus reform proposals to update such legislation, on the basis of statewide party discussion and open hearings and consistent with such official guidelines as may be voted by national party commissions.

Recommendation 3. The team approach to political and governmental problem solving should be vigorously developed by state and national party leaders.

One of the most promising avenues to building vital and effective parties lies in cooperative action and the pooling of resources of state leaders from the individual states. The team approach to state politics and government by governors, state chairmen, state legislators, and many other groups can be developed in several ways. State officeholders and party officials should establish active associations to develop, staff and fund interstate planning and action programs. Existing associations could sponsor or encourage cooperative action among other groups of state party leaders such as state party counsel, state reform chairmen and state platform chairmen.

These associations of governors, state chairmen and state leaders should recruit and develop their own staff for cooperative action. Operating staff could be assigned to the home-state office of the elected chairman of the association concerned as well as to a Washington liaison office. Full-time staff could be recruited through open national competition and supplemented by staff from the home-state offices of individual leaders on short-term assignment. In addition to staffing their own operations, such associations set up interstate personnel clearinghouses for state political executives and state party professionals, a vital function that has been neglected by the party national committees.

Such associations could also establish information clearinghouses and a system of flash bulletins to state offices. They could publish collected annual reports of the Democratic or Republican governors and of all the state party chairmen, undertake regular polls of state party leaders, and assist state leaders testifying before Congress or meeting with federal executive department officials.

Associations of state party leaders should develop existing and new forms of interstate communication on a cooperative basis. Republican or Democratic governors could, for example, experiment with various hot-line or Telex systems or remote terminal computers to link their state capitals. Such systems could be particularly useful in policy development and administration in state government, especially if they were connected to federal and private sources of information. Weekly telephone conference calls eventually extended to videophone or cable-television linkups could be an invaluable addition to the relatively infrequent formal conferences of state leaders.

Improved state facilities and staff in Washington could also increase the collective impact of state party leaders in national politics. State party leaders could make greater use of liaison offices in Washington. Large states could staff their delegations in Congress. Such state facilities might eventually be located in a central office complex where they could benefit from common-user services. Ideally, each state party should have the use of some Washington office where it can develop and maintain its own files and Washington information services. The state chairmen's associations of the two major parties could provide directories of such state facilities and staff located in Washington for the use of party leaders and interested citizens.

Interstate associations could be funded where possible by the states or by groups of states to ensure greater freedom of action and motivation. Central operating budgets could be raised by subscription of the members, by a number of state sponsors suggested by individual governors or state chairmen, or by direct mail to subscribing members of state parties. Funds should be obtainable for specific interstate projects as well. Governors and state chairmen can also make legitimate use of some state governmental and state party funds for interstate projects.

Recommendation 4. The national parties should develop a comprehensive program for state parties, including a national party commission on the states, multiyear planning and matching grants for state party development, pilot programs in key states, and state political information services.

The efforts of individual citizens, state party leaders and interstate party teams to inject new life into state politics can be greatly facilitated and strengthened by comprehensive national party programs for the states.

National party headquarters should first develop their own capabilities to serve and advise state party organizations. Through such means as state political files and a party library on the states they could collect and maintain current information on the organizational status, personnel, budget and programs of the 50 state parties. National party headquarters could compile and publish lists of party members and officials such as elected national committee members and state chairmen, national and state party professional staff, and professional political consultants who are particularly knowledgeable about the politics of individual states and who would be available to advise party groups. The national committees could also carefully appoint and make available the services of task forces on particular problems of interest to state parties. A new system of national party credits could be devised to recognize the contribution of party workers made in states outside their own.

The national parties should make use of the representative national party commission mechanism to undertake a thoroughgoing national inquiry into the problems of state party organization. A particular topic of investigation should be the effect of state laws on party organization and functions. A representative party commission could establish guidelines for model state and local party organizations, recognizing the diversity of party organizations but advancing national party goals such as in-

creased opportunities for participation and greater accountability of party officials.

The national parties could encourage each state party to prepare a multiyear plan for party development with the assistance
of a national committee task force. Adapting an approach used
effectively in federal-state governmental relations, the national
parties could develop a number of matching-grant programs
for state parties to encourage substantive as well as experimental projects such as the recruitment of state legislative
candidates or the development of direct-mail sustaining membership programs. The national committees could also fund
pilot projects in two or three states to test new party programs
and concepts. Successful prototypes could be demonstrated to
state party leaders and then made available to all states.

In order to overcome the relative lack of accessible information on politics within the individual states and between states,
the national committees, in cooperation with state chairmen,
governors, state legislators and other associations of state leaders, should develop political information services for the states.
National party publications could be designed with regional or
state inserts and indexed for later reference. State party libraries could be provided with basic reference materials on
state politics. Summaries of the proceedings of all the state
party conventions could be made available to the state parties
as a guide to developing their own conventions. National committees and major state party organizations with the necessary
resources could fully utilize advances in information and technology and cooperate in developing political information-
retrieval systems.

VI

A New Motivation
for Politics:
The Ability to Govern

The warning of the old machine politician George Washington Plunkitt that "if the parties go to pieces, the government they build must go to pieces, too,"[1] has more than a grain of truth in it. The crisis in American political parties is paralleled by a crisis in government. Godfrey Sperling, Jr., national political correspondent of the *Christian Science Monitor,* reports a "growing distrust of governmental processes." Management consultant Peter F. Drucker talks about "the sickness of government" and prescribes a "reprivatization" of many of the functions of government through greater reliance on the private sector. Columnist Holmes Alexander ventured the judgment that the country "now has had three Presidents in a row who seem unable to preside over the nation." President Nixon acknowledged the public disillusionment with government in his third State of the Union message: "Let's face it. Most Americans today are simply fed up with government at all levels. They will not—and should not—continue to tolerate the gap between promise and performance."

Representative government requires vigorous and healthy politics to function. Trained politicians with political skills and experience—elected and appointed political executives, legislators and their political staff and advisers—are even more essential than professional civil servants in providing policy direction and answering to the public for performance. Yet the

---

[1] *Plunkitt of Tammany Hall,* p. 13.

steady expansion of governmental power in recent decades has not been accompanied by a corresponding development in political leadership and self-government. Somehow Americans have lost sight of the positive connection between politics and government.

Among the definitions of "politics" that Webster offers are "the art or science of government; the art or science concerned with guiding or influencing governmental policy"; and, "political affairs or business, specifically . . . political activities characterized by artful and often dishonest practices." A "politician" is defined, first, as "one versed in the art or science of government, especially one actively engaged in conducting the business of government," and second, as "one engaged in party politics as a profession; one primarily interested in political offices from selfish or other usually short-run interests."

In common American usage, the second meanings clearly predominate. "Politics," "political," "partisan," and "politician" all tend to be dirty words. Newspaper headlines, editorials and columns constantly deprecate politics as though government, statesmanship and civic virtue were something above, and distinct from, politics. The citizen reads or hears about "political influence," "political considerations," "political reprisals," "political motives," "political expediency," all conveying the narrow, self-serving sense of the word. A cartoon captioned "High Road or Low Road?" depicts a Congressman facing two signs: "Passage of Vital Legislation" pointing upward, "Politics" pointing down. The Harris survey reports that sizable and growing majorities of the public are prepared to believe the worst about politicians, including the statement that "most politicians are in politics to make money for themselves." Correspondent Paul Niven once pointed out that "we dissuade our young people from going into politics and then we complain about the kind of government we get. We try to pretend there is some distinction between a politician and a statesman. Winston Churchill would know better; so would Charles de Gaulle, Konrad Adenauer and Nikita Khrushchev."

In continuing to denigrate politics, Americans limit the possibilities of government by denying the governmental process essential political leadership and support. At the same time, party politics without governmental purpose becomes a politics of manipulation, technique and style, encouraging a sense of hopelessness that people can do anything to influence their society. Real public policy problems and opportunities—economic recession and inflation, racial tensions and environmental degradation—are only compounded by this inability to relate government and politics constructively, this inability truly to govern.

A renaissance in American governmental institutions first requires that Americans rediscover the meaning and end purpose of party politics. In a century of civil service and governmental reform, Americans have systematically attempted to take partisan politics out of the governmental process. Parties were limited to contesting elections; they were not trusted with staffing and directing the government. Yet the political parties remain one of the few existing or potential institutions through which large numbers of citizens can have a direct impact on or involvement in the course of government.

Americans have begun to recognize the limitations of "the textbook presidency" which among other things is not even able to control the Washington bureaucracy. Congress, notwithstanding its representative and ombudsman functions, has insulated its party caucuses and policymaking bodies from citizen participation. Even the public interest movement, in its attempt to make government more responsive to unorganized constituencies rather than to powerful organized interests, is less an effort to involve people in government than it is to hold government technocrats responsible to an elitist conception of the public interest. Whatever merits they may have, other current answers to the crisis in government—the regionalization of federal programs, reprivatization of federal activities, massive revenue sharing with states and localities and the replacement of some social programs by income supplements—all try to reduce the size of government without increasing the political capabilities of citizens to influence governmental decision making.

The next step is for citizens to recognize that political parties are ready-made or easily developed instruments for exercising self-government, for channeling ideas and political talent into the governmental process, for bridging the gap between an ever more educated and politically capable citizenry and an ever more incomprehensible and seemingly impregnable hundred-billion-dollar governmental "system."

Once citizens discover the governmental purpose of politics they will have every reason to participate in it. Federal, state and local governmental agencies touch every aspect of American life from farm price-support programs to home mortgage rates, from air and rail passenger service, to the regulation of pension funds—an almost endless catalogue of concerns. The test of modernized political parties of the future—citizen parties—will be their capacity to involve citizen talents in government and to give citizens greater leverage on the permanent government of local, state and national bureaucracy: in brief, their ability to govern.[2]

An expanded party role in government, to be effective, requires a new issue-orientation and problem-solving motivation in the parties. In turn, the extent to which parties succeed in relating themselves to practical citizen concerns, in the way that the public interest movement has identified and dramatized problems in the regulatory agencies, will help to determine the levels of citizen participation and support political parties can enlist.

The Failure of the Old Politics: The Inattention to Government

American parties have had several plausible excuses for avoiding the responsibilities of government. Some scholars believe that America historically had less need for government than most other industrial societies.[3] With its natural wealth

---

[2] Stephen K. Bailey observed that modest party reforms could "greatly strengthen America's capacity to govern responsibly and effectively" more than 10 years ago. See *The Condition of Our National Political Parties*, An Occasional Paper on the Role of the Political Process in the Free Society (New York: The Fund for the Republic, 1959).

[3] As a result, according to Harvard Professor Samuel P. Huntington, the American political system was never fully "modernized." Sovereignty was and remains divided, power separated, and functions combined in many

and geographical isolation, the United States could afford throughout most of the nineteenth century the luxury of "non-government." The parties thus initially developed during a period when few governmental demands were made on them, and they could and did avoid the responsibilities of government. Laissez-faire capitalism, with its belief in a self-regulating system, assigned a minimal supportive role to government and politics and thereby exerted a further corrupting influence on both.

Although relatively decentralized and limited in national programs, the parties did provide the public a kind of direct access to and popular control of government through the appointment process and the spoils system. But as the nineteenth century drew to a close, a number of developments in the governmental system increased governmental policy output while limiting the functions of parties and their responsibility for governmental performance. The civil-service reform movement in particular worked to separate the spheres of partisan politics and governmental operations and weakened the already limited policymaking role of the American parties.

The objective of civil-service reform leaders of the post–Civil War period, almost exclusively white middle-class professional men often from established families, was the political neutralization of the government service.[4] The movement took the form of an attack on the spoils system, the reputed source of strength of the professional politicians. The practical effect of civil-service reform and later the reforms of the Progressive era was to deny political spoils to the new professional ethnic

---

different institutions—a kind of "quaintly old" latter-day Tudor polity. See Huntington, "Political Modernization: America vs. Europe," *World Politics*, April 1966, pp. 378–414. Also see Louis Hartz, *The Liberal Tradition in America: An Interpretation of American Political Thought Since the Revolution*, Harvest Book (New York: Harcourt, Brace & World, 1955), Ch. 1, "The Concept of a Liberal Society."

[4] See Ari Hoogenboom, *Outlawing the Spoils: A History of the Civil Service Reform Movement, 1865–1883* (Urbana: University of Illinois Press, 1961); and Herbert Kaufman, "The Growth of the Federal Personnel System," in Wallace S. Sayre (ed.), *The Federal Government Service*, Spectrum Book (2nd ed.; Englewood Cliffs, N.J.: Prentice-Hall, for the American Assembly, Columbia University, 1965), pp. 7–69.

politicians who were gaining political power in the populous urban centers.

The spoils system rested on the principles of appointment primarily for political considerations, congressional control of appointments (exemplified by the Tenure of Office Acts), and the rotation of officeholders with the change of administrations. It put at the disposal of Presidents the political resources to cement a decentralized party coalition and win support for legislation. At the same time, it gave Congressmen virtual control of the management of government personnel and effectively debased the standards of public service set during the Federalist and Jeffersonian eras. Scandals in the 1870's and 1880's, the assassination of President James A. Garfield in 1881 by a disappointed office seeker, in addition to the widespread practice of assessing public employees, provided excellent copy for the reform press, outraged the public and set the stage for broad reform.

The Civil Service Act of 1883 attempted to remedy such abuses by taking the civil service "out of politics." The power to make civil service appointments was transferred from the President (and Congress) to a bipartisan agency, a three-member Civil Service Commission. The law provided for "open, competitive examinations for testing the fitness of applicants for the public service now classified or to be classified hereunder." Political assessments by which public employees had been required to contribute time and money to party organizations were forbidden.

Since 1883, the percentage of public employees under the jurisdiction of the competitive civil service has steadily increased. By 1899, 44.8 percent of the public work force was covered; by 1910, 57.9 percent. The trend was temporarily reversed in the 1930's when President Roosevelt solved many of his program and patronage problems, and at the same time preserved the established classified service, by creating a new range of governmental agencies in parallel to old-line governmental departments and agencies. Between 1933 and 1936 public employment rose from 572,091 to 824,259, while the percentage of classified jobs dropped from 79.7 to 60.5. After 1936, New Deal agencies were gradually brought under the civil service, and by the end of the Truman administration some 86.3 percent of the 2.6-million public work force was under the classified service. The Eisenhower administration in 1953 introduced a new category of so-called Schedule C positions of a policymaking character, appointees to which served at the pleasure of the President. Schedule C appointments reached their highest level, 1,700, in the Nixon administration. According to an analysis by Herbert Kaufman, civil service classification is likely to remain at the 1960 level of 86 percent. The other 14 percent are largely "excepted" specialized or temporary positions, such as government lawyers, where competitive examinations have not been deemed necessary.

The Hatch Act of 1939, in part an effort to limit the political resources of President Roosevelt and in part a logical corollary of the Civil Service Act that barred political workers from the classified civil service, attempted to bar federal employees from taking an active role in the parties. The Hatch Act of 1940 covered state and municipal employees funded from federal sources. Among political activities prohibited by these laws were running as a partisan candidate for public office, serving as a party officer or member of a party committee, serving as a convention delegate, delivering political speeches, soliciting campaign contributions, propagandizing voters, and distributing political campaign literature. The Hatch Acts thus completed the theoretical separation of parties and the civil service. "Professionalization" of the public service became the dominant ethic; party loyalty was replaced by new program and professional loyalties.

At the same time as the creation of a classified civil service progressively restricted the party role in staffing government, the partisan politics of electoral competition and participation was being displaced by the rise of interest-group representation in government. Voluntary associations, corporations, labor unions, professional societies and a host of organized interests became competitors of the parties in the definition of public policy. Politics was steadily transferred from an electoral to an administrative context, with more limited party and popular participation. The complex decision-making calculus of the growing governmental bureaucracy and its interest-group clientele instead encouraged participation by specialized issue elites.

By the 1930's, with the significant increase in the federal budget and the "permanent government" of the classified civil service, interest-group liberalism was elevated to the status of a new public philosophy. The public interest and the agenda of public policy were to be defined in terms of the organized interests in society and administrative, technical and logrolling considerations, not through political parties and elections. "The public interest," observes political scientist Theodore Lowi, "would emerge from interactions between elites of skill and elites of interests"—the professional bureaucrats and the leaders of organized interests. The new arrangement, Lowi notes, meant "accountability to experts first and amateurs last"; it was "a conspiracy to shut out the public."[5]

Civil-service reform did not end politics in the public service but transformed it from the partisan politics of spoils to a new policy of politics based on individual agencies and programs of government. The insulation from political influence also meant an insulation from political control. Agencies developed an advocate role, selling and promoting their programs to Congress, the Cabinet secretary, the Bureau of the Budget and the public. Increasingly the governmental bureaucrat exercised enormous discretionary power and agencies functioned independently of presidential or party control, acting as self-directing bureaucracies and ignoring the leadership of political executives appointed by the party in charge of the government.

With the outbreak of World War II and the postwar international responsibilities of the United States, bipartisan policy elites, recruited from the government establishment and private sector and largely removed from congressional control and the arena of partisan electoral politics, further subordinated the party role in government. The effort to limit partisan debate of foreign and national security policy implied that political parties and the general public could make no positive contributions to policy development, an assumption that remained

---

[5] Theodore J. Lowi, *The End of Liberalism: Ideology, Policy, and the Crisis of Public Authority* (New York: W. W. Norton, 1969), pp. 205, 87.

unquestioned until the anti-Vietnam war and national priorities movements of the late 1960's.

Consensus politics, as practiced by President Johnson, brought political parties to their low point as active inter-mediaries between the people and government. Decision making in the Great Society was by private negotiation among economic, technological and administrative elites, not by public debate. "The President basically saw no constructive role for public debate in the formulation of national policy," observes David Broder, "and therefore systematically shut down public access to the plans he was making." Political parties were "un-wanted intruders on the process of consensus government."[6] Consensus government passed with the coming apart of the Johnson administration, but the problems of public access to government and the unwanted status of political parties con-tinue.

While the specter of the spoils system and patronage politics persists, the failure to develop legitimate partisan roles for parties in government has left the American people politically unprepared to deal with the new realities of massive govern-ment. During the 1960's, for example, federal grant-in-aid programs rose from an annual rate of about $7 billion to more than $25 billion, greatly strengthening new bureaucracies of federal-state-and-local specialists in areas like highways, health services, welfare and urban development. Mayors, county executives, governors and Presidents, the elected representa-tives of the people, have often had little control of the spread-ing intergovernmental bureaucracy. At one critical level of governmental development, the new system of federal regional offices, parties have not yet organized an effective public voice. Professor Harold Seidman of the University of Connecticut, formerly a top official of the Bureau of the Budget, concludes that "what we have been doing up to now has weakened central political authorities, strengthened the power of bureaucracies, and made the system more unmanageable without providing

---

6 David S. Broder, "The Fallacy of LBJ's Consensus," *Washington Monthly*, December 1971, pp. 12, 13. Also see Broder, *The Party's Over: The Failure of Politics in America* (New York: Harper & Row, 1972).

effective citizen participation or making government more responsive to citizen needs."[7]

Only a sustained public demand for improved governmental performance can strengthen political direction of the permanent government. As Harvard Professor Richard Neustadt has suggested, the great prospective struggle in American politics may well not be between the parties, or between President and Congress, but rather between "entrenched officialdom and politicians everywhere."[8] And the front line of battle will be the top appointive positions in federal, state and local governments which parties and politicians must fill.

Staffing an Administration: What Role for the Parties?

Nowhere is the failure of the parties to develop a capacity to govern more evident than in the staffing of the various positions available to a new administration in the top echelons of government. Critical though this relative handful of positions in the various agencies and departments may be to the implementation of a party or presidential program, the appointment process is surprisingly haphazard.

The second Hoover Commission in 1955 estimated that the number of political executive positions in the federal government open when the White House changes parties totaled 1,005, including about 250 non-civil-service bureau chiefs, 40 heads of substantive staff offices, 50 heads of departmental information offices, and 300 political aides and assistants. Expansion of the White House staff and creation of the Domestic Council and Office of Management and Budget under the Nixon administration have increased that number to 1,350. Counting only appointees requiring senatorial confirmation, however (Cabinet secretaries, under secretaries, assistant secretaries, agency

---

[7] See Harold Seidman, *Politics, Position, and Power: The Dynamics of Federal Organization* (New York: Oxford University Press, 1970), Ch. 5 and Ch. 9.

[8] Richard E. Neustadt, "Politicians and Bureaucrats," in David B. Truman (ed.), *The Congress and America's Future* (Englewood Cliffs, N.J.: Prentice-Hall, for the American Assembly, Columbia University, 1965), p. 119.

heads, some deputy agency heads, regulatory-agency commissioners, and a few individual cases like the Commissioner of Education and the Commissioner of Labor Statistics), and excluding ambassadors, flag-rank military officers and White House appointees, a President has between 250 and 300 top-echelon positions that he can fill.

In view of the importance of these political executives, the parties, incoming Presidents, and especially presidential staffs should know a great deal about them. Such is not the case. The appointment process in recent administrations has been characterized by last-minute intensive talent searches, the limited role of the parties, and the steady institutionalization of political personnel functions within the White House.

Executive recruitment rarely begins in earnest before a candidate has won election. In a study for the Brookings Institution, Dean E. Mann found that in both 1952 and 1960 little effort was made before November to prepare for the difficult job of recruitment. In the turmoil of the 1960 Kennedy campaign, "no staff member could be spared to consider matters that would be contingent upon the one major necessity: winning the election. One Kennedy staff member observed that if anyone had diverted his attention to such secondary matters, 'Kennedy wouldn't have won.' "[9]

Once the recruitment process begins, party involvement is circumscribed. Mann found that party officials had been chief participants in only four of 108 appointments of second-level political executives. The party national committees' function has been limited to clearance, i.e., ascertaining the political acceptability of candidates in their states, and even this may be pro forma. According to another Brookings study, parties tend to be concerned with specific personnel questions at a relatively low level in the administrative hierarchy. The study concludes that "one of the striking characteristics of American parties is the ineptness of party machinery in providing able candidates for executive positions who will be loyal to the

---

[9] Dean E. Mann with Jameson W. Doig, *The Assistant Secretaries: Problems and Processes of Appointment* (Washington, D.C.: The Brookings Institution, 1965), p. 72.

administration in office. . . . Parties have no mechanism for screening and recommending suitable candidates and no standards for judging executive competence."[10]

Left to their own devices, recent administrations have relied on a variety of means to recruit and screen executive talent. Harry Truman instituted a personnel office in the White House under presidential assistant Donald Dawson. The Eisenhower administration's staffing operation, assisted by a management consulting firm, McKinsey and Company, drew up a roster of 5,000 names from almost every state party organization. Although the roster was considered a shopping list of prospects, little background information was compiled on candidates and state parties did not follow through on recommendations, Cabinet officers soon turned to their own sources, and after six months the roster was forgotten. The Kennedy administration employed numerous policy task forces during the transition period, an approach that gave the President and his aides an opportunity to appraise potential candidates for federal positions and those who were selected a running start on their new jobs. Talent spotters in the private sector, a role long exercised by individuals like Bernard M. Baruch and Sidney Weinberg, were organized more formally into a network of 40 to 50 contact men by Special Assistant Dan H. Fenn, Jr.,[11] and his associates in the Kennedy White House. Months after taking office, however, the administration had no basic background files or evaluative information on its appointments. One Kennedy White House aide commented that "we didn't even know who the Under Secretary of the Air Force was." During Robert F. Kennedy's campaign for the 1968 Democratic presidential nomination, aides decided to get in touch with President Kennedy's appointees for support and found to their chagrin that no files had been kept on presidential appointees. "We didn't have the vaguest idea where people were," an aide said.

---

[10] Marver H. Bernstein, *The Job of the Federal Executive* (Washington, D.C.: The Brookings Institution, 1958), pp. 123–24.

[11] Fenn, now director of the John F. Kennedy Memorial Library and Lecturer in Business Administration, Harvard Business School, is completing a survey on presidential appointees since 1952.

The state of the art of staffing an administration and the minimal role of the national party organization were demonstrated in the appointment process during 1968 and 1969, the transition between the Johnson and Nixon administrations. As his chief personnel officer Nixon selected Harry S. Flemming, a Virginia Republican and son of Arthur S. Flemming, former Secretary of Health, Education and Welfare in the Eisenhower administration. Although Flemming had been an aide to Nixon's chief of field operations, Richard G. Kleindienst, at the Republican National Committee during the 1968 campaign, he lacked governmental experience before coming to the White House. Flemming and John W. Macy, Jr., who had served both as Chairman of the Civil Service Commission and as President Johnson's top personnel adviser, met only once for 15 minutes. The Nixon staff inherited the computer printout and programs for the executive talent bank that the Johnson administration had developed and received some general advice on filling the top 300 presidential-level appointments.

Nixon aides first had to ferret job descriptions out of the Civil Service Commission. Computer entrepreneur Sam Wyly of Texas and a working group tried to improve the Johnson executive-search computer programs, with little success. White House personnel staff proceeded to develop two separate operations, one a much-publicized computer talent hunt that solicited suggestions from state parties, the public and sources such as *Who's Who*, and the second a quiet search through personal Nixon administration contacts to fill political executive positions on a priority basis. (Neither operation, however, was able to recruit a sufficient number of Republicans to fill all the policy positions available in a critical department like Health, Education and Welfare.) The public operation served as a "smoke screen," according to one White House aide, "to help fend off the patronage-seekers. Don't get me wrong. Patronage in its place is functional. It keeps the political system going without screwing up government."

State party leaders soon saw through the smoke screen. One party professional and patronage contact from the Midwest made a concerted effort to recruit executive talent in his state, persuading one executive in the $100,000 pay bracket to consider a federal post at $25,000, only to find names submitted to Washington "lost in the shuffle." Other observers commented on the "ineptness" of the appointment process during the early months of the administration. According to one Nixon White House staff member, "They didn't even know where the key positions were. The Budget Bureau was a prime example. Secretary [of the Treasury David M.] Kennedy stipulated that he wanted Robert Mayo as Budget Director. He argued that he needed to work together with him to control inflation. The 'troika' [Robert Haldeman, Peter Flanigan, and John N. Mitchell] agreed to go along. It was the biggest mistake of the new administration. Nobody seemed to realize then that the Budget Director should be the *President's* man and what a critical role the Budget Bureau played in the government." President Nixon's early snap decision to delegate recruitment to his Cabinet officers and White House staff further reduced the President's leverage in appointments. When Labor Secretary George P. Shultz staffed most of the top of his department with Democrats or Independents, the President's party forfeited a rare opportunity to train Republican talent in a sector the party was attempting to add to a new Republican coalition.

Ironically, the President, among recent occupants of the White House generally considered the most partisan in his appointments, did not even consult his Republican National Chairman, Senator Dole, before announcing his controversial choice of Dr. Earl L. Butz of Purdue University to be Secretary of Agriculture in 1971. In fact, some system of party consultation might have spared President Nixon embarrassment in other appointments. "The disastrous [G. Harrold] Carswell appointment," commented Howard K. Smith on ABC News, "would not possibly have been made, had the President consulted a wider circle than his Attorney General." "The White House has a tendency to apply the same rule of secrecy [to high-level appointments] that you apply to intelligence operations," Senate Minority Leader Hugh Scott (R-Pa.) noted.

Liberal and conservative critics alike bemoaned the improvisations of the administration and the lack of a clear sense of direction from the party. James Reston of *The New York Times* criticized "the Nixon technique" for giving neither the Cabinet nor the civil service "a sure sense of where it is going."[12] Conservative columnist Kevin Phillips chided President Nixon for surrounding himself with managerial men who "lack the governmental experience to understand the realities of interest groups, Congress and political strategy" and are "principally concerned with efficient staff procedures, regulated paperflow, 'team play,' and public relations."[13]

At the spring 1969 meeting of the Republican National Committee, party leaders themselves were up in arms. White House aide Harry S. Dent met with national committee representatives and promised improvements in the patronage and other political reward systems but not until August, after more expressions of party dissatisfaction, did national committee headquarters add one full-time professional in charge of patronage, Howard E. Russell, Jr., a retired politician in the insurance business and former Republican state chairman of Rhode Island.

The limited view of the role the party could play in staffing a government was evidenced by the location and size of the Republican National Committee patronage office and by the patronage it handled. Located in a distant corner of the fourth floor of the Cafritz Building, two floors above what were then the main suite of the Republican National Committee, the operation was staffed by Russell, two full-time secretaries, and one part-time typist. Russell did not mind the inconspicuous location. "We handle what gravitates to us," he remarked. His office as a rule did not initiate searches for names; incoming requests for jobs were about all it could handle. "I understand Illinois has six full-time people working on patronage," Russell commented wistfully.

Most of the party patronage processed by the Republican National Committee and the White House concerned the prestigious, unpaid, usually do-little boards and commissions that

---

[12] James Reston, "The Nixon Technique," *New York Times*, August 16, 1970.
[13] Kevin P. Phillips, "The Plastic Empire," Washington *Post*, April 2, 1971.

abound within the federal government, such as the National Armed Forces Museum Advisory Board, the Annual Assay Commission, the President's Commission on Alcoholism, the Board of Foreign Scholarships, and the Board of the John F. Kennedy Center for the Performing Arts. The Nixon White House improvised other new forms of largely honorific patronage: Small Business Administration Advisory Councils, Regional Export Expansion Councils, rides on Air Force 1 and 2 with appropriate scrolls to the passenger. Some prominent party members not interested in honorific positions declined them, a fact that did not perturb the patronage dispensers since they could then offer the same job to several people. During the heat of the national committee revolt, the White House offered to place 10 names (largely to the honorific commissions) that each state submitted. "It took six months of follow-ups to get the names," a White House aide pointed out as evidence that "there was more complaining than a real problem." Communications with state organizations were so poor, however, that some party leaders did not recognize how choice some of the patronage plums were that they were offered, like berths on the Canadian Boundary Commission, which paid a full salary with virtually no duties.

In September 1970, Nixon administration personnel policy acquired a new "tough" line with the appointment of Fred Malek, a Nixon appointee at HEW, to head the White House executive recruitment program. Malek has given much closer and more systematic scrutiny to appointments within departments and claims to have more than doubled the number of women top-level appointees and recruited more blacks and Chicanos than any previous administration.

One senior civil servant who has observed top-level personnel recruitment in every administration since the 1930's pinpointed this basic deficiency in the appointment process and the need for a new approach: "Generally the people who apply for jobs with government are not the ones you want—yet they are the ones computer systems have in their files. The people you want are the type who lose more than they gain by taking high-level government jobs, who must have their arms twisted to take a job—and may or may not take it when offered. Except in times when there is great national excitement generated about government, you have to go out and look for men of this caliber. Again, 99 percent plus of those recruited by administrative machinery and schemes are useless."

Why have the parties ignored the problems of staffing and what can they do to improve the supply of political executives? Dan Fenn answers that the parties "simply don't have the people. It is a rare guy who comes up through a party or campaign organization who can be Assistant Secretary of Defense for Procurement." President Marver Bernstein of Brandeis has attributed the failure of the patronage system to supply suitable candidates in substantial numbers to the "lack of cohesion within the parties. National party committees are anchored in the state and local parties rather than in the presidential wing of the parties."[14] The Brookings task force, which Bernstein directed, was highly skeptical that political parties could do a better job in supplying competent political executives. Presidents or Cabinet members could not afford to delegate recruitment to such a decentralized party system, the task force argued, and officials not trained through the ranks of the party and believing "competence" and "party activity" to be incompatible would be suspicious of lists of candidates appointed by the party machinery.

Dean Mann's later study for Brookings supported this conclusion: "Party organizations are based on a substantially different substructure of American society than that from which political executives are recruited."[15] Mann does qualify his somewhat negative view by crediting the Democratic Advisory Council with providing a significant source of manpower at the beginning of the Kennedy administration. State governorships have also produced a number of top-level executives in recent administrations. Besides Abraham Ribicoff and Orville Freeman, who served on the Democratic Advisory Council, former governors include Walter Hickel, Luther Hodges, Douglas McKay, John Reed, Frank Murphy, George

---

[14] Bernstein, *The Job of the Federal Executive*, pp. 123, 169–72.
[15] Mann, *The Assistant Secretaries*, p. 273.

Romney and John Volpe. Richard Nixon recruited Robert Finch from the lieutenant governorship of California and Elliot Richardson from the attorney generalship of Massachusetts.

The arguments against an expanded party role in staffing government are not convincing. They assume a basically negative view of parties more appropriate to the era of the spoils system and completely ignore the positive governmental skills and talents found in state and municipal governments and linked, although somewhat ineffectively, through national party bodies. Party policy councils, such as the Democratic Advisory Council and the Republican Coordinating Committee, are only the beginning step of what parties could do to mobilize talent.

The basic problem cannot be attributed to a decentralized party structure or to the lack of party cohesion but rather to a lack of motivation and leadership. One career executive put his finger on the problem: "In my talks with party leaders, I usually find agreement that the party machinery ought to contribute to the supply of qualified executives, but rarely have I found anyone willing to take some concrete action."

Instead of the negative, limited role assigned to the parties in current personnel recruitment practices for government, the emphasis should be placed on positive leadership opportunities that the parties have to staff both the top-level policy positions in an administration and policy advisory posts throughout the government. So long as governmental leaders treat the parties as hordes of office seekers to be fended off or campaign contributors to be mollified with an engraved White House scroll, the potential for parties to contribute talent and substantive ideas to the solving of problems in government will not be realized.

Patronage politics admittedly survives in such widespread forms as governmental consultant positions, surrogate patronage and discretionary favors in construction contracts, insurance funds and franchise awards. That is not the issue. Some forms of patronage are an inevitable by-product of representative government. The question is how such governmental resources are used. As Martin and Susan Tolchin have pointed out in their study of the patronage system, "One can hope that a greater cross-section of the public will enter the two-party system—where the real allocation of rewards originates." Citizens can persuade their leaders "to use patronage more constructively and more equitably."[16] Citizens can also demand that party patronage be used in an open and systematic manner to develop the governmental capabilities of political parties at all levels.

Other Party Services for Government: An Unrealized Potential

Staffing is only one aspect of the problem. The inattention of the parties to the serious full-time business of government has also severely hampered the development and training of political executives. In 1955, the second Hoover Commission commented on both "the shortage of persons possessing both well-developed executive ability and well-developed qualities of political leadership and the failure to develop systematically in American life the capacities which are essential in political executives." Since then, a number of educational institutions and foundations have established or supported degree programs, such as the Harvard Ph.D. in Public Policy offered by the John F. Kennedy School of Government and fellowship or internship programs like the Congressional Fellowship Program of the American Political Science Association. Several governmental agencies such as the Peace Corps, the U.S. Information Agency and the Office of Economic Opportunity have set up intern programs for college and graduate students, although these are of limited value in staffing top political positions. The White House Fellowship Program begun in the mid-1960's has become the most prestigious of the executive branch's programs. Even the civil service recognized the need to train middle-level career executives and established Executive Seminar Centers with visiting faculties at Kings Point, New York (1963), and Berkeley, California (1966), and an advanced program at Charlottesville, Virginia (1968).

---

16 Martin and Susan Tolchin, *To the Victor,* p. 312.

Almost all of these efforts, however, are oriented toward government rather than politics. With the exception of a few relatively small university-affiliated institutes of politics like the Eagleton Institute at Rutgers University, the Hinckley Institute at the University of Utah and the Kennedy Institute of Politics at Harvard, and foundations like the Robert A. Taft Institute of Government in New York, party politics is largely ignored or given very limited treatment. Except for occasional workshops in campaign management and internal party management, the parties themselves have made no significant effort to train candidates, officeholders or political executives. New state legislators, governors, Congressmen and even Presidents arrive on the job with little if any formal training beyond their background experience and, if they are fortunate, a hastily improvised program of briefings by their staff or outside contacts. It should come as no surprise that with so little preparation so many successful candidates stumble or fall over the hazards of implementing policies and programs.

Even if political parties do little to prepare candidates for the responsibilities of public office during the primary and general election campaigns, they are in a unique position to help orient and train new political executives during the transition period and while the party is in office. Since, according to the Brookings Round Table, "most political executives and some career executives, particularly in emergency periods, are recruited from the business world, the universities, or other governments, with little or no previous contact with federal administration,"[17] effective orientation of these newcomers to the Washington bureaucracy is a pressing demand for all administrations. The rapid turnover in political executives (about once every two years on the average for under secretaries and assistant secretaries) only compounds such problems. The situation is similar in state capitals and county seats across the country.

Among the more perplexing aspects of the Washington community for the new political executive is the Congress,

---

[17] Bernstein, *The Job of the Federal Executive*, p. 176.

with its elaborate committee system, dual processes of authorization and appropriation, formidable prerogatives and powers of administrative surveillance and its institution of partisan criticism. Parties can provide an excellent bridge for establishing contacts, communication and reference points between an administration and Congress as well as with citizens and various interest groups. They can introduce Washington newcomers to the wealth of talented people from former administrations who still reside in the Washington community or visit frequently—the Averell Harrimans and Arthur Burnses of the Democratic and Republican parties. They can brief the political novice on the unique institutions of Washington and their connections with the politics of regions, states and cities—the national press corps, the national interest-group lobbies, the main Washington law firms and their latest counterpart, the public interest law firms.

As elementary as such orientation programs may seem, neither political party has instituted them in advance of taking office, in spite of the fact that since the Presidential Transition Act of 1963, $900,000 of public funds has been authorized to help defray the costs of party transition between the November election and January inauguration. Orientation seminars and introductory programs for new Congressmen and top-level administrators are left to outside organizations like the American Political Science Association and the Brookings Institution to initiate.

Parties remain almost totally illiterate when it comes to understanding the political and governmental importance of the civil service. Although there were more than three million civilian government employees in the federal executive branch in 1971 and an additional 10.1 million employees of state and local governments—about 16 percent of the total working force—neither party has established programs to define the party's role in reviewing the civil service or to monitor and upgrade the governmental service.

Because of its better communications with public employee unions, the Democratic party during its party reform hearings reviewed proposals to amend the Hatch Act so as to ensure civil servants greater political rights. Individual Republican candidates and campaign managers have raised questions about the political role of the postal unions, the most thoroughly unionized governmental service, but no party body has pursued the subject even though unions like the American Federation of State, County and Municipal Employees have begun raising a million-dollar fund for direct contributions to congressional and presidential campaigns,[18] and the American Federation of Government Employees has formed a political education committee to promote voter registration among its members.

While the White House has developed some data on presidential appointees and individual departments have compiled biographies and photos of top career-level staff, neither the White House nor political party headquarters has any idea who the top career civil servants are, during which administration they entered government, what their policy role has been, or what if any partisan involvement they have had during their careers. Parties, however, need such data on career civil servants to make intelligent political appointments within departments and agencies. If enacted, the Federal Executive Service proposed by the Nixon administration would require even greater presidential and party understanding of the career civil service. Under the proposal, the ratio of political executives to career executives would be set at 26 percent to 74 percent in the roughly 7,000 positions at the top three grade levels of government service (GS 16, 17 and 18). Career civil servants, now frozen into specific positions, could be kept in their current assignments, promoted to higher positions, moved to other posts in the government, or demoted. Some administration aides feel that the plan will enable the President to place political executives in positions most directly related to his programs at the same time that it will encourage a more responsible civil service. Others feel that the reform does not go far enough and that more than 26 percent of the top

---

[18] Charles Culhane, "Public Employees' Union Stresses Federal Action to Get More State, Local Clout," *National Journal,* October 16, 1971, pp. 2082–91.

positions of the government should be allocated for the President.

One senior civil servant has pointed to stagnation in the middle rather than the top ranges of the bureaucracy as "the greatest disaster area in government." Governmental personnel advance to the limit of their abilities and then are frozen into position through civil-service regulations. The steady unionization of these tiers of the bureaucracy has added further inflexibilities. An incoming administration is limited to bringing in political executives, often with little experience in government, at or near the top of a department or agency and is thus not able to penetrate, shake up or move the middle-level bureaucracy.

Insulated and unimaginative, the parties continue to ignore e *e and municipal administrations as a source of ideas, skills . levant problem-solving experience. Officeholders like emocratic and Republican governors and attorneys gen- or mayors and elected county executives do not funnel ble people in the party from county to state to national rnment often because of intraparty rivalries and insecurity. anizations like the Democratic and Republican Gov- ors Associations cannot sustain the simplest of clearing- se functions. Democratic and Republican mayors have both d to rely on the services of the National League of Cities– U.S. Conference of Mayors for basic staff services. Neither congressional party has developed a program for involving the talents of its governors, state constitutional officers, state legislators or mayors. Although Cabinet departments have federal–state liaison officers with the governors, incumbent administrations have not developed close working relationships between Cabinet officials and their party's governors.

In filling key positions and developing new policy ideas, the Democrats have made somewhat better use than the Republicans of the talented and experienced personnel in the universities and foundations—the so-called knowledge industry. Some Republicans, acutely sensitive to their party's failings in this regard, observe that the Democrats command a network in the universities, a feeder system of senior people and talent spotters with ties to Democratic administrations since the 1930's. The Democrats, they point out, are "smart enough to draw on schools of public administration" while the Republicans appear "afraid even to go near them."

Neither party, however, has systematically encouraged and engaged the creative resources of the major academic and research institutions in developing new approaches and party policies. Incumbent administrations have taken only marginal steps in this direction through presidential task forces, White House advisers (notably the President's Science Adviser and the Office of Science and Technology), and departmental staff; once in office the parties quickly disband any policymaking units they may have created, such as the Democratic Advisory Council (1956–60) or the Republican Coordinating Committee (1965–68). Almost by default, major private foundations have performed this policy-research role for the Democratic party. Some Republicans have accordingly pointed out the predominant position that Democrats enjoy on foundation boards and taken the opportunity to criticize foundations as an integral part of the "liberal establishment."

Patrick J. Buchanan, a Nixon adviser and a conservative Republican, agrees that most conservatives fail to realize the influence of the liberal academic institutions and foundations. "The Brookings Institution is almost a government in exile," he pointed out. "Their *Agenda for the Nation* is an alternative liberal program for government." Buchanan thinks that conservatives should establish their own foundations and institutes rather than seek token representation on the boards of liberal institutions. Melvin Laird, as Secretary of Defense, urged a group of corporate executives to contribute funds to the conservative think tank, the American Enterprise Institute for Public Policy Research, so that Republicans could support second-level Nixon administration appointees (if Republicans lost the 1972 election) to run their own government in exile.

A party's transition from government to opposition is almost as chaotic and wasteful as it is for a party coming from opposition to power. The party out of office never systematically prepares itself to govern. Neither major party has adopted the British "shadow Cabinet," although the new People's Party has debated the idea of such a party body to check on the departments of government. Proposals to strengthen the role of the opposition leader made more than 15 years ago have not even been discussed by the parties. The parties make virtually no effort to draw on the experience and talents of former members of an administration in order to develop alternative party programs and to prepare to run the next party administration on a national or state level. While it may be difficult to assemble talent and take control of government, it is nothing short of scandalous that the parties let recruited and trained talent waste away after leaving office. Commented an official in the Nixon administration, "Two years after you're out of office only 10 people will remember that you were an assistant secretary and five of them won't care."

Reform Democrats like Stephen Schlesinger, editor of the defunct *New Democrat,* have criticized their party's role as the "out" party. In 1971, Schlesinger reprimanded Democratic intellectuals for "not doing their jobs either. They should be, by now, rigorously goading the leadership into re-examining its own myths and they should be advocating fresh programmatic solutions. Their protean contributions to government both out of power, as a critical intelligence, and in power, as an idea bank for Democratic Presidents, seem to have dissipated in this new era."[19] According to Joseph Califano, former White House Special Assistant and party General Counsel, "What we Democrats need urgently is a Vatican II —an *aggiornamento*—to raise our vision and in turn provide hope for a troubled citizenry."[20]

Recommendations: A New Problem-Solving Orientation for Party Government

The demand for effective government in the 1970's provides important new opportunities and incentives for party develop-

---

[19] Stephen Schlesinger, "A Party Without Ideas," *New York Times,* January 9, 1971.
[20] Joseph Califano, Jr., "Vatican II for a Party," *New Democrat* (New York), February 1971, p. 11.

ment. Just as revelations of abuses in the selection of convention delegates in 1968 catalyzed a movement for party reform, so too can wider public knowledge of the dereliction of party responsibility for government inspire a public outcry for and insistence on dramatically improved governmental performance through modernized parties. American parties have always been more pragmatic than ideological. But in some respects parties have not been pragmatic enough. They have not taken the most elementary steps to build a capacity to govern; and until they do, better-articulated party programs by themselves will do little to solve the current crisis in government.

Recommendation 1. Parties should develop broad new tests of the ability to govern which would be applied as an integral part of the nominating and electoral process.

Before parties can assume new governmental responsibilities, they must take their traditional function of nominating candidates more seriously. Parties have presented candidates to the electorate without any discernible test of their qualifications to hold high elective office.

As an integral part of the nominating and electoral process, parties should develop broad new tests of the ability to govern and apply them to candidates they support. In the long run, the party will be held responsible at the polls for the performance of its elected officeholders. The party label or endorsement should mean that its candidates meet certain party-defined standards, that they are fit to govern. Some of the means for improved selection of presidential and vice-presidential candidates discussed earlier could be adapted for other offices. Gubernatorial and congressional candidates could, for example, testify before state party policy commissions, and representative citizen commissions on candidate recruitment could attempt to specify the necessary qualifications for state and local offices.

Party screening committees through open party hearings and field research could review the administrative and political qualifications of candidates seeking party nomination, as bar associations have done in screening prospective judges.

Although nominations would ultimately be made by the party primary or convention, the qualifications of candidates would be a matter of party and public record. A similar screening process for top political appointees could alert party leaders to conflict of interest situations and potential scandals before appointments were announced. Parties could encourage candidates to take an official leave of absence from public and party offices while campaigning for another office.

The parties should also face the difficult problem of the lack of any medical examination or test for candidates to public office.[21] Parties could, for example, request that their candidates take medical examinations, an accepted professional procedure in major American corporations, universities and other large organizations that would be in the interest of both the candidates and the public. Candidates with a history of medical problems would still be free to seek office but the public would have the benefit of such information. Parties could institute reasonable procedures for replacing incumbents who have become senile or physically incapacitated.

Candidates for major executive office, especially for President, Vice President and governor, could also be encouraged to make public the names and relevant political and governmental experience of their chief policy advisers and potential Cabinet choices, as George Wallace did provisionally in late 1971. Such information, while not committing a candidate to Cabinet and executive staff appointments before an election, would give party delegates and voters a more complete picture of the prospective administration they are being asked to nominate or elect.

Recommendation 2. Parties should promote a new concept of staffing an administration and develop long-range programs for identifying, recruiting and training political executives.

---

21 History affords abundant examples of how disease and ill health have affected national and international policymaking, especially during times of crisis and physical and mental stress on decision makers. See Hugh L'Etang, *The Pathology of Leadership: A History of the Effects of Disease on 20th-Century Leaders* (New York: Hawthorn Books, 1970).

At the heart of an expanded governmental role for parties is a new concept for staffing an administration. The parties have not been used effectively by Presidents, governors, mayors, Congressmen and other elected officials to recruit talent to government.

Elected officials and party leaders should work cooperatively to modernize the patronage function in government. Parties should function as talent hunters and talent brokers, identifying, recruiting and training talented individuals in the parties, the private sector and the government. One model of talent recruitment is provided by the experience of the Office of Strategic Services in the 1940's under the leadership of General William "Wild Bill" Donovan. Donovan succeeded in assembling some of America's most able men and women for critical national assignments, many of whom, more than two decades later, continue to serve their country at the highest levels of government.[22] Through their policy units and contacts with candidate organizations, parties could be constantly on the alert for new talent. Party offices for personnel development could assist in the scheduling and itineraries of party and government leaders to facilitate meetings with informed party members and citizens and the exchange of ideas whenever possible.

A party program for training political executives and staff could be implemented at several levels:

A national institute of politics with affiliated regional centers could be developed for the education and training of political executives as a matter of national priority. While the military bureaucracy has its service academies, the State Department its Foreign Service Institute and private graduate university programs, and the civil service its own elaborate educational complex, no institutions exist for the training of legislators, political executives and political staff. A national institute of politics could sponsor a range of programs, including academic courses leading to advanced degrees, special lectures and short-term workshops, summer-school sessions for national conven-

---

[22] See Corey Ford, *Donovan of OSS* (Boston: Little, Brown, 1970).

tion delegates, transition round tables for new state administrations and political internships with national and state parties.
It could also make its facilities available to the parties and the
public, perhaps developing extension courses for the Public
Broadcasting Service or experimenting with the "open university" concept of the British Broadcasting Corporation so
that interested citizens could enroll easily.

Parties themselves should also assume some formal responsibility for training as well as screening their candidates.
Party candidates in a general election (and where possible in
primary and convention contests such as the presidential
primaries) should be able to call on the national and state party
committees for briefings on public policy matters. Party committees, through their policy commissions or other means,
could organize pools of governmental and public policy
advisers to assist in the training of candidates for public office
and the briefing of newly elected officials in assuming their
responsibilities. Such advisers might run policy seminars for
candidates on a regional basis or be assigned individually or
in teams to specific campaigns. Candidates for major offices
could benefit especially from regular briefings on foreign-policy
issues.

A limited number of slots in the middle level of the bureaucracy could be reserved for political appointees beyond
the allotment of Schedule C positions of a top policy-deter-
mining character or requiring a confidential working relationship with a policy official. These middle-level positions could
be used by the parties to train personnel for policy positions in
future administrations at the same time that they could help
break tendencies toward stagnation in the middle-level civil
service.

An important actual and potential source of political executives and governmental personnel that could be developed by
the parties is the professional staff system of the Congress.
Previously recommended partisan congressional staff would
provide the parties with a government-wide reserve of trained
professionals and an excellent base for training party professionals for government. The party out of power could use the
partisan professional staff that is assigned to legislative com-

mittees to develop party policy alternatives and to assist party policy commissions as part of a shadow government.

Parties could take the lead in developing a reserve of political executives for appointment to national and state administrations. The National Defense Executive Reserve, a pool of some 4,000 men and women who are available to fill government positions in the event of a national emergency, could serve as a model for the parties. An administration could systematically use and develop the myriad advisory boards in government to give party members and interested citizens who wish to apply continuing experience and contact with government departments and agencies. Similar opportunities would also be afforded through new advisory committees to Congress.

Recommendation 3. Parties should assist government in policy implementation as well as policy formulation through such means as establishing permanent party policy commissions and developing effective transition and evaluation programs.

The current crisis in government is due as much to failures in governmental operations as it is to a lack of clear policy leadership. While government bureaucracies are charged with the responsibility of implementing policy determined by political executives, party responsibility should include the continuing evaluation of governmental performance. Party assistance in government operation could be provided at several points:

Permanent party policy commissions, recommended as part of modernized national committees, could provide the parties with a continuing base of experienced personnel and policy competence. When the party assumes control of the government, party policy commissions could serve as a source of political executives, party advisers and consultants. When the party leaves the administration, the commissions could serve as nuclei for alumni clubs or associations, such as "Republicans from Interior" or "Democrats from HUD."

Drawing on the resources of such party policy commissions, the parties could establish party boards of directors or advisers for individual government departments and agencies modeled on the experience of corporate boards of directors. These party advisers, served by full-time party professional staff, could meet four or more times a year with an agency head or Cabinet secretary and his top aides to review the programs and performance in relation to the party platform, identify problem areas and suggest appropriate party or administration action. Such advisers could serve as an "early warning system" to an administration that its programs were in trouble and as a source of ideas for new administration initiatives. They could also perform political intelligence and special assignments through party fact-finding teams that department heads would prefer not to give to the career civil service.

The parties need to develop more systematic methods for tapping the intellectual and personnel resources of the knowledge industry—the universities, private research organizations and foundation-sponsored research projects that comprise an ever more influential sector of American life. Party research staffs could, through personal visits and WATS line telephone calls, systematically interrogate public-policy experts on means for improving governmental performance.

Problem-solving research on public policy offers opportunities for bipartisan cooperation. The parties could jointly sponsor a series of issue-study groups to define major policy problems and alternative approaches for the 1970's. As an example, the Educational Staff Seminar of the George Washington University's Institute for Educational Leadership, funded in part by a Ford Foundation grant, has involved professional staff members from both major parties concerned with development of federal policy in the field of education in an ambitious program of Washington seminars and field trips.

At the beginning of a new administration, Cabinet and other key appointees could meet with party representatives to discuss their governmental responsibilities and relevant party policy interests. Representative party commissions with no formal authority in the appointment process could hold open party hearings during the confirmation period to enable party members to express their views, build lines of communication between the party and political executives, and familiarize appointees with legitimate concerns of parties in governmental performance.

As the federal government continues to decentralize its administrative structure along regional lines, national parties could establish similar regional party commissions to meet with appointees for regional office.

The parties could develop, fund and staff comprehensive transition and political orientation programs for new national and state administrations. Although the Presidential Transition Act of 1963 answers at least part of the problem, parties need to devote as much time and effort to transition programs as they give to staging party conventions and planning campaigns. National parties could offer transition assistance to state parties that request it through task forces of party staff, consultants and former officeholders in the same way that they offer technical campaign services.

The national chairman of the party in power could establish a party evaluation unit to review the overall governmental performance of the administration and report its findings periodically to the President and administration officials. The President and key White House staff are preoccupied with operational policymaking and hence lack the time to make such regular assessments and to maintain the extensive contacts with state and party leaders necessary to measure party reaction to administration actions.

The opposition party could undertake an evaluation of its own performance as an alternative government out of power instead of simply criticizing the administration's record.

The party in power could also undertake a full review of its governmental performance at the end of its second year in office, reassess administration program objectives, and set the major themes for the two years preceding the presidential election. Such a mid-term review could infuse new strength in an administration and might effectively be related to new interim national party conventions. Party advisory and evaluation units would accustom parties to think about their responsibilities for government on a continuing basis. Their successful operation could help to increase party responsiveness and problem-solving capabilities while establishing a new public reputation for the political parties.

Recommendation 4. The parties should explore and implement steps to build a party capability for providing party organization and information services to the government.

If parties are to assume a broader role in government, they need to develop means for increasing their involvement in and responsiveness to the executive and legislative process.

The national party in control of the presidency could, for example, establish and staff a party office in the White House to function as a party communications center and service bureau within the administration. Instead of occasionally visiting the White House, the national chairman could divide his time between the White House office and national party headquarters and work to improve the linkages between party and government. At least one deputy party chairman for governmental affairs could be appointed to assume responsibility for the day-to-day operation of the party White House office. The national chairman or his deputy could attend White House staff, Cabinet and subcabinet policy and congressional leadership meetings, including meetings on the preparation of the budget.

Party leaders and members could use the facilities of the office to make appointments and obtain background information on administration programs. The office could set up regular substantive briefings between White House political advisers, party leaders, national committee staff, and administration officials.

When a party is out of power, a smaller division for governmental affairs headed by a deputy chairman could carry on many of these functions in the party headquarters.

In view of the important party-related functions that the President's political advisers exercise, the parties could formulate and recommend to the President specific means to achieve greater party accountability on the part of White House political advisers. The parties could propose to the President more formal clearance procedures for such appointments, a party audit of campaign funds processed through the White House, and safeguards against conflict of interest and bonding requirements comparable to those instituted for party headquarters personnel.

The party national committees could establish party divisions on the civil service to study the political role of the civil service and to develop a broader party understanding of governmental bureaucracy. These party divisions could collect background information on top civil servants and agency performance to assist in the appointment process. They could study the involvement of civil servants in partisan politics and recommend appropriate changes in the Hatch Act rules. In view of the size of the governmental work force, the divisions could also assist in developing party policy positions and programs designed to attract the support of government employees.

Party national committees could assume the new function of serving as a repository for key administration records, to give the parties a permanent information base on the details of running a national administration. The decision of the Nixon administration to record documents on the Miracode information-retrieval system of the Republican National Committee is a commendable initial step in this direction. Retiring Presidents and their administrations could make the building of party capabilities for future administrations a major objective through the transfer of copies of pertinent documents and files to party headquarters and extensive debriefings with party personnel. Such a program of party information would supplement and need not in any way limit the usual procedures of transfer of information to government archives or presidential libraries.

VII

Citizens and the Parties: Can the Amateurs Play Politics?

The extent to which political parties can be made effective instruments of self-government depends ultimately on the level of citizen competence in politics and the willingness of citizens to invest political resources in the parties. Yet today most citizens are looking elsewhere than the parties. As a national survey by a Washington *Post* team concluded, Americans "want to believe that someone, or some group, will bring change. But they are no longer looking to the political parties as that vehicle."[1] At the same time, the record of organized citizen political activity in association with the parties or independent from them, of what might be termed the citizen sector, has not been encouraging.

Citizen politics in the United States has been a procession of temporary crusades for candidates and causes, tapping untold efforts, skills and financial resources, but too often with little sustained impact. The political landscape is littered with the bleached skeletons of citizen endeavors of every political coloration, from Barry Goldwater's Free Society Association for conservative political education to the Dissenting and Concerned Democrats of the last years of Lyndon B. Johnson's administration. Elaborate national citizen organizations for Eisenhower, Stevenson, Nixon, Goldwater and Humphrey carefully erected for lengthy presidential campaigns are among the first parts to be disassembled and forgotten. The "new politics" citizen

---

[1] David S. Broder and Haynes Johnson, "Voters Look to the Man, Not Party," Washington *Post*, December 16, 1971.

groups of the late 1960's and 1970's, with their emphasis on ad hoc organization and antibureaucratic forms of leadership, promise an even greater rate of organizational turnover and mortality. Scores of ad hoc antiwar and national-priorities citizen groups could spring up around the country and lay siege to the nation's capital to protest the American invasion of Cambodia, but one year later few traces remained of the citizen army of students, professors, lawyers, young professionals and housewives that had manned the organizational front.

To be sure, citizen groups have achieved limited and at times even notable successes, and talented citizen activists move from one generation of organizations to another, carrying their enthusiasm and experience. But in other important regards citizen politics has failed. It has certainly failed to realize the vital contribution that citizens can make to the political parties and the political process. It has failed to provide the basic elements of organizational permanence and continuity that can encourage and develop the spontaneity and vitality of citizen participation. It has failed by diverting scarce political resources of manpower and money that might have been spent for political reform and innovation to often ineffective letterhead organizations which have accomplished little. Perhaps the greatest failure of citizen groups lies in the disillusionment of highly motivated, enthusiastic members who have been lost to the political process for the future, in the growing number of Americans who are losing hope that they can ever influence their government through the political system.[2]

---

[2] In his study of changes in the American electorate, Philip Converse of the University of Michigan's Survey Research Center took note of "the sequence of national catastrophes, disruptions and blunders" that occurred during the 1960's—including the three shocking political assassinations, resentment in large sectors of the population concerning official pressures toward school desegregation, race riots and campus disorders, and the increasing weariness and frustration with the war in Vietnam that the government could not seem to win or otherwise terminate. These, he said, "seem adequate to account for a considerable loss of confidence in the government and politics on the part of the public." (Philip E. Converse, "Change in the American Electorate," paper prepared for inclusion in the Russell Sage volume *The Human Meaning of Social Change*, May 1970, p. 102.)

It is a primary thesis of this book that effective and responsive government and modernized participant parties cannot exist apart from vigorous organized citizen activity. Citizens in turn can increase their effectiveness in politics by modernizing and using the political parties rather than ignoring them. Party politics and a new sense of public citizenship can and should complement each other. The citizen does not face the antithetical choice of whether he should be active in the political parties or in citizen organizations. He can do both.

The development of the citizen sector is of vital interest to citizen parties. By helping to train people in political skills and building citizen competence in government, citizen organizations can become a primary source of new members and leaders for expanded party organizations. By involving citizens in practical governmental issues, such organizations can also help to introduce a problem-solving orientation to the parties. They can broaden the public constituency supporting party reform and improved governmental performance. And by preserving a degree of independence from the formal party organizations, they can provide public scrutiny conducive to new concepts of party accountability.

Ultimately the question is not whether political parties have lost their relevance to most Americans but whether citizens can develop the political competence to govern themselves, whatever organizational alternatives are involved. Representative politics has always been difficult, and it will become even more difficult in the 1970's as more groups of citizens demand more adequate representation. This is the central point: the only answer a democratic polity has to the problems of self-government is self-government. The development of citizen political skills is essential if Americans are to exercise their capacity to form and change their governments, to set the general directions of public policy through political contest and bargaining, and to influence the specific decisions of public and private institutions that affect their daily lives. The alternatives are either rule by political elites supported by a passive, acquiescent and/or alienated mass public or the suspension of politics itself in favor of some form of dictatorship.

Genuine citizen politics in the coming decade requires more

than aroused citizens willing to act. It requires a new group of political entrepreneurs and investors who can build appropriate party and citizen institutions, and it requires the systematic development and accumulation of citizen skills in politics as well as new means to increase organizational competence and continuity.

The Citizen Sector: "Tomorrow We Must Get Organized"

Whatever cohesiveness and continuity the citizen sector appears to have is given it by umbrella or national organizations that attempt to coordinate and focus the activities of member groups or a mass membership. Many of the umbrella organizations are identified with a particular part of the political spectrum and usually are aligned with one of the two major parties. The American Conservative Union works with conservative members of both major parties as well as conservative third parties at the state level, although its activities have been concentrated in the Republican party. In the early 1960's, the Republican Citizens Committee attempted to provide partywide services. The Council of Republican Organizations coordinated moderate Republican citizen groups in the post-Goldwater nomination period. The New Democratic Coalition has sought to organize the left liberal wing of the Democratic party. Common Cause was launched in August 1970 as a nonpartisan "third force" seeking to reform and revitalize the two major parties, although officials of one party at least consider it liberal Democratic in orientation.[3] The New American Movement is currently attempting to focus the political activities of the radical Left.

Other important national umbrella organizations coordinate the activities of cause groups. The Vietnam Moratorium during its short lifetime served as a national focus for the activities

---

[3] "Democrats Dominate Common Cause Vietnam Lobbying Effort," *MONDAY* (Republican National Committee, Washington, D.C.), May 31, 1971, p. 5; "Common Cause Continues to Parrot Democrat Line," *MONDAY*, April 12, 1971, p. 7; and John W. Gardner, "Charges of Partisanship Won't Deter Us," *Common Cause Report from Washington*, May 1971, p. 12.

of antiwar groups. The Leadership Conference on Civil Rights represents itself as "a coalition of 115 autonomous national civil-rights, labor, religious, and fraternal organizations seeking to secure full equality for all Americans through the enactment and enforcement of effective laws." The well-staffed and -funded Clergy and Laity Concerned conceived a whole series of coalitional efforts among militant antiwar groups and publishes a successful movement newspaper, *American Report*. The caucus form of umbrella organization characterizes much of the 1972 political action of women, blacks, Chicanos and youth.

Most umbrella organizations and coalitions, however, have failed to develop a lasting structure of communications and services in the citizen sector. They are essentially ad hoc and short-term in nature, forming and reforming with major new issues or cleavages within the parties. A closer examination of the recent experience of the conservative movement, the Democratic liberals and the Republican moderates demonstrates the uneven development and limited success of broadly based citizen efforts.

The conservative movement has been one of the more successful examples of citizen politics. With the founding of the *National Review* in 1955, publisher William A. Rusher recounts, "Conservatism began pulling away out of the Republican party." During the latter years of the Eisenhower administration, a well-financed network of conservative organizations, what can be described as the conservative apparatus, developed in parallel to the Republican party organization. In 1960, a conservative youth auxiliary, Young Americans for Freedom, was established. By early 1961, as the Kennedy administration came into office and the old machine of former New York Governor Thomas E. Dewey and former Attorney General Herbert Brownell, Jr., atrophied, conservative political strategists like Rusher and consultant F. Clifton White decided to return to the Republican party. "The Republican party was ripe for a change," Rusher observed. "It was ready to readjust its power structure for a new coalition." In Goldwater's nomination at the 1964 Republican convention, they won a stunning victory. Unlike other citizen movements which folded once their policies were adopted, the conservatives have remained a relatively cohesive force in American politics. After 1968, they maintained active pressure on an incumbent Republican administration, issuing periodic critiques and funding the challenge to President Nixon in some 1972 primaries by Congressman John M. Ashbrook (R-Ohio), a former Chairman of the American Conservative Union.

Conservative political groups have been relatively well integrated into a conservative apparatus that includes nominally bipartisan groups like Americans for Constitutional Action and Young Americans for Freedom; pressure groups like United Republicans of America which openly attempt to influence the course of the Republican party; nonpartisan tax-exempt foundations or research institutions such as the American Enterprise Institute, the Georgetown Center for Strategic Studies, and the Hoover Institute at Stanford;[4] and parts of existing Republican machinery such as the Teen Age Republicans, College Young Republicans and Young Republican National Federation, all of which receive substantial conservative financial and/or leadership resources.

The apparatus prints and distributes millions of pieces of conservative literature annually. *Human Events* serves as the movement's newspaper and the *National Review* its magazine. Conservatives target convention delegates, party officials, local community leaders and business executives for special distribution of material like *Republican Battle Line*, the newsletter of the American Conservative Union, and mass-produced paperback books. Arlington House publishes and the Conservative Book Club distributes to a national membership major conservative books like F. Clifton White's *Suite 3505: The Story of the Draft Goldwater Movement*, Kevin Phillips's *The Emerging Republican Majority*, and Peter Witónski's *The Wisdom of Conservatism*.

Besides their national organizations, conservatives have established political parties, conservative councils or conservative unions in a number of states. The Conservative Party of

---

[4] See Berkeley Rice, "The Cold-War College Think Tanks: Defense— or Offense?," *Washington Monthly*, June 1969, pp. 22–34.

New York, after successfully electing James L. Buckley in 1970 as the first third-party conservative U.S. Senator from a major industrial state, became a prototype for conservative pressure on moderate Republican state party organizations in such other states as Massachusetts and Michigan.

The strengths of the conservative apparatus are impressive: organizational ability, ideological commitment, a high degree of unity, powerful financial backing and tactical political skill. A number of factors account for its continuing impact. Just as the Republicans, in contrast to the Democrats, have developed a more professional party organization and closer relationships with the political consulting industry, it is reasonable to assume that a similar professional and businesslike orientation will characterize the more conservative wing of the party. The apparatus itself is bound together through interlocking director- ates and membership of key organizations. The roster of of- ficers, directors and speakers of the American Conservative Union reads like a *Who's Who* of the conservative movement.

Although engaged in a wide variety of activities, conserva- tive groups have also achieved an unusual degree of coopera- tion and coordination. Various organizations in the apparatus exchange or share staff, office facilities, guest editorials and feature columns, and there is even evidence suggesting an internal personnel promotion system. Regular staff communica- tion and strategy-planning sessions provide another important means of coordination. The informal specialization by function and constituency within the apparatus helps to minimize internecine warfare. The apparatus is well funded and the various organizations do not always have to compete with one another for survival. They share a valuable fund-raising re- source in Richard Viguerie, former executive director of Young Americans for Freedom, whose direct-mail political consulting firm works for conservative candidates and conservative organi- zations.

Perhaps the most important powerful unifying factor has been the conscious long-term effort to build an ideologically and organizationally distinct conservative movement in Ameri- can politics. Conservatives like publisher William Rusher, columnist William F. Buckley, Jr., and commentator M.

Stanton Evans have articulated a distinct conservative philosophy and political strategy to contest what they considered to be the domination of the political parties, media and other national institutions by "the liberal Establishment," to create a conservative base within the liberal-dominated citizen sector and to gain firm control of the Republican party. As a result, the conservatives during the 1960's systematically recruited and trained a citizen cadre that, though limited in its base, currently has no equal in organizational strength and capability in American party politics. One recent study concluded that the Republican party after the 1964 elections was "a high participation party with an amateur base composed of right wing ideologues."[5]

In contrast to the success of the conservative apparatus, the efforts of both Republican moderate and Democratic liberal citizen groups demonstrate many of the fundamental weaknesses of the citizen sector. As a result of the strong conservative movement in the Republican party and the associated intraparty struggle, numerous moderate Republican organizations were established in the 1960's including *Advance* magazine, the Republican Citizens Committee, the Ripon Society, the National Negro Republican Assembly, Republicans for Progress, the California Republican League, the Republican Advance, and the umbrella Council of Republican Organizations. By 1970 most of these groups had disappeared or become inactive. A few moderate Republican organizations, like the Association of Republicans for Educated Action in Philadelphia, were active at the state level, while a number of other groups merged as chapters of the Ripon Society, an organization of young Republican business, academic and professional men and women.

Because of its ideological position and its emphasis on research and publication, the Ripon Society has been given as much attention by the press as conservative groups such as the American Conservative Union and Young Americans for

---

[5] David Nexon, "Asymmetry in the Political System: Occasional Activists in the Republican and Democratic Parties, 1956–1964," *American Political Science Review*, September 1971, p. 717.

Freedom. With about a dozen chapters, however, the society cannot compare with the conservative apparatus. The Ripon *Forum*'s subscription base, considerably larger than the society's active membership, had not passed 2,500 in 1971. The Ripon Society, unlike the conservatives, has paid little attention to Republican party organization. During the 1968 campaign, its major party effort was the publication of a directory of national convention delegates. Ripon has sought instead to build its influence in research and policy on such topics as revenue sharing, the draft and Vietnam.

Since 1968, some Ripon leaders have attempted to define a more ambitious role for the society by lobbying in Washington through the post-Cambodia Project Purse Strings, by emulating the Vietnam Moratorium "network," and by sponsoring a conference of moderate Republicans in March 1970 at Airlie House in Warrenton, Virginia. Following the example of conservatives, Ripon leaders have also set up a separate tax-exempt foundation for policy research (the Sabre Foundation) and a fund-raising mechanism for moderate Republican candidates (the One Per Cent Club). In mid-1971, the society hired its first full-time paid political director and began a three-year program of political organization budgeted at $150,000.

The visibility of the Ripon Society and the ability of moderate Republicans to maintain an electoral base in key industrial states and a voice in the U.S. Senate have distracted attention from the growing organizational vacuum in the moderate Republican citizen sector. A more accurate estimate of the effectiveness of moderate Republican groups is found in the losing convention platform and nomination contests of 1964 and 1968, in their declining influence on Republican National Committee programs such as big cities and minorities, and in the absence of a fund-raising letter for moderate Republican candidates in 1970 for the first election in more than a decade. In spite of the continued organizational weakness of moderates, however, there are apparently still enough substantial financial contributors to moderate Republican candidates and causes to sustain Ripon and individual special projects as well as to have funded modestly the 1971–72 national presidential campaign of Congressman Paul N. McCloskey, Jr.

Whether moderate Republicans can build a broad base of citizen involvement and organizational competence during the 1970's remains to be proved.

The liberal Democratic side of the citizen sector since the late 1960's has included the McCarthy campaign of 1968, the cluster of citizen and official Democratic party bodies and commissions dedicated to party reform, the Vietnam Moratorium, and the post–Cambodia-Kent student and citizen groups that worked in the 1970 campaign and youth registration efforts for 1972. The most ambitious of these was the New Democratic Coalition, which set out after the 1968 election with a commendable catalogue of objectives: to provide an information clearinghouse for news of politics and issues; to provide staff and program assistance to selected candidates and projects; to disseminate educational materials on important areas of political, social and economic concern; to identify, help organize and charter indigenous leadership and grass-roots participation in every state; and to develop, through study groups, programs for the 1970's. In mid-1969, the NDC claimed affiliates in 32 states and a membership of 65,000, but by early 1970 the organization had accumulated a $20,000 debt, closed its national office in Washington, and lost its first and second executive directors. Since its Chicago convention in February 1970, the NDC, under a new chairman, Marvin L. Madeson of St. Louis, has resisted attempts of some Democrats and the national press to bury it as a functioning national organization. It issued an informative 50-page booklet and began publication of a national newsletter. Individual state organizations such as those in Iowa and Washington have also continued their programs and newsletters.

Although hampered by financial and organizational problems, the NDC has had some impact on all levels of Democratic party organization. It pressed the Democratic National Committee on party reform and won representation on both the McGovern and O'Hara reform commissions. Much of its reform activity, however, has taken place at the state and local level, reflecting the regional and local autonomy of the organization. It successfully challenged regular party organizations, capturing party chairmanships in the largest counties in New

Mexico and Washington. In New York, the NDC is regarded by some as the most powerful single faction in the splintered state party.

During its relatively short existence, the NDC has also established an innovative political internship program in the 1970 campaigns, cosponsored with a committee of physicians a conference on the public policy aspects of medicine, endorsed black organizational efforts in Alabama, and set up a legal defense fund for students arrested in Berkeley in the spring of 1969.

In spite of these accomplishments, the New Democratic Coalition remains, according to New Jersey leader Daniel M. Gaby, "a white, suburban, middle class operation." Another state chairman characterized the NDC as "a movement without an organization that had still not solved its organizational problems." It has not successfully established a national head-quarters to focus the activities of a confederation of state organizations. Former NDC Co-chairman Paul Schrade, Western director of the United Automobile Workers, has expressed his deep concern that the NDC has been unable to mount an effective challenge to the policy positions of a Republican adminis-tration or to organize the Democratic party's most loyal constituencies (black, brown, liberal and blue-collar) to par-ticipate fully in electoral politics. Even its major program emphasis through 1972—assistance in the implementation of the McGovern Commission guidelines—has been taken over by such other organizations as the Americans for Democratic Action, the Center for Political Reform, and Common Cause.

In addition to the NDC, the most important organization to survive the anti-Vietnam war movement is "the network," as it is referred to, a group of about 50 activists and another 500 part-time associates who are scattered around the country but who can be mobilized by telephone for future organ-izational activity. What form such activity might take is unclear from the statements of two Vietnam Moratorium leaders. David Mixner believes that citizens can be recruited for politics only through periodic "waves" of involvement, such as the McCarthy campaign, the Moratorium and the 1970 con-gressional elections. Sam Brown has concluded that "not enough

students have the stature, capacity, or inclination to run a
tightly disciplined peace movement."[6] He argues that the new
peace leadership should be composed instead of Senators,
Congressmen, governors, mayors and businessmen and that the
renewed peace movement should take the National Rifle Association as an organizational model, though an "unpleasant" one.

Aside from the network, the loose structure of the New
Democratic Coalition and the interconnections of old liberal
establishment groups like Americans for Democratic Action,
civil-rights organizations and various trade unions, there is little
evidence of an infrastructure comparable to that of the conservatives among the recent generation of liberal Democratic
activities. To date, the McCarthy-Kennedy-McGovern constituency of 1968 has not developed a mass circulation newsletter or
national subscription membership organizations, a technique
that George Wallace has used effectively to finance his movement with more than 300,000 continuing supporters. A Mc-
Carthy historical unit, however, succeeded in collecting and
archiving files and documentary materials of the 1968 campaign, but the defunct magazine *The New Democrat* in vain
struggled to become a live disseminator of information and
criticism for Democratic reform elements. Both of the new
Democratic citizen organizations set up during the 1970
campaign failed to establish any genuine citizen base. The
Committee for National Unity was strictly a limited-purpose
organization created by Democratic reform leaders to fund
the election-eve broadcast of Senator Edmund S. Muskie to
reply to President Nixon. Congressional Leadership for the
Future was established to supplement the work of official
party campaign committees in electing talented new Democratic members of Congress, but its impressive Citizens
Advisory Committee had only limited involvement and the
group remained essentially an initiative of its chairman, former
Ambassador R. Sargent Shriver.

On the basis of their organizational record, there is a real
question whether the liberal Democrats can match the effec-

---

[6] Sam Brown, "The Politics of Peace," *Washington Monthly*, August 1970,
p. 42.

tiveness of the conservative movement within the Republican party. Diagnosing the disarray of liberal political forces in early 1970, Senator Harold Hughes observed: "There are numerous causes going with good political activists working in these causes. But there is no central thrust, no overview to unite them and stir them to concerted action. The amalgam is lacking." Like the conservatives, however, the moderate Republican and liberal Democratic citizen groups have brought new generations of political activists into the parties that must be taken into account in the politics of the 1970's.

Why Citizen Politics Has Failed

As politics becomes more complex and broader in scope, the question remains whether citizens can devise effective means for ongoing amateur involvement. A review of the checkered history of citizen groups suggests some recurring obstacles to effective citizen politics. Citizen politics on a national scale has been beset by a number of problems that could be remedied with adequate planning and cooperation.

Citizen groups have often been publicly launched before they have established a political base and a plan of operation. Without such preparation, citizen groups waste resources and as often as not repeat the mistakes of the past. They may be drawn into public controversy before they have mobilized their membership. They may take on issues indiscriminately instead of evaluating their objectives and their actual and potential citizen and financial resources.

The well-financed Republican Citizens Committee, for example, which was announced with fanfare at the All-Republican Conference in the summer of 1962, had still not decided what role it wanted to play in the Republican party at its last formal board meeting in December 1965. Common Cause succeeded in establishing a membership base before it had developed plans for involving local members. Chairman John W. Gardner announced that the citizen lobby would not adopt a local chapter form of organization. "Nor do we want members to launch local actions that are not part of a national effort that Common Cause is making," he told the membership.

"Uncoordinated local initiatives would dissipate the power that Common Cause can exert when all members act together."[7] In reply to questions of restive members, Gardner ventured that "perhaps in a couple of years when we have more confidence and solidity we can deal with more issues." In December 1971, however, faced by difficulties in soliciting new memberships and sustaining membership renewals, Common Cause publicly announced a shift to grassroots activism in order to satisfy "activist-oriented" members eager to participate in Common Cause state chapters. The actual form of local initiatives was not specified.

Another problem common to many groups is the lack of permanent professional staff and facilities. Citizen groups have suffered from a Paul Revere mentality, confident that citizen minutemen can be rallied to the occasion on a moment's notice. Most fail to realize that professional staff can provide organizational stability and continuity at the same time that it can facilitate involvement of citizens on a part-time basis. Instead, they believe that such essentials to effective action as permanent staff facilities, files and records run counter to the amateur spirit. Vietnam Moratorium organizer Sam Brown argued in this vein: "The national Moratorium office was more of a burden on the local groups than a help. We were in danger of becoming peace bureaucrats. . . . So we decided to do what all stale organizations should do—disband and let the good local groups survive on their own and the bad ones fade away."[8] Within days of the formal closing of the national office, however, the Cambodian-Kent crisis caught the national peace leadership unprepared. Common Cause has sought to avoid this problem. According to its president, former United Automobile Workers executive Jack T. Conway, "You have to learn as you go how to develop an effective citizens' organization, but the key to it is a highly professional staff in Washington and an active constituency in local areas locked right into it."

Most citizen groups have ignored their many common

---

[7] John W. Gardner, "Success Depends on Solid Foundations," *Common Cause Report from Washington*, March 1971, p. 8.
[8] Brown, *Washington Monthly*, August 1970, p. 42.

interests apart from ideological or issue differences and tended to operate in isolation, joining forces only for limited and specific purposes. Accordingly, citizen resources are largely fragmented and common facilities or cooperative services have never been developed on a continuing basis. At the local level, many groups are often unaware of the existence of other groups and of other resources in the private and independent sectors, such as business and labor-union programs and foundation-supported research.

A related problem is the lack of information on citizen activity in politics. Only scattered sources provide any reliable information about the citizen sector, such as the series of organizational profiles published by the *National Journal* as part of its coverage of Washington interest-group activities.[9] Group Research, Inc., a specialized reporting service primarily engaged in a monitoring role for clients, maintains a 3,000-page directory service on right-wing organizational activity with detailed profiles of about 100 organizations and more than 250 individuals and some 20 special reports on specific organizations or topics like the finances of the political Right.

But in general, the citizen sector and individual citizen groups lack essential and readily available information about their own resources. At the end of its first year, for example, Common Cause had no profile of the characteristics of its reported 200,000 members. The organization did not know how many Democrats, Republicans, Independents or others it had attracted or any personal data on educational background or occupational skills that might be relevant to Common Cause political action. Chairman Gardner cited the concern of members about bureaucratic snooping as one reason its computerized membership information had been limited to names, addresses and telephone numbers.

Lack of money is another frequently cited reason for the failure of citizen efforts. Citizen organizations are highly vulnerable to debt. Unlike the parties, citizen groups do not

---

[9] The editors and reporters of *National Journal*, Judith G. Smith (ed.), *Political Brokers: Money, Organizations, Power and People* (New York: Liveright, 1972).

enjoy such protective advantages as deferred debts and settlement of outstanding bills at reduced rates. Office facilities, staff and travel expenses are among the first casualties of a financial squeeze. A citizen organization cannot survive with a debt of $50,000 or $100,000, while a national party can continue to operate with a multimillion-dollar debt.

The long-term success of fund-raising groups like the National Committee for an Effective Congress as well as the enormous sums that can be raised quickly for a cause group like the Vietnam Moratorium suggest that political money is available in sizable amounts for citizen organizations. Most groups, however, have not developed systematic fund-raising techniques or shared expertise in this area, for example in direct-mail membership fund-raising campaigns. They also expend funds as rapidly as they are raised instead of budgeting their activities on a long-term basis.

Most citizen groups fail to involve their membership systematically and effectively in the organization's development and programs. Few groups circulate well-prepared agenda before meetings or distribute minutes with reminders of deadlines afterwards. Leaders often do not encourage members to contribute their ideas, skills and other resources, to undertake specific assignments, or to take part in policy and platform decisions. Some citizen organizations are consciously elitist in their approach to politics, among them the National Committee for an Effective Congress, which was structured to ensure that effective control remained in the hands of the professional staff and a few key officers and that the contributor base had no voice in the organization's operation.[10] Few groups have been creative or imaginative in developing new organizational and communications patterns that facilitate participation of citizens on a part-time basis. Even Ralph Nader's Public Citizen, Inc., while seeking financial contributions to create new citizen awareness and support full-time "public citizens," offers no participatory role for its citizen members.

---

[10] Harry M. Scoble, *Ideology and Electoral Action: A Comparative Case Study of the National Committee for an Effective Congress* (San Francisco: Chandler, 1967).

As a result, dedicated people who join organizations expecting to accomplish something soon become discouraged. In other instances, the lack of effective contact between the leadership and membership has contributed to the irrelevance and eventual failure of many groups even though they may continue as letterhead or paper committees. Without citizen participation and feedback, an organization soon loses the motivation of its members, its sense of purpose and its credibility.

Other national citizen organizations have failed because of their inability to relate national programs to constituent state and local groups. National offices have devoted insufficient resources to field staff and have been relatively uninformed about or insensitive to local needs and opportunities. Local citizen organizations in turn have seen little benefit to be gained from an association with a more broadly (and vaguely) conceived national organization. In deciding initially to organize from the top down, Common Cause postponed answering the question of local chapter organization and relationships with already established local citizen groups. The New Democratic Coalition, with its "from the bottom up" approach and suspicion of a national hierarchy, has not solved this organizational problem either.

Instead of concentrating on action-oriented members and programs, citizen groups have placed too much faith in their educational and propaganda roles and in education as a prerequisite to civic and political action. They have failed to recognize the need for citizen action skills developed through such means as systematic training conferences and workshops. In comparison to the candidate and staff training schools organized on a continuing basis by a wide variety of party organizations, the occasional conferences used by the New Democratic Coalition or by Republican moderate organizations are insignificant.

Rather, citizens and citizen groups are often satisfied with apparent or "symbolic politics" and do not pursue issues through the complex political and governmental machinery where they are resolved. Citizens have been content to become passive consumers of politics, regarding the media as substitutes for rather than guides to action. "Receiving 'information,' sharing a newscaster's, columnist's or Senator's indignation and venting it to friends is for most of us vicarious action, our only sustained 'action' on a public matter," observes Alexander Klein.[11] For many citizens, politics stops with the television screen or the editorial page, a phenomenon that has been quietly noticed by politicians with their image and media strategies. The "new politics" of technique affords everyone a box seat, but the ball game continues to belong strictly to the professionals.

Citizen political activity is further hampered by a persistent anticitizen bias on the part of party professionals and the lack of party organization support. Outside of their own women's and youth auxiliaries and limited minority-group and ethnic programs, the parties make little effort to involve citizen groups in party affairs. As the minority party, the Republican party could benefit from broader group affiliations, but it persists in treating independent citizen initiatives as divisive splinter efforts. Although the Democratic party is more heterogeneous and enjoys better communications with the citizen sector, it provides essentially no party support or services for citizen groups. Neither party has a responsible top-level official with a staff and budget to keep in touch with citizen organizations and develop opportunities for cooperative projects.

Both national parties, moreover, have discouraged financial contributions to citizen groups. Republican national chairmen have frequently warned party contributors not to be "fooled" by independent citizen groups bearing Republican labels. In 1965, Republican National Finance Chairman Lucius D. Clay attempted to dissuade prominent Republican citizens from co-signing a fund-raising letter for the moderate Republicans for Progress. In 1970, Democratic National Chairman O'Brien attempted to undercut Sargent Shriver's Congressional Leadership for the Future before it could get established financially, although later he worked out an accommodation with the group.

For their part, citizen groups often share an antiparty tradi-

---

[11] Alexander Klein, "A New American Politics," *Current*, September 1970, p. 5. See also Murray Edelman, *The Symbolic Uses of Politics* (Urbana: University of Illinois Press, 1964).

tion and have not pressed the parties to develop programs or services to facilitate citizen involvement. They also run the constant risk of having key leaders absorbed by the parties and the political system. Party professionals use political appointments to neutralize the effectiveness of citizen groups, a tactic that has been employed effectively by both Democratic and Republican administrations. The rapid turnover of organizations and key leaders and the consequent loss of valuable experience have exacted a heavy toll from citizen politics.

The Citizen Sector and the Parties: Prospects for the 1970's

The stirring of the public interest movement and the proliferation of issue-oriented citizen groups suggest that the United States is entering a new era of citizen involvement and political reform in the 1970's. Citizen politics will undoubtedly shape the new political alignments and institutional forms of the decade. Citizens may turn increasingly to temporary organizations or ad hoc coalitions directed toward specific problems in much the same way that parties and candidates are relying on temporary campaign organizations created by professional political consultants. The rapid increase in temporary organizations will present a tremendous new challenge to coordinate activities among groups and organizations.[12] At the same time, citizen organizations, while limited in many of the ways noted above, will have at their disposal new forms of technology and communication such as computer-based mailing operations, telephone banks and two-way cable television through which specialized citizen constituencies can be linked and specialized working teams can be assembled quickly for virtually any project.

The new nonpartisan, bipartisan and multipartisan groups of the citizen sector will have a significant impact on the po-

---

[12] See Warren G. Bennis, *Changing Organizations: Essays on the Development and Evolution of Human Organization* (New York: McGraw-Hill, 1966). Also see Warren G. Bennis, "A Funny Thing Happened on the Way to the Future," *American Psychologist*, July 1970, pp. 595–608.

litical parties of the 1970's, whether they become integrated into and work through modernized party structures, whether they coalesce as a new political force, perhaps as a new reform party, or whether they fall by the wayside and merely contribute to citizen disillusionment with the political process. Common Cause itself bears a great burden in this regard. "It will hurt the whole public interest movement, civil rights, consumerism—you name it—if they fail," observed a Washington lobbyist. In a sober address to an overflow audience of more than 2,500 members and friends of Common Cause in Boston, John Gardner admitted, "It is the essence of citizens' organizations to come and go. The essential thing we want to leave behind is a concern for the public process." (In its subsequent policy shift to local activism, Common Cause abruptly terminated its voter registration and campaign-financing national headquarters staff, letting go some of its most competent personnel.) Common Cause President Jack Conway expressed hope that "an effective citizens' lobby will discipline the parties and make them more effective and open. If the parties don't respond, the Independent and unaffiliated vote will grow. At some point it will congeal in some form of organization."

Sensitive to the past weaknesses of citizen politics, Ralph Nader has attempted to give the public interest movement a broad citizen base of "public citizens" beyond its cadre of public interest lawyers and full-time professional citizen advocates. "The idea that you can have any public-interest mechanism operate in government without a renewed or different brand of citizenship is absurd," states Nader. In improving governmental performance, however, Nader, like Progressive reformers before him, has ignored the potential contribution of the parties. "A good politician is not considered even as good as a good citizen," Nader remarked in repudiating a partisan political career.

At the present time, the Democratic party is in a position to gain much more support from citizen groups than the Republican party. Democratic party reforms in guidelines for delegate selection to the 1972 convention, combined with activities of the National Women's Political Caucus, the National Youth Caucus, and the Black Caucus based in the House of Representatives, should effect significant changes in the composition of state party delegations. The Democratic National Committee and Democratic state organizations have briefed a wide range of public interest groups with citizenship programs for their members, encouraging them to become involved in the selection of convention delegates. The Republican convention, operating under no comparable mandatory instructions to state parties, stands to remain more white, middle-class and middle-aged in delegate composition.

Apart from the different responses the parties have made to the issue of party reform, other factors favor an alignment of more citizen groups with the Democrats than with the Republicans. More of the nominally bipartisan or multipartisan citizen organizations are in fact liberal Democratic in orientation. Their boards of directors are predominantly Democratic or Independent, with a place or two reserved for a token (usually liberal or moderate) Republican. Their professional staffs are usually Democratic in background or orientation.

Although formally a bipartisan group, the National Committee for an Effective Congress, for example, has an overwhelmingly Democratic board and a professional staff with a long-term involvement in Democratic party affairs. Although NCEC endorses occasional Republicans for Congress and has made grants to moderate Republican organizations such as the Wednesday Group in the House of Representatives and the Ripon Society, its financial contributions and staff resources are directed primarily to liberal Democratic candidates for Congress. Other technically bipartisan groups make no pretense concerning their party orientation. During the early 1960's, the Leadership Conference on Civil Rights, for example, was closely connected with the Democratic leadership in the White House and Congress and in 1964 went so far as to exclude from its deliberations on civil-rights strategy moderate Republican staffers with legislative responsibilities for civil rights.

Many of the new generation of peace, national priorities and environmental organizations—groups like the Movement for a New Congress, the Bipartisan Congressional Clearing House, the Universities Antiwar Fund, the Congressional Action Fund, and Environmental Action—have made pro forma efforts to be bipartisan in their board appointments and their endorsements and financial contributions. But the impact of their activities during the 1970 campaign was overwhelmingly on the Democratic side. The Movement for a New Congress, for example, endorsed 65 Democrats and only one Republican. The Bipartisan Congressional Clearing House was organized and staffed by young Democrats and provided services almost exclusively to Democratic campaigns. The nominally nonpartisan National Youth Caucus, organized by former Congressman Allard K. Lowenstein in late 1971, has concentrated its efforts almost exclusively in winning delegate strength at the 1972 Democratic National Convention and registering young voters to "Dump Nixon" in the November elections.

The reasons for this partisan imbalance are complicated. Liberal Democrats have clearly taken more initiative in picking up issues like peace, women's rights and the 18-year-old vote and organizing appropriate citizen activity. Many groups initially started by liberal Democrats have defined programs, positions and leadership that narrow their potential appeal to Republicans and make it difficult for Republicans to affiliate after the group is established. Liberal Democrats have also produced a greater number of activists trained in the organizational politics of citizen movements than have the Republicans. Although conservative Republicans have developed citizen cadres and have espoused an activist conservative philosophy, they have only occasionally joined broad-based citizen organizations like the National Taxpayers Union and the Committee to Repeal the Draft.

As noted earlier, moderate Republican ranks have been steadily eroded during the 1960's. The Goldwater citizen movement drove many moderates from the party and out of leadership and staff positions while giving the national Republican party a more conservative cast on civil rights, social welfare and foreign-policy issues. The polarizing strategy articulated by Vice President Agnew during the 1970 election campaign further alienated party moderates as well as peace, national-priorities, black and student organizations.

Thus far, the net effect of these factors has been to make the Democratic party more attractive than the Republican party to many cause and reform-oriented groups of citizens. If the current antipathy between national Republican leaders and major citizen groups continues and if the Democratic reform movement succeeds in opening up the convention process, the Democratic party may broaden its coalitional base substantially during the 1970's and the Republican party find itself consigned to a perpetual minority status.

Recommendations: Developing the Citizen Sector

The citizen sector, to be effective in the 1970's, must organize and advance a broader definition of citizen interests in politics. Disenchanted amateurs "waiting for some candidate to emerge with a new philosophy for the coming age," observes James Reston, may wake up too late to the importance of political organization and finance.[13] Individual citizen groups each pursue their own factional and issue objectives, fight their own organizational battles, and in time die. The political parties and government bureaucracies may endure such groups for a while but can afford to discount most of them as any long-term factor in politics.

While bitter antagonists on some issues, diverse citizen groups do have common interests. All have the same interest in being more effective in achieving organizational goals. All have an interest in improving the access of their members to government. In view of the underlying interest of the amateur citizen in politics, cooperative citizen programs dedicated to serving, encouraging and enhancing citizen political activity offer the most promising direction for developing the citizen sector of politics as an essential resource for self-government and party modernization.

Recommendation 1. Citizen clearinghouse facilities for information, action and communication among citizen organizations and individuals should be established in Washington. Citizen groups should also develop cooperative programs for fund raising.

---

[13] James Reston, "The Forgotten Battle," *New York Times,* November 17, 1971.

In order to provide more centralized information and services to the citizen sector and to expand and enhance effective citizen participation in politics, groups of citizen organizations could pool resources on a long-term basis as "citizen consortia" or "citizen conglomerates." The cooperative efforts of conservative citizen groups provide one model that could be developed by other organizations. Another example is the office complex maintained in Atlanta for a number of years by several progressive "New South" organizations like the Southern Regional Council, the American Civil Liberties Union (Southern region), the National Sharecroppers Fund, and the Voter Education Project. Eventually, cooperative citizen activities might evolve into a structured national citizen center with permanent facilities in Washington and a representative board of user organizations servicing a variety of common organizational needs.

Citizen clearinghouse operations could provide a number of essential information services to widely scattered groups and individuals. Citizen computer data banks could be developed with proper safeguards on the collection and use of information as one of the most important resources of the citizen sector.

A comprehensive directory of citizen organizations, for example, could be compiled and printed quarterly by a computer which could also be used to answer specific inquiries on organizations, their officers, the nature and location of their facilities, and their programs and services. Citizen clearinghouses could also provide a political opportunities alert service giving citizens weekly or even daily calendars of events of political meetings, political broadcasts on radio and television, and other political events. With timely information on opportunities for participation or action, citizen groups could mobilize members more effectively to participate in events they consider important. Citizens could also be encouraged to alert each other nationally to political opportunities they might see in their own community or area of experience.

A citizen talent-bank operation could provide a job notification and referral service and could assist organizations, parties, and national, state and local governments in searches for specific skills in the citizen sector. Through a political idea bank, ideas, recommendations and suggestions submitted by citizens, ranging from practical nuts-and-bolts politics to public policy issues, could be entered on permanent file with a formal credit to the citizen and referred to potential users, including party commissions, campaign committees, and party and governmental policy task forces and officeholders.

The citizen center could assume primary responsibility for collecting, compiling and/or developing and making available a series of guides to effective citizen action, master checklists, or standard operating procedures for group functions. New citizen groups could obtain technical assistance on organizational problems ranging from fund raising to program implementation. A citizen clearinghouse could retain a press clipping service and develop a telephone network, systematically employing WATS lines across the country, to increase the current political intelligence available to citizen organizations. A citizen newsletter providing news on the activities of political organizations and information on political services available could be published regularly, perhaps biweekly.

Citizens could cooperate in sharing specialized skills. For example, a citizen legal service, a pool of legal talent at national and state levels, could assist citizen groups in dealing with legal aspects of party and governmental structure such as party reform and convention delegations and also with litigation in policy areas such as voting rights. A citizen legal service could help open the political process to greater citizen participation at the same time it gave citizens access to an increasingly important instrument of political reform. Similar services could provide technical assistance in other areas of common interest, such as fund raising and training and recruitment.

In order to develop a broad, stable base of financial support and to increase the public's long-term financial support of politics, citizen groups could experiment with new fund-raising approaches and techniques. A group of organizations could cooperate in establishing a united citizen political fund, drawing on the experience of civic United Fund or Community Chest drives. Citizens could be given a number of options for earmarking contributions for specific activities. Other citizen groups could jointly retain consultants on political fund raising, especially direct-mail solicitation, and sponsor workshops or training programs on fund-raising techniques. A citizen sponsors program might also be established, involving a number of contributors who regularly donate large sums of money to individual candidates or cause groups and who would be willing to fund specific projects in the citizen sector.

Citizen groups could also encourage the establishment of citizen political archives to preserve the documentary history and records of as many citizen organizations as possible and to sponsor basic research on organizational effectiveness in politics, including the systematic interrogation of past officials of citizen organizations. A series of case studies and analyses of citizen action in politics by individual citizens and scholars could be published.

Recommendation 2. Citizen organizations could develop the political and organizational skills of their members through the use of professional field staff and consultants, an annual conference of citizen groups, regional workshops, and special training programs for potential citizen leaders.

More effective citizen politics requires a major upgrading of the political and organizational skills of citizens. Clearinghouse and information services can help individual organizations develop citizen skills through guides and training materials, but significant improvement depends on cooperative action by citizen groups themselves. Citizen groups could pool their professional and staff resources to develop and fund a professional field staff on a regional basis. Professional staff could train citizens in specialized skills, undertake independent evaluations or audits of group performance, and facilitate exchanges of information, ideas, and personnel between various organizations. Citizen groups could also supplement their own professional staff resources for special projects through greater use of political consultants, especially during nonelection years.

Citizen groups could experiment with large working conferences as well as more specialized workshops. A national conference of citizen groups with as comprehensive group representation as possible is one such innovation that deserves several serious tries. A citizen convention could be of special value in defining the role of citizen groups in politics; identifying common needs in membership, communication, political strategy and fund raising; indicating concerns and possibilities for cooperative action; and establishing new friendships and relationships among diverse citizen groups and their leaders.

Citizen groups could organize their own cooperative political training seminars and internship programs as well as using the formal training opportunities provided by the political parties. Citizens could also take full advantage of the excellent informal opportunities for practical political training afforded at party meetings and conventions, reform-commission hearings, governors' and state legislators' conferences and meetings of political consultants and other groups active in politics.

Of central importance to any citizen training program is the identification, training and long-term development of the self-starters, the citizen-entrepreneurs of politics. Every active citizen organization or movement has such individuals who imaginatively devise the means to accomplish their goal in spite of the opposition or indifference of established parties and institutions. Their accomplishments could receive more formal recognition through an annual citizen honor list or comparable awards designed to enhance the public status of citizens who choose to make politics a noble and honorable avocation.

Recommendation 3. The political parties should take positive steps to achieve greater citizen involvement and to encourage continuing communication between citizen groups and party leaders.

In order to meet the demands of citizen volunteers for a more meaningful role in party affairs and to determine the supporting role party organizations can play in the growth of citizen politics, the Democratic and Republican parties could appoint representative party commissions to study the citizen's role within the parties and recommend detailed programs for citizen involvement. These party commissions could conduct hearings and field investigations to study practical and effective means for involving citizens in party activities and to evaluate specific innovations such as the Urban Action Centers program of the Republican National Committee and the citizen caucuses developed in Democratic congressional and presidential primaries in Massachusetts. The commissions could prepare and publish an extensive list of activities or political investment opportunities to stimulate citizen initiative within the parties, such as providing open forums for candidates for elective and appointive office, developing testimony for party platform hearings, attending party meetings and conventions, preparing political education programs, and evaluating major party programs like the 1970 Democratic closed-circuit TV campaign caucus, the Republican Mission 70's project, and various election campaigns.

A number of reforms in traditional party structures could serve the common interests of citizen groups and the parties themselves by building vital citizen lobbies into the political parties. The national committees could each name an assistant chairman for citizen affairs responsible for increasing citizen involvement in the parties. Divisions for citizen affairs at the state and national party headquarters level could maintain liaison with citizen groups and organize conferences or workshops in which citizen group and party representatives could exchange views. Citizen organizations could be invited by party organizations, for example, to cosponsor research and policy studies and to participate actively in implementing party reforms such as the equitable representation of various population groups.

Recommendation 4. Citizen organizations can encourage innovation and reform within the political parties through independent initiatives in critical new areas such as the development and application of cable television and the use of political data banks as well as in such traditional areas as candidate recruitment.

Just as political consultants are shaping managerial aspects of future party organization, citizen groups can play an innovative role in developing the participatory aspects of future party structures. Innovations by citizen organizations in recent years suggest a range of functions that participant parties could incorporate: the Congressional Action Fund's model of participatory fund raising and allocation; the Movement for a New

Congress's computerized techniques for coordinating and linking college campuses and keeping track of a highly mobile student population; and Common Cause's development and use of telephone networks for citizen lobbying.

A more organized citizen sector could also take initiatives in major new areas being ignored by the parties. Citizens could give special attention to the information and communications technology of the 1970's and its potential for greatly increased citizen participation. The regulation of cable television, for example, has significant potential consequences for citizen politics in the possibilities for electronic town meetings and other community-based use of media and eventually in the linkup of national or regional television audiences of specialized citizen activist groups. Citizen initiative in establishing a national citizen study of cable television might encourage the political parties to pay greater attention to the implications of CATV.

The very advances in information technology that will permit new forms of citizen participation in politics also pose serious threats to privacy through the collection and use of information on individual citizens and private organizations by federal, state and local governmental data banks and by employers, powerful, private interests and political parties. A citizen commission on privacy could review legislative and administrative action in this area and press the political parties to give such problems serious attention.

Citizens can move independently to correct the repeated failure of the parties to name candidates or contest elections for scores of congressional and hundreds of state legislative seats as well as many more lesser offices. A coordinated citizen effort in candidate recruitment could guarantee every citizen the right to a choice between at least two candidates. Citizen groups could sponsor Independent candidates as a form of political antitrust action whenever the parties act in such a way as to eliminate or minimize electoral competition. If nomination procedures or costs should prove a serious barrier to such Independent candidates, citizens could initiate appropriate court tests.

VIII

The Media: Information Brokers for Politics

The media occupy a critical position with regard to the current functioning and future development of American politics. As the principal information brokers in the political system, the media can serve to open up the political process through alert investigative reporting, through public review of governmental and political performance and ethical standards ("accountability" in its broad sense), and through providing at least some sense of citizen involvement. The coming dramatic expansion in the number of channels for electronic media and the development of a two-way communications capacity in mass media afford both the media and the political parties even more important opportunities—political, public service and commercial—to build specialized attentive and informed audiences in politics and to enable citizens to participate more directly and fully in the political system.

By and large, the media have not faced up to the responsibilities for informing the public they have inherited with the enormous expansion in communications technology and with the accelerating pace and greater complexity of news developments. Admittedly there have been major advances in the reporting of political news since the emergence of an independent press and reporting profession after the Civil War and the introduction of electronic media. But the fact remains that the American political system operates on far too low levels of information for its own health.

The citizen who wants to be informed on politics faces two distinct problems in getting political information and analysis from the media.[1] First, in the face of the so-called information explosion, the literal flood of news produced and processed in our high-paced society, the citizen will find few means to help him locate political information relevant to his needs. *The New York Times* is exceptional among newspapers in providing a daily index. There is no political newsletter or publication that extracts or indexes major news stories relating to party politics. Basic political news organized and indexed for citizen use is currently not a part of the public domain.

At the same time, however, the critical problem is not one of too much information but of too little systematic, comprehensive reporting on and analysis of political news. Major political news developments can go unreported and important parts of the political system are rarely examined. In 1968, for example, the national news media were months late in reporting the early phases of the Wallace organization that won spots on all 50 state ballots, and even after this remarkable political accomplishment offered little insight on key Wallace staff members and their successful operation. Between 1968 and 1972, the media gave little attention to the Democratic National Committee's record $9.3-million-dollar debt and how it was being handled by party officials. More than one year after Republican National Chairman Dole and Republican National Committee Cochairman Anne L. Armstrong took office, no

---

[1] It is important to note that there are several distinct audiences for political news: 1) the mass audience of politics, ranging from the about 70 percent of eligible voters who vote in presidential elections to the more than 98 percent of the population that owns television or radio and follows major public events; 2) the attentive audience of politics, a sizable and growing minority of the public, estimated by V. O. Key, Jr., at 15 to 20 percent of the population in 1961, that follows political news in some detail; and 3) the activist-party elite audience characterized primarily by its active involvement or participation in party politics and numbering from a fraction of one percent to a few percentage points of the population depending on the criteria of participation used.

The attentive public provides a much closer review of governmental performance than does the general public, and its needs and expectations of media coverage of politics are accordingly much greater. The activist-party elite audience acts upon political information on a continuing basis, and its highly specialized and often immediate informational needs are frequently met by informal personal "networks" of communication within the parties and related political groups.

major news agency had released an analysis of the new party administration. Many topics covered in this book, such as the insulation of the congressional parties from public scrutiny and the developing relationships between parties and political consultants, have remained largely unexamined in the media.

The ultimate loser from the gap in political information and analysis is the citizen himself. The deficiencies in political reporting discussed in this chapter breed public apathy and cynicism, contribute in a substantial way to closed, unresponsive parties, and seriously handicap effective citizen action in politics and government. In the absence of systematic political news coverage by the media, political information has become a largely private political resource for use by party professionals and others inside the system.

The media, of course, share the responsibility for promoting public involvement and understanding of the political system with many other institutions in American society, including the schools, the political parties, corporations, labor unions and citizen organizations. Nor can the political parties be excused from a necessary supporting and potentially innovative role. At the same time, however, improvements in media performance and political reporting need not wait for and can even encourage the process of party modernization.

Political Reporting: From Parties to the Media

The importance of political news and information for both electoral participation and continuing citizen involvement in politics and the parties raises the question of who bears responsibility for keeping the public informed and how well they have performed these functions.

During the first half of the nineteenth century, while the American system was being democratized, the new party organizations and partisan press performed the function of informing the rapidly expanding electorate. Only five percent of the newspapers in 1850 could be considered neutral or independent; the party press accounted for the majority. Each party organization and faction within the states had its own official organ. Martin Van Buren, then a New York State party leader, admitted the importance of the press in maintaining state party control: "Without a paper thus edited [i.e., 'soundly and discreetly' edited] at Albany, we may hang our harps on the willows."[2]

With the emergence of the penny papers after 1830, advances in journalism during the Civil War and the growth of an independent press during the 1870's, news as such began to replace party propaganda and editorial comment as the leading function of the American newspaper. The changing concept of news and development of a reporting profession gradually shifted the control of news from politicians to reporters and newspaper journalism steadily established itself as an independent institutional force. Already in 1870, an English observer could generalize that "the American reader will abandon a paper of his own political creed for one that has superior enterprise in publishing the latest and fullest items of events."[3]

The print and later the electronic media greatly expanded the mass audience for politics. By 1900, daily newspaper circulation had reached 16 million; by 1950, 54 million; and by 1968, 62.5 million. With radio and television in 98 and 97 percent of American homes respectively by 1970, for the first time in the history of a major country the potential audience for news extended to almost the entire population.

In addition to the media, other institutions have attempted, unsuccessfully, to assume certain aspects of the informing, educational function once provided by party organizations. Although civics courses in elementary and secondary schools supposedly educate youth for adult citizenship, the low scores in recent survey data on relatively simple questions about the government and the Constitution reveal the deficiencies of such attempts. Courses of this type also devote relatively little time to the study of party politics and means of participation in the political process.

---

[2] Quoted in Frank Luther Mott, *American Journalism, A History: 1690–1960* (3rd ed.; New York: Macmillan, 1968), p. 253.
[3] Quoted in *ibid.*, p. 385.

The academic profession of political science has devoted some resources since the early part of this century to education in the public service and to informative political analysis. Unfortunately, the potential contribution of political science to broad citizen understanding of the political parties has been limited. While the subject matter of politics is intrinsically interesting to many laymen and -women, the professional literature on parties has become increasingly quantitative, interlaced with jargon, and incomprehensible to the general public.

Citizen organizations, business and labor bipartisan programs in political action and the new profession of political consultants have also sought to provide various forms of citizen education in politics. Since the decline of the partisan press, however, the political parties have done relatively little to illuminate their activities or to inform citizens about ways they can use the political process.

Each party has a clear interest in improved reporting of politics and in assuring that news of its candidates and programs and its leaders in government are reported adequately and fairly by the media. Yet, apart from criticism of the media by powerful Congressmen and administration officials in both parties, neither party has developed through its national committee headquarters or other appropriate party body a systematic public procedure for monitoring the media and making periodic suggestions for more balanced and thorough news coverage.

Instead of operating like public mass-membership organizations eager to get their message to the broadest possible public audience, the parties have tended to insulate themselves from public scrutiny and to behave more like private elite clubs. Party meetings are closed, party documents classified, reporters made to feel unwelcome at national party conventions, news opportunities frequently neglected.

One consequence of the failure of parties to service the media adequately or to develop informative party publications and political education programs has been to limit citizen access to the parties. As a foreign observer, Moisei Ostrogorski, noted more than 50 years ago: "Left without guidance by those who could or should have supplied them with a clue to the

labyrinth of political affairs, American citizens have no means
. . . of acquiring the rudiments of political knowledge."[4]

Another consequence has been the assumption of the political reporting function in most of its aspects, almost by default, by television, radio and the print media.

The Current State of Political Reporting: Television, Radio, and the Print Media

Television, which is the source of most news for 60 percent of Americans and the exclusive source for 31 percent, has perhaps the greatest responsibility among the media to present regular and accurate information on politics. The major television network news bureaus have in the space of roughly two decades gained enormous power in the communication of news. During the 1960's, television replaced newspapers as the most widely followed media by a 6–5 margin, with more people watching the CBS or NBC evening news than read the top 10 newspapers combined. Television was also rated the most believable news source by Americans by a 2–1 margin over its nearest competitor, newspapers. The anchor men of their evening news programs, moreover, have emerged as opinionmakers of unprecedented influence. "Certainly the thinking of a third of the politically articulate American public is shaped by Mr. Cronkite," observes Joseph C. Harsch, the *Christian Science Monitor* editorial-page chief, and "well over half is influenced by Mr. Cronkite, David Brinkley, Harry Reasoner, and Howard K. Smith."[5]

Television, like radio, has also accelerated the pace and obsolescence of news. What audiences witness or hear via these two media or what commentators report in the evening and morning news programs may have a far greater influence on the public's interpretation of political events than the reporting

---

[4] Moisei Ostrogorski, *Democracy and the Party System in the United States: A Study in Extra-Constitutional Government* (New York: Macmillan, 1910), p. 192.

[5] Joseph C. Harsch, "Mr. Nixon vs. Mr. Cronkite," *Christian Science Monitor*, April 8, 1971.

and analysis printed many hours or days later. One study of split-ticket voters ranked television news and television documentaries and specials as the two most important influencing factors in the voting decision, followed by newspaper articles, newspaper editorials and television editorials.[6]

Television reporting has obviously added a significant new visual dimension to the news. "Movement politics" in the 1960's used the mass media to short-circuit the representative party and electoral processes and to dramatize causes and issues directly to the public, Congress and top governmental officials. Dr. Martin Luther King's march on Selma, Alabama, gave almost instantaneous national visibility to the demands of the civil-rights movement for new voting-rights legislation in 1965. Similarly, the Vietnam Moratorium of October 15, 1969, succeeded in mobilizing massive antiwar rallies virtually overnight, thanks in part to the access to the media Moratorium leaders enjoyed. Televised reports of the war in Southeast Asia and the Democratic National Convention of Chicago in 1968 conveyed information via the screen to more Americans with much greater impact than did print media in their voluminous background reports and documentation. (The accuracy of the picture conveyed is, however, a subject of continuing controversy.[7]) Television reporting has also subtly transformed the style and expectations of politics into a "contest of visibility," according to public opinion analyst Samuel Lubell. "Increasingly voters have come to believe that things happen because they are made to happen, which often encourages further voter activism and make-happenings."[8]

Considering the tremendous communications power of the electronic media, how well have radio and television covered

---

[6] Walter DeVries and V. Lance Tarrance, Jr., *The Ticket-Splitter: A New Force in American Politics* (Grand Rapids, Mich.: William B. Eerdmans, 1971).

[7] See the special section of eight articles "Vietnam: What Lessons?" in *Columbia Journalism Review*, Winter 1970–71, pp. 7–46; Jules Witcover, "The Press and Chicago: The Truth Hurt," *Columbia Journalism Review*, Fall 1968, pp. 5–9; and Edwin Diamond, "Chicago Press: Rebellion and Retrenchment," *ibid.*, pp. 10–17.

[8] Samuel Lubell, *The Hidden Crisis in American Politics* (New York: W. W. Norton, 1970), p. 67.

politics for the mass and attentive audiences of political news?

Although the parties function year-round and significant events in the party political process occur almost daily, television and radio news treat politics as a seasonal phenomenon, mobilizing their resources for blitz coverage of the national conventions and elections. This cyclical, sporadic attention to politics is accentuated by the failure of the networks to add full-time political reporters and analysts to their broadcasting and news-bureau staffs who can provide continuous in-depth coverage of politics. While a few individual television stations, such as KSL in Salt Lake City, have added their own full-time political analysts, only ABC of the three commercial television networks had a political editor, William H. Lawrence, and even his title was changed to National Affairs Editor. Instead, the networks have supplemented their staff elections and conventions units with political consultants who periodically offer comments during the extended coverage of the conventions or election returns but who are rarely called upon for regular network news programs. The almost inevitable consequence of leaving political coverage and commentary to the network anchor men is a superficial treatment of political news.

The news that is presented is also circumscribed by current news-gathering practices of the networks, which rely on a limited number of correspondents, news teams and camera crews, usually based in Washington and a few major cities. As a result, television and radio tend to cover only scheduled political events or depend on the wire services rather than undertake in-depth, investigative journalism. According to Fred W. Friendly, former president of CBS News and Edward R. Murrow Professor of Broadcast Journalism at Columbia University, the three major networks and United Press International (which serves independent stations) each select 10 to 12 stories they will cover each evening, usually with considerable duplication of effort, and "that decision automatically eliminates some twenty-five or thirty stories."[9] Television news may further limit itself to events that can be filmed.

---

[9] Fred W. Friendly, "Pooled Coverage: Small Step to a TV News Breakthrough?," *Columbia Journalism Review*, May/June 1971, p. 50.

If a group of governors is holding a series of meetings, for example, the networks may dispatch only a camera crew for the concluding press conference without an advance political reporter to prepare background news and interpretation.

Finally, television and radio have downgraded their coverage of politics by relegating political news and public affairs programs like "Meet the Press" (NBC), "Issues and Answers" (ABC), and "Face the Nation" (CBS) to the Sunday ghetto, and even then they are frequently bumped by sports events or grade B movies. The media have continued to rely on the argument that the general public is not seriously interested in improved news and public affairs broadcasting. A recent survey, however, revealed that 22 percent of the American public desired more news and public affairs broadcasting while only 10 percent wanted the amount reduced. The growing potential audience of politically aware Americans has been demonstrated by the success of such efforts as the all-news programming of several radio stations like WTOP in Washington, and WCBS and WINS in New York City, public television's regular programs like "Washington Week in Review," the local news and investigative reports of WGBH Boston's "Reporters," WCVE's live coverage of city council meetings in Richmond, Virginia, and various political documentaries.

Television and radio have not given more systematic and continuing coverage to political news for several reasons, some of which are defensible or understandable, others of which are not. Radio and television are not the media for public record or for conveying large quantities of political information to the public on a day-to-day basis. Even the 30-minute national news broadcast with 22 or 23 minutes of actual news time can report, in bulletin form, about as much text as is printed on half of a front page of *The New York Times*. Moreover, television and radio news is highly perishable. Newspapers and magazines can be clipped or books annotated, but transcripts or tapes of broadcasts on electronic media are much more difficult to obtain.[10]

---

[10] Vanderbilt University in Nashville, Tennessee, has been unique in recording and maintaining a library of videotapes of network news shows,

Television in particular has also been limited by the economics of newsgathering. While a major newspaper can assign one or more reporters for the cost of the reporters alone, a television crew at $500 a day can shoot only a few film sequences in a workday, many of which may not be used. Proposals for pooled coverage through a television news service which would give the networks greater flexibility have met with a cool response. While the radio and television news producers may have their own network of contacts, bureau chiefs and correspondents in Washington and other major cities, they are largely dependent for many of their news leads on a few daily newspapers, notably *The New York Times* and Washington *Post*, and the wire-service tickers. "The *Times* is a bulletin board for the news community," observes Edwin Diamond, radio-TV commentator for WTOP News in Washington. "It's the campus newspaper. It's the one document you know all the news executives have read."

Limitations of time and space, reporting resources and original material, however, are only a partial explanation of deficiencies in television and radio news. More fundamental are the amounts of time and program resources budgeted for political news and public affairs and assumptions made about news audiences. Television and radio have not adequately defined their own responsibilities in communicating political information to the public. Until they do, their programming is unlikely to be guided by a greater sense of the importance of politics and public understanding of the political process to the effective functioning of government.

While television news in particular has captured a large segment of the audience of politics, the print media—newspapers, magazines, books, and other publications—retain a major responsibility for providing information and analysis on politics. Newspapers remain in a strong competitive position, as shown by a 1969 Louis Harris survey for *Time* magazine that found that almost 90 percent of Americans read a news-

---

although Senator Howard H. Baker (R-Tenn.) has introduced legislation to authorize the Library of Congress to develop a similar national depository.

paper regularly. The print media devote a fair amount of resources, both in space and in manpower, to the coverage of politics at the national, state and local level. In turn, much of the best reporting on politics originates from the dedicated "pencil-and-paper" reporters who cover politics on a year-round basis.

Reporting resources are highly concentrated on and oriented to the eastern seaboard, with most news organizations based in Washington and New York. National politics is covered by the Washington correspondents of the national news magazines and more than 500 of the nation's newspapers, by the news or wire services and by some 65 nationally syndicated Washington-based columnists. Virtually all of the almost 2,000 daily newspapers use at least one of the three major wire services (Associated Press, United Press International and Reuters), which provide a steady flow of news copy that may be selected and edited for local use, and many newspapers rely exclusively on the output of these wire services for their news on national politics. AP and UPI regional and state wires are also a major source for political news at the state level. Leading supplemental wire services are operated by *The New York Times–Washington Star*, Los Angeles *Times–Washington Post–Long Island Newsday*, the Chicago *Daily News–Chicago Sun-Times*, the Knight and Newhouse newspapers, and the *Christian Science Monitor*.

A surprisingly small number of correspondents, an elite of the Washington press corps, are actually experienced full-time political writers—25 at the most, according to Philip Potter, Washington bureau chief for the Baltimore *Sun* and one of the select few himself. Another observer credits only one or two score Washington correspondents with original probing and writing, with the rest of the more than a thousand Washington press corps duplicating their stories.[11]

A particularly strategic position is occupied by the nationally

---

[11] See William L. Rivers, "Appraising Press Coverage of Politics," in Richard W. Lee (ed.), *Politics & the Press* (Washington, D.C.: Acropolis Books, 1970), pp. 35–56; and Philip Potter, "Political Reporting: The Criteria of Selection," in *ibid.*, pp. 105–16.

syndicated political columnists and some of the by-line political reporters or Washington bureau chiefs for key daily news-papers and news magazines whose columns and analysis are distributed on various news wires. While they may add depth and breadth to the editorial pages or news analysis, these columnists are also among the leading political opinionmakers in the country. They evaluate the performance of Presidents and, as already noted, serve as a screening committee for presidential hopefuls. They can give political causes visibility or respectability as the fashion leaders of politics.

How well, then, do the print media cover politics? In spite of some outstanding examples of political journalism, there are major deficiencies in the overall quality of their political re-porting.

The importance of in-depth reporting, of putting events in perspective, is usually overlooked. "Extraordinarily few journals, either daily newspapers or magazines, act as agencies of political criticism," V. O. Key concluded in his classic study of American public opinion. For the most part, he said, "the grand problems of the political system . . . escape their critical attention."[12] In-depth reporting in the form of political series has only infrequently been used by a few papers like the Washington *Post* to cover political subjects. Teams of reporters like the Spotlight team of the Boston *Globe* are rarely used to provide political coverage and analysis. Not enough papers follow *The New York Times*'s practice of regularly assigning reporters to research particular issues without an immediate schedule of publication. An optimistic effort in this direction was *The Morning News,* slated for publication in late 1972, which planned to devote the bulk of its news space to analytical or investigative stories, a significant recognition of this defi-ciency in the media. The project died aborning.

Even though news staffs are much larger in the print media than in broadcasting, political journalism is not recognized as a specialized field. Unlike editorial writers, cartoonists, sports writers or art critics, there is no professional association

---

[12] V. O. Key, Jr., *Public Opinion and American Democracy* (New York: Knopf, 1961), p. 281.

or easily identifiable corps of political reporters at the state or national level. Anyone interested in servicing the media has to construct painstakingly his own list of political reporters and editorial writers covering politics.

Nor are there formal political beats or systematic coverage of politics comparable to police reports, the stock market, sports, fashions or the theater. There is no evidence, for example, that the Washington press corps regularly visits the headquarters or major divisions of the parties or the offices of citizen groups, political consultants or similar sources that should comprise a Washington political news beat.

Even the performance of many political columnists leaves much to be desired in terms of information, insight, and analysis of politics. "One gets the feeling reading some columnists that their sources do not extend much beyond a careful reading of the *Post, Star, New York Times,* and *Wall Street Journal,*" observes Julius Duscha of the Washington Journalism Center. Some columnists are seldom seen where news is being made, while others "spend most of their days on the telephone with 'sources,' a euphemism for friends in government or on Capitol Hill."[13] Los Angeles *Times* correspondent Jules Witcover has pointed out another deficiency in Washington news. Describing the overworked AP and UPI staffs trying to cover congressional committee hearings, he observed: "Far from its being digging reporting, it is not even routine reporting. It is skimming, and yet the results of that time-honored procedure go out over the wires to editors who think they are getting solid committee coverage."[14]

The failure of the print media to develop political beats, coupled with the limited availability of specialized newsletters and the absence of a political news service to alert them to political trends and upcoming events, contributes to the non-

---

[13] Julius Duscha, "Washington Columnists: The Star Attractions of Spiro Agnew's Eastern Establishment Media Menagerie," *Washingtonian,* July 1970, p. 62.
[14] Jules Witcover, "Washington: The Workhorse Wire Services," *Columbia Journalism Review,* Summer 1969, p. 11. See also Michael Green, "Obstacles to Reform: Nobody Covers the House," *Washington Monthly,* June 1970, pp. 62–70.

reporting of much political news. The print media respond more often to easily recognized news events, press conferences and statements and rarely pay attention to subtle but often significant decisions and occurrences (like the failure of both national committees to meet during or within a reasonable period after the 1970 election campaign), although such events or nonevents may themselves constitute important news.

Although modern survey techniques are available, only a few papers and television stations retain professional polling firms to conduct state or metropolitan-area political polls.[15] The national wire services with their networks of state offices limit most of their political surveying to election years, although Ray Lahr of the UPI's Washington bureau has begun surveys of national committee members and other state leaders prior to meetings of the national committees. Walter R. Mears of the Associated Press also makes occasional national round-ups. Godfrey Sperling, Jr., national political correspondent of the *Christian Science Monitor*, operates the only regular national surveys of top political leaders, and even they appear infrequently. "We would publish them oftener," admits DeWitt John, former editor of the *Monitor*, "but frankly it is a question of cost."

Politics outside of Washington, where there is no comparable concentration of political figures or reporters, is even less adequately covered. Although members of the national press corps try to attend major meetings like governors' conferences and party conclaves where large numbers of party politicians congregate, only a handful of news bureaus free reporters for early and periodic political tours through the states, and these correspondents often lack adequate background on the politics of states they are visiting and writing about. National news organizations like *The New York Times*, *Newsweek*, *Time*, the *Congressional Quarterly*, and the *National Journal* do have state stringers, but these publications can devote only limited space to the highlights of state politics.

---

[15] See *Congressional Quarterly*'s survey of state polls, "Published Polls: Techniques and Results, by State," *Congressional Quarterly*, September 18, 1971, pp. 1931–34.

Although a few statewide and regional publications like the *Texas Observer*, the *Intermountain Observer*, the Pacific Northwest's *Argus*, and the *Maine Times* have established high standards, political reporting for the most part is even weaker at the state level, a factor that adds to the lack of the public's understanding and its motivation to participate in state politics and state party organizations. During recent statewide campaigns, for example, major daily newspapers in states as diverse as New Jersey, Texas and Kentucky did not send out reporters to cover state and congressional candidates. Instead they relied on prepared statements and press releases from candidates and telephone reports from campaign press aides for details on candidate appearances.

These weaknesses in the coverage of politics by the print media are accounted for in part by the economic downturn that began in 1969 and by the changing structure of the newspaper industry itself. Leading news bureaus have instituted a series of economy moves, including substantial reductions in travel budgets for reporters covering national political meetings or interviewing in the states. At the same time, mounting wire service and personnel costs have increased the pressure on editors of major dailies to use standardized prepackaged news from the various news services instead of staff-originated news. Such economic pressures account for the decline of the individual journalist and the rise of subadministrators or deskmen who sort "ready-made copy by the pound, neatly ground to fit particular editorial percolators," according to Professor John Hohenberg of the Columbia Graduate School of Journalism and Administrator of the Pulitzer Prizes.[16] John Rothchild, managing editor of the *Washington Monthly*, observes that "the growth of specialization in newspapers has brought many advantages in the quality of regular coverage, but it also means there are less floating reporters who are free to investigate and create their own news."[17] Still to be evalu-

---

[16] John Hohenberg, *Free Press/Free People: The Best Cause* (New York: Columbia University Press, 1971), p. 478.
[17] John Rothchild, "The Stories Reporters Don't Write," *Washington Monthly*, June 1971, p. 24.

ated in terms of their impact on news coverage are the longer-term trends toward consolidation of newspaper ownership and the growth of chains, already evidenced in the control of more than one-quarter of the nation's daily and Sunday newspapers by the seven largest newspaper groups in the country.

The elite character of the Washington press corps and the private nature of its political news sources also hamper full and critical coverage of politics. The relationship between reporter and politician may become too close, the columnist assuring himself of good leads and the politician often screening himself from public scrutiny and even winning plaudits in the press. Government and party officials invite select members of the corps to news "backgrounders" where information is freely divulged but no named sources may be used, just "a White House spokesman" or a "knowledgeable authority at the national committee." One of the most exclusive Washington press institutions is "Breakfast with Godfrey," begun in 1966 by Godfrey Sperling, Jr., of the *Christian Science Monitor*. Twice a week 20 or so newsmen are invited to interrogate a guest, usually a politician or government official, for 75 minutes. Some newsmen who could find no room at Godfrey's table have set up at least two other breakfast groups in competition. The small size and in-group quality of the top political reporters also tend to discourage forthright competitive journalism and to overlook the expression of the viewpoints of women, blacks, youth and other groups.

Compounding such weaknesses is the critical problem of information accessibility and retrieval, both for political activists and reporters and commentators. News organizations lack the facilities and personnel to process and make use of the increasing volume of political information available. Mass-circulation magazines and Sunday newspaper supplements sometimes carry excellent political features; other magazines like the *New Yorker*, *New York*, the *Washington Monthly*, the *National Journal* and the political-science journals often publish lengthy profiles and perceptive articles on various aspects of American politics; and the partisan press provides informative material on party politics and often outspoken interpretive reporting. Such material is widely scattered, however, and

with the absence of a medium that reproduces, digests, or
even indexes the key articles on politics that regularly appear
in print, relevant political developments or important antecedents to current events are for practical purposes inaccessible
to most reporters and their audiences. More important, even
though newsletters are "the fastest growing medium in communications," according to the Newsletter Clearinghouse, and
specialized newsletters have proliferated in recent years on
topics other than politics, there is no news service or major
newsletter that attempts to provide regular and comprehensive
reporting and analysis of state and national politics. The few
newsletters in circulation that devote substantial attention to
politics are a helpful beginning but still do not provide even
basic political information services.[18]

Developments in communications and computer technology
are, however, gradually making more political information
more readily available to the working press and the public.
The New York Times's computerized index and information
service is an important step in this direction. The Republican
National Committee has used its Miracode retrieval system to
provide members of the press with documentation on policy
positions of the Nixon administration. Although the current
costs of storage and operation limit its use, Project NEWS at
the Massachusetts Institute of Technology, sponsored by the
American Newspaper Publishers Association, has developed
information retrieval programs that can file, store and retrieve
wire-service stories directly from the news ticker. In the meantime, the far more simple information-retrieval problems remain to be solved.

---

[18] Newsletters by political columnists and commentators include the
American Political Report (Kevin P. Phillips [ed.]), the *Evans-Novak Political Report,* and Fulton Lewis III's *Exclusive Digest and Analysis of*
Washington Intelligence. The American Association of Political Consultants has recently begun an association magazine, *Polite'ia,* and Campaign Associates of Wichita, Kansas, circulates a newsletter on political
consulting, *Campaign Insight: A Monthly Overview of Political Techniques.* However, the only regularly updated calendar of political events
circulated nationally is prepared by Miss Josephine L. Good of the Republican National Committee.

Efforts to Reform the Media

Dissatisfaction with the performance of the media has led to a number of efforts to broaden the current range of political news and commentary and to upgrade the quality of political reporting.

Some efforts to improve journalism have been initiated within the news media themselves. The Louisville *Courier-Journal* and *Times* have opened an ombudsman office to answer questions or complaints about news coverage and to help readers with "problems requiring the attention of any top management personnel." Reporters on various papers have begun revolting against what they consider unwarranted censorship of their material and lack of representation in editorial and general newspaper policy. Reporters at the Minneapolis *Tribune*, for instance, demanded a voice in the running of their newspaper and received an advisory role in the appointment of assistant city editors.

Widespread uneasiness about the state of journalism has also found expression in the journalism reviews established in the last decade. *Columbia Journalism Review* in 1961 noted its concern "not over any supposed deterioration [of journalism] but over the probability that journalism is not yet a match for the complications of our age."[19] *Chicago Journalism Review*, founded in 1968, was the first of some 10 local journalism reviews whose aim was to point out the deficiencies and prejudices of the established press as well as instances of good reporting. *Columbia Journalism Review's* "Darts and Laurels," New York–based [*MORE*]'s "Hellbox," and *Hawaii Journalism Review's* "Knocks and Kudos" give pointed and brief comment on specific media practices.

Other efforts have been directed at the broadcast media from outside. In *How to Talk Back to Your Television Set*, Federal Communications Commissioner Nicholas Johnson has urged citizens to make full use of FCC rules and regulations

---

[19] "Why a Review of Journalism?," *Columbia Journalism Review*, May/June 1971, p. iv (reprinted from pilot issue, Fall 1961).

which assure adequate and unbiased programming in the public interest and provide a number of routes for appeal and action by concerned citizens. His advice on "what you can do to improve TV" includes such activities as petitioning to deny renewal of broadcast-station licenses, filing competing applications, seeking transfers of ownership and control and directly negotiating with local stations. Marsha O'Bannon Prewitt, a former aide to Johnson, has prepared a 44-page "Guide to Citizen Action in Radio and Television" outlining steps for combating inadequate or biased programming.

Another approach, that of systematic public monitoring of the broadcast media, illustrates the potential for citizen action. Working with three tape recorders, Edith Efron of *TV Guide* transcribed all the prime-time TV network news programs from mid-September to election eve in 1968. Her analysis of the data and findings of bias in news coverage have been published as a book, *The News Twisters*, which has provoked wide public discussion.[20] A somewhat different news-monitoring project, the Alfred I. DuPont–Columbia University Survey and Awards, recognizes excellence in broadcasting. A national network of 60 DuPont correspondents, supplemented by a large group of volunteer monitors from the American Association of University Women and by exchanges with more than 400 individual broadcasters, supplies the DuPont jurors with the best material throughout the country that the broadcasting industry is producing. Accuracy in Media (AIM), a nonpartisan, nonprofit citizen organization founded in response to media coverage of the disturbances at the 1968 Democratic National Convention, monitors the coverage of specific events and has gained the bipartisan backing of conservatives in Congress.

---

[20] Edith Efron, *The News Twisters* (Los Angeles: Nash Publishing Company, 1971). Harvard Professor Paul H. Weaver noted that the book's "supporters and detractors have quickly assimilated it to their own polemical purposes. This is a pity," he said, "for the book . . . presents for the first time an extensive and tolerably reliable body of evidence on the content of television coverage of the presidential campaign in 1968." (Paul H. Weaver, "Is Television News Biased?," *Public Interest,* Winter 1972, p. 60.)

Party efforts to improve media coverage of politics have generally been extremely lax. While national chairmen and the national committees have petitioned the FCC for national air time to answer presidential addresses, they have not regularly monitored network and local broadcasts to ensure fairness and equal time to party views. One of the most comprehensive and constructive party initiatives, a press project proposed in 1965 by Congressmen Thomas B. Curtis of Missouri and Bob Wilson of California, was initially authorized by the House Republican leadership but then terminated before it could be funded. In addition to an ambitious monitoring program, the project sought to improve press coverage of politics by disseminating minority-party views, statements and background information to the media.

One of the most effective expressions of public dissatisfaction with the performance of the established media has been the rapid growth of alternative media, such as the so-called underground or people press, student newspapers reaching down into the secondary school level, and FM underground stations. At its best advocacy journalism, at its worst irresponsible and inaccurate, the people press presents a fresh alternative to political reporting, particularly at the state and local level. Papers like the Los Angeles *Free Press*, the *East Village Other* and *Rolling Stone* reached an estimated circulation of almost five million in 1970. Topics of direct concern to many citizens but largely ignored by the conventional dailies receive extended coverage in the people press. Boston's *Phoenix*, for example, undertook a lengthy report and analysis of the politics and administration of justice in the Massachusetts judiciary and then turned its attention to Cambridge real-estate profiteering. The 60-station Moratorium Radio Network provided broadcasting's *only* sustained coverage of the April 1970 antiwar activities. The technology for low-cost people's television already exists, and groups like People's Video Theatre in New York and San Francisco's Mobile Muck Truck are taking their television gear in mobile units to the public and developing new interviewing and programming formats. This experimental medium has thus far produced publications like *Radical Software* and *Source* (a catalogue serving 500 radical print and media groups) and organized a national Alternative Media Conference.

Because they generally operate on extremely low budgets, publications of the people press face some serious handicaps in covering politics, especially national politics. Since many people-press reporters are not paid and their papers have not received second-class mailing privileges, they are denied accreditation to the Senate and House galleries by provisions that a reporter's principal income must be obtained "from news correspondence intended for publication in newspapers entitled to second-class mailing privileges" and that members of the press gallery are to be "bona fide correspondents of repute in their profession."[21] In turn, they cannot gain accreditation to the national party conventions, which is normally assigned to representatives of these same galleries, and at times political parties have set up additional procedures for accreditation that virtually exclude these media from party meetings. These rules have yet to be tested in force by underground-press reporters, although a single representative of the Underground Press Syndicate was given credentials to the House and Senate galleries by a 3–2 vote of gallery representatives.

Cable Television: The Sleeping Giant

Efforts to reform the media through alternative media, monitoring and journalism reviews could soon be dwarfed by the sweeping impact of cable television and its potential for new forms of communication and participation. According to one survey, cable television could develop into "a complete communications service" that would make the immense power of present television look "trivial in scope."[22] *Columbia Journalism Review* described the laying of the foundations of the

---

[21] Rules 4 (a) and 3, respectively, "Rules Governing Press Galleries," *Official Congressional Directory, 92nd Congress, First Session, convened January 21, 1971* (Washington, D.C.: United States Government Printing Office, 1971), p. 801.

[22] *On the Cable: The Television of Abundance,* Report of the Sloan Commission on Cable Communications (New York: McGraw-Hill, 1971), p. 167.

"wired nation" as "a technological development of historic moment" and pointed out that "the stakes are enormous—not only the control of television signals but also facsimile reproduction (including newspapers, books, and mail), banking and other marketing functions, computer research, possibly even election balloting."[23]

Cable television, or community antenna television (CATV) as it was initially labeled, has grown rapidly in the past 20 years, reaching about nine percent of the nation's 60 million television households in 1971. By 1980, 40 to 60 percent of American homes could be wired for cable reception.

Because the cables now in use have roughly a thousand times the carrying capacity of telephone wire, the channel capacity of television can be enlarged significantly. In August 1971, the FCC proposed a minimum capacity of 20 channels for future CATV systems, and several communities like Akron and San Jose are already developing 40 or more channel systems. Cable experts project the eventual possibility of hundreds of local channels, with modern satellites easily providing 40 or more new coast-to-coast channels.

During this first phase of development, cable television for the most part is still aimed at general audiences, in this case to everyone connected to the system, although a much larger variety of programs can be made available. This potential alone has obvious and significant consequences for news broadcasting, public affairs programming and the direct political use of television. FCC deliberations point toward even further decentralization and diversification by encouraging greater local programming and community use of cable television and barring certain forms of cross-ownership of CATV. The commission has, for example, proposed that systems with 20 channels reserve one free and noncommercial public-access channel available on a nondiscriminatory basis, a second for educational uses, a third for state and local government and politics, and several leased or common-carrier channels for commercial users. The television of abundance will open up significant

---

[23] "CATV: Coverage Now," *Columbia Journalism Review,* Winter 1970–71, p. 4.

new political resources and possibilities. Eugene V. Rostow, Yale law professor and former chairman of President Johnson's Task Force on Communications Policy, forecast in 1970 that cable television "should reduce the cost of access to television by all kinds of interests and groups, and make local politics, at least, feasible again at a reasonable cost."[24]

The second and truly revolutionary stage of cable development will follow once one-way cable is converted to a two-way communications network with a switching capacity similar to the telephone system so that the viewer will be able to send communications out of his home via television. The FCC has already proposed that future cable systems make provisions for limited two-way communications to enable the subscriber to send at least a nonvoice signal to his local program origination point.

The implications of this development are staggering. If cable-system operators can receive, broadcast, originate and store in libraries a sufficient range of television programs from VHF and cable networks, independent producers and broadcasters, viewers will have unprecedented choice both as to what they view and when they view it. Ralph Lee Smith, who has written a basic primer on cable TV for the Fund for Investigative Journalism, predicts that with two-way cable "every home and office will contain a communications center of a breadth and flexibility to influence every aspect of private and community life."[25] In addition to standard television broadcasts, such a system could provide: 1) home library services permitting page-by-page viewing and facsimile recording of the contents of libraries stored on microfilm or videotape, 2) facsimile data service which would furnish the subscriber with computer printout summaries of new information and events of interest, 3) mail delivery within minutes anywhere in the United States, 4) home crime detection and prevention, 5) home business conferences via videophone, and 6) consumer

---

[24] Eugene V. Rostow, "The Future of Cable Television," address to the annual convention of the National Cable Television Association, Chicago, June 8, 1970.

[25] Ralph Lee Smith, "The Wired Nation," *Nation*, May 18, 1970, p. 582.

shopping from the home with a central accounting computer to adjust bank and store-account balances. Ben Bagdikian has suggested that cable connected to computers will also revolutionize the nature of advertising by permitting exact audience measurement: "It will not be difficult to feed into the computer data about each household connected to the cable, so that among other things the computer will show the economic, educational, occupational, and other characteristics of households listening to each program."[26]

Several other applications of cable television suggest the power of the new medium and its potential impact on American politics. Broad-band two-way communications offer an alternative to physical movement and costly transportation. Citizens will be able to engage in politics from their homes in the same way that they will be able to shop, bank, conduct business with clients, "visit" doctors, and so forth. Political parties or cause groups will be able to lease common-carrier network channels that will enable them to mobilize entire constituencies rapidly or to put together national meetings, conferences and strategy sessions in the homes of the members concerned. Party reform commissions in the 50 states could lease time for national and regional cable TV workshops. Annual meetings of citizen groups could be broadcast live to the national membership. Party educational programs could be programmed for cable-television distribution. Individual citizens could initiate contacts or meetings with citizens of similar interests through cable-TV subscriber services.

Candidates for public office will benefit directly from the new broadcasting pattern of small cable systems since they will be able to reach small local television constituencies on free time or at a small fraction of the current cost of commercial television time. Political consultants, working with parties or independently, will be able to link up cable television with current computer programs for specialized media strategies using direct mail and telephone.

Community political and governmental meetings are already

---

[26] Ben H. Bagdikian, *The Information Machines: Their Impact on Men and the Media* (New York: Harper & Row, 1971), p. 255.

being broadcast on cable systems and this use is expected to expand. With two-way communication it will be possible to stage electronic town meetings. Many municipalities have made provisions in their leases of cable franchises for channels to broadcast municipal and educational services.

In the near future, all-news and all-public-affairs national cable networks linking separate cable systems by satellite will be able (with appropriate permission) to broadcast live sessions of Congress and its committees and state and local legislative bodies, governmental and party leaders' press conferences, and a wider range of news and public affairs programs.

Citizens will have much greater access to current political news. Some cable systems are devoting one channel to a wire-service ticker where the subscriber can see the same Teletype messages that are being typed out in newsrooms across the country. Eventually viewers will be able to obtain facsimile reproduction of particular news stories of interest. When computerized information systems are economically feasible, cable will provide convenient access for citizens who want to use them. Although most experts do not expect home newspaper facsimile until the 1990's, the distinction between printed and broadcast news will increasingly be blurred in the intervening decades.[27]

Current telephone and mail polls used on various local radio and television news and talk shows will be replaced by direct audience polls by two-way cable. National cable networks will in time be able to take instantaneous national surveys on political poll questions, and network analysts could subdivide audience response for more extensive analysis and interpretation. With proper safeguards for voter identification, it would be technically feasible for the individual voter to receive facsimile ballots and background information in his home and to vote in elections at all levels without leaving his residence.

---

[27] According to Bagdikian, "Newspapers will have to decide whether they are printing factories or analysts of daily political and social information." (*Ibid.*, p. 283.)

There are, of course, many developmental problems ahead. The second phase of cable development will require supporting computer technology to give it a sufficient switching capability, a requirement that may delay its full impact for a decade or two. A more immediate problem is the quality of programming. In 1970, before the FCC ruling that cable systems with more than 3,500 subscribers had to originate local programming by April 1971, only five to ten percent of cable systems offered live programming of local origin. News programs are often limited to ticker-tape news, and news services like Documentary Broadcasting Syndicate, which projected 11 hours of daily live nationwide news programming, have failed in their initial efforts to obtain financing. Professor Amitai Etzioni of Columbia has raised the possibility that "lacking a source of funds to support public and educational CATV programming, these channels may be incredibly dull."[28] Other observers fear that commercial interests and cultural-junk tastes will corrupt the potential of cable TV for diversity of expression.[29]

One of the most serious implications of cable television is that it will reinforce some current trends toward stratification and fragmentation of American society. The affluent population that is able to afford the extra costs of cable and special pay-television features, as well as the future electronic appliances of the home communications center, will increasingly be able to live, work and enjoy recreation *within* the insular household in physical isolation from the urban ghettos and problems of urban living.

At the same time, however, groups that have been denied access to mass media stand to gain influence. Black Efforts for Soul in Television (BEST) sees cable television as a significant opportunity for blacks and other minority groups and neighborhoods to gain a voice in their community government. Some

---

28 Amitai Etzioni, "CATV: High Potential, Many Problems," *Wall Street Journal,* September 8, 1970.
29 See Stuart P. Sucherman, "Cable TV: The Endangered Revolution," *Columbia Journalism Review,* May/June 1971, pp. 13–20; and Judy Strasser, "Smoke Screen Cloaks Cable-TV Czars," *Christian Science Monitor,* August 7, 1971.

cable owners see CATV developing as a group of "community networks." Social and political institutions like the political parties may, however, be able to use the new media to increase communication and understanding among the separate communities and cultures within America, for example, through cable-television hearings on state and national party platforms or through participation by cable in party caucuses and conventions.

Regardless of its current state of development, the future of CATV raises fundamental questions of public policy and new definitions of the public interest that should concern citizens in general and the parties in particular. Such discussions, however, have been left in the hands of a tangled complex of Washington lobbying and interest groups, the FCC, the White House Office of Telecommunications Policy, the cable-television and over-the-air broadcasting industries, and government officials with ownership interests in radio and television stations. Some of the biggest American corporations are already investing heavily in the cable TV industry—Time Inc., General Electric, Kaiser, Gulf & Western, Hughes Aircraft, General Instrument, General Tire and Rubber, Westinghouse, American Telephone and Telegraph and General Telephone and Electronics—and the intensive politics of who receives which license or franchise and what laws, rules, regulations and court tests guide the struggle only occasionally come into public view. The FCC, under Chairman Dean Burch, held an unprecedented series of public panels on the future of cable television to satisfy the regulatory agency's hearings requirement and encourage greater public discussion of the issues involved.

Some citizen organizations like Americans for Democratic Action and the American Civil Liberties Union have joined the dialogue, and the United Church of Christ has begun an advisory service designed to inform citizens, especially minorities and the poor, of their rights with regard to cable television. A coalition of more than 40 education, public service and community organizations known as PUBLICABLE has organized in Washington to assure wide public involvement, and major foundations, including the Ford Foundation (through grants to the RAND Corporation) and the Alfred P.

Sloan Foundation (through the establishment of a Commission on Cable Communications), have sponsored research and advanced public policy discussion. The parties, however, appear to remain blissfully ignorant of the revolutionary era in media that lies ahead. Neither major party has taken steps to appoint a party study group or to submit party-approved views or recommendations on cable television to the FCC. Meanwhile, the potential of cable television for new forms of communication and participation remains largely undeveloped, waiting like a sleeping giant.

Recommendations: Media Responsibility in a New Political Era

The media's performance of their responsibility for communicating political news and background information and analysis and the potential impact of the coming communications revolution will have far-reaching consequences for the nation's political development and for the progress of party modernization. Although the parties themselves can do much to improve media coverage through an open information policy and more aggressive and informative party communications, expanded and systematic political news coverage and more readily accessible and retrievable information on politics are essential and attainable objectives for the 1970's.

The communications media have given little systematic or focused attention to the political responsibilities their power entails in a democratic society. The specific recommendations advanced below assume that professional associations and publications within the media will review their responsibilities for developing citizen competence in politics and government and in so doing assign a much higher priority to the reporting and analysis of politics.

Recommendation 1. The media could take the lead in improving public access to and retrieval of information on politics and introduce such improvements as new information formats, comprehensive political information indexes, and a political news and information digest.

To keep pace with the continuing information explosion, the media could take the lead in structuring and presenting political news and information to make this valuable resource more accessible and understandable to those interested in politics. Newspapers could develop convenient new information formats to present political news stories, features, columns and other information for those citizens who want to follow local, state and national politics. Regular notice columns could list radio and television news, commentary and public service broadcasts, forthcoming party and other political meetings and the schedules of candidates and party officials. The current status of party reform commissions, convention arrangements, delegate selection procedures and court cases relating to politics could be conveniently presented in summary tables.

More comprehensive indexing of political information is essential to ensure its ready accessibility. The daily news index format of *The New York Times* and the multiple index format of the *National Journal* (with personal name, private organization, and geographical indexes included weekly and additional government organization and subject indexes printed quarterly) could be adapted by other publications to help readers locate political news and background items. Current books on politics should be well indexed by subject matter as well as names to increase their usefulness. A political news and information digest modeled after *Atlas* or *Current* could be established which would list and reprint key political news articles, analyses, and book reviews from other media.

The media, parties, academic institutions and private organizations could also take joint steps to deal with the longer-term problems and applications of information retrieval in politics and to develop basic libraries on politics and political data banks and ensure their availability to a wide range of organizations and individuals.

Recommendation 2. The media should take steps to substantially improve political news coverage for the attentive and activist audiences of politics through such means as political news services, specialized newsletters on politics, an association of political writers, greater use of political analysts and consultants, and new polling and survey services.

The major news organizations should further expand and broaden their capabilities for reporting and analysis of all aspects of American politics. The news media, in particular television and radio networks that do not already do so, could designate and publicly identify full-time political reporters to cover specific beats such as the party national chairmen and national committees, state parties, the congressional parties, political consultants, and citizen organizations active in party politics. In order to build their audience as well as to inform the public, news media could assign special investigative teams and devote periodic series of articles or programs to major developments like the party reform movement, the growth of national convention arrangements and security precautions, and the pervasive new role of professional campaign consultants.

Specialized news services focusing primarily on politics should be established to cover political personalities and events, party meetings and publications and other news sources only skimmed by the established national wire services. A national political news service similar to the Religious News Service (RNS) or Science News Service (SNS) could assign reporters and investigative teams at both the national and state levels and distribute their stories to interested media. The Democratic and Republican parties could establish party news services to perform similar functions both for the news media and the party media, helping thereby to build up party publications as an alternative means of communicating political news to party members.

A comprehensive political newsletter and audiocassette service should be established to provide political reporters, news organizations, party activists and interested citizens with information on national and state party politics as well as short but incisive analyses of a range of political topics. Both the newsletter and cassettes could include news items on party activities and personnel, summaries of important political

sessions, an inclusive political calendar and original investigative reporting. The newsletter could also refer its readers to
other sources of political reporting and offer reprints of key
news articles and political documents.

Even before such political news services are established,
individual newspapers and other subscribers could make
greater use of the news resources available to them and improve the media coverage of politics by requesting more
political features, surveys, and investigative reports from the
national wire services and special Washington news services,
by urging syndicated columnists to analyze political topics of
interest to their local readership and by exchanging ideas for
political coverage of national and state politics with their
Washington bureaus or representatives of the various news
services.

The media could expand their use of outside political analysts
and consultants such as political scientists, professional campaign managers and party and citizen activists to provide background analysis for editors, commentators and reporters and to
participate directly in expanded convention, election and political news coverage. Advisory panels like *Time*'s board of economic advisers, which meets periodically with the magazine's
editors to discuss economic affairs, could be appointed to perform such functions on a regular basis.

Since polls have become an important source of political
information to the media as well as to the parties and candidates, the major wire services, radio and television networks
and newspapers could sponsor regular national polls or develop
or contract for independent polling and survey services on
topics of particular interest to their audiences. The wire services
through their state bureaus could also expand their periodic
surveys of political leaders in the 50 states as well as within
individual states.

At the same time, the media should ensure that their staffing
and top-level assignments are more nearly representative of
the population as a whole. Panels on network news programs
could be expanded, regional anchor men could be appointed
in such cities as Los Angeles, Denver, Chicago and Atlanta, and
a broader range of outside political analysts could be used

in order to afford more opportunities for women and minority-group representatives.

An association of political writers and commentators could be established to encourage public awareness of and support for the functions and responsibilities of political reporting and to provide a forum in which political writers could exchange ideas, work for the solution of common problems facing the media, set standards for the profession, and recognize outstanding examples of political journalism. An association could facilitate adequate distribution of political news through such steps as publishing a current directory of political reporters.

Recommendation 3. Citizen groups, political parties and public interest advocates can encourage improved media performance, especially at the local and state levels, through the establishment of citizen media councils, news monitoring programs, action guides and additional journalism reviews.

Citizen groups, the political parties, particularly at the state and local level and public interest advocates could take several steps to improve news and public affairs programming. Citizen media councils could be formed to study and report on the quality of political reporting and to promote more adequate media coverage of politics. Media councils could coordinate bipartisan, independent and citizen efforts such as community forums for the exchange of views with the management of local media outlets, volunteers for public service programs, letter-writing campaigns requesting more political news and analysis in newspapers and on radio and television and financial contributions to public television.

Party organizations, media councils, or other citizen groups could establish monitoring programs to ensure adequate and unbiased media coverage of political news and public affairs. Monitoring could be accomplished through national, state and local press and clipping services such as Press Intelligence, Washington, D.C., which can provide relevant clippings on specific topics; through broadcast monitoring services such as Radio-T.V. Reports, New York, which can provide videotapes, tapes, stills, or transcripts of radio and television programs; or through citizen monitors. A correction mechanism for errors in political reporting could be developed, going beyond the current use of the *Congressional Record* by individual members of Congress, including expanded use of the letters-to-the-editor format.

Media councils, other citizen groups, or the parties could also develop and provide their members with action guides, similar to those developed by lawyers and researchers in the public interest movement, which would detail specific information necessary for effective citizen action, such as lists of the owners and responsible officials of broadcast stations and newspapers, dates and places of the annual stockholders' meetings of companies controlling various media, dates and procedures for challenging FCC license renewals, and recommended procedures for submitting documented complaints and suggestions to such groups.

Members of the journalism profession themselves can provide a degree of internal self-discipline and set specific standards for political reporting through their professional associations and the various journalism reviews. Additional reviews could be established in the major regions of the country lacking them to provide working reporters and more citizens the opportunity to comment on news coverage and analysis by all media.

Recommendation 4. Citizens, community groups and the political parties should take an active interest in the development and regulation of cable television during its introductory stages to ensure broad citizen participation and improved political and public affairs programming.

Whether cable television realizes its full potential will depend in good measure on the initiatives of individual citizens, citizen groups and political leaders. The political parties in particular should commit themselves publicly to the goals of improved political and public affairs programming, greater public service and increased citizen participation in the development of cable television. Modernized political parties could benefit directly from an expanded activist audience able to participate in politics and government through cable television in such new ways as electronic town meetings or party caucuses.

In view of the likely impact of cable television, the political parties should assign high priority to the careful study of the development, potential and regulation of CATV. The parties should appoint representative party commissions on cable television to conduct public hearings and staff investigations so as to define party policy objectives for the new medium and to recommend action programs that can be implemented at the national, state and local level. The commissions could, for example, make recommendations concerning the reservation and use of cable channels and networks for political and public affairs news and programming and urge party and citizen groups to work for their adoption. Citizens, party reformers and party organizations could be kept informed on pending decisions and procedures of the FCC concerning requirements for the control and regulation of CATV.

The parties could develop long-term political information, education and training programs adaptable to CATV and cooperate with the media to establish libraries of videocassettes for use on cable television. Party meetings, conferences, reports, conventions, interviews and other political events could be videorecorded, indexed and distributed to cable libraries for later viewing at the convenience of the citizen.

IX

Political Consultants and the Technology of the "New Politics"

America has discovered the political consultant. The banner in an article in the *Potomac* Sunday magazine section of the Washington *Post* proclaimed, "Political Consultants: Their Tentacles Grow and Grow." Joe McGinniss's *The Selling of the President: 1968* topped the nation's nonfiction bestseller lists for weeks. Top consultants charged $500 or more per day for their services in the 1968 and 1970 campaigns. President Nixon's media consultant Roger Ailes offered a $12,000 package entitling clients to 12 eight-hour sessions of coaching, videotaping and media advice plus "consultation and emergencies" during the campaign. Many consultants took a 15 percent cut of the huge media advertising budgets they helped to place.

When the 1970 election returns were in, the process of deflation quickly began. "The image makers struck out, didn't they?" captioned the Boston *Globe*. "Box scores" for the big names like Joseph Napolitan, Roger E. Ailes, David Garth, Charles Guggenheim and Harry W. Treleaven, Jr., were compiled by Bernard Nossiter of the Washington *Post*. One of the largest firms—Bailey, Deardourff & Bowen—could not show a single winner among its major Senate and gubernatorial races. The losses of the big media spenders, Richard L. Ottinger in New York, Howard Metzenbaum in Ohio and Sam Grossman in Arizona (all Democratic senatorial candidates), were object lessons that political office should not be purchasable with high-priced consultants and media blitzes. At the same time that the press was burying the consultants, however, the American Association of Political Consultants was meeting in New

York for a two-day seminar analyzing the 1970 campaigns—a type of exercise the political parties themselves have seldom attempted. The newly self-conscious profession of political counseling pushed ahead with plans for its own publication (*Polite'ia*), a permanent secretariat, a fellowship program, possible alignment with a university or an institute of political studies, research projects sponsored by foundations or industry, a job-referral service and marketing opportunities.

In the past decade, consulting firms have proliferated both in number and in specialized services.[1] Consultants have started business in virtually every state and region of the country. In Vermont, New England area pollster and consultant John F. Becker gave critical strategic advice to the late Republican Senator Winston L. Prouty in his tight 1970 race with former Democratic Governor Philip H. Hoff. Deloss Walker & Associates, a 14-man media firm based in Arkansas and Tennessee, helped Democratic political novice Dale L. Bumpers oust Arkansas' Republican Governor Winthrop Rockefeller. The total number of firms involved in providing campaign services of all kinds probably exceeds 300, although no accurate figures are available, a problem the Association's first president, Joseph Napolitan, remarked upon: "We keep turning up new people." Individual firms have begun to handle more campaigns and accounts over longer periods of time, to develop extensive subcontracting arrangements with other firms, to extend campaign services to new areas such as state legislative and municipal races, and to work on school-bond issues and for bipartisan cause groups.

At the same time that political consulting has become a

---

[1] See David Lee Rosenbloom, "Managers in Politics" (unpublished Ph.D. dissertation, Massachusetts Institute of Technology, 1970); James M. Perry, *The New Politics: The Expanding Technology of Political Manipulation* (New York: Clarkson N. Potter, 1968); Dan Nimmo, *The Political Persuaders: The Techniques of Modern Election Campaigns,* Spectrum Books (Englewood Cliffs, N.J.: Prentice-Hall, 1970); Robert L. Chartrand, *Computers and Political Campaigning* (New York: Spartan Books, 1972); "Professional Managers, Consultants Play Major Roles in 1970 Political Races," *National Journal,* September 26, 1970, pp. 2077–87; and "Campaign Management: Expertise Brings Dollars," *Congressional Quarterly,* May 1, 1970, pp. 1183–91.

truly national phenomenon, top American consultants have internationalized their operations. Americans helped to shape the International Association of Political Consultants. A combine of the best-known American political consultants, including such figures as Lawrence F. O'Brien (who went on leave to become Democratic National Chairman), Joseph Napolitan and F. Clifton White, organized an international consulting firm, Public Affairs Analysts, that has sought clients among major international corporations. An American consulting firm has a substantial contract with a leading party of one Western European country to develop advanced campaign simulation techniques (which in turn can be applied by the same firm in this country).

Recent public fascination with the political consultants has both overestimated and underestimated their growing influence. Political consultants are clearly not a new "magic" quantity in politics. The area of political counseling is as old as politics, and the campaign manager or the "professional" in politics has long been on the scene. What, then, is really different or new about political consultants and campaign-management firms and what effects have they had on party politics?

Unlike party organizations and most candidates, campaign-management firms are not tied to a single geographical political base. They deal with clients across the country or within a region, specializing in the building of temporary limited-purpose organizations, i.e., political campaigns. Political consulting firms can and have at various times provided every service a party organization has traditionally supplied. In Nelson Rockefeller's California presidential primary campaign in 1964, Spencer-Roberts literally constructed a primary organization from the precinct up. Matthew Reese has been selling precinct organization services and telephone "bucket shops" to Democratic candidates across the country for years.

The political consulting firms can be viewed as new forms of entrepreneurship and venture capital in politics. Their growth has corresponded with the development and adjustment of the parties to new technologies of communications and organization in American politics. They have stepped in to fill what could be described as the wasteland of American party politics created by the changing political environment and ignored by the parties. A number of factors, including the erosion of patronage-based party organizations, the growth and increased mobility of the American population, the development of the mass media, advancing political technology and mounting campaign budgets, have combined over the past few decades to produce this significant organizational and communications vacuum in American politics.[2]

Political consultants now constitute one of the most important agents of change in the political system. They have become both innovators and brokers serving to bring new technologies, such as television and automatic data processing, into politics. While many observers talk of the need to reform the parties or create new parallel structures in politics, the political consultants are in effect doing just those things.

Over the coming decade, the supply of political consultants will probably grow sufficiently to provide any user the consulting services for which he or an organization is willing to pay. Consultants can be used by insurgents seeking to elect "cause" candidates and reform institutions or by party regulars seeking to reinforce the established order.

Professional campaign-management firms, an effort by candidates to add certainty to their campaigns, constitute a new element of uncertainty in the political future. On the one hand, the political consulting industry may reinforce the existing party *structure* at the same time that party identification within the electorate has been weakening. The substitution of professional staff, consultants, communications and information technology

---

[2] See Harold Mendelsohn and Irving Crespi, *Polls, Television, and the New Politics* (Scranton, Pa.: Chandler Publishing Company, 1970). Professor Richard Jensen of the University of Illinois (Chicago Circle) dates the beginning of the "mercantilist" style in American politics with the presidential campaign of 1916, well before the advent of radio and television. (See Richard Jensen, "American Election Campaigns: A Theoretical and Historical Typology," paper prepared in May 1968 for delivery to the Midwest Political Science Conference, Chicago.)

and money for the old party pros, amateur participation and a popular organizational base is most clearly reflected in Republican state and national party organizations. An alternative direction of development of consultant use is suggested by the Democrats, emphasizing candidates instead of party organization and involving organized labor and other groups aligned with the party. Still another possible direction of development is the use of political consultants by citizen organizations apart from the two major parties.

As a new and generally available political resource, political consultants open some exciting possibilities for modernization of the parties. At the same time, their advent poses important new issues. Will the significant increase in political power represented by the political consulting industry and the political technologies it is developing and applying be subject to public and party regulation? And can the trend toward greater professionalization in party politics now being encouraged by consultants be counterbalanced by greater citizen involvement and participation in the use of new political technology?

The Republicans: Toward Technocratic Politics?

The developing relationships between political consulting firms and the parties are most clearly illustrated by what has been happening in the Republican party. The Republican experience has been one of a developing party-consultant relationship of mutual dependence, with each partner specializing in what he does best. Almost every significant firm dealing with Republican candidates now has competed or is competing for contracts with national, state or county Republican organizations. Several factors explain this close relationship.

The relationship has been economically beneficial to both principals. The Republican party organization, with its continuing access to funds, and growing financial base contrasted to its relatively weak organizational base, has recognized the need and desirability for outside technical assistance. The consulting firms provide a variety of specialized services, some of which are quite new to volunteer-based parties. It makes economic sense for the parties to contract for some of these services as they are needed rather than to attempt to build them into the party structure. For example, in 1969 the Republican National Committee under National Chairman Morton announced an organizational shift toward "a consultant concept" of contracting out specialized national committee services.

The management firms for their part need the economic stability and the continuing financial support that party organizations can provide. Some consultants feel that party state committees are much better financial risks than candidate organizations and prefer to handle candidate services through the state party. Accordingly, a number of firms have sought long-term relationships with national and state party organizations.

The consulting firms and party organizations have also found it mutually advantageous to specialize in certain areas. The economic law of comparative advantage is at work: the specialized skills that consultants represent are still in limited supply and the parties still have considerable resources in volunteer workers. Consultants seem to agree that party organizations are potentially most effective at systematic fund raising and precinct organization, voter registration, canvassing and getting out the vote. "Management firms will show us how to make better use of local organizations," observed one Republican party official. "They will not replace local party organization; they'll strengthen it."

An important form of specialization that has linked the consulting firms and the party organizations is basic research and innovation. The consulting firms concentrate their resources on research and development of services for the parties which are gradually incorporated into the party structure or bought as standardized services. The Republican National Committee and the Republican organizations in several large states, such as California and Minnesota, have invested initially in consultants with the longer-term objective of building their own professional capability. Richard B. Wirthlin of Decision Making Information admits, "You've automatically created a competitor over the short run, but we have everything to gain and nothing to lose by aligning with state committees. This is an evolving and changing field. We're interested in taking the next step—simulation. Let the party backfill in what has become standard or routine. We've given state committees the responsibility for about half of what we were doing two years ago."

One problem that consultants are quick to recognize concerns how long the process can continue. "It works fine as long as there is a frontier," Wirthlin remarks. "Right now we have more things that we want to get into than we can handle in the next five years." A critical factor, of course, is how much money is available for research and development. The Republican National Committee has invested large sums in contract research, and the Nixon campaigns of both 1968 and 1972 financed the longest, most expensive and most complex political polling operations in campaign history.[3] The American Medical Association Political Action Committee has invested an undisclosed amount, estimated by some to be in the hundreds of thousands of dollars, in basic research by Decision Making Information, formerly a subsidiary of Spencer-Roberts, which works almost exclusively for Republican candidates. AMPAC has encouraged other Republican-oriented consultants, underwriting, for example, the development of some imaginative new survey research techniques by Professor Dan Nimmo of the University of Missouri and Roy Pfautch for Civic Service Incorporated.

The consultant–party relationship constitutes an important new mechanism for involving talent and creativity in politics in a way that is mutually exciting and satisfying to the participants. The advent of the consultant firms has broadened participation in the top echelons of party politics in two important ways. It has helped to breed a new generation of party professionals who have entered politics and been trained through the parties at the same time that it has made it possible for talented professionals to stay in politics at salary levels and under nonparty organization working conditions that meet

---

[3] See Andrew J. Glass, "Pollsters Prowl Nation as Candidates Use Opinion Surveys to Plan '72 Campaign," *National Journal*, August 14, 1971, pp. 1693–1705.

their demands. The old party boss who worked his way up in the organization and his circle of trusted political cronies have been replaced by the fast-moving team of the professional full-time paid state chairman or executive director and the political consultant who function almost as alter egos.

For their part, party officials are conscious of their role in developing consulting talent and encouraging it to stay in Republican politics. Former Republican National Committee Deputy Chairman and political consultant James N. Allison, Jr., sees the Republican National Committee's role as building a reserve of trained professionals: "We must first analyze who the good ones are and then find ways to keep them intact between elections either in industry or through patronage." During his tenure, the RNC distributed to state parties a list of computer firms approved as technically competent and politically secure to handle redistricting after the 1970 census. Several Republican consultants have been awarded government contracts or consultantships by the Nixon administration to take up the slack of nonelection years, among them Harry Treleaven, a partner in Allison's firm of Allison, Treleaven & Rietz, who was retained by Secretary of the Interior and former Republican National Chairman Morton to advise him on the department's information programs.

The consultants themselves share with the party leadership the objective of building political parties into more effective organizational forces. Many of the Republican consultants have a party background either as professional staffers or through volunteer organization work. Consultants have a direct business interest in getting to know party officials and their problems, and some make it a practice to attend meetings of state chairmen, the national committee and professional staff and research conferences, as well as state party meetings in areas where they have clients.

Consultants see part of their role as bringing rationality to party organization. Spencer-Roberts worked closely with California Republican leaders in developing the CALPLAN, a multiyear plan designed to build party strength in the state legislative districts and targeted for the 1970 legislature, which would handle state legislative redistricting. The plan actually ran ahead of schedule, with Republicans winning control of both houses of the legislature through special elections in 1969. In 1970, however, all the planning of CALPLAN and the re- sources of Spencer-Roberts could not offset the weakness of keeping incumbent Republican Senator George L. Murphy at the head of the ticket, and the relatively disorganized and understaffed California Democratic party won both houses of the legislature.

Consultants see logical economies in centralizing under strong state party organizations some party functions such as research, polling, computer data analysis and services, ad- vertising research, and fund raising and budgeting—a view shared by many state party chairmen. "The party is the ideal mechanism for continuity in politics, not the officeholder," commented one consultant specializing in survey research. "Survey research and electronic data processing give the party a lever to bring candidates together." Consultants also see the programmatic value of strong parties. "The party is a hell of a vehicle to get control in a state and keep it. You can't do that through a candidate."

Some of the implications of the developing consultant-party relationship for the future of the Republican party should already be clear. Given the growing financial base of the party, a continuing relationship should mean both further party investment in the industry and the steady professionalization of the Republican party structure. Republican consultants see the national and state parties emerging as "giant service bureaus or agencies" providing a wider range of services than they ever have before. The parties are developing a new in- formation base, observes Richard Wirthlin and "party head- quarters staffs will perform the central brokerage for these information sources and computer programs." One Western Republican state chairman described the process of organiza- tional development as "drawing the lines and filling the squares on the grid of a checkerboard."

The direction and rate of this significant innovation in American party politics are controlled partly by the Republican party leadership and partly by the consultants themselves. The task of probing the political frontier, of deciding how much to invest in simulation versus media analysis and motivational research, for example, has fallen to the consultants. Theirs is the longer time horizon. To stay in business, they always have to be one step ahead of the politicians. The Republican-oriented consulting firms are well into planning for the later 1970's, defining a new information-based model of the political party.

The fluidity and dynamic character of the political consulting industry obscure some significant trends toward concentration. There is evidence that the industry, especially on the Republican side, may be dominated by something new in American politics, the consulting conglomerate working exclusively for one of the national parties. (For reasons discussed below, the Democratic party may pool comparable consulting resources in quite different ways.)

The conglomerate as an organizational form has evolved gradually over the past decade as the result of a number of conscious decisions by individual consulting firms. The first prototypes were the Spencer-Roberts/Decision Making Information complex[4] with a base in the West and South, and Market Opinion Research/Bailey, Deardourff & Bowen in the Midwest and Northeast. At this stage, one or two other complexes could still emerge on the Republican side if someone with the necessary capital resources were able to consolidate some of the smaller independent firms and consultants.

The pattern of development for the conglomerates has had the following elements. The firms have decided to work exclusively for one party, i.e., to develop a long-term relationship with one of the major parties based on mutual familiarity and confidence of key consulting and party officials. In so doing they have gained access to the innermost circles of party strategy making. In return, the parties have gained some assurances of continuity and security.

---

[4] Decision Making Information recently repurchased the 20 percent of its stock that had been owned by Spencer-Roberts. DMI subsequently acquired CMP Research of Phoenix, which specializes in survey research and financial surveys and has broadened its scope of operations to include advertising. "We are actually doing twice the amount of work in January 1972 that we were doing in 1970," states Vincent Barabba of DMI.

The firms have expanded the services they offer by such means as forming new subsidiaries, buying into other firms, subcontracting to smaller firms and maintaining senior consultants. Interlocking directorates, shared facilities and continuing networks of professional contacts link the conglomerates and their satellites.

The range of capabilities of the conglomerate is determined by its long-term corporate objectives and planning. A first step has been to link a general campaign management or consulting capability with a polling capacity and/or an electronic data-processing capacity. Spencer-Roberts, through the establishment of Datamatics (later reconstituted as Decision Making Information), moved in this direction. Bailey, Deardourff & Bowen (formerly Campaign Consultants, Inc., then Campaign Systems) has moved in the direction of media and political advertising. The first agency-structured political advertising firm in the industry, BD&B aspires to becoming "the premier political advertising and consulting firm in the United States." Its connection with Market Opinion Research Corporation (which owns a quarter of its stock) gives it access to a major Republican polling capacity. MORC's president, Frederick P. Currier, has built a media market-analysis capability in the firm that is unique in the industry. MORC in turn has sub-contracted some of its computer systems work to Politicon, an upcoming but still small firm based in Pittsburgh.

The political objectives of the conglomerates have escalated with their capabilities. Both consulting complexes, while maintaining ties with regular state party organizations, worked with Republican presidential nominating campaigns in 1968, Spencer-Roberts/Decision Making Information with Ronald Reagan and the Republican conservatives, MORC/BD&B with George W. Romney, Nelson Rockefeller and the Republican moderates. Both would like to elect a future President, although each has a different view of the kind of Republican candidate it would like to support.[5] The MORC/BD&B team makes no

[5] Peter A. Herrndorf and C. Edward Ward, Jr., "The Business of Politics: The Economics of the Political Consulting Industry" (unpublished research report, Harvard Business School, 1970).

secret of its plans to be around after the Nixon administration. Members of "the combine" (as they sometimes refer to themselves) view one another as "right-thinking guys" and admit that a common philosophical orientation is "an overriding consideration" in their joint enterprise. "We have the same vision of where the goal line is," one observed. By 1976 they expect the leadership of the Republican party to accrue to the moderate Republicans.

Neither group of firms, whatever its preference for the national ticket, wanted to undertake the challenge of an incumbent Republican administration, especially one which was demonstrably able to pour millions into its campaign budget. In looking beyond 1972, the conglomerates are likely to continue developing their differential political and competitive advantages. The new consulting team that emerges from the Spencer-Roberts/DMI reorganization might logically develop an organization-oriented strategy directed to Republican growth areas in the West and South. In 1968, Datamatics served as the purchasing agent for a nationwide series of polls commissioned by the Republican Congressional Campaign Committee. Although the experiment was a disappointment, it represented the first step toward a comprehensive Republican party data bank. DMI is in a good competitive position to assist the national organization in this type of development.

MORC/BD&B works for candidates from moderate Republican states and districts, some of which have tended to be suspicious of the national party organization since the Goldwater period. MORC would go into a national Republican data bank only if it were given some "protection" with regard to the future use of its data. The firm believes that conservative Republican Congressional Campaign Committee staff have discriminated against it in awarding contracts because it was regarded as "too moderate." "The combine" has kept its lines open, however, to the administration and the Republican National Committee. MORC/BD&B, with its media emphasis and geographical base (which includes the weak or nonexistent Republican organizations of some of the Northeastern states), might logically develop a candidate-oriented as opposed to an organization-oriented strategy.

The Democratic Counterpart:
Pooling the Resources of the Coalition

"The Democrats are behind four or five years," observes one Republican consultant, "and it's our job to keep them behind." This impression of Republican superiority in the technology of the new politics was confirmed at the two-day seminar on "Information Systems, Computers, and Campaigns" presented by the American Association of Political Consultants at Lincoln Center in New York in March 1970. Winn Martin, president of Winn Martin Associates of Atlanta and former director of data processing for the Republican National Committee, was fielding questions when a participant asked for more information about statewide computer canvassing:

> CONFEREE: *Can you tell me where? I'm from Iowa and I've never heard of it.*
> MARTIN: *Are you a Democrat or a Republican?*
> CONFEREE: *Democrat.*
> MARTIN: *Well, that's the reason you never heard of it (laughter). I'm sorry I got the parties involved!*[6]

How serious is the gap in technical capabilities between the parties and what has the Democratic party done to close it? Many observers expect that the effects of new technologies will be neutralized as soon as both sides acquire them. The parties will be playing the same competitive game, only better. Most consultants working for the Republicans expect the Democrats to professionalize their party and are surprised that they have been so slow in taking pages from the Republican book. In fact, as more than one Republican state organization has learned to its chagrin, the Democrats have greater consulting resources than their depleted party treasuries and organizational disarray suggest. At the same time, Democratic party development appears to be taking a distinctive course that has escaped most Republican observers.

Several important factors should be taken into consideration

---

[6] Transcript of a two-day seminar "Information Systems, Computers, and Campaigns" presented by the American Association of Political Consultants, New York, March 20–21, 1970, p. 22.

in assessing Democratic party effectiveness. First, the Democratic National Committee since 1968 has made genuine efforts to professionalize its staff and build some in-house professional capability. Both the DNC and the Democratic Congressional Campaign Committee have used consultants to supplement party staff and to run campaign seminars. During his term as Democratic National Chairman, Fred Harris brought young professionals like Mark Shields (campaign management) and Peter Hart (polling) into his top-level staff. "Fred Harris understands the need for professionalism," remarked one Democratic consultant, "but he just doesn't have the money."

The situation improved somewhat under National Chairman Lawrence O'Brien, although John G. Stewart, director of the Office of Communications, admitted that the DNC was not coming anywhere near what the Republicans were doing in helping state organizations. The national committee did, however, develop successfully a computerized data bank of voting statistics, regional socio-economic data, survey research data and other critical information for use in the 1972 campaign. The committee has also developed a computer-based voter-identification system.

Under the Democrats, consultant services have been used more in developing media strategy than in the broad range of organizational services to state parties that has characterized Republican efforts. The Democrats have utilized consultants like Joseph Napolitan, Robert D. Squier and Tony Schwartz, who masterminded the media strategy for Hubert Humphrey's dramatic recovery in the 1968 presidential election. To date, nothing approaching the corporative complexes of Spencer-Roberts/Decision Making Information and Market Opinion Research/Bailey, Deardourff & Bowen has emerged as a consulting resource to the Democratic party organization, although some rate media consultant David Garth and his team (including Robert Kennedy's advance man Jerry Bruno, speechwriter Jeff Greenfield and on some campaigns television buyer Ruth Jones) as a major political force that several Democratic presidential hopefuls besides Garth's client, New York Mayor John V. Lindsay, would have liked to enlist.

While the Republicans have made an in-depth investment

in consultants, attempting to limit the number of major campaigns a firm can handle, Democrats have spread their consultants thinner to permit piggybacking so that more than one candidate within a state can use the services of the same consultant. The Democratic approach has its difficulties, however. It is impossible for most candidates even on a shared basis to afford both the media skills of a Charles Guggenheim and the organizational assistance of a Matthew Reese. As a result, a candidate usually hires one or the other, with the consultant trying to cover as best he can a field that is not his specialty.

Second, Democratic consulting resources have been directed more toward a candidate-focused media strategy rather than toward party organizational development for other significant reasons. Liberal Democrats, as in the case of the congressional parties, have often found it easier to set up parallel and independent or quasi-party fund-raising and organizational mechanisms like the Democratic Study Group than to reform and broaden party campaign committees. Fund-raising committees like the nominally bipartisan National Committee for an Effective Congress and the Committee for the Democratic Process and newer peace and national-priorities fund-raising groups have added to the fragmentation of fund raising for Democratic candidates at the very time Republican fund raising has become more institutionalized within the party.

Some of the implications of this trend toward candidate-centered campaigns for Democratic party–consultant relationships are illustrated by the record of NCEC. To a degree, NCEC has assumed some of the screening of consultants for Democrats provided by the party organization on the Republican side. As a policy, NCEC will not finance a campaign where there has not been a good polling operation. The committee has served as a broker between consultants and candidate organizations, paying for services directly, earmarking campaign contributions or routing funds from big contributors to candidates. NCEC has provided candidates with the varied services of Robert Squier, Charles Guggenheim, Oliver A. Quayle III and John F. Kraft. NCEC Executive Director Russell Hemenway himself serves as a member of the board of directors of the American Association of Political Consultants.

Hemenway has little use for party organizations, having come up through Democratic insurgent politics in New York City. "For all intents and purposes," Hemenway observes, "the Democratic and Republican parties don't exist. There are only individuals and professionals." NCEC has worked with liberal groups within the congressional parties, notably the Democratic Study Group, but its political strategy has been to aid individual liberal candidates, mostly Democratic. NCEC has gained considerable leverage in individual campaigns by its ability to commit tens of thousands of dollars of early money to hard-pressed candidates.

Following the 1970 elections, in which it distributed more than $830,000, NCEC announced a major shift in emphasis in its strategy. In 1972, it would concentrate on key primary contests against senior members of the House of Representatives in an effort to break the back of the seniority system. The NCEC stated that it would provide its candidates "who may number anywhere from 5 to 30, access to research, consultants to equip them with sophisticated campaign technology, and, most important, substantial financial assistance." The committee, noting that its role "must be invisible in specific primaries, because it would be obviously self-defeating to hand a targeted incumbent the issue of outside interference," asked its 80,000 supporters to contribute not to specific candidates but to a new "campaign method."[7] The implications of the new strategy for intraparty Democratic politics, especially the position of Southern Democratic leaders, were clear.

Third, organized labor occupies an increasingly strategic position in the future development of the Democratic party. "Organized labor is the guts of the Democratic Party," asserts James M. Perry of the *National Observer*, an authority on the technology of the new politics. "Organized labor supplies the Democrats with muscle and with cash; without labor, there is no Democratic Party."[8] With the formal party structure lacking the financial base and resources to make substantial investments

---

[7] NCEC press release, December 22, 1970.
[8] James M. Perry, "Can Labor Trump Nixon's Trick?," *National Observer*, September 18, 1971.

in service packages for party organizations and candidates or to build computerized information systems to support them, organized labor is the only part of the normally Democratic party constituency that can fill the competitive gap with the Republicans. Labor-employed consultants could be an important source of technical campaign advice for the Democrats in the 1970's.

The breakdown of Democratic party organization in some states and localities has left labor virtually in charge of some campaigns. The Montana 1970 Senate campaign of Democratic Majority Leader Mike Mansfield, for example, was run by the secretary-treasurer and the political action director of the state AFL-CIO. Some labor leaders with a national view, like James Cuff O'Brien, political action director of the United Steelworkers, are appalled by the dimensions of the problem. "The party system definitely needs strengthening. The advantages of such party strength for labor far outweigh the minor disadvantages," O'Brien points out. "In an ideal system, labor should be doing about 20 percent of the total job for the Democrats—20 percent of the manpower, money, work—in the states where labor has strength."

Various elements of labor are currently developing more specialized capabilities and skills. At the forefront is the Committee on Political Education, the political action arm of the AFL-CIO, which has local committees or special activists in almost a thousand cities. COPE Director Alexander E. Barkan boasts: "There's no party that can match us. Every election it gets better and better. Give us 10 years or 15 years and we'll have the best political organization in the history of this country."[9] COPE has a staff of seven professionals, another 16 staff assistants and 18 field representatives. The committee runs an almost continuous series of conferences in election years, taking a staff of six to eight experts on tour around the country. Delegates to these regional conferences are trained in workshops that include outside speakers and experts on

---

[9] Jonathan Cottin and Charles Culhane, "COPE's Political Craftsmen Build Smooth Organization," *National Journal*, September 12, 1970, p. 1965.

public opinion polls, research and media strategy. COPE representatives also claim to have the best political-research files in Washington.

COPE staff resources are matched or exceeded by some of the international unions. The United Automobile Workers maintain a year-round political and educational staff of 35 that has risen to as high as 60. UAW Political Action Director William Dodds states that the union is "committed to the need for a professional group of people—all of them up out of the union shops—trained to cope with modern political technique." The Teamsters maintain about 30 political staffers locally. The United Steelworkers build their political staff to about 25 or 30 for the six months preceding elections. The Machinists alone assigned 60 full-time workers to the 1969 California special election for Congress between Democrat John K. Van de Kamp and the winner, Republican Congressman Barry Goldwater, Jr. Reed Larson of the National Right to Work Committee estimates labor spending on politics not reported as direct dollar contributions to include in personnel time the equivalent of 20 to 50 percent of the more than $750 million in salaries at all staff levels.

Labor's first major ventures into the new politics have been through computer voter identification and polling. COPE's computerized voter identification program (VIP) now includes more than five million names of union members with pertinent data stored on magnetic tape and processed on computers owned by the International Association of Machinists. James Cuff O'Brien estimates that about 12 to 15 states, with Pennsylvania and Ohio in the lead, have first-rate VIP computer operations, with another eight to 10 close behind. Working experience with the program over the past four to six years is beginning to pay off.

Labor has also coordinated and shared political polling with the Democratic party for years and presumably is capable of generating the base of comparable polling data now available to the Republicans. COPE may, for instance, contract for 50 to 70 polls at a time with large polling firms to get a better price. COPE has also been experimenting with its own in-house telephone polling techniques. In states like Michigan and

Minnesota, the unions have worked cooperatively with Democratic-oriented academicians with extensive research experience
in polling and voting analysis. The Industrial Union Department of the AFL-CIO is developing a sophisticated information system with computer "fingerprint" cards on every
American manufacturer, capable of detecting trends in various
industries and providing information for several union interests,
among them legislative lobbying.

The real payoff for the Democrats and organized labor, however, may not come in the advanced techniques the Republicans have been developing but in the elementary steps
of voter registration and turnout. Alan Otten of the *Wall Street
Journal* reports that "Democrats seem finally to be recognizing
the computer as a tool potentially far more valuable for them
than for the Republicans." A disproportionate share of those
who do not register or vote are Democrats. "Any device that
makes it easier to prod men and women to register and vote,"
Otten concludes, "is almost bound to help Democrats more
than Republicans."[10]

Consultant Matthew Reese, director of operations for the
Democratic National Committee from 1961 to 1965, agrees that
registration is crucial to the Democrats. Reese coordinated
efforts to add two million new Democrats to the registration
rolls in 1964, a feat that prompted James H. Rowe, Jr., coordinator of National Citizens for Johnson and Humphrey, to
credit him with "the single most proficient performance in
the 1964 campaign." Reese feels that "the computer will be as
important in the 1970's as TV has been in the 1960's." A significant breakthrough, in his estimate, will be a computer
program that combines precinct targeting, polling and telephone research.

Fourth, although the Democratic party has not had the
financial resources to support and develop consultants on the
scale the Republicans have, it enjoys a number of compensating
advantages, including the predominant support of political
and social scientists in the academic community. Firms founded

---

[10] Alan L. Otten, "Computing Democratic Winners in '72," *Wall Street
Journal,* December 11, 1970.

by university professors, such as Simulmatics (now out of business), Decision Technology, Inc., and Participation Systems, Inc., while less closely identified with partisan politics than the campaign management firms, afford the Democrats ready access to new technologies. Other new firms like Valentine, Sherman & Associates, which was highly effective in 1970 gains by the Democrats in Minnesota, also have roots in the academic community.

Political scientist Robert Agranoff of Northern Illinois University, who worked with Valentine, Sherman & Associates and Minnesota's Democratic-Farmer-Labor party, described the DFL's program of campaign assistance to state legislators as "a comprehensive package of research, technical assistance and finances" and "one of the first efforts by an American political party organization to employ a small number of specialists for the purpose of applying new campaign techniques in a large number of campaigns."[11] Besides directing central party headquarters efforts in research and planning, developing a computer data bank of 85 percent of the state's electorate, and combined fund-raising and direct-mail operations, the DFL/Valentine, Sherman team used consultants in workshops and five full-time field men to give candidates personal access to experts on a cheaper, pooled basis.

Uninterrupted Democratic control of the Congress and its committee system for almost two decades has permitted Democratic campaign committees and individual Democratic members to develop and keep ample professional political talent on congressional staffs. Democrats, as the majority party, have also enjoyed an advantage in officeholders and attractive candidates for higher office. Republican gains at the state organizational level, reflected in the sharp rise of Republican governorships during the 1960's, only temporarily offset this advantage.

The Democratic reform movement has introduced a whole new set of organizational questions and concerns that appear

---

[11] Robert Agranoff, "Managing Small Campaigns," in Ray Hiebert and others (eds.), *The Political Image Merchants: Strategies in the New Politics* (Washington, D.C.: Acropolis Books, 1971), pp. 204, 184.

to have been excluded from the agenda of technocratic political reform. Some DNC spokesmen like John Stewart view this basic overhaul of the party structure and delegate selection process with its thrust toward *"humanizing* the party structure" as potentially "the most effective brand of new politics for the 1970's. We believe . . . that we are way ahead of the Republicans on this score . . . just as they are ahead of us in the sophisticated use of computers and polling techniques." Elly M. Peterson, a former assistant chairman of the Republican National Committee, has warned her party of just this danger: "I don't think future elections will be won solely by computerized records and electronics—no one ever wanted to join a party because they were attracted by their voter identification records or wanted to be a computerized card. For a long time I've maintained the Republican Party needs to broaden its base. Unless we include the non-traditional Republican we are going to grow old and obsolete."

The use of political consultants by independent citizen organizations apart from the two major parties is still in its early stages. There are already, however, some significant examples that suggest the potential for development in this direction. The 1970 Senate campaign of James L. Buckley, masterminded by consultant F. Clifton White and built on the framework of the New York Conservative party, molded a coalition of ethnic groups, Democrats, Republican, Independents, labor and farmers, breaking in the process many historic group ties with the two major parties. Between 1968 and 1972, George Wallace professionalized his third-party citizen movement with the help of National Fund Raising, Inc., a Texas consulting firm, and McDill Corp., a Montgomery, Alabama, computer firm. Another example is the decision of black elected officials and leaders to develop independent political organizations with consultant help. The Joint Center for Political Studies, a service organization for black elected officials established in Washington in 1970, has developed with the political consulting firm of David Hackett Associates a plan to provide blacks with computer-designed redistricting plans for congressional and state legislative races. The Hackett firm expects that the plan could add five or six black congressional seats in the House of Representatives over the next decade. This number could be doubled with the building of new minority coalitions with Mexican Americans in the Southwest. The Black Caucus of the House of Representatives also retained a political consulting firm to organize its $250,000 Washington fund-raising dinner in June 1970.

Some consultants who have tended to work with one or another of the parties have developed citizen-oriented services that could easily be contracted by new political organizations. Richard Viguerie and Associates has been advancing direct-mail techniques in fund-raising efforts on behalf of conservative candidates (such as 1968 California Republican Senate candidate Max Rafferty, Judge G. Harrold Carswell in the 1970 Republican primary for the Senate from Florida, and Illinois Congressman Philip M. Crane) and more than 40 conservative citizen organizations. Viguerie has built up a computer-tape file of almost a million names of contributors to conservative causes.

One consultant who is explicitly developing new techniques for citizen participation is Dr. Chandler H. Stevens, president of Participation Systems, Inc., of Concord, Massachusetts. Stevens, who developed a citizen feedback system for the governor of Puerto Rico and the Commonwealth of Massachusetts and a new politics system based on a massive door-to-door canvass for the Father Robert F. Drinan for Congress Committee in the Third Congressional District of Massachusetts, would like to use computers and interactive media to build an active citizen role in government and politics. Computer terminals in the voter's home, telephone linkups and cable television provide, in his view, the practical means for "participatory democracy" in the future.[12]

Another example worthy of note is the direct establishment

---

[12] See Chandler Harrison Stevens, "Citizen Feedback System" (paper prepared for the Eastern Regional Conference on Science and Technology for Public Programs, April 2–3, 1970). See also Hazel Henderson, "Computers: Hardware of Democracy," *Forum 70*, February 1970, pp. 22–51; and Donald L. Michael, "On Coping with Complexity: Planning and Politics," *Daedalus,* Fall 1968, pp. 1179–93.

of consulting firms by prominent citizens who wish to have an impact on party politics. A prototype of the citizen consulting firm is Potomac Associates, founded in 1970 with the support of Indiana industrialist J. Irwin Miller and some associates. The firm, represented at meetings of the American Association of Political Consultants, among its first projects has sponsored and published a major polling study of American political attitudes.[13]

Political Consultants, Computers, and the Future of Party Politics

Political consultants are using information and computers at two substantially different levels of sophistication: the clerical and production level and the modeling or strategic planning level. The first group of applications is relatively simple to understand. These clerical and production applications do not require the use of a computer, although there are substantial advantages in using one. The information stored in a computer bank (characteristics of voters and precincts, records of past contributions, volunteer lists, etc.) could just as well be stored in filing cabinets or on a cardex system. In one sense, the computer is a glorified filing clerk and filing system. Its advantages, however, are high speed, accuracy, the ability to handle multiple cross-referencing of individual entries and the ability to link files that are widely scattered geographically. A computerized information-retrieval system is thus a major advance in the selective and intelligent use of information.

Campaign managers who have used computers in such applications believe them to be an economic allocation of campaign resources. John Marttila, manager for Father Drinan's 1970 congressional campaign in Massachusetts and the 1971 reelection campaign of Boston Mayor Kevin H. White, credits the computer with a secondary campaign role. "We could have done it without computers but that would have been silly.

---

[13] Albert H. Cantril and Charles W. Roll, Jr., *Hopes and Fears of the American People* (New York: Universe Books, 1971).

The really hard work was canvassing and the computer set people free to work on 'people work.' In politics, the simple rule is to apply your resources intelligently."

The real clerical advantages of computers comes in production-line applications where the computer is used as a lightning-speed typewriter and routing or dispatching clerk. After retrieving information and lists of names, the computer can mass-produce individually typed personalized letters (including as much individual personal information as the sender has available on file and wants to incorporate in the specialized computer typing instructions), dial selected telephone numbers that will receive a prerecorded campaign message, and print gummed labels for mailing and lists for all types of campaign use. Used in this way, the computer is the most powerful campaign "worker" a party or candidate can hire.

Some specific examples of current computer applications suggest the impact that computerized information systems are already having on American politics. Data banks have been constructed for local, congressional and statewide districts that include information on every potential voter in the district. Consultants have used computers for determining the vote potential of precincts, precinct priority lists for the candidate's and campaign workers' attention and areas with large numbers of ticket splitters. COPE and the Democratic National Committee have developed computer programs that spot unregistered voters, map door-to-door routes for union canvassers, print out telephone lists for election-day calling and prepare lists for union poll watchers. Republicans are using computers to analyze legislative voting records. One Republican firm has produced a "target area graph" of incumbents' strength and weaknesses. Computers have also been employed to select recipients and type letters for specialized mailings. Some consultants in fact consider direct mail the most powerful campaign instrument there is, next to face-to-face contact with the voter. According to Peter Iovino of Datatab, "Some candidates [can] win with just one worker—[the] computer."[14] A number

---

[14] Interview published in *Campaign Insight* (Wichita, Kans.), November 1970, pp. 1–2.

of research applications of computers have already been developed. The Republican National Committee Miracode system, which uses computers and microfiche, incorporates several hundred thousand documents which can be photoreproduced without losing original copies.

The use of computer-information systems in strategy applications, which are more complex and potentially far more powerful than the clerical-production applications, assists the politician and his campaign manager in making decisions. Most of these techniques incorporate models or mathematical representations of the real world which can be quite simple expressions of rules of thumb or complicated dynamic systems with multiple variables. In campaign applications, the use of computer models, on the one hand, forces the candidate and his manager to determine the key factors or variables that should be taken into account in campaign decisions. Such models, on the other hand, enable them to test various ideas or strategies before their actual use in a campaign. For example, how different voting groups would react to a proposed increase in taxes or to a major change in the welfare system or how the campaign media budget should be allocated to reach those voters most responsive to the candidate and his program.

Computer models have originated information requirements in politics that go well beyond the traditional party organization's precinct lists, election returns and voting records of officeholders. Sophisticated polling data, cost-effectiveness information on campaign techniques, market-segmentation research and motivation studies have become essential tools for the political consultant. Again, specific examples of this use of computers suggest their potential. The most dramatic illustration of computer modeling is the simulation of elections through the use of data banks to represent the electorate and its response to various candidates, issues, and strategies.[15] Consulting firms working for Republicans have already begun linking survey data into a national data frame, and the Repub-

---

[15] See Ithiel de Sola Pool, Robert P. Abelson, and Samuel L. Popkin, *Candidates, Issues, and Strategies: A Computer Simulation of the 1960 and 1964 Presidential Elections* (Cambridge, Mass.: M.I.T. Press, 1965).

lican National Committee expected to achieve in the early 1970's the first national capacity for large-scale modeling. A number of firms have also developed computer models for state legislative redistricting after the 1970 census. A variety of media analysis and time-buying models are already in use. Participation Systems, Inc., has applied a computerized planning system at the congressional level to select and schedule media for an advertising campaign based on such criteria as the media alternatives available, their costs, the campaign budget and the relative vote potential of various identifiable population groups. Another consulting firm, Decision Technology, Inc., has developed a simulation model that will enable a national party to test the media effects of national television coverage of its national convention. The model would help the party plan its convention program schedule and content for the maximum possible favorable media impact.

The profession, while investing heavily in simulation modeling, does not want to oversell the technique's potential in politics. The unpredictable strategy of the opposition and the unexpected interjection of issues and events in campaigns place outside limits on the usefulness of election simulations. The Republican failure to revise 1970 campaign strategy to take account of shifts in the importance of the economy and the so-called "social issue," for example, might have been averted with better polling and simulation techniques. Individual consultants like Walter DeVries, senior consultant of DeVries and Associates, and Roy Pfautch, president of Civic Service Incorporated, caught the shift at the state level, but most Republican consultants accepted the White House–national Republican party line. The likely development is that limited simulation exercises will be run to help in formulating campaign strategy and in allocating campaign budgets. As the cost of campaigning mounts, however, the managerial, resource-allocation aspects of politics will gain in importance. Legal limits on the amounts of television and radio campaign advertising a candidate can purchase will force candidates and the consultant to decide 1) how the effectiveness of television and radio advertising can be maximized within those limits, and 2) where the remaining campaign budget can be spent most effectively. Computer consultant Winn Martin concluded: "I don't think the computer will ever in 1970 design a campaign strategy. It is a tremendous tool for assisting you in implementing the campaign strategy you've decided on in the most efficient manner. So, I hardly ever look to the computer to tell me what needs to be done, but rather to tell me how to do it best; or how to allocate my funds."

The Expanding Role of Political Consultants: New Issues for Party Responsibility

Unless the political parties modernize themselves in the coming decade, consultants could assume many of the functions now exercised by the parties. The consultants have already introduced new expectations and demands for party performance and their role will continue to expand into new functional areas in the 1970's. Consultants, for example, will play a critical role in determining how open or closed the presidential selection process will be. A successful preconvention strategy now requires professional advance work and planning in both primary and party convention states as well as a sizable convention-city operation and convention strategy. In the 1970's, polls and simulation will be even more important in weighing alternative candidates and strategies. Consultants, trained in the party process and familiar with party politicians in a wide number of states, will be among the relatively small number of people capable of mounting presidential campaigns for either major- or minor-party candidates.

If the national parties do not develop effective, integrated national headquarters, operations centers and communication nets, the major consulting conglomerates themselves could begin to fill *national* party roles. Suggested party reforms could in many instances be just as easily adapted for use by a large consulting complex with clients over a sufficiently broad geographical region. The multifunctional conglomerate consulting firm is thus a serious competitive rival to unreformed national committees.

If party politics remains fluid and temporary coalitions

replace the still dominant New Deal Democratic party coalition, consultants will play an increasingly crucial role in negotiating with various elements of prospective party coalitions. New York City and New York State politics provide a ready example with a four-party framework, numerous extra party lines added to the ballot and enormous shifts of voting blocs between parties, depending on the candidate choices offered. If party activists become more ideological and issue-oriented in their approach to electoral politics, more neutral actors will have to assume the brokerage role traditionally performed by a broad-based two-party system. The alternative to coalitions within the parties is some form of multiparty system, an option that would afford consultants a new range of opportunities.

Consultants will also be the political brokers of cable television, perhaps the most important political media innovation of the coming decade.

The continued growth of the political consulting industry raises major new issues for party responsibility. To the old problems of making officeholders and party officials accountable for their actions in a decentralized party and governmental system that diffuses lines of responsibility, there has been added the new factor of an echelon of political professionals with no formal public or party accountability either in statutory or party rules. The professionalization of the parties will have the added effect of concentrating new political resources in national and state party committees with wide discretionary authority in hiring trained professionals who often have little or no public visibility.

As consultants have become a quasi-staff arm of the parties and as complicated new relationships have evolved, new forms of political unaccountability have emerged in the clear absence of any clear party guidelines on the use of political consultants. Several examples indicate the potential conflicts of interest.

A consulting firm retained in several major 1970 election campaigns by candidates at the state level received directions from national party headquarters recommending that it shift key personnel from one race to another. Since the party served

as reference for the consultant in the first place and controlled
national funds going to these and future races, the consultant
had little choice but to comply with the recommendation.

A state party precluded by law from making preprimary
endorsements used consultants as a front to back candidates in
primaries that it favored. In another instance, a candidate
discovered that a polling firm he had retained to do surveys
was also doing polling work for the opposition party and sitting in on strategy sessions with his opponent.

Besides participating in campaign decision making and
operations, consultants are shaping the parties and the decision-
making structures of the future, but no representative agency
is overseeing and/or participating in this process of political
modernization.

Another problem is the broader responsibility of the consultant for the functioning of the governmental process. These
are not entirely new problems for representative government,
but the growth of the consulting industry and the new techniques it is introducing to party politics have made them
urgent topics for public and party discussion. From where is
political leadership to come, with the ever more sophisticated
means to find out what people are thinking and then communicate campaign appeals back to them to maximize votes?
Moreover, as one party official notes with concern, "If more
and more legislators, if governors and even Presidents, gain
public office as men running against the machine—the established party—the governmental process is bound to become
more and more fragmented and disjointed. These public officials
are likely to assume an increasingly self-centered view of their
public responsibilities, in a period when our democratic
system can least afford the luxury of such fragmentation."[16]

Recommendations: Regulating the Consultants

The political consulting industry already is a substantial
independent force in American politics and one of the surest

---

[16] John G. Stewart, "Humanizing the New Politics," in Hiebert, *The Political Image Merchants,* p. 29.

areas of political growth in the 1970's. During the past decade, political consultants and the parties have developed a modus vivendi of mutual dependence. Unless parties come to terms with the potential of the industry, consulting firms may expand into functional areas ignored by the parties, in time becoming competing political structures. The best defense for popularly based parties is internal party reform supplemented by careful party and public review of the consultants' role in politics.

Recommendation 1. Representative party commissions of the Democratic and Republican National Committees should study the role of consultants, data banks and polls in party politics and develop party guidelines for the use of political consultants and the investment of party funds in the new political technology.

The Democratic and Republican National Committees should establish representative party commissions on political consulting and technology to study the role of consultants, data banks and polls in the party politics of the 1970's. The commissions could develop through field investigations and open party hearings a series of party policy guidelines on the use of consultants, data banks and polls that could be published and distributed to all party organizations, candidates, consultants, the media and the interested public.

The guidelines on consultants could cover such subjects as hiring, clearance and reference procedures, means for ensuring open and competitive bidding, recommended ranges for fees, performance standards, a code of ethics and a complaint and appeals procedure. The guidelines on political data banks could include specific procedures to safeguard individual rights, to determine what information should or should not be collected and stored, to ensure that designated party officials regularly monitor all information used in the data bank, and to provide for formal review of all studies, analyses and reports produced with the data-bank facilities. In addition to developing policy guidelines for the use of political data banks under direct party control, the national parties could review the use of data banks by Congress, the federal administration and state governments to ensure for legitimate political and governmental research the right of party access to relevant data resources. The set of guidelines for polls (developed in cooperation with the polling profession and the media) could apply to all publicly distributed polls and call for background information on who commissioned or completed the poll, the sample size and the margin of error.

The commission should also have the authority to enforce standards and to review all party investment in new political technology to ensure the proper use of party funds. Such a review could be a prerequisite to future funding. The commission could also encourage investments that would contribute to the broader development of the party and emphasize party participation and the development of issues in addition to efficient management. The commission could serve as a continuing party watchdog, overseeing any concentrations of consulting or polling contracts or possible cartel-like operations involving party funds. The commission could encourage equitable access to party-consultant resources for all major party factions or candidates for the party's presidential and vice-presidential nominations.

Consulting relationships with individual candidates, their managers and top party officials often bypass the national committees, state committees and local party members. The parties could require that both the national and state committees be periodically briefed on the status of campaigns using party services or funds and special party projects involving consultants.

Recommendation 2. All political consulting firms and polling organizations working for candidates in primary and general elections for federal and state office should be required by appropriate legislation to file public reports on the extent of their campaign involvement.

Some candidates, to avoid the issue of using out-of-state consultants, hide their consultants from public view, a practice that has extended the cloak of secrecy and mystery surrounding the profession. In view of the power that consulting and polling organizations exercise in electoral politics, some form of public regulation is both desirable and necessary. Public reporting and information on the use of consultants in primary and general elections for federal offices should be regulated by statute. Such reports could take the form of reports that election committees are required to file with the Clerk of the House of Representatives under the Corrupt Practices Act or of the registration requirements of lobbyists under the Legislative Reorganization Act. Similar state statutes could be adopted to cover state elections. Ideally the reports should include information on the candidates and candidate organizations contracting for consulting and polling services, the extent of involvement of the consultant and the terms of the contract. They should be filed at three stages in a campaign: a preliminary report two to three months in advance of the election concerned, a preelection report about 10 days before the voting, and a complete postelection report.

It is unrealistic, however, to expect stronger regulation of a quasi-private industry than it has been possible to achieve with regard to parties. Until parties themselves are required to publish meaningful financial statements and to open their books to audit, probably the best that can be expected is for the industry to extend the practice of a few consultants who undergo a voluntary audit of their books.

While there admittedly are loopholes in any reporting system, public reports filed at specified intervals would make more information available about professional political consultants and their involvement in party politics. But in view of their growing influence in the political process, a comprehensive and informative directory of political consultants is also needed. This directory could be published and updated at regular intervals as necessitated by the rapid changes in the profession. It could include biographical and professional summaries and photographs of all consultants, similar to various directories currently available on members of Congress and congressional staffs and listing all services offered by individual consultants and firms. The directory service might also develop a standard classification of services to assist the potential user.

•

Recommendation 3. To balance the trend toward greater
professionalization of parties, citizen groups and private
individuals and organizations should develop ways to encourage citizen involvement and participation in the use of
the new political technology.

Lack of public information and public misunderstanding of
polls, computers and the technology of the new politics only
serve to increase the influence and mystique of the pollster or
consultant. Many of the applications of computers to politics,
for example, are straightforward and easily understandable if
intelligently presented to the interested citizen. A public guide
to polling and the new technology of politics could be prepared and published as a paperback book presenting in non-
technical language the various new techniques being developed
and applied to politics.

A new mechanism and motivation for introducing such
innovations as the modern digital computer, cable television
and interactive media into citizen-oriented politics will have to
be found that parallels the close relationship between profit-
oriented consulting firms and managerially oriented party
professionals. Research and development of information systems
that would encourage citizen involvement in politics should
receive priority attention by foundations, private contributors
and possibly government sources.

Another way to encourage citizen involvement and participation in professionalized politics would be for major reform-
oriented contributors to contract directly with consulting firms
for specific innovations or studies they would like to see made
available to the parties or citizen or cause groups. Individuals
and citizen groups could also invest in the stock of a consulting
firm. A group of such investors could, perhaps through an
annual meeting of stockholders, help to offset any tendency
toward the development of a closed party-consultant relationship.

Library and other reference facilities should be encouraged
to develop their collections on the new political technology
to serve both the general public and interested citizen groups.
One private collection of political TV spot advertisements,

begun by Julian Kanter in 1952, now includes spots from 206 candidates in 154 races, a unique and invaluable resource for students of the evolution of the new politics.

All public polls could be collected by an institute of politics or other independent body which could publish periodic comprehensive reports of poll results for the use of party leaders, the media, and interested citizens.

Recommendation 4. Political consultants should take initiatives to increase public understanding of their role in politics and to continue to improve and upgrade their profession.

Political consultants bear the principal responsibility for increasing public understanding of their role in politics and for improving and upgrading their profession. The adoption by the American Association of Political Consultants in March 1971 of a Statement of Purposes and Code of Ethics was a first step. The new political quarterly of the association, *Polite'ia,* should also increase public understanding of the profession.

Consultants could work to upgrade the parties and the political process. They could develop, through seminars and publications, greater professional and public awareness of the relationship between politics and government and party responsibility for governmental performance.

Political consultants ought to follow the example of the legal profession in performing pro bono or public interest work. They might also become affiliates of such firms or specific cause groups. The announced educational and research programs of the AAPC could be expanded and formal resolutions could be adopted to further such activities. The profession could devote attention to the participatory as well as the managerial aspects of politics, sponsoring research, for example, on the reasons for nonvoting. Political consultants could also exert a constructive discipline on the parties by investigating complaints of unfair party practices and suits against clients filed by firms or individual consultants and encouraging new and constructive party procedures.

X

Alternative Futures for American Politics

In much the same style as various scenarios have been fashioned for presidential campaigns, political strategists, publicists and scholars have defined a wide range of alternative futures for the political parties in the 1970's and beyond. About the only thing on which these observers agree is that the Democratic Roosevelt coalition that has dominated American politics since the 1930's is nearing its end and that some new party alignment or political system will take its place. Political pollster and analyst Samuel Lubell has observed that in the past, majority-party coalitions have lost their "timeliness" and periodically been shattered to the core and then "reshuffled." Such realignments, according to political scientists and historians, have occurred at about 30-year intervals since the American two-party system was firmly established during the Jacksonian era.[1] "The drama of American politics is transformed," states Lubell. "Figuratively and literally a new political era begins."[2] These critical realignments, Massachusetts Institute of Technology Professor Walter Dean Burnham concludes, constitute "a political decision of the first magnitude and a turning point in the mainstream of national policy formation" and may well be regarded as "America's surrogate for revolution."[3]

---

[1] See V. O. Key, Jr., "A Theory of Critical Elections," *Journal of Politics*, February 1955, pp. 3–18; and Walter Nisbet Chambers and Walter Dean Burnham (eds.), *The American Party Systems: Stages of Political Development* (New York: Oxford University Press, 1967).

[2] Samuel Lubell, *The Future of American Politics*, Harper Colophon Books (3rd ed., rev.; New York: Harper & Row, 1965), p. 195.

[3] Walter Dean Burnham, "Party Systems and the Political Process," in Chambers and Burnham, *The American Party Systems*, p. 289.

There is little consensus, however, on what shape the contemporary American political revolution will take, although the efforts of Republican conservatives to recast the national Republican party, the challenge of liberal Democrats against big-city, labor and Southern power within the Democratic party, the Wallace campaign, nationwide activities to enfranchise and register 18-to-21-year-olds, and reform of party conventions and delegate selection procedures are all indications of the tremendous energies many Americans have been willing to invest in trying to anticipate and shape the political future. Several possible alternative futures can be delineated: a renewed Democratic coalition, an emerging Republican majority, a multiparty system, the decline of political parties or politics without parties, technocratic authoritarianism, and party modernization and the development of citizen or participant parties. Our own preference—for modernized political parties which offer extensive new opportunities for citizen participation and a much greater competence to govern—is a sixth alternative.

Just as the New Deal coalition established a new agenda of party and public policy goals and reshaped governmental institutions, so too could the party configuration that evolves from the current flux of American politics have profound consequences for every American for decades to come.

Alternative Future 1. A Renewed Democratic Coalition

One possibility for a future ordering of American politics is to reconstitute the liberal, labor and black elements of the old Roosevelt coalition on a new basis. One of the most articulate political strategists developing this option is George Agree, former executive director of the National Committee for an Effective Congress, who now heads a number of Democratic fund-raising efforts, including the Committee for the Democratic Process.

Agree asserts that two broad demographic trends have profoundly undermined the traditional Democratic coalition. First, there has been the growth of a new class, an educated elite who lean toward the Democratic party but whose life style

has little in common with working-class Democrats. These
self-styled New Democrats have forgotten how to count, according to Agree. "They feel they comprise a majority of the
public, but they simply won't win elections without organized
labor. They are concerned with issues not central to most
people. This is the problem with the 'liberal constituency.'
They have no real 'interests' but politics is mostly interests.
Their concern with 'great big issues' makes them susceptible
to a 'politics of rhetoric.' They go wherever their emotions take
them. They are most naive about the acquisition and use of
power."

Second, the ramifications of the migration of blacks in the
North and South pose the critical problem for the Democratic
coalition and for American politics in the years ahead. "America's response to the Negro is the fundamental issue of our
times," states Agree, "and the Democratic party can be the
only vehicle for that response. Republicans do not owe it to
their party." The Negro migration created an "uprooted
peasantry" in the cities which found the routes of economic
mobility followed by earlier generations of immigrants virtually
closed to unskilled or semiskilled black workers. Lower-income,
lower-status whites, the very groups that already paid a disproportionate share of taxes and whose real income held steady
or declined in the past decade, found their schools and neighborhoods bearing the principal impact of this migration. At
the same time, the American black's self-perception was changing radically as passivity gave way to activism and militancy.

These trends, according to Agree, helped to dissolve the
cement of the New Deal coalition and to produce a pattern
of Northern politics mildly reminiscent of the traditional Southern politics in which the race issue overshadows economic
issues. "If the pattern of dividing lower income whites and
Negroes politically is allowed to harden or fix," Agree warns,
"the Democratic party is sunk for a long time." The Republicans
have deliberately and understandably sought to exploit these
developments through initiatives like the "Philadelphia Plan"
which guaranteed quotas for black construction workers on
public projects and through appeals for labor-union support.
"The line of opportunity is so glaring it is almost inescapable,"

Agree points out. "It's the northern part of the Southern Strategy to keep the blacks and labor apart, fighting each other."

When the Vietnam issue dealt the final blow to Lyndon Johnson's Democratic coalition, Agree attempted to formulate a strategy for a renewed Democratic majority coalition. Outlining a campaign strategy based on the slogan "Order and Progress" for the 1968 elections, he argued in a memo to the President that the only issue on which Johnson could win a powerful affirmation would be that of "ending racial injustice and violence and building a viable and humanly satisfying multi-racial society in America."

After Richard Nixon was elected and inherited the problem of Vietnam, Agree stressed that the primary task for Democrats was to rebuild the old liberal-labor-black coalition. By emphasizing economic issues, he said, the Democrats can exploit a natural Republican weakness and at the same time unite working-class whites and blacks. "Labor," he said, "is the largest, most integrated mass organization for political impact in American life. It is more integrated than any of its critics." As to the new-politics Democrats, Agree assumes that in the long run they will once more identify themselves with the lower-income classes of the Democratic coalition, since to a great extent conscience is the emotional basis of their continuing involvement in politics. He would, however, institute an Eleventh Commandment for the Democratic illuminati similar to Parkinson's law, first enunciated by California Republican State Chairman Dr. Gaylord Parkinson and instituted by the Republicans after the 1964 election: "No Democrat shall fight another Democrat unto the death. Otherwise the whole damn thing will fall apart."

Agree's prescription for a renewed Democratic coalition has been advanced by a number of other Democrats. Bayard Rustin, civil-rights leader and executive director of the A. Philip Randolph Institute, has called for strengthening the coalition of labor, minorities and liberals that has "brought about every progressive change since Franklin Delano Roosevelt"; and Vernon Jordan, executive director of the National Urban League, has concluded that "the labor movement, despite its well-advertised faults, is still a major member of the coalition for change that could turn this country around."[4] Michael Harrington, chairman of the Socialist party, has defended the labor movement to Democratic intellectuals as "the largest, most effective force for social change" in the country and an essential element in a new majority coalition.[5] Richard M. Scammon and Ben J. Wattenberg in *The Real Majority* advised liberal Democrats before the 1970 elections "to split off the Race Issue from the Social Issue,"[6] that is, those aspects of social change (like crime, student radicalism, racial tension, changing social values and street riots) that were causing growing anxiety among voters and to appeal to both black Democrats and white Democrats in inner-city neighborhoods, the so-called ethnics, through a pro–civil-rights party and a strong law-and-order stand.

The possibility of a renewed liberal-labor-black Democratic coalition has, however, been seriously criticized both by the new-politics Democrats and by the proponents of black and women's political power. Some new-politics Democrats, like political science professor Arnold Kaufman, who helped organize the New Democratic Coalition in 1968 to emphasize an alternative direction for the Democratic party, have seen the NDC as an effort to create "a permanent left in the Democratic party." From this viewpoint the NDC can coexist, at times uneasily, within the renewed Democratic coalition, serving as a reform agent. Other new-politics Democrats like Richard N. Goodwin disagree.[7] Goodwin sharply criticizes older intellectuals raised in the Roosevelt liberal tradition whose ideas

---

[4] Vernon Jordan, "Labor Remains Blacks' Ally," *Citizen Register* (Ossining, N.Y.), December 2, 1971.

[5] Michael Harrington, "A Radical Strategy—Don't Form a Fourth Party, Form a New First Party," *New York Times Magazine,* September 13, 1970, pp. 28, 128, 132–35. See also Harrington, *Toward a Democratic Left: A Radical Program for a New Majority* (Baltimore, Md.: Penguin Books, 1969).

[6] Richard M. Scammon and Ben J. Wattenberg, *The Real Majority* (New York: Coward-McCann, 1970), p. 285.

[7] David Gelman and Beverly Kempton, "New Issues for the New Politics: An Interview with Richard N. Goodwin," *Washington Monthly,* August 1969, pp. 18–29.

"are not wrong; they're just irrelevant or inadequate." Instead of first formulating the new issues for a future political coalition, they induced the NDC to declare its adherence to the Democratic party and thus to surrender any bargaining position it might have had. Goodwin also questions whether either existing party can become a truly "modernizing" party or whether a new party must serve this need. Citing George Wallace, he muses that "maybe a third party doesn't have to win the Presidency to have an important impact."

The advocates of black political power are more actively seeking to break out of the Democratic coalition. Herbert Hill, national labor director of the National Association for the Advancement of Colored People, has argued for a number of years that Negro participation in the old Democratic coalition was based on the powerlessness or impotence of the blacks and that only by breaking away could they cast off the coalition's "noose round the black's neck—in urban renewal, public construction, jobs in the public sector, in enforcement of the whole complex of civil rights legislation." This is now possible because of significant demographic movements confirmed by the 1970 census, "a document of monumental importance" for the black people, according to Hill. For the first time in American history, more blacks are living in the North than in the South, and a higher proportion of blacks than whites are living in urban areas. These and other trends, such as increased black electoral participation and a significantly lower median age for the black population, have given blacks new political power and the potential to withdraw from the Democratic coalition and to build an independent political base and enter new political coalitions that would serve their community interests more directly.

The real tragedy of Nixon's political strategy, in Hill's interpretation, is that it appears for the time being to have severely limited the potential for political flexibility of the black voter. Hill expects that blacks will now concentrate on municipal, state and selected congressional elections where their power can be maximized.

Black political action independent from the Democratic party has been supported by the Reverend Jesse Jackson, director of Operation PUSH (People United to Save Humanity), who has urged a "progressive third force" or "rainbow coalition" of blacks, Chicanos, women, the unemployed and young voters to push for a greater share of economic and political power for poor people. Other significant black political initiatives have been independently financed and staffed, such as the Black Caucus of the House of Representatives and a series of local black caucuses and black conventions. Blacks have also defected from the traditional Democratic coalition to help elect Republican governors like Linwood Holton of Virginia and William G. Milliken of Michigan.

The civil-rights movement, black political independence and the separate caucus form of political organization have provided models for other social and political movements in the 1970's, notably women's liberation. The National Women's Political Caucus has announced plans to organize multipartisan groups in every state, a move that could further limit the base of a renewed Democratic party coalition. A symbol of greater independence within the party, Congresswoman and National Committeewoman Shirley Chisholm, became the first black woman to seek a major party's presidential nomination. Asked if she would take part in a third-party movement, Mrs. Chisholm replied, "The Democratic Party is in very serious difficulty and the presence of Shirley Chisholm has nothing to do with it."

What in fact are the prospects for a renewed Democratic coalition? Pollster Louis Harris has reported a steady slippage in Democratic party identification to below the 50 percent mark in 1970 for the first time in the modern political era. Samuel Lubell, who after the Johnson landslide of 1964 forecast a restored and substantially enlarged Democratic coalition based on the white middle class and blacks, found the semisectional and polarized alignment of the two major parties in 1970 too narrow to support a truly national majority coalition.[8] AFL-CIO President George Meany has proclaimed the Demo-

---

[8] Lubell, *The Future of American Politics*, pp. 1–19; and Lubell, *The Hidden Crisis in American Politics*, p. 68.

cratic party "in a shambles" and almost under the control of "extremists" or "so-called liberals or new lefts."[9] The *New Democrat* in 1970 had editorially charged National Chairman O'Brien and Treasurer Robert S. Strauss with policies that "risk reopening the wounds of 1968, throwing away dissenting intellectuals, castigating the McCarthy-Kennedy forces, and taking the entire party down the road of Neo-Nixonism."[10] *New York Times* columnist Tom Wicker saw the probability of either a radical Democratic or a conservative Democratic split from the coalition. "It's very hard for me to see at this point how Democrats can be unified in 1972, and the possibility of a fourth party candidacy is strong."[11]

Our estimate of the future of the Democratic party coalition is more hopeful. While the Democratic coalition is admittedly under severe strain and events could produce sizable defections to a number of possible third-, fourth-, or more party candidates at the presidential level, several factors favor a renewed Democratic coalition.

First, survey data show continued basic Democratic party strength in spite of the massive decline in the vote for the Democratic presidential ticket from more than 61 percent in 1964 to less than 43 percent in 1968 under the impact of both Vietnam and George Wallace. In its analysis of the 1968 election, the Michigan Survey Research Center stressed the continued stability of partisanship below the presidential level. Democratic strength in the House of Representatives declined only two percentage points, from 57 percent in 1966 to 55 percent in 1968. Democratic control of state legislative seats remained virtually unchanged at about 57.5 percent. A post-1970 analysis by a team of political scientists found no massive conversion of voters in terms of party identification since the 1930's, although the composition of both parties had drastically

[9] Damon Stetson, "Meany Sees Democrats Losing Workers' Support," *New York Times*, August 31, 1970.

[10] "The Galbraith Purge," *New Democrat* (New York), October 1970.

[11] Address to Summer Arts Festival, Orono, Maine, reported by Kent Ward, "Times Editor Talks of Muskie in '72," Bangor (Me.) *Daily News*, July 14, 1970.

changed.[12] The Democratic party successfully transformed itself into the party of the American middle class, changing its
tone and style as the socio-economic status of Democrats rose
and a new professional and managerial middle class rapidly
expanded. The Republican party in turn had adopted neo-
populistic rhetoric in an effort to win marginal segments of
the Democratic coalition. The study concluded that "much
of the current dissatisfaction with the major parties is strictly
short-term, and will pass with changes in leaders and policies
(especially, with an end to the war in Vietnam)," although
the electorate would continue to grow more independent of
the parties. James L. Sundquist, senior Fellow of the Brookings
Institution and author of a major historical study on party
realignments,[13] predicts that in the next few years an alignment of the major parties on an "activist-conservative" line
of cleavage will be reinforced through the rise of new polarizing
issues relating to the role of government. "When this happens,"
Sundquist states, "the parties will recover a considerable
proportion of the meaning they have lost during the period
since the 1960's when cross-cutting issues have been dominant."

Second, the Democratic party has excelled in playing coalition politics in the past and the coalition-building skills of
Democratic party leaders will be an important resource in the
1970's. The party is still able to accommodate the interests of
big-city, Southern, black and liberal Democrats in maintaining
control of the Congress and its powerful committee system.
Even John Kenneth Galbraith, who has criticized his party as
"a device for keeping in power the most regressive part of
the American political community,"[14] has praised the Democratic organization for its virtue of being "accessible to every-

---

[12] Everett Ladd, Jr., Charles Hadley, and Lauriston King, "A New Political Alignment," *Public Interest*, Spring 1971, pp. 46–63. See also Philip
E. Converse and others, "Continuity and Change in American Politics:
Parties and Issues in the 1968 Election" (paper prepared for delivery
at the American Political Science Association Annual Meeting, New York,
1969).

[13] James L. Sundquist, *Party Alignment and Realignment in the United
States* (to be published by the Brookings Institution).

[14] John Kenneth Galbraith, *Who Needs the Democrats?* (Garden City,
N.Y.: Doubleday, 1970), p. 48.

body." Galbraith rules out opting for a small, uncertain fourth party when instead "you can have a piece of a large successful one."[15] Faced with the prospect of electing a Republican President by splitting the Democratic vote, many new-politics Democrats will go along with the party. Far from being the death knell of the Democratic coalition, the strength of such widely varied presidential hopefuls as Jackson, Mills, McGovern and Lindsay can be interpreted as a sign of strength and renewed vitality in the coalition.

Third, unlike the Republicans, the Democratic party has maintained ties with many of the new independent political forces in the country and their organizational leaders. Groups like the Black Caucus, the National Women's Political Caucus, the Vietnam Moratorium, Common Cause, Project 18, Environmental Action and a variety of public interest groups have much closer connections with the Democratic than the Republican party and are in many instances led and staffed by partisan Democrats. While it may appear that these independent organizational efforts are fragmenting the Democratic coalition, they may actually be broadening the base of a more loosely structured Democratic majority coalition in the 1970's. In any event, Democratic party access to such political skills and organizational talent will be an invaluable resource.

Fourth, if the movement within the Democratic party for reform of delegate selection procedures and national convention rules achieves its goals and is extended and expanded to review internal party structure and functions, the party will have drafted the equivalent of a new party constitution by the 1976 convention. A partywide consensus on fair procedures could provide new bonds for the diverse and seemingly irreconcilable elements of the Democratic coalition. How candidates are nominated and platforms drafted and debated may become even more important for many Democrats than who is nominated and what platform planks are incorporated. Reform Democrats who have worked within the party since 1968 may find their legitimate grievances with the party organization

---

[15] Warren Weaver, Jr., "Galbraith Predicts No New Left Party in 1972," *New York Times,* September 22, 1970.

substantially relieved as the decade progresses. The future tests of party reform are closely related to the prospects for a viable Democratic coalition.

Finally, if the Democratic coalition is able to bridge the divisive issue of race and win the allegiance of sizable elements of the new political generation, it stands to gain long-term strength in American politics. As Richard Scammon points out, "The desire for social peace is an articulate, non-negotiable demand of the American people." "In the long run the political future belongs to the forces of unification," adds Samuel Lubell. Beyond the number of voters it would gain directly through a broad coalitional strategy, a renewed Democratic party may have the best prospects for unifying the country and winning a broad national base of support.

Alternative Future 2. An Emerging Republican Majority

As the majority party coalition since the New Deal era, the Democratic party has, at least until 1968, felt less need than the Republican party to develop future coalitional strategies. The Republican party, on the other hand, has been torn between two strategies for its future—a "modern" Republican strategy designed to combine progressive Republican strength with new voting blocs such as the blacks and with disaffected elements of the Roosevelt coalition, and a conservative Republican strategy seeking a clear ideological differentiation from the Democratic coalition, "a choice not an echo," as Senator Barry Goldwater and his supporters put it.

Led by men like William Rusher of the *National Review*, conservative strategists have consistently argued the desirability and inevitability of a realignment of American political parties along more ideological lines, that is, an ideologically conservative Republican party and an ideologically liberal Democratic party. The modern Republican case against the conservative approach was stated by New York Governor Thomas E. Dewey in a series of lectures on the two-party system delivered at Princeton early in 1950:

These impractical theorists with a "passion for neatness" demand that our parties be sharply divided, one against the other, in interest, membership and doctrine. They want to drive all moderates and liberals out of the Republican party and then have the remainder join forces with the conservative groups of the South. . . . The results would be neatly arranged, too. The Republicans would lose every election and the Democrats would win every election.[16]

The election results of Goldwater vs. Johnson in 1964 appeared to vindicate Dewey's forecast. Yet less than five years later a sophisticated, heavily documented statement of the conservative strategy, *The Emerging Republican Majority* by Kevin P. Phillips, was receiving widespread attention and acclaim. Marshaling extensive data (143 charts and 47 maps) to prove his case, Phillips argues "that a liberal Democratic era has ended and that a new era of consolidationist Republicanism has begun." The principal force that has broken up the Democratic New Deal coalition has been "the Negro socio-economic revolution and liberal Democratic ideological inability to cope with it." The result has been an "emerging Negro-Establishment entente" in the industrialized urban Northeast and the increasing alienation of many traditional Democrats from their party "by its social programs and increasing identification with the Northeastern Establishment and ghetto alike." In the South, Phillips foresees rising Negro political strength taking over the Democratic party in many areas and creating "a partisan politics reflecting racial cleavage."[17]

If, as this analysis suggests, the Democratic party has become the vehicle for Negro advancement, other more significant demographic trends will ensure a dominant Republican majority. During each new era, Phillips argues, "the ascending party has ridden the economic and demographic wave of the future." Since the nation's fastest-growing areas are, in his view, strongly Republican and conservative—Phoenix, Dallas, Houston, Anaheim, San Diego, Fort Lauderdale—a "demographically ascendant" Sun Belt stretching across the South

---

16 John A. Wells (ed.), *Thomas E. Dewey on the Two-Party System* (Garden City, N.Y.: Doubleday, 1966), p. 9.
17 Phillips, "A New South?," *Human Events* (Washington, D.C.), June 12, 1971, p. 6.

and West will gain electoral votes and national political power at the expense of the decaying urban Northeast.

The Negro revolution, Sun Belt migration and economic boom conditions, suburbanization and urban decay have all combined to set in motion two great shifts in party identification that are reversing and obliterating the regionalism of Civil War loyalties, long the basis of American voting patterns. The civil-rights revolution "cut the South adrift from its Democratic moorings" and drew the Yankee Northeast toward the Democrats. It also increased the Southern and Western bias within the Republican party to the point, the Goldwater nomination, where the Republican party "decided to break with its formative antecedents and make an ideological bid for the anti-civil rights South." Phillips sees the 1968 election as a ratification of "the basic geopolitical trend spotlighted and accelerated in 1964." In retrospect, the Goldwater nomination and defeat, while disastrous in the short term, were essential to the conservative strategy of realignment.

Phillips treats the Wallace American Independent Party as a transient third-party phenomenon, an example of "an electorate in motion between major parties." The vote against Hubert Humphrey and the Democratic administration (57 percent) represents "an obvious inchoate Nixon constituency" and a Republican opportunity to fashion a dominant electoral majority. Since this new popular majority is white and conservative in Phillips's view, a program of "successful moderate conservatism" can attract the Northern blue-collar workers who flirted with Wallace and unite white Protestants and Roman Catholics (exemplified by "the New York City Irish"). Phillips pointedly rejects the liberal Republican strategy of "mobilizing liberal support in the big cities, appealing to 'liberal' youth, empathizing with 'liberal' urbanization, gaining substantial Negro support and courting the affluent young professional classes of 'suburbia'" as "one of the greatest political myths of the decade." None of its elements is essential to a new Republican majority: "Obviously [in light of the 1968 election returns], the GOP can build a winning coalition without Negro votes." The leading big-city states are no longer necessary for a Republican majority since an ascendant Republican party "can easily afford to lose the states of Massachusetts, New York and Michigan—and is likely to do so except in landslide years."

Phillips dismisses arguments against a strategy of "polarization." Racial and ethnic polarization, he believes, is "a long-standing hallmark of American politics, not an unprecedented and menacing development of 1968," and has "neither stopped progress nor worked repression on the groups out of power." Although too innovative to win a presidential majority, the new Democratic liberalism, however, will inject "a needed leavening of humanism into the middle-class realpolitik of the new Republican coalition."

Such a strategy as advocated in *The Emerging Republican Majority* clearly represents a turning point in national policy formulation and a significant political decision with considerable stakes. This is one reason the Phillips thesis has stirred such controversy. The book has been billed as "the master plan that won the White House" and "the political Bible of the Nixon era." Its ideas were expressed during the 1970 campaign when Vice President Agnew claimed the working man for the Republican party as the "cornerstone" of a "new Majority."

In his newspaper column, Phillips endorsed the new Northern, blue-collar and Roman Catholic phase of Nixon-Agnew campaigning as a "post-Southern Strategy" predicated on the surmise that Republican success in Dixie was already assured. Republicans, not Democrats, would benefit from the "social issue" (identified by Scammon and Wattenberg in *The Real Majority*) by a strong stand for law and order and opposition to permissiveness, campus anarchy and racial engineering.[18]

What are the prospects for an emerging Republican majority? Some critics of this statement of conservative strategy argue its implausibility but concede that it may succeed, at least in the short run. The Republican alternative, they point out, does have the advantages of a relatively clear and cogent statement and of the potential leadership of an incumbent President. Samuel Lubell already credits the Nixon coalition with effect-

---

[18] Phillips, "Post-Southern Strategy," Washington *Post*, September 25, 1970.

ing a "startling departure" from the traditional broad-based nature of American political parties. A narrow-based coalition
built on a politics of polarization, he admits, could win elections and hold power, although its ability to conciliate conflict
would be limited.[19]

The problems of the New Deal coalition and a gradual decline in Democratic party identification, however, do not
automatically assure a "new era of consolidationist Republicanism" in which the emerging Republican majority simply re-
places the Roosevelt coalition as a cohesive dominant party.
The case can in fact be made that a Republican majority in the
early 1970's, if it is achieved, will be an ephemeral or unstable
majority quite unlike the New Deal coalition. Phillips assumes
a continuity in ethnic, racial and cultural bloc voting and the
formation of new strong party identifications and gives little
attention to the steady increase in Independent party identification, split-ticket voting, and the nationalizing impact of mass
media. The Harris data on party identification since 1968, for
example, show no significant growth in Republican identification (although Independents have gained some five to six
percentage points at the expense of Democrats). Nor do Republican weaknesses in the Congress and state legislatures,
the party's sharp reverses in gubernatorial races in 1970 and
1971, and the post-1970 census legislative redistricting augur
well for a new majority. Phillips avoids the problems posed
by 1970 by claiming that his theory does not deal with congressional, gubernatorial and local politics "except in a very
corollary way." The very movements he identifies in the
electorate may, however, indicate the end of old-politics bloc
voting rather than a realignment of voting blocs.

At a number of points in his analysis, moreover, Phillips
assigns an inevitability to trends that cannot be supported by
existing data. He relies heavily for evidence on voting shifts
that occurred between 1960 and 1964 and between 1964 and
1968. However, a change of nominees in either 1964 or 1968

---

[19] Lubell, *The Hidden Crisis in American Politics,* pp. 267–68.

could easily have produced quite different results in the major two-party vote. Again, the contingency of two assassinations and an unanticipated war on the Asian mainland greatly affected the composition of Democratic electoral support during the decade. The past may be irreversible, but it is less clear that the political trends of the 1960's, measured by presidential election statistics, were inevitable.

Phillips also makes assertions about the elements of his future majority that are more in the nature of self-fulfilling prophecies than research-based and projected trends. Perhaps most important are the assertions that the Wallace vote will move almost intact into the Nixon column and that Republicans can do little to win the black vote, in view of the identification of black political interests with Democratic welfare liberalism. But the motivations of voters, white and black, are more complicated and sophisticated than these assertions suggest. Wallace had a strong populist appeal that assumed the continuation and even expansion of many programs of welfare liberalism. Unlike Goldwater, he made deep inroads among working-class Democrats. How transferable is this vote to a Republican party identified with budgetary restraints, high unemployment and economic recession? And as long as George Wallace or a successor persists as a presidential candidate, can any national Republican candidate compete with him for the white segregationist vote? Phillips also ignores data that indicate the independence of black voters and the potential for middle-class black support for the GOP.

The prospects for a Republican majority may be questioned on a number of other grounds. Republicans have yet to solve the problem of how to broaden and hold together a coalition that includes more diverse groups. The emerging Republican majority that Phillips projects is a unique combination of two American political mainstreams—the populist South, West and lower middle-class urban electorate, and the rural, small-town and suburban North. They have never meshed before in any lasting way. Will the socially self-conscious white Protestant Republican bourgeoisie be comfortable with anti-establishment popular insurgents? Can the Republican coalition be broadened to a lower middle-class constituency? Unless a "popular, progressive conservatism" works, Phillips concedes, "this could be a short-lived Whig era, a basic marking of time, . . . a mere rearranging of existing programs and institutions that breaks no really new ground."[20]

The issue of race, which Phillips assumes will be as important a determinant of new party identifications as Civil War loyalties and the Great Depression were in the past, poses still more problems for the Republican majority. If the civil-rights revolution has made impossible the coalition of conservative white Southern Democratic interests and self-conscious black power, it has also raised the salience of civil rights as an issue within the Republican party. Phillips, however, sees few costs to the Republicans (and conversely gains for the Democrats) in the movement of white Southern Democrats into the Republican party, overlooking the fact that the resistance to making the Republican party an all-white and implicit antiblack coalition extends well beyond the liberal progressive wing of the party. A former California Republican official, James W. Halley, argues that "it is impossible to create permanent philosophical coalitions of people who disagree on anything as fundamental as human rights. . . . Men who earnestly believe in constitutional government, fiscal responsibility, limited budgets, campus peace and law and order may find a forced alliance with segregationists impossible to bear. There is a fracture point between the red neck vote and the traditional conservative vote." The Democrats for their part disdain Phillips's assessment. Liberal Democrats in Congress like Representative Richard Bolling of Missouri have encouraged Southern Democrats to cross the aisle. Democratic strategists in the South see their long-term future in a new coalition of liberal and racially moderate whites with blacks, while in the North they count on a Republican Southern strategy to yield them the strategically situated black urban vote plus white moderate support.

The prospects for an emerging Republican majority may be

[20] Phillips, "A Blueprint for a GOP Era," Washington *Post*, March 8, 1970.

questioned on another ground—the appeal to "the great silent majority" and the conscious neglect of major politically active and growing groups in the population. Phillips shares with Richard Scammon of the Elections Research Center the estimate that the decisive political majority in the United States is "un-young, un-poor, and un-black." He discounts the political impact of youth, noting that voters under 25 cast only 7.4 percent of the vote in 1968. Data analyzed below, however, suggest the much greater significance of young voters both qualitatively and quantitatively on the political system. Republican leaders have similarly ignored women's-rights and minority groups and the peace and public interest citizen movements. The net effect of Republican inattention and Democratic initiative has been to ally much of the membership and organizational resources of a wide variety of new-politics cause groups with the Democratic party coalition of the 1970's, hardly a promising development for a party that remains an almost permanent minority.

Finally, the Republican majority must be constructed from a minority position under severe constraints. At this moment of history, the leadership of the new Republican coalition falls to Richard Nixon, who lacks both the charismatic appeal that has been an important ingredient to previous populist movements and the electoral and congressional margins that Franklin Roosevelt enjoyed in the 1930's. Instead, the Republicans have turned to "populism via bureaucratic procedures," an alternative noted by Professor Andrew Hacker of Cornell which involves accelerating the "polarizing process by administrative means," for example, a mixture of action and inaction on the part of administration officials supplemented by the political spokesmanship of the Vice President.[21]

The President's partisan role is limited, however, by the requirement that he govern the country effectively. Even if he could achieve a partisan majority through the politics of racial and ethnic polarization, he must weigh the national costs of dividing rather than unifying Americans. This restraint is that

---

[21] Andrew Hacker, "Is There a New Republican Majority?," *Commentary*, November 1969, pp. 68–69.

much more salient when the projected political minority includes much of the nation's youth and a militant black population.

Alternative Future 3. A Multiparty System

A third alternative encompasses a cluster of multiparty possibilities. The Wallace campaign in 1968, politically conscious groups like blacks and women that may field their own presidential candidates, national opinion polls and survey data on youth all indicate the potential for at least third- and fourth-party movements during the 1970's. Several observers have specifically discussed the likelihood of a multiparty system. Senator Mark O. Hatfield expects that frustrations with the two major parties will produce such a system by 1976. According to Samuel Lubell, a four-party politics much like New York State's may develop as a result of the continuing polarization of American politics and the narrowing coalitional bases of the two parties.[22] Frederick G. Dutton, Assistant Secretary of State in the Kennedy administration and Democratic party professional, sees a three- or four-way split in the presidential politics of the 1970's leading to either a multicandidate (rather than a multiparty) arrangement or a realigned two-party system.[23] Tom Wicker anticipates "a proliferation of political parties by the end of the century."[24]

The two most serious contestants for national third- and fourth-party status at the moment are the Wallace movement and the still largely unorganized "modernizing" or "reform" constituency identified in the 1968 presidential campaigns of Eugene McCarthy, Robert Kennedy, and, in a different manner, of Nelson Rockefeller. Although McCarthy and Rockefeller did confer after the 1968 national conventions, the only organiza-

---

[22] Lubell, *The Hidden Crisis in American Politics*, p. 68.

[23] Frederick G. Dutton, *Changing Sources of Power: American Politics in the 1970s* (New York: McGraw-Hill, 1971), p. 242.

[24] Bangor (Me.) *Daily News*, July 14, 1970. Wicker also predicts that "turbulence and a demand for participation can be expected to continue for many years. . . ." (Tom Wicker, "The Politics Before Us," *New York Review of Books*, February 11, 1971, p. 14.)

tional expression of the modernizers has been the still headless fourth-party movement, the New Party or People's Party of Dr. Benjamin Spock, Marcus Raskin and their associates. On the other hand, George Wallace's 1968 efforts represented a historic breakthrough for national third-party organizations. The Wallace "ballot brigade" of more than 25 attorneys directed by four young lawyers from Alabama and South Carolina visited some 45 state capitals, researched relevant statutes, and quietly organized an impressive national campaign that netted an estimated 2.7 million signatures on Wallace petitions. The Ohio law that required petitions signed by 15 percent of the last vote for governor, or 433,100 persons, an almost impossible hurdle for third parties, was ruled unconstitutional in a landmark Supreme Court decision in mid-October 1968, thereby ensuring Wallace a position on the ballot in all 50 states. In November, Wallace, running under at least six different party names, managed to capture 13.5 percent of the vote (in comparison to the Republicans' 43.4 percent and the Democrats' 42.7 percent). Wallace also demonstrated the feasibility of a presidential campaign financed by small contributors and by state and regional candidate-appreciation dinners. "We raised more than the Democrats did from small contributions," observed Wallace adviser and Alabama newspaper publisher Dick Smith. In one 14-day period with 52 scheduled speeches, Wallace erased a sizable debt and banked $268,000, raising $67,000 in one Memphis speech alone.

Although Wallace himself has stressed the difference between his movement ("the Wallace campaign") and the American Independent Party, the party remains essentially a presidential ballot-line phenomenon, and followers of the Alabama governor have had little success in transferring his strength to state and local AIP candidates. Identifying another major problem facing Wallace, Seymour Martin Lipset and Earl Raab concluded after analysis of the 1968 data that Wallace appealed to two very different groups—economic conservatives who were concerned with repudiating the welfare state, and less affluent supporters of the welfare state who were affected by issues of racial integration and law and order. According to the study, appeals to what the authors termed the economically liberal working-class intolerants on the basis of welfare measures lost Wallace the middle-class conservative intolerants: "These data point up the dilemma facing a racist third-party candidate in becoming a viable alternative to the two major parties."[25]

Consistently underestimated by his detractors, the Alabama governor, prior to the assassination attempt made on him, joined the field of 1972 Democratic presidential contenders by entering the primaries, accumulating delegate strength for the convention and retaining his loyal personal organization for any eventuality.

Wallace's success in influencing both parties from the right simply by the fact of his candidacy, apart from his actual vote, provided an example for possible adaptation by the left. Strategists of the modernizing constituency, however, remain divided, as they were in 1968, between two courses: 1) taking over the Democratic party on the model of the Goldwater movement and remaking it into a radical-modernizing party; or 2) writing off chances for reforming the two existing parties and making a direct appeal to the growing college-educated, Independent-oriented sector of the electorate and allied minority groups. To solve the problem, some Democrats have suggested working for Democratic party modernization, while at the same time keeping open the option of a supplemental presidential line on the ballot as a contingency plan.

A new-party coalition appealing to those disaffected by the traditional two-party system (and not attracted by the Wallace alternative) could on the basis of current polls probably win popular support roughly equivalent to the Wallace vote, although less concentrated regionally (and accordingly with fewer votes under the Electoral College system). Dr. Martin Peretz of Harvard, a close McCarthy adviser and activist in a variety of causes, cites survey data from states like California that indicate "a steady and consistent number of people who are ready to throw both the parties out." Some new-

---

[25] Seymour Martin Lipset and Earl Raab, *The Politics of Unreason: Right-Wing Extremism in America, 1790–1970* (New York: Harper & Row, 1970), p. 412.

party enthusiasts see a major opportunity in the reform of the Electoral College to permit direct election of the President with a runoff if no candidate receives 40 percent of the vote (the proposal of Senator Birch Bayh). John O'Sullivan, a student activist from the McCarthy campaign and the Vietnam Moratorium, outlined one scenario: "If we had the direct election of the President with a 40 percent runoff provision in 1972 there would be a four-party race. Assuming Nixon runs for re-election, the Democrats nominate Humphrey or Muskie, and George Wallace goes again, we would almost surely be able to pull Nixon under the 40 percent line and we would have an excellent chance of being runner-up. In the runoff we could beat Nixon." Other new-party planners like Marcus Raskin see a presidential campaign as a means to build local organizations for postelection social-service and action programs rather than as a bid for national power.

The viability of a new modernizing party as a serious competitor to the two major parties depends largely on the existence of a sizable constituency outside the traditional parties. Whether the generational revolution and the massive influx of new young voters who do not identify themselves with either major party will provide this base is not yet clear. Apart from the one-time expansion of the national electorate in 1972 to include 18-to-21-year-olds—the much-heralded 25 million first-time potential voters from 18 to 25—election analysts like Richard Scammon, pointing to the tendency of young people to vote as their parents do and to the low rate of registration and voter turnout among those under 30, predict little change in the traditional two-party system. However, Samuel Lubell and California pollster Mervin D. Field anticipate a significant shift of young voters in favor of the Democrats.[26] The 3–1 Democrat-to-Republican registration ratio among new voters has become "a matter of great concern" among Republican leaders in the states, such as Alexander M. Lankler, the Maryland party chairman.

---

[26] Samuel Lubell, "The 18-Year-Old Vote Could Beat Nixon in '72," *Look*, July 13, 1971, pp. 64–66; and "Politics: A Quiet Revolution?," *Newsweek*, June 14, 1971, p. 37.

According to some scholars, the revolutionary political potential of youth lies less in their numbers than in the new cultural values they will bring to politics. Kenneth Keniston, professor of psychology at the Yale Medical School, has argued that the well-born, talented and privileged youth in technological postmodern (or postindustrial) societies have been able to define a distinctive postmodern style of life, the so-called youth culture.[27] The values of today's youth, shaped by rapid social change, automatic abundance, and a preoccupation with the issue of violence, nonetheless have a highly idealistic, humanistic, moral component, frequently expressed in postconventional moral reasoning that challenges existing community standards.

According to Theodore Roszak, a young historian at the California State College at Hayward, the contemporary youth culture is actually a counterculture, radically disaffiliated from the cultural imperative of the scientific revolution and its organized social form, "technocracy" or the "regime of experts."[28] More than a political movement, the alienated young are a cultural phenomenon that extends beyond the level of class, party, institution, or ideology to "the level of consciousness, seeking to transform our deepest sense of the self, the other, the environment." As to the future, Roszak is confident that a new "politics of consciousness" will grow. "The ethos of disaffiliation is still in the process of broadening down through the adolescent years, picking up numbers as time goes on." For those concerned with radical social change, "the young have become one of the very few social levers dissent has to work with."

The new politics of the youth culture, however, may not be compatible with the coalitional politics of the traditional political parties. Keniston suggests the tensions between the two revolutions in American society, the unfinished revolution of social and economic justice, and the new revolution of post-

---

27 Kenneth Keniston, *Young Radicals: Notes on Committed Youth*, Harvest Book (New York: Harcourt, Brace & World, 1968).
28 Theodore Roszak, *The Making of a Counter Culture: Reflections on the Technocratic Society and Its Youthful Opposition*, Anchor Books (Garden City, N.Y.: Doubleday, 1969).

modern youth.[29] Roszak foresees the possibility of ad hoc liaisons with workers and exploited minorities—the poor and the disadvantaged seeking entrance to technocratic affluence—but doubts the feasibility of any enduring alliance since the disadvantaged can be too easily co-opted into the very system that disaffiliated youth reject. Charles Reich, the Yale law professor who has popularized the values of the new generation (what he calls Consciousness III) in his book *The Greening of America,* goes so far as to say that political activism within the system is irrelevant.[30] "For one interested in basic change," Reich states, "law and political institutions are virtually irrelevant (except as theatres in which to stage exemplary battles of consciousness)." Instead of structural or institutional solutions, Reich advocates "revolution by consciousness," a statement of new values and a new way of life for the future society.

Survey data by Daniel Yankelovich, Inc., and Louis Harris and Associates, Inc.,[31] published in 1969 and 1970, present another picture of the political attitudes of youth. First, their findings supported the general interpretation of a youth counterculture. The Yankelovich surveys found a sharp division on the college campuses between what they termed "career-minded" students and a "forerunner" group less concerned about making money. Two motivations enjoyed exceptional

---

[29] Kenneth Keniston, "You Have to Grow Up in Scarsdale to Know How Bad Things Really Are," *New York Times Magazine,* April 27, 1969, pp. 27–28, 122–30.
[30] Charles A. Reich, *The Greening of America* (New York: Bantam Books, 1971).
[31] "What They Believe [survey conducted for Fortune by Daniel Yankelovich, Inc.]," *Fortune,* January 1969, pp. 70–71, 179–81; *Generations Apart,* A study of the generation gap conducted by Daniel Yankelovich, Inc., for use in the CBS News series "CBS Reports: Generations Apart" broadcast May 20, May 27, June 3, 1969 (New York: Columbia Broadcasting System, Inc., 1969); *Youth and the Establishment,* A Report on Research for John D. Rockefeller 3rd and the Task Force on Youth by Daniel Yankelovich, Inc. (New York: The JDR 3rd Fund, Inc., 1971); and *A Survey of the Attitudes of College Students,* a survey commissioned by the American Council on Education at the suggestion of Chancellor Alexander Heard of Vanderbilt University, Nashville, Tennessee, conducted by Louis Harris and Associates, Inc., June 1970.

strength among forerunner students: a private motivation toward personal self-fulfillment, self-actualization and creativity and a public motivation toward building a just and brotherly society. The forerunners questioned almost every major American institution, the objectives of American foreign policy and the racism, unequal distribution of wealth and economic soundness of American society. Career-minded students, on the other hand, expressed views more similar to noncollege youth, although the sharpest cleavages were between the forerunner students and noncollege youth. Not surprisingly, 30 percent of noncollege youth admired George Wallace (only seven percent of the forerunners did) and 65 percent of the forerunners admired Eugene McCarthy (compared to 24 percent for noncollege youth).

Most significant was the size of the forerunner group. Surveys taken in 1968 had estimated that student activists constituted less than two percent of the college population and that only 20 percent of college undergraduates had engaged in protest activity. The Yankelovich survey suggested that "behind the small and highly visible activist minority is a much larger and generally 'invisible' minority of forerunners holding similar dissident attitudes." It is in this forerunner group, "a universe of some 2,300,000," that a profound challenge to democratic and capitalist institutions is centered. Yankelovich found that between 1969 and 1970, forerunner students were moving toward "a deepening sense of alienation and apartness" and he predicted that the student rebellion would not be a transient phenomenon.

Second, youth, especially the forerunners, were highly critical of the traditional political parties. Between 1969 and 1970, the percentage of forerunners who felt the political parties should be "done away with" rose from 11 to 26. Among all students, 67 percent favored either "fundamental reform" or abolition of the parties in 1970. Half of the forerunners strongly agreed that the present two-party system did not offer any real alternatives. These findings have been supported both by a *Newsweek* poll in the fall of 1969 in which only 18 percent of college students gave a favorable rating to the political parties, by far the lowest rating of our major institutions, and by a 12-campus survey in June 1971 by the *National Review*.

Third, while critical of the parties, youth were more optimistic in their evaluation of the political process. Asked by Yankelovich if "the American system of representative democracy can respond effectively to the needs of the people," 43 percent of the young people strongly agreed, 46 percent partially agreed, and nine percent strongly disagreed. Harris found that 63 percent of students agreed and 33 percent disagreed that "the democratic process is capable of keeping up with the pace of events and with the need for action." His student sample also rated "working to elect better public officials" as the most effective means to bring about real improvement. Contrary to Reich's depreciation of political activism, both surveys found students willing to work within the system. Yankelovich found college youth preferred almost 3–1 (and forerunners more than 2–1) to work with the establishment rather than protest organizations, and Harris found that only three percent would become apathetic if they failed to elect candidates they supported for public office. At the same time, both reported the student opinion that protest to force change within institutions would continue and grow even after the ending of the Vietnam war.

Whether these attitudes and tendencies among the young and much of the upper middle class will coalesce into the "third force" described by Frederick Dutton that does not fit into either conservative or traditional liberal patterns[32] can be determined only by developments in the 1970's. In the meantime, what are prospects that third and fourth parties might pose a serious competitive challenge to the two-party system, perhaps even displacing one of the two major parties? Most national and state political leaders do not anticipate a serious third- (or fourth-) party challenge to the two-party system, although some concede that minor parties could establish themselves as electoral pressure groups on the left and right of the two major centrist parties. We are inclined to agree with this estimate for several reasons.

---

[32] Dutton, *Changing Sources of Power*, p. 63.

The two existing political parties are built into the political and governmental system at the national, state and local level through a series of legal and traditional means. They are vested interests that can be displaced only with an enormous investment of time, energy and financial resources. Detailed state laws regulating the parties give the existing two parties a complicated, decentralized first line of defense against any third-party movements. Single-member (as opposed to proportionally representative) districts for Congress and most state and local legislative bodies also make it hard for splinter parties to establish a base. Even within the Congress, traditional operating procedures with majority and minority leaders in each House and the complex committee system reinforce the hold of the two broadly based competitive national parties. Through their control of state and national legislatures, the major parties are able to adjust their statutory defenses, making it more difficult for third parties to get on the ballot or to endorse major-party candidates through use of a supplemental line.

A principal argument against the $1 tax-checkoff proposal for financing presidential elections, for example, has been that it would bring about a splintering of the major parties. The plan, now postponed until at least 1976, could have provided each major party in 1972 with $20,400,000 and Governor Wallace with some $6,000,000. Other new parties could receive funding for the election after they had demonstrated their ability to win at least five percent of the vote. "If we should find that we have done too much for a third party," stated Russell B. Long, chairman of the Senate Committee on Finance, "it would be easy enough to correct that in the near future. The potential third parties are represented by a mere handful of votes in either House of Congress and can rely on nothing more than the good conscience of the Senators and Congressmen belonging to the two major parties, as well as the Supreme Court, to assure them fair treatment." Proposals to reform the Electoral College so as to neutralize the Wallace threat afford another example of two-party cooperation at the national level.

The two major parties can rely on preemptive tactics to undercut the electoral appeal of a third party. Kevin Phillips foresaw that Nixon would get the border states Wallace vote. A new-politics Democratic presidential candidate or platform or reform efforts within the Democratic party can limit the electoral success of a new modernizing party. Even with too broad and diverse an electorate to be satisfied by only two centrist choices for the presidency, the two major parties still have the initiative in choosing candidates, issues and strategies that can maximize their own appeal and the two-party share of the vote.

Direct election of the President (i.e., abolition of the Electoral College) would probably not change this situation. Neal R. Peirce, author of *The People's President,* the definitive analysis of the Electoral College, believes that direct election would probably discourage regional-based third parties like the Wallace movement or Senator Strom Thurmond's Dixiecrat effort in 1948, since there would no longer be blocs of electoral votes they could obtain for bargaining purposes. Nor does Peirce see direct election as the key factor in the possible development of a presidential multiparty system. "If the major parties are truly unresponsive, there will be minor parties running for the Presidency whether there is still an electoral college or not. On the other hand, reasonably open and responsive major parties under relatively stable social conditions will quickly engulf minor parties, simply because the major parties are where the action—and the jobs—are."

Finally, there is no evidence yet that third- and fourth-party advocates are systematically developing party cadres or institutions that in any way rival or challenge the dominant position of the two major parties. The Wallace campaign, while professionalizing its Montgomery headquarters operation, did not develop a national field organization within the states and fourth-party planners continue to seek a charismatic leader. Even if one grants, as Frederick Dutton contends, that "vastly more money and muscle are available even now for starting an independent party than for reform of either of the major parties,"[33] the strategy for converting those resources into a viable, sustained political force is not yet evident. Be-

---

[33] *Ibid.,* p. 241.

cause of their preference for ad hoc organizational styles, new-politics amateurs are currently limited to a kind of guerrilla warfare against the parties rather than functioning as an effective third force nationally. None of these citizen groups has yet advanced a serious plan for developing a modernizing party coalition in American politics or even seriously directed its energies toward modernizing one (or both) of the existing major parties.[34]

Alternative Future 4. The Decline of Political Parties: Politics Without Parties

Another interpretation, one that differs markedly from the various coalition strategies, stresses the long-term decline of parties as effective intermediary structures in American politics and offers various views of a future politics without parties. Whether a new party alignment can emerge in American politics is seriously questioned by Walter Dean Burnham.[35] Although political parties are the only means thus far devised whereby individual voters can mobilize their collective power to check the power of elites, he observes, party-related identification and voting choice may in fact already have dissolved to a point where a large enough or stable enough long-term party majority can no longer be constructed, a development that would "in itself mark one of the great turning points in the history of American politics." If the trend toward independent voting and "politics without parties" continues and if parties disappear without new structures being developed to assume their intermediary role, Burnham warns, power will inevitably concentrate in the hands of economic, technological

---

[34] Josiah Lee Auspitz, former president of the Ripon Society, has projected the possibility of two broad coalitions, one of which would be modernizing and decentralizing (and presumably moderate Republican), but moderates have given little indication of developing the necessary strategy and organization for such a realignment. (Auspitz, "For a Moderate Majority," *Playboy*, April 1970, pp. 89–90, 94, 186–90.)

[35] See Walter Dean Burnham, "The End of American Party Politics," *Trans-Action*, December 1969, pp. 12–22; and Burnham, *Critical Elections and the Mainsprings of American Politics* (New York: W. W. Norton, 1970), especially pp. 173–74.

and administrative elites. Public policy in turn would become "as system-maintaining or 'conservative' for its time as was that of the 1920's for that time, even though punctuated from time to time by fire-brigade rescue operations." Burnham offers few projections beyond this, although he does note that a "countermobilization" for self-defense by the threatened American "great middle," outside of the traditional parties, could occur and become a factor that might break the system altogether.

Political consultant William E. Roberts posed the question of what is going to take the place of parties. "The end of the parties is fine as long as there's something to replace them, to maintain a choice, to give people an alternative. But it bothers the hell out of me because, without the parties, I can't see how we can guarantee ourselves alternatives at the polls in November."[36]

A decade of "rootless politics" is predicted by Yale Professor Robert E. Lane, a former president of the American Political Science Association, who points out that such cues for voting as party and social class are being reduced at the same time that the voter is required to make more decisions.[37] Although rootless politics will open up the possibility for both mood politics and reasoned argument through the media, Lane also expects the 1970's to be a decade of protest politics in which submerged groups, including women, Chicanos, Indians, the rural poor and underemployed professionals will adopt the techniques pioneered by blacks and students during the 1960's. New responses to protest like ombudsmen and legal aid in the ghettos will meet some of these new group demands, but, he cautions, society "cannot underestimate the power of either violence or repression." One group Lane doesn't include, Americans over 65, who constitute an estimated 17 percent of

---

[36] "Now Is the Time for All Good Men to . . . What's That?" (interview), Washington *Post*, December 19, 1971.

[37] Robert E. Lane, "Alienation, Protest, and Rootless Politics in the Seventies," in Ray Hiebert and others (eds.), *The Political Image Merchants: Strategies in the New Politics* (Washington, D.C.: Acropolis Books, 1971), pp. 273–300. See also Jean-François Revel, *Without Marx or Jesus* (Garden City, N.Y.: Doubleday, 1971).

registered voters, has begun to mobilize its political resources in earnest. Membership in politically active groups like the National Council of Senior Citizens and the American Association of Retired Persons has already reached some 6,000,000.

Other observers have also indicated that instead of a dominant party majority capable of governing the country, the United States may face a sustained period of politics without parties and the development of new competitive forms of political organization. Parties may, according to Samuel H. Beer, be gradually replaced by "a new type of political formation consisting of a coalition of voters united by a common attitude toward a major problem, but dissolving and re-forming as such problems changed."[38] In another direction, more differentiated political organizations like consulting firms and ad hoc citizen organizations are increasingly assuming functions once provided by the parties. Political consultants, professional campaign-management firms and the new consulting conglomerates can provide virtually the complete range of party functions. One observer of the consultant industry has suggested that consultants may be capable of managing "parties without people."[39] The objective of organizing information *about* people would replace the traditional methods of precinct, ward and county organization of people through the political parties. The professional party organization of the future requires only a strong central committee staff (and supporting consultants) and an up-to-date political information-management system. This new resource base becomes the key to planning election strategy, organizing a professionally managed campaign, recruiting and screening candidates and raising political funds. In addition to professionalized organizations, ideologically based electoral interest groups can raise funds through direct mail to aid endorsed candidates and causes. Pools or networks of issue-oriented citizen activists can be rapidly mobilized to

---

[38] Samuel H. Beer, *British Politics in the Collectivist Age* (New York: Vintage Books, 1969), p. 432. See also Moisei Ostrogorski, *Democracy and the Party System in the United States: A Study in Extra-Constitutional Government* (New York: Macmillan, 1910), pp. 442–44.
[39] David Lee Rosenbloom, "Managers in Politics" (unpublished Ph.D. dissertation, Massachusetts Institute of Technology, 1970), pp. 258–61.

work in presidential primaries or congressional elections, and public interest law firms and citizen feedback systems can be developed to counterbalance the influence of elected officials and governmental experts.

But there is no conclusive evidence of the prospective end of political parties. While party identification in the electorate may be declining, parties still perform essential electoral and governmental functions that make them (or an equivalent organizational form) a permanent factor of political life. The Democratic and Republican parties are built into the political system and as such they are almost impossible to eradicate or displace. As columnist Roscoe Drummond observes, "Even if the parties were dead and buried, they would rise again on the third day." "Inconvenient and often stupid as American politics and the two-party system is," remarks Walter Lippmann, "it's better than any alternative anybody has to offer."

Instead of the demise of political parties, we conclude that in many instances broader and more systematic management, financial and program approaches are instilling new vigor into party bodies. Far from supplanting county, state and national party organizations, consulting firms have in many instances developed mutually supportive working relationships with them. In another direction, the party reform movement, although still limited in focus, has dealt with some highly visible abuses of and public grievances with party organization politics, thereby increasing the acceptability of party organizations to the general public. We expect that the two major parties will survive the turbulent decade of the 1970's and probably a good deal longer, although in a context of greater citizen independence and activism.

Alternative Future 5. Technocratic Authoritarianism

The most pessimistic alternative is based on the assumption that our political system will be unable to cope with the problems of governing postmodern America and the fear that the ensuing decline or fragmentation of the parties could lead to political *immobilisme* and ultimately an authoritarian solution. Although the nature of American coalition politics has so far managed to retard the growth of political disorganization, it does not, as Lipset and Raab point out in their study of right-wing extremism in the United States, "guarantee such stability." Changes in party coalitions come through crisis; and until the delicate task of building new party coalitions is completed, Americans can expect "the formation of movements operating outside the normal rules of the game of two-party electoral politics."[40] At some point, parties might simply be suspended by technocratic elites, perhaps with the aid of a power-frustrated President, or nullified by the pronounced tendency, pointed out by British observer Henry Fairlie, of the American presidency to evolve into Caesaropapism, "the most refined of all absolutist systems."[41]

One picture of the 1970's, described by Dr. John R. Everett, president of the New School for Social Research in New York, suggests a massive disintegration and reorganization of the American myth structure as a virtually certain product of an accelerating rate of change. The dangers in such a process are immense, warns Dr. Everett. One could be the unraveling of the essential faith that has made the American political system work, the casting aside of such basic beliefs as the one that "the general political process, leading to the nominating conventions, would in some mysterious and unspecific way produce nominees which each party was convinced was the best person to manage the country's destiny." Tactics of terror and violence would be used increasingly by revolutionary groups bent upon undermining existing authority structures. The polarization of power in such a "coming-apart" of the system would be multipolar. "Relatively small groups will seek the power to determine the thrust of our society by making and breaking uneasy alliances with each other as their special interests coincide and diverge."

Unless a new myth structure based on decentralization or powerful community control can be devised, Dr. Everett foresees the likely development of "technocratic fascism" which

---

[40] Lipset and Raab, *The Politics of Unreason,* p. 512.
[41] Henry Fairlie, "Thoughts on the Presidency," *Public Interest,* Fall 1967, p. 44.

places the essential power of government and social order generally in the hands of those power elites which are capable of operating the enormously complicated system of public-private corporate power.[42] Many of the futurist descriptions of the year 2000 are also technocratic in their assumptions. Zbigniew Brzezinski of Columbia University foresees a long-term evolution toward a "symbolic" presidency where functionally necessary experts replace parties and elected governments. The President will no longer be able to adjust and interrelate "all the functionally specialized interests that will evolve" and the representation of interests in the legislative process will become far more abstracted, "involving the weighing of interrelationships within the society and within the technological processes."[43]

A more chilling view of what the technocratic future might hold has been provided by Bertram M. Gross, Distinguished Urban Affairs Professor at Hunter College, City University of New York.[44] Gross believes that a distinctive American "techno-urban" fascism could develop as a cancerous growth within present institutional structures. The present military-industrial complex would be broadened into a faceless and widely dispersed complex including three new component bureaucracies—police, welfare and communications. New "control networks" would include selective repression operating through and around the constitutional system, indirect controls like rationed welfare-state benefits (made conditional on good behavior) and "credentialized" meritocracy or a kind of status slavery, and co-optation of new elements into the leadership. Charismatic dictators, one-party rule, or mass fascist parties would not be needed. Multiple scapegoats would serve to divert public energy and deter opposition. The new techno-

---

[42] John R. Everett, "The '70s: Battleground for Old Myths," *Think* (Armonk, N.Y.), January–February 1970, pp. 11–14. See also, Beer, *British Politics in the Collectivist Age*, pp. 428–30.

[43] "Working Session One: Baselines for the Future, October 22–24, 1965 (Commission on the Year 2000, American Academy of Arts and Sciences)," *Daedalus*, Summer 1967, p. 671.

[44] Bertram M. Gross, "Friendly Fascism: A Model for America," *Social Policy*, November/December 1970, pp. 44–52.

cratic ideology which carried "rationality" to an extreme would spell the end of political ideologies. A culture of alienation would encourage the breakdown of political trust and possibilities for organized action in a society of repressed isolates.

Although few Americans have delineated this possible alternative as comprehensively as has Gross, many have expressed serious concern about the possibility of a successful fascist movement in American politics. President Nixon cited the possibility of a domestic right-wing protest movement against an American defeat in Vietnam as a major reason for his policy of gradual troop withdrawal. George Wallace has justified his movement as a legitimate expression of popular opinion within the democratic system and as the best defense against an anti-democratic movement and an American Hitler. William L. Shirer, author of *The Rise and Fall of the Third Reich,* soberly cautions that "perhaps America will one day go fascist—democratically, by popular vote."[45] Political figures like John Lindsay already warn of the threat of a "new repression," and Louis Harris reports that 58 percent of students agree (and 20 percent strongly agree) that "the United States has become a highly repressive society, intolerant of dissent." Critics of the revolutionary tactics of the New Left and the intellectual community's fascination with social-fascism like Arnold Beichman, Theodore Draper, and Norman Podhoretz of *Commentary* remind us that American democracy, like the Weimar Republic of Germany, can effectively commit suicide at the same time that it is being murdered.

The alternative of a right- or left-wing take-over of the American political system appears to be the least likely of those considered in the short term. The American two-party system, with its broad party coalitions and pragmatic, largely non-ideological orientation, has in the past demonstrated an unusual capacity over time to absorb or co-opt protest movements and to serve as a stabilizing influence against political movements of the right or left. Organized labor working within the Democratic coalition in 1968, for example, was the most effec-

---

[45] Quoted in Albin Krebs, "After 2 Tomes, Shirer Leans Back Thinking of No. 3," *New York Times,* December 29, 1969.

tive counterforce to George Wallace's American Independent Party.

European observers like the British team that analyzed the 1968 elections in *An American Melodrama* found that American fears of fascism are greatly exaggerated, especially in the connotation of physical repression. The American system, with its institutionally buttressed constitutional safeguards, relatively open politicized bureaucracy and principle of civilian control of the military, cannot begin to be compared with earlier European forms of fascism. Yet the possibility of a distinctive and advanced form of technocratic fascism by bureaucratic extension, remote as it may be, delineates most clearly the challenge faced by the traditional political parties and the urgent need for party modernization and/or the introduction of new political means for the popular control of government in the 1970's.

Alternative Future 6. Party Modernization and the Development of Citizen or Participant Parties

These five alternative futures, of course, do not exhaust possible political futures. A split in the Democratic party, for example, could produce quite different coalitional strategies in the Democratic and Republican parties, depending on which elements bolted in which direction. A Republican President in the moderate Eisenhower tradition could broaden the Republican coalition in directions conservatives are ideologically predisposed to ignore. None of these alternatives, however, adequately describes or analyzes the functions that political parties can or will perform in the future. The citizen is left only with reshuffled party coalitions, one or more parties that are largely limited to the politics of presidential elections, the decline of parties with no clear indication of what will replace them, or a new technocratic order that makes party politics superfluous.

There is another alternative, one that is both realistic and feasible, namely, the possibility of modernizing party structures and improving their political and governmental effectiveness. What we have defined as citizen or participant parties represents a potentially new stage in American political development as significant for democratic participation in politics and direction of government as the construction of popular political parties in the Jacksonian era. These participant parties assume both a new level of citizen competence in politics and a new citizen demand for competence in government.

Some of their possible characteristics have been suggested by this book. Within the decade of the 1970's, citizens working through local party reform groups could use the rapidly expanding potential of cable television to rejuvenate local politics, county-level party organizations and municipal government, creating a vital national reform movement. Citizens could study the statutory base of the parties in the states, develop model state-party reforms, and revitalize state-party politics and government. Taking advantage of the latest advances in communications technology and transportation, citizen parties could assemble interstate problem-solving task forces, under party auspices, to investigate and recommend policy initiatives with regard to virtually any problem of public concern.

New criteria for the nomination of presidential and vice-presidential candidates within the convention framework, giving attention to the needs for national political leadership and executive ability, could be developed by citizens. Party commissions on convention modernization could design the first modern party conventions equipped to serve as representative governing bodies for the parties, with two-way televised communications between state delegations and their constituencies. Interim national party conventions could be held at citizen demand to develop timely party positions on significant national issues and to give added impetus to party reform. The Democratic and Republican National Committees, with their membership reformed on a population basis and including representatives of all major national population groups, could become important party representative assemblies between conventions, with a new breed of activist national committeemen and committeewomen exercising a greater leadership role in party politics and government.

The significant Democratic party innovation of representative party commissions operating as party study and rule-making bodies under the authority of the national convention and offering new means for grass-roots citizen involvement in the parties could be applied to a broad range of topics, such as methods of recruiting party candidates for state and national legislatures and guidelines for the party use of political consultants and new political technologies. New national and state party administrations could undertake a national talent hunt through the party organization to locate and train political executives. Party advisory committees throughout the executive and legislative branches could involve tens of thousands of citizens in the workings of federal and state government, providing valuable lay opinion while developing executive reserves for the parties and government.

The alternative of participant parties is not necessarily an exclusive one. Either or both of the major party coalitions could be modernized. The Democratic party has made the beginning steps in this direction, but it is too early to conclude that a fundamental restructuring will necessarily follow. Nor can the possibility be ruled out that the Republicans will adopt a strategy of modernization and leapfrog the Democrats.[46] While we do not subscribe to or advocate any particular coalitional alignment of the parties, it is our assumption that the major parties can be modernized, that modernization is most likely to be effected through one of the major parties, and that reforms in one party will in turn encourage reforms within the other major party. Also, the relatively secure position of the two major parties and the limited progress of third-party movements do not preclude the possibility that a third party might adopt a strategy of modernization and develop new party structures and functions in the process of broadening its appeal to Americans disaffected with the traditional parties.

The alternatives of politics without parties or technocratic

---

[46] Frederick Dutton has suggested that Republicans have a potential advantage in courting young voters. "The more articulate young people now see liberals as sometimes talking a good game but only infrequently playing it and therefore, worst of all in their view, full of hypocrisy—people who daily put aside their social convictions for careers and comforts that leave them shallow and dull." (Dutton, *Changing Sources of Power,* p. 60.)

authoritarianism are clearly antithetical to the direction of
party modernization. In the absence of new representative
structures equivalent to the traditional political parties, both
alternatives reduce the possibilities for citizen participation
and efficacy and insult the growing competence of citizens to
act in politics by assuming that they will abdicate control of
the political future to technocratic and bureaucratic elites.
Those who would consciously undermine, dismantle, or attempt to destroy the political parties without defining a replacement for them should consider the consequences of such
actions for the continued functioning of representative democracy in America.

The political future may well combine aspects of all of
these alternatives. Fundamentally, however, the choice facing
the American people remains whether or not they will demand
a greater voice in decisions directly affecting the world in
which they live or whether they will leave such decisions to
professional party elites, officeholders, bureaucrats, or others.
If they choose to take destiny in their own hands, modernized
citizen parties would be a serviceable instrument for political
and governmental action.

XI

Strategy for the Seventies: Investing in Party Politics

> "I declare it's marked out just like a large chess-board!" Alice said at last. "There ought to be some men moving about somewhere—and so there are!" she added in a tone of delight, and her heart began to beat quickly with excitement as she went on. "It's a great huge game of chess that's being played—all over the world— if this *is* the world at all, you know. Oh, what fun it is! How I *wish* I was one of them! I wouldn't mind being a Pawn, if only I might join—though of course I should *like* to be a Queen best."
>
> LEWIS CARROLL, *Through the Looking-Glass*

The game of politics offers excitement, challenge and endless fascination to those who would play it. It is also a game with high stakes—the direction of our government and society— and that is what the game of party politics is all about. Policies, programs and leaders emerge from the periodic contests of elections and day-to-day skirmishes of partisan politics. Individuals engaged in politics, whether as part of organized party teams or through independent action, *can* make things happen. The game is wide open to anyone who wants to join.

Yet for many Americans today the game seems pointless and closed. Presidential campaign games fill the toy shelves of department stores and public television borrows from Monopoly in designing a big Polopoly board for its in-depth analysis of presidential-year politics. But as David S. Broder and Haynes Johnson report in their national survey of the American electorate for the Washington *Post*, "The voters see little hope that . . . [the] presidential election will provide the answers they want."[1] Neither the politicians nor the people seem to have a clear sense of political direction or know where to find it.

Herein lies the key. One major reason why politics seems to offer no answers or possibilities for change to many Americans is the absence of activist strategies that get results either by the major parties or by individuals or groups of citizens acting in politics. By and large, the concept of strategy is missing from American politics. We have strategyless parties and partyless strategies. Much of the incapacity of our politics rests on the central fact that it is a politics without party strategy.

Politics without strategy begins to resemble the surrealistic world of *Through the Looking-Glass,* with its Red Queen running as fast as she could to stay in place and its White Knight thinking best when hanging head-downwards. Only it is worse. Alice did manage to win her game of backwards chess in 11 moves. The striking quality of contemporary American politics is how little has changed in spite of all that has occurred in the rest of American society in the past two decades.

The national and state party committees rarely meet, and when they do the subject of party strategy somehow is seldom on the agenda. Presidential politics is full of classic "moves"—entering or avoiding primaries, favorite-son candidacies, bandwagons, alliances and occasional dark-horses, to mention but a few[2]—but neither party has developed a strategy for governing once in office. The Democratic party had no discernible

---

[1] David S. Broder and Haynes Johnson, "Americans Still Looking for a Leader: Future May See New Coalitions, Groupings—Even Parties," Washington *Post*, December 19, 1971.

[2] Nelson W. Polsby and Aaron B. Wildavsky, *Presidential Elections: Strategies of Electoral Politics* (2nd ed.; New York: Scribner's, 1968), especially pp. 3–6.

strategy for paying off its 1968 debt of more than $9 million. The Republican party has no clear strategy for redressing loudly proclaimed grievances with the media's coverage of political news. Although parties control access to the key positions in government, most citizen organizations have no long-term strategy for influencing the parties.

Such party strategy as may exist is made in the hidden recesses of the parties by faceless individuals with no broad accountability for their decisions and actions. There are no long-term party goals, no party discussions or debates, no public hearings, no formal decision-making procedures or mechanisms for drafting strategy. Without broad party participation in the definition of goals, there is little impetus to develop party strategy. Instead, low standards of party performance and low expectations of change are generally accepted. But in politics, as in other games, well-defined strategies—carefully thought-out courses of action consciously pursued toward specified goals—are a precondition for success. Although it is possible to design a strategy for any political situation to deal with any problem or goal one may have, no one can guarantee that a strategy by itself will work—inevitably there are both winners and losers in political contests. But the party or candidate or citizen who thinks and acts in terms of strategy is well ahead of the opponent that does not.

Strategy for Citizen Parties

The modernization of American parties will require sustained strategies to further citizen participation and party accountability for their political and governmental performance. Formally structured strategy mechanisms and consultative procedures are particularly essential to involve a broad cross-section of the party in the strategy-making process.

Strategies presuppose the existence of some strategy-making group or "think-tank" whose members have time to read, weigh and develop plans that often require considerable lead time to implement—factors rarely taken into consideration in the current style and pace of party politics. Parties are more often than not bankrupt in ideas, in part because they have no systematic means for evaluating their performance and generating strategies and tactics. Following the practice of top corporations, the parties could free top-level personnel from operating responsibilities to concentrate on long-term planning. New strategy mechanisms would give parties the opportunity to plan for the future, replacing the tendency of party leaders simply to react to events.

One of the best approaches toward assuring that parties will develop effective strategies is through the establishment of sound procedures for decision making and communication within the parties. The absence of party reports, budget hearings, financial reports and campaign post-mortems only frustrates the review and planning that is a prerequisite to meaningful party strategy. Many of the recommendations suggested in this book are in the nature of such procedural reforms and related structural changes in the parties. Party members should have a voice in determining strategy through open hearings, adequate discussion and recorded votes. A much broader and tougher definition is also needed regarding what decisions are in the public domain, which party meetings should be open and which held in executive session, what records should be available for inspection, etc. The Freedom of Information Act at the federal level and comparable state statutes from California to Florida have set public information standards that could be adapted for party use. The examples of bipartisan cooperation to improve rules and procedures in the Congress, including the significant rules change requiring public "teller" votes in the House of Representatives, and the Democratic party procedural reforms in delegate selection are instructive. Procedural reforms such as these can have important qualitative effects on political outcomes. The cumulative impact of such changes can steadily open the parties and the processes of party decision making to greater popular scrutiny and participation.

At the same time that more formal procedures are built into the parties, means for enforcing these reforms must also be included. Unless there is a widespread expectation that procedural changes are going to remain in effect for the foreseeable future, they will not be taken into account. A certain measure of discipline can be incorporated through legal requirements and penalties. The recently adopted New Mexico presidential primary law, for example, imposes a penalty of up to $1,000 and/or 10 days in jail for convention delegates who do not vote as bound by the primary. Parties could also establish internal sanctions for enforcing procedural rules.

Before the game of politics can be played vigorously by all who would like to participate, adequate political information and intelligence are needed by citizens and party activists alike. Even the most basic directory type of information on party committees and staff, state parties, political consultants or citizen organizations is not available. Party files, background memoranda and news clippings are rarely available when decisions are made. Party organizations quickly lose touch with former leaders and experienced party workers who are an invaluable party resource. Media coverage of politics gives only fragmentary information on which to base intelligence for strategy, and the problem of sorting, locating, filing and retrieving such information is at least as serious.

Parties themselves will thus require substantially improved intelligence- and information-retrieval services and internal party communications to keep members abreast of relevant political developments. Informed citizen participation in party strategy decisions requires both improved media coverage of politics and more specialized approaches, such as new and expanded political newsletters, access to political data banks, case studies and recorded oral histories of successful and unsuccessful political strategies, and political refresher courses eventually through videocassettes and cable television.

Strategy also requires a new concept of timing and the use of critical periods of time. The postelection months of November, December and early January before a new Congress convenes, for example, pose some of the most important opportunities for party evaluation, updating and future planning, but they are rarely used for this purpose by either the party establishment or party reformers. They are a kind of extended "lost weekend" of American politics. The periodic congressional recesses, now including the formal summer break, afford regular opportunities to involve members of Congress in party

planning at the state and local level. The experience of the
Democratic reform commissions also suggests the crucial importance of the period preceding the national party conventions
in planning strategy, drafting proposals and mobilizing support. Although probably two or three conventions are needed
to establish firmly a basic change in party structure, conventions also impose a four-year cycle and provide sufficient lead
time to initiate, implement and gain general understanding
and acceptance of party reforms. While the media and in turn
much of the public may follow politics on a seasonal basis, a
strategy-conscious party will define its own political calendar
and make full use of periods like these.

Strategy at its best requires individual talents and leadership
qualities, sheer intellectual force, candor, imagination and
creativity, courage, and a fine sense of timing. Effective strategy
requires highly selected and trained teams of leaders, whether
it be for developing cable television, expanding the base of
party contributors, or designing new issue and service functions
to attract citizens into the parties. Modernized parties could
serve an important broker role in identifying citizens with
critical political skills and in helping teams of party members
get together for specific strategy purposes.

Politics could also take on a new vitality if the players learned
how to use available instruments more effectively. One obvious
example is found in the new technologies of communications
and information processing. The slow response of party politics
to the strategic potential of mass media and to communications
and management systems pioneered in the private sector has
opened a major gap between current party operations and
potential performance. What is most startling about political
technology is not the futuristic possibilities of home communications centers and computer modeling but the lack of
imagination within the parties in the use of such elementary
communications techniques as the telephone conference call.
The party or groups that apply existing and emerging technologies to politics—from direct mail and WATS lines to computers and cable television—can achieve significant strategic
breakthroughs.

Similarly, media strategies by parties and citizen groups

represent important "leverage" potential in politics. The strategic importance of the media in communicating political news and information makes them a necessary aspect of any party planning. Citizens have been well ahead of the parties in understanding the power of the media in influencing public opinion through such projects as the massive multimedia campaign, "The Unselling of the War," conceived and planned by a 20-year-old Yale student and a group of fellow students and faculty members. Commenting on the enormous media exposure of Earth Day 1970, Stephen Cotton, press director for Environmental Action, candidly admitted, "We developed the strategy of the self-fulfilling press release. We produced confident accounts of how the crusade was growing. And as the press churned out mountains of newsprint, interest indeed perked up."[3]

The phenomenal recent growth and expansion into almost every field of the public interest lawyer has underlined the importance of an understanding of law to the future as an instrument of political strategy. It is only a matter of time before party reformers, such excluded groups as women and blacks, and public interest lawyers and organizations begin to design effective legal strategies for opening the parties. Parties themselves, aware of their exposed position and the pending challenge, have an added incentive to initiate their own reforms.

Effecting these changes in the strategic framework of party politics and the way the game of politics is played is basically the work of the players and the party teams themselves. It can, however, receive a valuable assist through an independent institutional catalyst. While parties develop their internal capabilities, there is a crucial supporting role that can be performed in political research and development and idea generation and in the implementation of strategies of party modernization by an independent political institute.

The potential contributions of a national institute of politics funded on a multiyear basis and with permanent, full-time

---

[3] Stephen Cotton, "Earth Day Got a Good Press," Washington *Post,* April 18, 1971.

staff analyzing the functioning of the political process are extensive. An institute could initiate public discussion on party reform topics through the sponsorship of conferences, panels and special weekend and one-week programs. It could encourage the reporting and evaluation function within the parties by serving as a multipartisan, impartial, candid outside monitor, issuing its own regular reports. One of its most valuable functions might be in initiating political directories and other political-information clearinghouse services that could introduce new ideas and citizen talent into the parties.

The Need for Major Investment in the Parties

Strategies for party modernization, even if they fulfill all these requisites, will still require massive and concentrated funding if they are to change party performance measurably. Americans spend relatively little on politics. The weak and ineffective political parties of the American states and the nation are in part a product of a deep antiparty tradition that has discouraged investment in party institutions. Herbert E. Alexander, director of the Citizens' Research Foundation of Princeton, New Jersey, concludes that in this country "politics is not overpriced. It is underfinanced."[4]

Neither the public nor anyone else has a realistic concept of the cost of politics in the United States. The cost of politics should, but does not, include the costs of operating the political parties as ongoing organizations and the costs of party operations in government, such as the staffing of new administrations and the work of party caucuses and policy-research groups in the legislature. Virtually no efforts have been made to collect data on the financing of presidential transitions and congressional-party operations, critical sectors of American politics which remain seriously underfinanced in spite of recent increases in funding levels (including some government financing in the Presidential Transition Act of 1963).

Walter Pincus, associate editor of *The New Republic,* is a

---

[4] Herbert E. Alexander, Statement Before the Subcommittee on Communications of the Senate Committee on Commerce, April 1, 1971.

member of the woefully small group of investigative journalists reporting on money in politics, and he bluntly contends that "there are fewer than a dozen men living today—Democrats or Republicans—who fully understand the intricate processes of loans, debts, cash, multiple committees, and contribution techniques that have supported national campaigns in the past," and that none of them made their knowledge available to Congress during the drafting of recent campaign reform legislation.[5]

Research in this area has itself been fragmentary and underfinanced. The books and monographs of the thinly staffed Citizens' Research Foundation and a few studies by political scientists over the past decade exhaust the serious literature on the subject. There is no newsletter or regular reporting service covering this complex and rapidly changing area. The lack of basic information on the subject, however, has not deterred extensive editorial comment and advice in the media.

Political finance is thought of merely in terms of campaign finance, that is, the amount, sources and uses of the money used in campaigning for public office. Challengers, incumbents and citizens alike are voicing alarm about the costs of campaigning. Many decry the "national scandal" of "skyrocketing costs"; others say that elective politics will become the "special preserve of the wealthy" and warn that "the price of campaigning has risen so high that it actually imperils the integrity of our political institutions."[6]

Most public discussion of political finance continues to center on increases in campaign spending. An estimated $300 million was spent in 1968 in campaigns for nomination and election by candidates for more than 500,000 public offices at all levels, representing an increase of 50 percent from the $200

---

[5] Walter Pincus, "Campaign Funding: Bogus Reform," *New Republic*, December 11, 1971.

[6] See, for example, Haynes Johnson, "Rising TV Spending Adds to the High Cost of Campaigning," Washington *Post*, November 22, 1970; Senator Mike R. Gravel (D-Alaska), "Introduction of a Bill to Strengthen Confidence in the Political Process," *Congressional Record—Senate*, 92nd Congress, 1st Session, January 25, 1971, p. S 18; and "High Cost of Politics in '68," *U.S. News & World Report*, August 5, 1968, p. 38.

million spent in 1964 and more than 100 percent since 1952, when the first national estimates of $140 million were compiled. The figure is expected to be up to $400 million in 1972.[7] Nominating and electing a President cost an estimated $17 million in 1956, $25 million in 1960, $35 million in 1964, and $100 million in 1968 (a good part of which went for expensive preconvention drives by unsuccessful aspirants Rockefeller, Romney, McCarthy and Kennedy). Democratic aspirants actually spent more money in seeking the nomination in 1968 than the party nominee, Vice President Humphrey, could raise for his entire postconvention campaign. One preliminary estimate, made well before the Democratic National Convention of 1972, reckoned that preconvention spending among a half dozen serious Democratic contenders could easily top $50 million.[8] Postelection estimates amount to about half.

The dramatic increase in campaign spending, especially at the presidential level, however, should be considered in perspective. The total of $300 million spent for political campaigns in 1968 is approximately *one-tenth of one percent* of the $282.6 billion spent in fiscal 1968 at all levels of government, only slightly more than Procter and Gamble's $270-million advertising budget for 1968, and less than is spent annually on chewing gum or cosmetics in this country.[9] With all the public discussion about reordering national priorities, the American people

---

[7] Alexander Heard, *The Costs of Democracy: Financing American Political Campaigns*, Anchor Book (Garden City, N.Y.: Doubleday, 1962); Herbert E. Alexander, *Financing the 1960 Election* (Princeton, N.J.: Citizens' Research Foundation, 1962); Herbert E. Alexander, *Financing the 1964 Election* (Princeton, N.J.: Citizens' Research Foundation, 1966); Herbert E. Alexander, *Financing the 1968 Election* (Lexington, Mass.: D. C. Heath, 1971); Paul Hope, "For the '72 Campaign: Democrats Learning Money Is Tight," Washington *Star*, February 23, 1971; and "The $400 Million Election Machine," *Newsweek*, December 13, 1971, pp. 23–32.

[8] Washington *Post*, January 30, 1971.

[9] "Political Perspective: Money and Political Campaigns," taped interview of Herbert E. Alexander by Torrey Baker for the League of Women Voters, reprinted in Remarks of Fred Schwengel (R-Iowa), *Congressional Record—Extensions of Remarks*, 91st Congress, 1st Session, November 25, 1969, p. E 10073; and Alexander, Statement Before the Senate Subcommittee on Commerce, April 1, 1971.

have in fact devoted relatively few resources to participatory politics, in theory *the* means most available to them for influencing the priorities of government. Even if the unreported and unmeasured political expenditures of parties and citizen groups were added to the total of estimated campaign spending, the question whether Americans are spending enough on politics would still have to be raised.

Political costs since 1950 have not risen as fast as increases in national wealth and income, although they have increased at a faster rate than the prices of nonpolitical goods and services purchased by consumers. Yet they do not appear to be overpriced. David Adamany has shown, for example, that while the cost per vote of presidential elections rose from an estimated $2.27 in 1952 to $2.83 in 1964, when stated as a ratio of the average hourly wage of industrial workers this index of political expenditure actually declined over the same period from 1.36 to 1.12. A cost per vote of roughly one hour's wages to conduct elections does not seem "too high" when contrasted with expenditures for other purposes. Nor do these costs appear high when compared to a similar index of political expenditure for other countries.[10]

Several factors have contributed to the increasing dollar costs of political campaigns. Since 1952, there has been a greater reliance on the use of mass media, especially television. While the value of labor contributed by party ward organizations and volunteers and allied groups like organized labor is extremely difficult to estimate, it is apparent that with the shift from party organization campaigning (noncash) to media campaigning (cash), the percentage of cash costs has risen steadily. Campaigning in the United States is increasingly dependent on avenues and mechanisms requiring money rather than donated labor and goods. The use of new campaign techniques, such as public opinion polls and computerized voter analysis, has clearly added to cash costs.[11]

---

[10] David Adamany, *Financing Politics: Recent Wisconsin Elections* (Madison: University of Wisconsin Press, 1969), pp. 56–57.
[11] "Campaign Costs: More Specialization, More Dollars," *Congressional Quarterly,* September 11, 1971, pp. 1912–16.

Individual constituencies have become larger and more complex with population increases and the expansion of the suffrage. When the current size of the House of Representatives was set at 435 members in 1911, the average population of a district was about 210,000. By 1970, with a total population of almost 205 million, the average stood at more than 470,000. By 1980, each Representative will have acquired another 100,000 constituents. State legislative districts have undergone even more dramatic changes with reapportionment. The number of contacts a candidate needs to make have increased, together with travel and staff costs required to canvass larger constituencies. In addition, the number of federal and state offices seriously contested by the two major parties has increased with the decline of one-party dominance in most states, including the once solid Democratic South. Political costs, however, appear to rise sharply in relation to the growth of strong two-party competition.[12]

Alexander Heard's conclusion in 1959 that such costs are not a high price to pay for the means of freely choosing our leaders was reaffirmed by Adamany a decade later: "By most measures Americans pay a small cost for the maintenance of an adversary political process in a complicated federal system with its many elective offices at a variety of levels of government.[13]

Although Americans have spent comparatively little on politics, there are indications that they are willing to spend more. Since 1953, Gallup polls have consistently shown 30 to 40 percent of Americans expressing a willingness to make a political contribution if asked. Yet according to studies of the Gallup organization and the Survey Research Center of the

---

[12] Adamany, *Financing Politics,* p. 85. Citing his research in Connecticut and Wisconsin, Adamany suggests that "after a very sharp acceleration in the rate of spending during the transition from one-party to two-party competition, there is a flattening of the rate of increase. Nonetheless, Connecticut's higher per vote costs suggest that costs in dollar terms are likely to be much higher in areas with established two-party competition than in either non-competitive situations or transitional jurisdictions." (*Ibid.,* p. 86.)

[13] Heard, *The Costs of Democracy,* p. 11; and Adamany, *Financing Politics,* p. 244.

University of Michigan, no more than 12 percent of the population has contributed to a political party or a candidate.

Two examples from different ends of the political spectrum show that the public is responsive when asked. Barry Goldwater's presidential campaign in 1964 met with unprecedented success in attracting large amounts of money in small sums. The employment of two previously unused techniques for mass fund raising in a national campaign, direct mail and radio and television appeals, was responsible for the outpouring of some 650,000 individual contributions to Goldwater, with an estimated 560,000 people sending in contributions of $100 or less. In response to one half-hour appeal and several shorter appeals by actors John Wayne and Ronald Reagan, more than $2 million was collected within five days before the election. Reagan and another actor, Raymond Massey, were credited with bringing in 134,000 individual contributions of $100 or less. At a cost of $1 million, 15,000,000 pieces of direct mail were sent out and the response was a record-breaking 380,000 donations totaling $5.8 million. The campaign ended with a $1-million surplus.

A half-hour television appeal by five antiwar Senators in May 1970 to help finance a campaign to halt the Vietnam war by congressional action brought a blizzard of contributions and letters of support from across the nation. Contributions of cash and checks ranging from less than $1 to $5,000 amounted to more than $100,000 within a week and $480,000 in total. After spending $355,000 on television and radio commercials in the following months to marshal public support for an amendment to end the war (which was subsequently defeated by the Senate 55–39), the Senate doves still had a surplus of $125,000 when Congress adjourned.

In most cases, however, fund raising simply has not kept pace with rising costs. A plethora of autonomous committees, inefficient overlap, multiple solicitations and tired techniques have characterized the financing efforts of the parties. In large part their financial structure and funding operations have been a reflection of their focus on campaign fund raising, with the need to solicit and distribute money to endorsed candidates.

A serious impediment to popularly financed parties and a major factor contributing to the negative public image of "political money" is the failure of either major political party to consider itself financially accountable to its membership, much less to the public. Each year millions of dollars pass through party treasuries in the form of cash, checks and loans. Yet despite the requirements of good business practice as well as state and federal law, less than a handful of people know how these funds were raised and spent or the status of various accounts and party programs. Such practices foster exactly the secrecy and hypocrisy which only reinforce the public's suspicions about political finance. The lack of party-enforced disclosure of political contributions leaves the parties wide open to charges of "dirty money" in politics, thus tainting legitimate contributions in the process.

More systematic fund raising and disclosure are only partial answers, however. Fund-raising success may actually reinforce the closed nature of the political parties. The Republicans, for example, have made significant progress in establishing a self-sustaining financial base on traditional appeals, with no reporting to or participation of sustaining members concerning expenditures of party funds. The parties have not even begun to develop participatory fund-raising programs that could attract a sizable number of new contributors.

The goals of party modernization can be presented to the American people in such a way as to attract impressive new financial support. In politics, as in any other sector of the real world, the citizen generally gets what he is willing to pay for. The citizen who wants more choices among better-qualified candidates for public office must pay the costs of recruiting them and getting them on the ballot. The citizen who wants to be better informed about candidates and party programs during campaigns and about their performance in office must support the costs of independent political news coverage and analysis. The citizen who wants open political parties with greater opportunities for citizen participation in party politics must finance party reforms to accomplish these ends. The citizen who wants political parties to develop a more active problem-solving orientation in government must subscribe the resources with which they can act. All these worthwhile goals require more political financing. Whether political funds are raised by voluntary contributions, tax credits or tax deductions or public subsidies, it is still the citizen who must ultimately pay the cost. The approach of campaign spending limitations and regulation, without adequate attention to the real costs of politics and who must pay them, offers only an illusory solution of cut-rate politics. But there are no bargain-basement routes to increased political participation and improved governmental performance. Financing quality politics will be expensive.

Our suggestions for party modernization require varying amounts of political investment. Where considerable resources are already spent to convene national committee meetings and national and state party conventions, situations in which party resources are put to incredibly poor use, significant improvements could be realized through better planning and leadership. Where little money has been previously invested, as in setting up functioning associations of state party officials and interstate project teams, a modest level of investment should yield impressive returns. Other innovations like more frequent extended national committee meetings, regional party offices, interim party conventions, matching grants to state parties, party news services and an independent political institute require significant increases in party budgets and/or private funding of specific projects. Overall, a major advance in American political parties will require extensive financial investment.

A New Approach to the Funding of Politics

If there is to be a substantial improvement in American politics in the decade ahead, either through strategies of party modernization or through alternative approaches such as new parties or citizen movements, Americans must be willing to invest substantially more than they now do in politics—in their time, attention, skills and financial support.

In contrast to the current wave of public sentiment for limiting campaign spending, we believe that the flow of money in politics must be increased. Political contributions need a new legitimacy. As Alexander Heard has pointed out, "The giving, receiving, and handling of political money is a unique and especially important form of political action."[14] Private contributions, financial and other, are one of the basic resources through which citizens can change politics.

Politics, the art and science of government, should be upgraded to give it a status in a democratic society fitting the responsibilities of modern government. It is ludicrous to maintain a nickel-and-dime politics where campaign expenditures are regulated by so many cents per vote in an era of hundred-billion-dollar government. Such a course limits or restricts the very means by which citizens can participate in and influence government. A society of big government, big business, big education, big labor, of big institutions generally, is a society that requires big politics and big spending on politics.

"Limitations on political party activities, particularly as they limit access to the costly mass media, which are not balanced by similar restraints on the large private interests in our society, can only further weaken the public interest component in the policy-making process," concludes political scientist and former Humphrey presidential-campaign staff member Vic Fingerhut.[15] To those who would replace private contributions with public financing, *New York Times* columnist Tom Wicker puts this question: "Won't total Federal financing of a Presidential candidate or for that matter any candidate tend to make him less, not more responsive to the public will and to the play of interests and political forces in society?"[16]

Instead of their current preoccupation with cutting dollar costs and eliminating "the corrupting influence of money in elections," American political leaders and reformers should be drafting and discussing long-term party development programs and growth budgets. Instead of handing out embossed menus at $500- and $1000-a-plate campaign fund-raising dinners, party treasurers and dinner committees could distribute pro-

---

[14] Heard, *The Costs of Democracy*, p. 1.
[15] Vic Fingerhut, "A Limit on Campaign Spending—Who Will Benefit?," *Public Interest*, Fall 1971, p. 12.
[16] Tom Wicker, "The Checkoff System," *New York Times*, November 21, 1971.

gram budgets for the upcoming campaign and postelection period. To date, no one has calculated what such a program might involve. But if major individual American universities have undertaken fund-raising programs of up to $100 million and citizen groups have proposed multibillion-dollar budgets for reclaiming America's urban centers, a *minimum* 10-year national party development budget of $1 billion would seem to be a reasonable objective. (For comparison, total campaign spending for the three presidential campaign years 1960, 1964 and 1968 was estimated at $675 million.) Such large sums of political money are necessary to make our complicated political system function. More money will be required as Americans expect and demand more from politics.

Once we have accepted the necessity and desirability of big spending in politics, two major problems remain—how best to raise such substantial sums and how best to oversee the use of money in politics. Both subjects deserve the full attention of party working conferences and discussion groups, not merely the limited attention of closed party finance committees. During the entire congressional debate on campaign finance limitations, neither party has developed a constructive policy statement presenting the party's positions and recommendations of increasing the flow of funds in politics within a system of public accountability.

A new approach to long-term party finance in addition to the tax credits and deductions enacted in 1971 by the Congress might include several of the following features:

- Intensified efforts to broaden the financial base of political participation especially in state parties through direct mail, newspaper advertisements, telephone and door-to-door canvasses to enroll dues-paying members.

- Greater ease of contribution for the citizen through bipartisan or multipartisan fund-raising drives or payroll checkoff systems at his place of work such as have been attempted successfully by some corporations in California.

- An open budget process within the parties that affords citizens information on how funds are allocated and expenditures are reviewed.

- Opportunities for citizens to express their choice on how political funds are to be expanded, through earmarking funds for specific uses or projects and testifying before party budget committees.
- Accountability of responsible party leaders for all funds under their supervision, including the bonding of key officials who handle political funds.
- A party-enforced system of full disclosure and reporting of political contributions for all party committees and candidates.
- An information-retrieval system maintained by a private nonpartisan agency or with government support, capable of storing, analyzing, and printing out the massive data on political contributions and expenditures for scrutiny by the public and the media.

Such a general approach of more systematic solicitation, citizen participation in funding decisions and full and accurate party reporting of all political funds can help to build public confidence in political finance at the same time that it increases the amount of funding available for urgently needed innovations and improvements in politics. The Federal Election Campaign Act of 1971 makes liberal provision for public disclosure, including the availability for public inspection and copying of all information filed under the act. However, it places an enormous burden of detailed reporting and record keeping on candidates and political committees and may well result in established committees like COPE, AMPAC, and NCEC setting up separate so-called "educational" and campaign committees, further complicating public understanding of political campaign financing. Its workability remains to be tested.

One vital step each citizen can take is to make a contribution, however small, in support of the party, principle, or candidate of his choice. Only if millions of Americans do so, and then demand accountability, will parties truly reflect their wishes and flourish as free institutions.

While a long-term solution to the problems of political finance requires a broadened and open base of party finance, private foundations, organizations and citizens contributing individually or in association can provide seed money and concentrated funding for some vital aspects of party modernization. Ford Foundation support of a two-phase project by the League of Women Voters and the National Municipal League "to encourage and insure greater citizen participation in the electoral process," initially funded at $613,000, suggests the possibilities for foundation initiative. Ford's $30-million five-year appropriation to support an independent police foundation for experimental improvements to law enforcement and its $1.2 million, three-year support of the Native American Rights Fund, a public interest law firm (which Ford helped establish) to defend the rights of American Indians are examples of the massive long-term funding that foundations could provide new institutions like a national political institute. Yet another example is Ford's $820,000 two-year grant to help found the Joint Center for Political Studies to assist black elected officials. It should be possible to develop a number of foundation-backed programs in support of party modernization and to advance citizen participation in politics within the provisions of the Tax Reform Act of 1969, which restricts the involvement of foundations in politics such as lobbying for legislation or conducting voter-registration drives except under limited circumstances. For example, a number of our proposals for improving the capabilities of the parties for government and media coverage of politics could be funded by foundations on a nonpartisan or multipartisan basis.

The role of major foundations in initiating institutional change in other sectors of American society through multimillion-dollar contributions of seed money has been critical. Comparable private investment in the political sector could greatly facilitate the modernization of American party institutions.

Making a Personal Investment in Politics

One of the warnings we have encountered from sages of American politics is not to take the political parties too seriously. Considering their current performance, there is some

merit to this judgment. Unlike the opposing armies of Clause-
witzian warfare, the American political parties are a noisy and
colorful rabble. They have plenty of (although often not
enough) people and money and candidates but operate without any discernible strategy. They wander aimlessly from
election to election, periodically experiencing disaster at the
polls, periodically inheriting a government that they treat like
an accidentally acquired kingdom. If the purpose of politics
were not so important, the ragamuffin parade and the whole
directionless game would strike the outside visitor as hilarious.
Many Americans have in fact already rendered that verdict.

Much more is at stake today, however, than the future of the
political parties. Their incapacity has a depressing effect on
the process of politics itself and restricts all those who take
politics seriously enough to engage in it. Admittedly there is
nothing sacred about political party institutions or even the
framework of the venerable two-party system. Parties are
merely instruments for realizing political ends, like pieces on
a chessboard to be used or bypassed as they suit specific
purposes. But they are also one of the few means free men
have developed historically to establish common purposes and
direction.

The message of this book is one of the unrealized *potential*
of the political parties for a new era of citizen politics. Politics
is and should be a major growth industry with expanding
financial and human resources. It is possible to play politics
and win, to accomplish serious purposes and experience fun
and satisfaction at the same time. Politics can have clout as
well as color.

We do not underestimate the massiveness of the work to be
undertaken in modernizing American political institutions. If
easy total solutions were available, they would have been tried
long ago. Individual parts of the task, however, are simple to
do. Plunkitt of Tammany Hall got his start in the business of
politics with the loyal following of one cousin. "I got a
marketable commodity—one vote. Then I went to the district
leader and told him I could command two votes on election
day, Tommy's and my own. He smiled on me and told me to

go ahead. If I had offered him a speech or a bookful of learn-in', he would have said, 'Oh, forget it!' "[17]

There are all kinds of action opportunities for enterprising citizens who want to invest in the parties. Few other personal investments today can yield comparable returns. A dedicated group of party activists can reshape a state party organization. A small group of citizens with appropriate legal advice can initiate court tests that can break through decades of party inertia and inaction. Ten Texans recently succeeded in winning court approval of their proposal for state legislative redistrict-ing, a decision that threw out the redistricting plan of the state's powerful legislature. With relatively minimal efforts it is pos-sible for citizens with a strategy to reach and influence any party or government official in the United States, even the President, with a message or proposal for action. It is often surprisingly easy to gain acceptance of good individual ideas within the parties and government.

Possibilities for action presented throughout this book are summarized and grouped in a concluding Action Guide. Strategies can link these and other initiatives together so that they have a lasting impact on party politics. People can be more readily activated and involved in politics if they see some direction and progress as a result of their efforts. Vague, directionless calls for citizen action only add to public cynicism and a sense of hopelessness about politics.

New, developed political institutions will provide far greater opportunities for involving the constructive talents of citizens in politics on a systematic basis. Even exceptionally talented men and women can waste their energies in politics if they do not find greater form and direction in political action.

The modernized parties suggested here assume a consider-able expansion of party machinery, commissions and working teams in each case to provide a specific function or service or to study and move an important problem closer to solution. If parties are to do more, they must be equipped with the

---

[17] *Plunkitt of Tammany Hall,* p. 9.

necessary institutional means. Just as reforms in the delegate selection process would not have moved within the Democratic party without the work of the national and state Democratic reform commissions, so too it is unrealistic to expect parties to develop strategies in other areas without some party body being charged specifically with the responsibility. Strategies and movement in politics do not just happen by themselves.

We have pointed the direction toward a new conception of political parties, but more importantly toward a renewed conception of politics. To the ancient Greeks of the *polis*, politics was the noblest form of human endeavor. Civic virtue was to be found in the practice of politics, not its disparagement. Today we urgently need to rediscover the possibilities of politics as a genuine living expression of the best of American society and its people and as a means for shaping our destiny. Part of that rediscovery will come through a new level of development in our party institutions. But ultimately the rediscovery of politics must be the personal experience of individual men and women who care enough to leave the sidelines and participate in the serious business of parties and government.

Action Guide

Having read this book you have seen that many political opportunities, big enough to be worthwhile and clear enough to be grasped, are within reach. Remember that a few dedicated reformers and activists, as in the case of the Hughes Commission at the 1968 Democratic National Convention, can have a tremendous impact in politics. You can influence government; you can elect candidates and party officials of your choice; you can promote issues of your choice. *Parties* offers a constructive range of alternatives that can be readily implemented.

The recommendations at the conclusion of individual chapters contain practical, operational ideas to make the political system work better for you. To save space and increase readability we found it necessary to condense what were initially hundreds of specific recommendations into these shorter groups of general recommendations. The Action Guide gives you suggestions for using those ideas effectively in politics.

Parties is written for many different people: citizen activists, party professionals, candidates, political consultants, media representatives, party fund raisers, researchers and speechwriters, etc. Different people will use the book for different purposes. In reading it, we hope you have begun to develop connections between its ideas and your own situation. We have included "Suggestions for Individual Users" below to illustrate the possible multiple use of various chapters. There is no corner on the market as far as good ideas are concerned. *Parties* will hopefully trigger many new ideas, variations and original applications.

Parties stresses the urgent need for developing new forms of part-time citizen participation in politics and government. You need not approach this book or politics in general on an either/or basis. You can make a valuable contribution to politics without being a full-time activist. You can help implement ideas through contributing time, giving money, lending your name. If you cannot do something yourself, you can go to someone who can and offer your support and recommendations. Watch for those ideas that can increase your own involvement and effectiveness and press for their adoption.

Each local situation is unique. Analyze the major political needs in your own community or organization. As you have read *Parties* we hope you made up your own list of needs and possible courses of action. Simply by doing this you may surface important opportunities and problems that have gone undiscussed or unrecognized.

Begin to think in terms of major themes or concepts, such as the ability to govern, the importance of fair procedures and accountability, the need for improved political information and analysis, etc. You will see that ideas fit together in a related set of reforms. Then apply these same concepts to your own situation.

Review the table of contents and note those chapters that were most directly relevant to you. Since this book offers a wide range of subject matter and specific recommendations, it might be helpful to select two or three areas which interest you most and promise to be the most personally rewarding or fun to do. Get a like-minded group of people together to discuss some of these ideas and to develop strategies to implement them in your locality. (See pp. 353–60 for the discussion of the importance of strategy.)

The success of an organization or cause ultimately depends on the core of activists who are willing to make a dedicated commitment to political action. Identify other activists in the parties and citizen groups and join with them or give them your support. Form your own action group if necessary. Look for new talent for political action in other civic activities in your community.

In order to increase your personal effectiveness and keep abreast of new political developments and opportunities, read as extensively as you can and discuss politics regularly with interested friends. Draw on the knowledge and experience of the older generation of political activists. Share subscriptions

and prepare your own mimeographed or offset political newsletter tailored to the needs of your community. Learn how to
communicate most effectively with busy people in politics.

Effective use of the law can help you get results in politics.
Invite a public interest lawyer, individual attorney or law
students to become affiliated with your group. Develop contacts with knowledgeable state legislators and city councilmen.

Develop a greater awareness of all types of media in your
locality, including newspapers, periodicals, radio and television. Bring your ideas and action plans to the attention of the
media. Never underestimate the power of ideas in politics.

Finally, one of the best rules in politics is to be candid about
what you want and persistent in going after it. Be flexible in
your tactics. You may be fortunate enough to succeed the first
time around—or it may take two, three or even more tries to
achieve success. In the final analysis, it is *you* who can make
the political system work.

Suggestions for Individual Users

Listed alphabetically below are groups of prospective users:
candidates, citizen activists, convention delegates, media representatives, etc. There is considerable overlap in these user
categories. You will probably find several of interest in your
particular situation. It should be stressed that the ideas listed
in each category apply in varying degrees to local, state *and*
national political campaigns and party organizations. Remember, the suggestions are only a sampler of the ideas and useful
information in *Parties*. They are meant to guide you to pertinent
analysis and recommendations and to indicate other relevant
approaches and material.

Candidates and Campaign Managers

- The ability to govern—a new theme for your campaign
  based on your qualifications for office and how you would
  staff and operate government (Chapter VI).

- How you can institute guidelines for open recruitment of
  candidates (pp. 148–49, 17–23).

- Weaknesses in the reporting of political news and the importance of news monitoring—key points to keep in mind in developing political intelligence on your opposition (pp. 251–62, 264–65, 277–78).
- How cable television will transform political campaigning at the local and state levels (pp. 266–73).
- Political consultants—new issues of accountability, screening and regulation by parties (pp. 306–11).
- How national and state parties can be effective service bureaus for your campaigns (Chapters III and V, especially pp. 110–19, 172–82).
- For more campaign-related ideas, see Fund Raisers, Personnel Recruiters, Press Secretaries, Research Chairmen and other categories in the Action Guide.

Citizen Activists and Citizen Groups
(see also Minority Groups, Party Activists, Political
Action Groups, Women, Youth in the Action Guide)

- How you can get started in local and state party organizations; importance of county party organization as point of access (pp. 170–72, 176–77).
- What you as a citizen can do to promote party reform; the goal of citizen parties (pp. 47–49, 7–12).
- The public interest movement and some successful techniques of political action (pp. 37–42).
- The importance of the individual convention delegate, and ways you can participate in preconvention and convention politics (pp. 60–61, 69–70, 82–91).
- How national committee meetings, party policy commissions and budget finances can be opened up to real citizen participation (pp. 112–14).
- Steps you can take to build party and leadership accountability by demanding reports, roll-call votes, open party meetings, etc. (pp. 85–86, 114–15).
- How citizens can be involved in government on a part-time basis through the parties to build citizen advisory com-

mittees and a citizen executive reserve (pp. 212–13).

- Why so many citizen organizations fail, and steps you can take to make your organization more effective in politics; the importance of strategy in politics (Chapter VII and pp. 353–60).

- How citizens can improve the quality of presidential and vice-presidential candidates (pp. 75–79).

- How citizen lobbies and activists can penetrate the congressional power structure and how the legislative parties can become new problem-solving vehicles (Chapter IV).

- Practical steps citizens can take to improve the way the media cover and report political news (pp. 277–78).

- The coming revolution in cable television, and what you can do *now* to advance and safeguard your interests and those of your community (pp. 266–73, 278–79).

- How citizens can counterbalance the new power of political technology and political consultants (pp. 308–13).

- Opportunities to reshape parties at the state and local level through the law (pp. 157–60, 167–70, 179).

Congressmen and Congressional Staff

- The chapter on congressional parties (Chapter IV) includes extensive recommendations for increasing the responsiveness and effectiveness of congressional parties, including caucus reforms, the modernization of the office of the Speaker and the wider use of congressional action groups.

- The contribution Congressmen can make to their party's ability to govern (pp. 148–51, 211–12).

- How Congressmen can support the party reform movement (pp. 45–46).

- The growing involvement and need for regulation of political consultants in congressional campaigns (pp. 137–38, 306–11).

- The potential for interstate party problem-solving teams— an idea that congressional action groups could develop (pp. 172–74).

- Cable television networks—a way to bring Congress, state, legislatures and city councils directly to the people (pp. 269–70).

Consultants

- The consultants chapter (Chapter IX) analyzes the development of consultant use by the Republican and Democratic parties and the new issues this poses; it includes among its recommendations steps political consultants can take to upgrade politics and their own profession (p. 313).

- *Parties* is virtually a catalog of entrepreneurial opportunities for political consultants looking for new ideas to develop for parties, candidates and citizen organizations: transition programs for parties assuming governmental office (p. 214); legislative action groups (pp. 151–52); multi-year development plans for state parties (p. 182); communications systems to link state delegations at national conventions with their home states (p. 89); potential applications of cable television (pp. 269–70); citizen clearing-houses or consortia (pp. 239–42); etc.

- What alternatives exist to traditional party coalitions?—a question that political consultants are often asked and that they ask themselves (Chapter X).

- Is "winning" enough?—how candidates and parties fail the test of the ability to govern (Chapter VI).

- How the party reform movement is changing the rules of politics (Chapter I).

Convention Delegates and Planners

- How party conventions can be modernized as new governing bodies of the parties, and how this will completely change the role of the convention delegate (Chapter II); the ideas of this chapter can be adapted to state and county party conventions, Young Democrat and Young Republican conventions, and a wide variety of citizen conventions.

- How reformers used the 1968 and 1972 national conventions to launch Democratic reform (pp. 14–16, Addendum), and the importance of representative party commissions acting under convention mandate (pp. 17–22, 80).

- Interstate party teams—a way that several state parties can share ideas, planning and experience in modernizing their conventions (pp. 172–74).

- The potential of two-way electronic communications in party conventions (p. 89).

- Limitations in media coverage, and what you can do to improve reporting and public understanding of conventions (pp. 251–62, 89–91, 47–49, 118–19).

Foundations

Ideas for party modernization that are potentially of interest include:

- The creation of a national institute of politics to monitor and analyze political developments and prepare training programs and courses (pp. 210–11, 359–60, Addendum).

- Bipartisan-issue study groups to enhance the parties' ability to govern (p. 213).

- Programs to improve political news reporting and increase the accessibility of usable political information for citizens (pp. 273–79).

- Research and development of communications and computer technology to further citizen participation in government and politics (pp. 312–13).

Fund Raisers

- A new approach to the funding of politics; party development budgets and reasons why citizens should increase political contributions (pp. 367–70).

- The ability to govern—a rationale for party fund raising before and after elections (Chapter VI).

- How to build responsible planning and party involvement

into party finances—the idea of an open budget committee (pp. 112–19).

* Party audits, reporting and appeals procedures as ways to increase the legitimacy of citizen financing of politics (pp. 114–15).

* Special projects for parties and/or citizen groups that can raise money: permanent party headquarters (p. 178); guest houses and meeting facilities on Capitol Hill (pp. 144–45); legislative action groups (pp. 151–52); interstate party problem-solving teams (pp. 172–74); etc.

* Matching grants from national and state parties to encourage local effort (p. 182).

*Governors, Mayors, State Legislators, and
State and Local Party Officials*
(see also Party Organization Leaders
and comparable national officeholders in the Action Guide)

* The chapter on state parties (Chapter V) includes numerous recommendations for developing state and local parties, including revision of state statutes, state parties as service bureaus for citizens, cooperative projects among governors and other elected officials, interstate problem-solving teams, and the use of developmental matching grants.

* Ways that state party delegations can gain new political skills and training at national party conventions and stay in touch with home-state constituencies (pp. 83–84, 89).

* The ability to govern as a new motivation for modernized state and county party organizations (pp. 178, 207–16).

* The importance of electing activist national and state committee members who can make national and state party organizations more responsive to state and local needs (pp. 110–12, 159–60).

* Opportunities to develop state and local parties through party regional offices (pp. 117–18) and party offices in each congressional district (p. 143).

* Cable television and its potential for upgrading media cov-

erage of state and local politics (pp. 259–60, 266–73).

- Political data banks as a vital new source of ideas and talent for state and local parties (pp. 240–41).

Lawyers, Party Counsel and Public Interest Advocates

- How the public interest movement can provide major new organizational and personnel resources for party reform (pp. 38–42).
- Developing the general counsel's office at the party national committee (p. 117).
- Establishing a public interest law unit at the national conventions (pp. 85–86).
- The importance of pooled citizen legal services for political action (p. 241).
- Law as a means for modernizing state parties and elections (pp. 179, 87).

Media Representatives and Commentators

- The chapter on the media and information in politics (Chapter VIII) analyzes the performance of the media in reporting politics and includes extensive recommendations for the media, parties and citizens to upgrade the coverage of political news.
- The need for new priorities in the presidential selection process and in media coverage of preconvention and convention politics (pp. 68–69, 75–79).
- Background on the party reform movement and its impact on the major party conventions (pp. 14–37).
- How the national party conventions could be modernized by 1976 (pp. 79–91), including televised state delegation reports from the convention city.
- Why the congressional party establishment has been able to insulate itself from press and public scrutiny and citizen political action (pp. 123–32).

- The new political consulting conglomerates—much more than image makers (pp. 289–91).

- Where are American parties heading?—six alternative futures (Chapter X).

- Why we need a major increase in citizen spending in politics (pp. 360–67).

Minority Groups
(see also Citizen Activists and Citizen Groups in the Action Guide)

Also of interest:

- New means to broaden minority-group participation in parties: representative party commissions (pp. 43–45); at-large members to national, state and local party committees (pp. 111, 116–17); permanent policy commissions (p. 112); citizen advisory committees in government (pp. 212–13); etc.

- Guidelines for the open recruitment of congressional (and other) candidates (pp. 148–49, 17–23).

- How to broaden the number and kinds of candidates considered for President, national and state offices, including open competition for the vice presidency (pp. 75–79).

Party Organization Leaders (*Party Chairmen, Committee Members and Professional Staff*)

In addition to the various chapters dealing with formal party bodies, also see the various specialized functions included in this user list. Of particular interest are the following ideas for strengthening party organizations:

- How party conventions can function as governing bodies for the parties with the use of mandated party commissions and interim conventions (pp. 80–82).

- Open national committees with active national committee memberships as a model for central committees at all levels of the party (pp. 110–19).

- How a party office in the White House and party division on the civil service can contribute to the party's ability to govern (pp. 215–16).

- How strong national parties can help staff a new national administration and help it govern more effectively (pp. 209–15).

- Developing the office of the Speaker to serve as a major party leadership position (p. 146).

- The importance of majority and minority party staff and a vigorous congressional opposition to the party's ability to govern (pp. 149–51).

- The need for 24-hour operations centers at national party headquarters and under the congressional parties (pp. 118, 146–48).

- Why national committees should recruit and elect full-time national party chairmen, convention directors, and other top professionals (pp. 100–101, 115–16, 84).

- How state parties and party programs can be developed through matching grants (pp. 181–82).

- The developing relationship between political consultants and party professionals, and what it means for the parties (pp. 284–300, 306–11).

Party Activists, Party Reformers and Party Reform Groups
(see also Citizen Activists and Citizen Groups in
the Action Guide)

- See especially Chapter I on the different progress of and opportunities for party reform in the two major parties. Note especially the need to renew and extend party reform mandates and the importance of well-developed strategies at the 1972 party conventions (pp. 28–29, 37, 46–47). Note the many places where representative party commissions like the McGovern-Fraser and O'Hara Democratic reform commissions can be applied to specific opportunities and problems facing the parties: national convention modernization (pp. 79–80); national committee modernization (p.

111); an inquiry on state parties (pp. 181–82); a study of new means of citizen participation in the parties (pp. 243–44); the development of party policy on cable television (p. 279); a review of party relations with political consultants (pp. 309–10).

- Relate party reforms to the needs of different users in this guide. You can build a much broader constituency for party modernization than you ever imagined.

Personnel Recruiters (Education and Training)

- How parties can define a new positive function for patronage—recruiting talent for government (pp. 209–12).

- Some model talent hunt operations: a citizen's commission on presidential selection (pp. 77–78); recruiting a national chairman and key party professional staff (pp. 115–16); recruiting qualified candidates for *all* congressional and state legislative seats (pp. 148–49).

- New sources of talented men and women for campaigns, party operations and government: the party reform movement (pp. 23–24); public interest law firms (pp. 40–42); the new breed of convention delegate (pp. 60–61, 236–37); party commissions and advisory committees (pp. 112, 212–13); political talent banks for state parties and citizens (pp. 240–41); a national conference of citizen organizations (pp. 242–43).

- Unused opportunities and resources at party conventions to train party workers and citizens (pp. 88–89).

- How a national institute of politics could help fill the urgent party and governmental need for advanced training in politics (pp. 210–11).

Political Action Groups (Business and Professional Groups, Labor, Teacher, Homeowner Associations, etc.)
(see also Citizen Activists and Citizen Groups in the Action Guide)

- A new way to rate candidates and parties—tests of the ability to govern (pp. 208–209).

- Running your own delegates for party conventions and platform committees—new rules open the parties (pp. 18–19, 31–32).

- Opportunities for developing new campaign and polling techniques with the help of political consultants (pp. 286, 295–98, 301–302).

- Getting the best results in Congress and state legislatures —the unused potential of legislative parties (pp. 139–52).

Press Secretaries, Public Relations Men and Speechwriters

- How limitations in the media's coverage of politics (Chapter VIII, especially pp. 251–62) give you the opportunity and the responsibility to make political news come alive (pp. 118–19).

- The political public relations potential of the party reform issue (pp. 26–27, 47–49).

- Making party publications more useful and responsive to party members (pp. 97, 118, 182, 262–63, 275, 89–90).

- How party operations centers and press rooms in Congress could improve party news coverage (pp. 146–47).

- How to upgrade parties and politics in the public image: an open information policy for the parties (pp. 85, 114); full financial reporting (p. 115); party ethics committees (p. 115); party screening of candidates and appointees (pp. 208–209).

Research Chairmen (Campaign Research Directors, Party Policy Commissions, Platform Chairmen and Citizen Cause Groups)

- Permanent party policy commissions—an essential ingredient to the ability to govern (pp. 112–13, 212–13).

- How candidate testimony and cross-examination can be built into party conventions (pp. 75–76).

- Ways to involve citizen research groups and talented citizens in party research units (pp. 243–44).

- New instruments for party research: congressional and state legislative action groups (pp. 151–52); interstate party teams (pp. 172–74); representative party commissions with regional party hearings (pp. 43–45); computerized information retrieval (pp. 273–74, 309–10).
- The importance of debriefings, oral history and archives (pp. 115, 216, 242).

State and Local Party Officials
(see Governors, etc., and Party Organization
Leaders in the Action Guide)

Women
(see also Citizen Activists and Citizen Groups,
Political Action Groups in the Action Guide)

- The potential for women as a majority group to reshape the traditional political parties in the 1970's (pp. 108–10).
- How women can open up the presidential and vice-presidential selection process (pp. 75–79).
- Party reform guidelines for equitable representation of women (pp. 18, 31–32) applicable to all party offices, commissions, programs, etc., suggested.

Youth
(see also Citizen Activists and Citizen Groups,
Political Action Groups, Minority Groups in the Action Guide)

- Youth attitudes toward the parties and politics, and how this can transform the two-party system (pp. 335–39).
- The problems of ad hoc new politics organization and suggestions for more effective citizen politics (pp. 229–35, 239–43).
- Public interest research groups as a model for youth participation in the parties (pp. 39–40).

Outlook: Parties in Practice

The experience of the 1972 national party conventions and elections has emphasized both the current deficiencies of American party politics and the prognosis that the parties can be modernized to serve the needs of a new generation of citizen politicians. The American body politic, while evidencing impressive signs of new vitality in its party institutions, shows, however, no progress in other indicators of political health. Our assessment of the potential for citizen parties remains optimistic, but we are concerned that the political system continues to suffer from some basic debilities.

The most spectacular advances in 1972 occurred in party reforms dealing with the organizational structure and internal procedures of the Democratic party. Some critics of party reform have argued that the reform commissions on delegate selection and national party structure headed by Messrs. McGovern, Fraser and O'Hara allowed an elitist minority to capture the Democratic party, with disastrous consequences.

There is an element of truth in this interpretation. The Miami Beach Democratic National Convention, while it was the most representative of party conventions by its composition of women (39.7 percent), racial minorities (15.2 percent black, 5 percent Latino, 1 percent Indian), and young people under 30 years of age (21.4 percent), was also a predominantly middle-class, affluent, college-educated convention which underrepresented other elements of the traditional Democratic coalition. Senator McGovern's aides, with the support of a dedicated grassroots movement in much the same manner as the Goldwater citizen politicians before them, mastered the art of nominating politics but were incapable both of uniting the Democratic party for an effective national campaign and of running a presidential campaign.

With the exception of the Presidency, however, the Democratic party in 1972 won a landslide victory at all levels. The commission authorized by the 1972 Democratic convention to review and evaluate the McGovern-Fraser guidelines for delegate selection, and chaired by Barbara Mikulski of Maryland, will almost certainly find that Democratic candidates for congressional, state and local offices benefited directly from the surge of new people into the opened Democratic party caucuses, conventions and delegate slates. Similarly, the party won a massive victory in registration (61,793,000 Democrats; 35,624,000 Republicans; and 5,000,000 "others"), in part through the millions of Americans who came into the Democratic party to participate in the selection of its presidential nominee.

Unlike the Goldwater movement, Democratic party reformers between 1968 and 1972 restructured their party as well as nominated a candidate of their choice, assuring in the process at least "four more years" of Democratic party reform. Already accomplished are the McGovern-Fraser guidelines broadening representation in the party and the enlarging and restructuring of the Democratic National Committee for the first time in over 10 years.[1] The reformed Democratic convention of 1972 also mandated a party charter commission (headed by former Governor Terry Sanford of North Carolina) charged with considering and recommending a permanent charter for "the Democratic Party of the United States" and planning for a national party conference in 1974 on "Democratic Party organization and policy." In addition, the convention required a new system of proportional representation in delegate selection for 1976, changes in state laws to eliminate winner-take-all primaries and crossover voting, a national party fund to defray expenses of delegates attending

---

[1] The Democratic committee, as approved by resolution of the 1972 convention, consists of the following: 1) the chairman and the highest ranking officer of the opposite sex of each recognized state Democratic party sharing one vote, 2) additional members with a total vote of 150 apportioned to each state on essentially a population basis, 3) the chairman and two others designated by the Democratic Governors Conference, 4) the Senate and House Democratic leaders and one more from each body designated by the respective caucuses, and 5) additional members not to exceed 25 added by the foregoing to provide balanced representation of all Democratic voters. An executive committee of not more than 25 members shall be elected which reflects the composition of the national committee.

conventions and convention committee meetings, and serious consideration of a university campus site for the 1976 Democratic convention.

Democratic party reformers face an ambitious schedule and some serious problems in the years immediately ahead, but the Democratic party after 1972 is far healthier and has invested more soundly in its long-term future than most post-election analyses have suggested. The coalition of elements that nominated McGovern must still come to terms with organized labor and the forces of Alabama Governor George Wallace, both of which are capable of waging a long-term struggle for control of the national Democratic party. The discovery of the preliminary strategy sessions of the labor-staffed and -funded ABM (Anybody But McGovern) coalition of Humphrey, Muskie, Jackson and Wallace forces in Miami Beach was an early indicator of what was ahead. The post-election formation of the Coalition for a Democratic Majority, involving many alumni members of ABM and the use of a Wallace Washington office, are additional signs that the losers at the 1972 convention do not intend knowingly to repeat the same mistakes.

Democratic party reform has gone too far in any event to be undone. Senator Walter F. Mondale (D-Minn.), while concerned that rules changes gave an impression in some states that working people, labor leaders, farmers and regular Democrats were not wanted or needed, believes that "in the long run those particular rules are fundamental, important, and I hope no one tampers with them." The 1972 convention has already broadened the McGovern-Fraser guidelines for the projected 1974 national party conference "to assure fair representation . . . of all Democratic voters on the basis of sex, age, race, and *social and economic status*" (emphasis added). Former Democratic vice presidential nominee Senator Thomas F. Eagleton concludes that "rather than changing the procedures, labor and other groups are going to have to work harder within the confines of those rules to see that they are more fully represented at the next Democratic National Convention." The failure of Humphrey, and Wallace in particular, to translate their 1972 popular vote in the primaries into comparable delegate strength by joining and working in the reform process earlier effectively gave the nomination to George McGovern.

The process of drafting a national charter will force some important and difficult issues into the open well before 1976. Just as the innovative platform drafting procedures used by the Democrats in 1972 introduced a new candor and openness in terms of issue politics with an over-all favorable public response to the way the Democrats handled their open convention,[2] so too does the hammering out in public of a representative national party structure stand to strengthen the Democratic party in the long run. It has been suggested that the reform movement has created two Democratic parties, which must now come to terms with one another. To the traditional Democratic party—a loose federation of state and local parties that coalesced and disbanded once every four years to nominate a President—the reforms have added, through an open delegate selection process, a new presidential nominating party not formally connected to the organizational base of the party but with a life extending well beyond the immediate task of nominating and electing a President. Further complicating the drafting of a party charter is the role of organized labor in the Democratic party. While labor is in a period of political and personnel transition marked by greater independence from the Democratic coalition as well as more independent action by individual international and local unions, both party and trade union leaders will have to give much more explicit recognition to the position of organized labor in the Democratic coalition.

The Democratic reform movement may lose some of its momentum now that the powerful impetus of the 1968 Chicago convention has been largely spent. Democratic reformers did not fully succeed in institutionalizing party reform even in 1972. Among the first casualties in the cuts of Democratic National Committee staff ordered by Chairman Jean Westwood after Miami Beach were, ironically, the two remaining top staff members of the McGovern-Fraser commission, Robert

---

[2] Pollster Louis Harris found that "by 52 to 25 percent a majority of Americans had a highly positive reaction" to the convention.

Nelson and Carol Casey: the campaign critically needed their knowledge of the national party. But most party leaders now appear committed to party reform, and even more importantly the reforms themselves have enabled experienced reform-oriented citizen politicians to replace many former opponents.

Republican party reform, in spite of the low profile and limited work of the Delegates and Organizations Committee and no visible support or substantive input from the White House, made some surprising gains at the Republican Miami Beach convention. The tradition of closed executive sessions of both Republican reform and Republican convention committees was broken by the initiative of Rhode Island House minority leader Frederick Lippitt, who successfully challenged the closed-door policy of Rules chairman former Florida Congressman William Cramer. As a result, some 10 days of crucial Republican rules debate were open to the public and press, assuring a much fairer hearing for Republican reformers.

Republicans voted for a continuing reform commission and opened its membership to a broad cross-section of the party. The complicated rules of the House of Representatives that govern Republican national conventions are scheduled to be replaced by 1976 with the more widely understood Roberts Rules of Order. The party also approved a rules change requiring the Republican National Committee and the Republican State Committee of each state to "take positive action to achieve the broadest possible participation by everyone in party affairs, including such participation by women, young people, minority and heritage groups and senior citizens in the delegate selection process."

Rank-and-file Republicans accordingly now have significant new opportunities to press local and state party leaders for participatory reforms and to become delegates and alternates themselves. Responsible conservative leaders such as Congressman John M. Ashbrook of Ohio have long argued for the elimination of favorite son candidacies and "instructed" state delegations that vitiate grassroots participation in the presidential selection process. An open competition of ideas, for example, to encourage the modernization of the 1976 Republican National Convention and for a new selection procedure for the Vice President could be a constructive part of Republican nominating politics cutting across old ideological lines.

But old ways are hard to change. The selection in 1972 of the new chairman of the Republican National Committee, George Bush, came as an announcement by the outgoing chairman, Robert Dole. Granting his qualifications, the opportunity for members of the Republican National Committee to consider, interview and then choose anyone else was apparently not to be theirs. In contrast, the contenders for the chairmanship of the Democratic National Committee caucused widely for weeks preceding the election on December 9, in which Robert Strauss emerged as victor among several candidates.

Another impressive advance toward reform was the Democratic National Convention of 1972 itself, which went a fair distance toward the goals of convention modernization recommended in this book. The national party convention as a representative and authoritative decision-making body for American parties came of age in 1972 as the Democrats, in committee and full convention, handled with remarkable fairness and lack of rancor an unprecedented volume of platform amendments and minority reports, credentials challenges and rules changes. Concluded roughly two weeks before the full convention in Miami Beach, the innovative two-part convention, with committee sessions in Washington, D.C., was an effective "working convention." Yet the Democrats have only begun to realize the potential afforded by the national convention. Little effort was made to relate and communicate convention deliberations to party rank and file in the states. The inept scheduling of day, evening and all-night sessions cost the Democratic party more than a prime-time audience of the McGovern acceptance speech; it effectively shut out millions of Americans who had worked to make a reformed open national convention a reality. The parties may have to solve this communications problem in 1976 without the extensive television coverage they have taken for granted. The end of gavel-to-gavel coverage by the major commercial networks at future conventions has become a likely development. The roles of the policy-making Corporation for Public Broadcasting and the technical Public Broadcasting Service are still to be defined.

The Democratic convention of 1972 failed to meet the potential of a modernized convention in its most important function: the nomination of the presidential–vice presidential ticket. The case for the open convention selection of the Vice President was made persuasively by the Eagleton affair. A major party crisis and personal tragedy were needlessly precipitated by the "hasty, haphazard selection of a candidate whose background received less scrutiny than that of a lowly government clerk."[3] Instead of setting a new politics precedent by suggesting a new format for convention nomination of the Vice President, the McGovern staff at incalculable cost to their national campaign was forced just a few weeks later to establish an even more difficult precedent of admitting a major error in staff work and judgment and removing a convention-endorsed nominee from a national party ticket. A Democratic commission on the selection of the Vice President chaired by Senator Hubert Humphrey was subsequently established to report with recommendations to the Democratic National Committee by January 1974.

The results of these reform commissions are both full of possibilities and fraught with troubles. As they proceed, it will prove useful to monitor their work closely in order to ascertain the direction in which it is carrying the parties and what effects it might eventually have on political figures and causes on all levels, citizen groups, labor, business, women, blacks, etc.

One of the more important advances of 1972, largely obscured by the uninspiring presidential campaign, was the infusion of new bipartisan talent into the House of Representatives. Some 70 new members, almost one-sixth the membership of the House—the great majority replacing retiring senior members or members seeking higher office—took office in January 1973. The influx might have been even greater but for the fact that Republicans still left 37 House districts uncontested (11

---

[3] Frederick H. Sontag and Lark Wallwork, "McGovern Should Involve Committee in Selection," *Los Angeles Times* News Service, August 4, 1972, Part II, p. 7.

in Texas alone, where Senator John Tower insisted on the concentration of party resources for his own re-election campaign). Democrats failed to contest only eight districts.

The House, an increasingly strategic point of entry for young men and women into national politics, could become a major new front for party modernization well before the party conventions of 1974 and 1976. With the steady change in House membership since the Democratic congressional landslide of 1958, the opening up of the insulated congressional parties to new citizen involvement—from open party caucuses to congressional action groups—is now a real possibility.

Another sign of new vitality in American politics was the success of the National Women's Political Caucus in its first venture into convention politics. The caucus form of organization, working inside both major parties, proved to be about the most effective form of citizen political action in 1972. Women organized themselves into political caucuses and won a record 39.7 percent of the delegate seats at the Democratic convention and 34 percent at the Republican convention. Women's issues such as day care and abortion were discussed at length and voted on for the first time at the platform committee meetings. After the conventions, however, neither presidential candidate appealed directly to women. Women, who felt ignored by the vestiges of old party politics in 1972, can be expected to continue working for a new politics concerned with human priorities, with issues such as pollution, equality, abortion and the quality of life in general.

New *opportunities* for party modernization, as yet largely untapped, were opened up by political developments during the election year. The passage by Congress in modified form of President Nixon's multi-billion-dollar revenue sharing plan, a policy initiative that will almost certainly be expanded by a second Nixon administration, has significantly increased discretionary funds available to state and local government and, accordingly, the stakes of state and local politics. The McGovern defeat and the ending of the war in southeast Asia may have the coincident effect of making new political resources available to the reform of state politics.

Growing voter selectivity among candidates and issues and

the higher levels of voter understanding of and interest in politics that this implies have opened other significant opportunities for modernized party organization. The commonly held interpretation that "ticket-splitting" is an anti-party phenomenon that will steadily weaken the political parties does disservice to both the aspirations of the American voters and the capabilities of public-spirited party organizations. The message Americans gave to the parties in 1972 was: "Give us better candidates and a better statement of the issues." The decline in party identification among the general electorate marks only the passing of older traditional forms of party organization and loyalty. The sophisticated American voter is defining higher standards of performance for Presidents, Senators, Congressmen, Governors and state officers, and Mayors and elected municipal officials in a new multitrack approach to elections. Greater citizen competence in politics requires increased party responsiveness and effectiveness if this healthy development is to be encouraged. When the voter's choice for any office is reduced to "the lesser of two evils," one obvious need is party reform in candidate selection, training and campaign support.

The remarkable scale of the 1972 Nixon victory both geographically and across a range of population groups suggests that the President and his associates better understood the changing expectations of the American electorate than did their Democratic opposition. They addressed their masterfully executed presidential campaign strategy to the political concerns of a "new American majority" that transcended one political party. But the Nixon landslide was also a continuation of a massive citizen protest against the national Democratic party and its failure to develop new programs with a clear sense of direction and convincing promise of performance if returned to office. In 1972, voters weighed platforms, issues and party performance rather than the personalities of the candidates.[4]

---

[4] For analysis of the Democratic and Republican platforms see Frederick H. Sontag and Lark Wallwork, "The Parties," in League of Women Voters of the United States, *Pick a President* (Washington, D.C., 1972),

The outcomes of the 1972 elections do not substantially change our estimates of alternative futures for the American party system. The Democratic coalition, midway through an historic process of self-reform, has added new voting groups while as yet not permanently alienating organized labor or splitting the Democratic party organization as such. The stunning Nixon sweep in turn has yet to produce a Republican majority at any other level of government. The new wave of young voters made some important advances *within* the two-party system but not at as rapid a rate as some anticipated. There was relatively little innovation in political institutions or new coalitions to replace existing party alignments either by citizens or consultants. Extremes of the political left or right received relatively little attention or popular support. Progress toward significant party modernization and increased citizen participation, while impressive, still fell far short of the potential.

Major new developments to be watched are the accelerated pace of change in organized labor and its relations to the major parties and the enlarged options of Governor Wallace. Neither the parties nor the media have given adequate attention to the changing political face of labor, the future of COPE, the separate political activities of individual unions, and the new generation of union leaders who will replace the current leadership of the AFL-CIO. The late 1972 surprise announcement by Wallace national campaign director Charles S. Snider that the Alabama governor might run as a Republican in 1976 opens some intriguing new possibilities. If the Wallace–American Independent Party constituency numbering at least one in every 10 voters were mobilized on a neo-populist legitimate non-racist appeal, Wallace supporters might have an even greater impact on the numerically weak Republican party organizations of the southern, border and some northern industrial and western states than they could

---

pp. 5–9; and Sontag and Wallwork, "The National Political Parties: Where They Stand on the Major Issues—A Concise Comparison," *Greenville 1972 Election Guide* (Greenville, S.C., Chamber of Commerce: October 23, 1972), pp. 26–27.

have within the reformed Democratic party. Such a change in major party coalitions would require, among other things, a sufficient level of economic prosperity under the new Nixon administration to make the Republican party an attractive political target and a remarkable new feat of organizational leadership by Wallace himself. The very possibility, however, underlines in yet another way the potential for citizen action through the political parties.

These optimistic estimates on the prospects for party modernization must be tempered by the admission that some basic political weaknesses identified in this book remain unchanged.

Perhaps most disturbing has been the failure of party activists and professionals within the party to initiate action in behalf of stronger, more effective party organizations. The elected national committees sat out most of the year as though there were no conventions or elections, when only a handful of concerned national committee members could have demanded special meetings and an active role in convention and campaign planning. When President Nixon and the Republican hierarchy decided unofficially to support incumbent Democratic Senator James O. Eastland of Mississippi *and* deliberately to undercut the campaign of Republican candidate Gilbert Carmichael (who ultimately managed to win 40 percent of the vote), there was no national committee protest. Thirteen Republican Senators, representing almost the full ideological spectrum of the party, had the courage to endorse Carmichael against the wishes of the White House. However, no similar group of Congressmen, Governors, Republican National Committee members or other influential Republicans spoke up or took specific actions. This example illustrates the more general problem, as other cases did not surface and were not discussed or acted upon.

In neither the Democratic nor the Republican party in 1972 was there an identifiable body of men and women willing to speak out on principle for what was good for their party in the face of egregious violations of the parties' (and the nation's) long-term political health. The Committee to Re-elect the President took over the fund-raising mechanism of the Republican

National Committee and diverted funds from other party campaign organizations to the presidential campaign. Republican Senators, Congressmen and Governors failed to develop their own cooperative candidate- and issue-research support capabilities long after it was evident that the President had decided *not* to campaign for a Republican Congress or Republican state tickets. Individual complaints after the election were no substitute for coordinated party activity when it could have done some good.

The value and effectiveness of such ad hoc committees as the Committee to Re-elect the President will be judged finally by how they either supplement or detract from the work of the parties' national, congressional and gubernatorial campaign committees.

McGovern forces under National Chairman Jean Westwood dismissed two-thirds of the professional staff of the Democratic National Committee as a supposed presidential campaign economy move. Democratic loyalists who had worked since August 1968—when Hubert Humphrey found the national committee cupboard bare—to build a first-rate party headquarters capability that could be transferred to the nominee in 1972 witnessed the disemboweling of the DNC. Both the Re-elect and the McGovern committees were disbanded without so much as a report from their staffs to the respective party national committees. Republican party professionals remained silent at reports of the Re-elect committee's involvement in the Watergate break-in and "political sabotage" operations, situations that in the course of time could seriously undermine the administration's ability to govern. If party professionals and candidates exercise so little intelligent self-interest in using party organizations, it is little wonder that so many people refuse to take the parties seriously.

The citizen sector, with the notable exception of the National Women's Political Caucus, showed little improvement in organizational effectiveness in 1972. John Gardner's well financed and much publicized third-force citizen's lobby, Common Cause, devoted most of its energies to trying to police the cumbersome new Federal Election Campaign Act with little discernible positive public benefit to the level of election-year politics. In spite of losses in membership and an announced shift to grassroots activity in order to provide greater member involvement, Common Cause's national staff remain firmly opposed to the chartering or encouraging of local groups with "independent political agendas." Effective control of the organization's "national response mechanism" is still in the hands of the Washington headquarters and its professional staff. The impact of Ralph Nader's report on Congress and profiles of incumbent Congressmen released just prior to the election has yet to be effectively measured. Nader's student Public Interest Research Groups were extended to some 50 campuses with total budgets of more than $1 million during 1972.

The New Democrat, an important and interesting effort in party-oriented journalism, was allowed to die by reform Democrats after the Democratic convention. The Ripon Society slowly ventured into the Republican Rules Committee fight on convention apportionment for 1976 to suffer a not too surprising reverse at the hands of a quietly but effectively organized conservative whip operation directed by Mississippi Republican chairman Clarke T. Reed; Ripon sought a Federal court injunction against the new delegate apportionment formula immediately after the election. Once again the conservative citizen organizations functioned most smoothly. The American Conservative Union, for example, ran a clearinghouse for conservative lawyers, businessmen, graduate students and administrators interested in working for newly elected members of Congress and circulated more than 500 job resumes. A conservative publication gave an inside preview of Republican congressional leadership fights in far more detail than the regular press.

One of the most disappointing aspects of the election year was the media's coverage of party politics.[5] With the Republican convention and the presidential election outcome mostly

---

[5] See "The Report on Network News Treatment of the 1972 Democratic Presidential Candidates," available from *The Alternative*, RR #11, Box 360, Bloomington, Indiana, a study prepared by Professor Paul Weaver of Harvard University.

a foregone conclusion and with an economic recovery well under way, the broadcast and print media had abundant mobile resources to do imaginative in-depth reporting, surveys and background analyses. Indeed, the three major television networks signed off their $10 million combined cost coverage of national and state returns at 2 a.m. election night.

With a few exceptions the print media did little to advance public information and understanding of party politics. A citizen-sponsored workshop conference and task force for the media on new approaches to election-year coverage could be a valuable undertaking both for the public major news bureaus and for individual reporters. Media managements clearly need the continuing services of public affairs consultants for research and program development as much as do the parties, candidates and issues they will be reporting on in the years to come. There was little coverage in depth of the successful Nixon field operations either in the primaries or general elections in spite of the importance of the 1972 campaign staff to the politics of 1976 and the Nixon succession. No comprehensive state-by-state lists of campaign personnel for either party were published.

Many interesting political situations were left virtually untouched: the intimate tensions between the Republican national and state committees and the Committee to Re-elect the President, the national deployment of political consultants by the two parties, coordinated coverage of the Nixon "surrogate candidates," the conservative whip operation in the Republican rules fight prior to and at Miami Beach, the Wallace and American Independent Party field operations, the reactions of Democratic intellectuals to the development of campaign issues by the McGovern braintrust and campaign staff, the whereabouts of Humphrey and Muskie staff during the fall campaign, the relations between the McGovern campaign and black political organizations like the black caucuses, the "absence" of key Democrats and their allies, the timely analysis of the multi-million-dollar presidential campaign budgets, etc. Particularly missing were staff biographies and interviews of anyone besides the principals and top campaign managers.

Finally, the new campaign spending limitation and disclosure law had a number of negative and depressing effects on the political process that deserve the attention of party reformers and the Congress. The law proved so complex that a Common Cause board member and a reform lawyer on the Democratic National Committee who were handling finances at the state level reportedly made errors and omissions in their finance reports and were investigated by a Federal attorney. Well-meaning candidates who accidentally overlooked provisions of the law were "exposed" via unchecked press releases by at times overzealous monitoring units set up in the states by Common Cause. One party group which has consistently invited the participation of members and interested persons through its publications, the College Republican National Committee, revealed that no Nixon campaign materials were available through its national headquarters due to campaign spending limitations required by the law. Besides imposing real additional physical, financial and mental costs on political participation, campaign-spending-limitation legislation has been designed with the long-term goals of forcibly reducing or eliminating private individual and organizational contributions and instituting Federal, state and local funding of political campaigns to be paid by the taxpayers on a compulsory basis. Some observers have argued that the use of taxpayer-provided funds must be mandatory if elections are truly to be financed by the public, and Common Cause has begun organizing a citizen lobbying effort for Federal tax funding of general elections to national office. The League of Women Voters, the National Committee for an Effective Congress, the Committee for the Democratic Process and some citizen groups may be expected to lobby for similar, taxpayer-financed expenditures on the national, state and local levels.

The parties themselves have continued to feel this essentially negative impulse by the way they have handled their own finances. The Democrats claimed to have reduced their $9.3 million debt to under $5 million at the end of 1972 by settling outstanding debts with non-regulated industries with 25 cents on the dollar. (Regulated industries such as telephone companies and airlines were able to hold out for full settlement.) The financial transfers reportedly linking the Committee to Re-elect the President with the Watergate affair seriously undercut Republican party credibility. Neither party articulated any case in favor of increased financing for party politics.[6]

The approach of restrictive and compulsory politics extends far beyond limiting campaign spending. Under the rationale of supposedly streamlining American politics and perhaps reducing costs, reformers would eliminate or severely reduce the opportunities for participation afforded by the existing system of state presidential primaries and conventions and national party conventions in favor of a single national primary, cut the formal presidential campaign itself from 10 weeks to approximately one month to bring the United States more in line with short parliamentary elections in Great Britain, Canada and other foreign countries, and in the extreme impose compulsory voting (under penalty of fine) in general elections. Little attention has been given to likely consequences of such restrictive changes: the strengthening of already well-entrenched incumbents, the splintering of parties in government by direct subsidies to candidates, the even greater difficulty in defining and discussing issues and testing candidates, and above all the undermining of voluntary direct and vital participatory politics.

We have advanced the case for *increased* political contributions by citizens to support party modernization. The urgent, primary need is to invigorate and broaden the base for a quality politics that measures up to new citizen capabilities instead of playing down to increasingly outdated and negative prejudices against politics. The art of raising—not limiting or subsidizing—money and other resources has always been an integral part of politics and it should be an active part of the new citizen politics. One sign of the vitality of the McGovern movement was its ability to raise a record $14 million in small contributions for the presidential campaign—about triple the

---

[6] See John S. Saloma III and Frederick H. Sontag, "More Money to the Politicians," *The New York Times* (Op-Ed page), September 3, 1972, p. 13.

previous record of grassroots gifts (albeit in inflated dollars) set by the Goldwater campaign in 1964.

None of these deficiencies in American politics is fundamental or irremediable. There are hundreds and probably thousands of party leaders in the states who could stimulate the party national committees, and with proper training the number could be multiplied rapidly. A growing and talented citizen army, ignored and underestimated by the parties, most existing citizen organizations, and the media, is looking for effective political means to express its views in local, state and national politics. The level of political information available to both individual voters and the public and retrievable for use in politics can be significantly increased by more effective use of existing media resources. And Americans, with a healthy civic motivation, are easily capable of financing quality politics and extensive party modernization.

What then is missing? One answer suggested by several commentators is political leadership to challenge the best that is in Americans. Admittedly, President Nixon, if he were to make party modernization part of his new American Revolution for 1976, could encourage extensive political change. But the President, preoccupied with the heavy, time-consuming affairs of state, has shown little inclination to strengthen the party to which he belongs and on whose ticket he ran. Nor has the leadership of younger generations of Americans yet emerged in either party in significant numbers. The parties have done little to advance new leadership, such as task forces to recruit candidates, citizen talent banks and executive reserves, and training to develop critical leadership skills.

Citizens by themselves can do a great deal in their local communities and in selected areas of state and national politics, but unaided they do not seem capable of undertaking on any discernible timetable the range of reforms projected in this book. We must reluctantly and candidly conclude that amateurs and even party professionals probably need a good deal more formal training and encouragement than they can now readily obtain in order to have a significant impact on the governmental and political systems.

One of our major recommendations is directed to this very problem, the establishment of an independent Institute of Politics (or a number of such institutes). An Institute of Politics chartered to assist citizens and party leaders in modernizing American political institutions and properly funded toward this end could serve major needs, three among many which are not now being met adequately by any existing institution.

First, an Institute of Politics could develop educational curricula in practical politics to train and accredit citizens for specific political responsibilities in the parties and government. It could offer courses and workshops at regional, state and local community centers accessible to interested citizens. In addition to its own educational and training programs it could develop materials for, encourage and publicize political-education programs in parties, citizen, business, professional and labor organizations, and in the educational system.

Second, an institute could generate citizen and party initiative in party modernization through conferences, research monographs, experimental and demonstration projects, consultant services, development grants, fellowships for innovative politics, special action programs, and a continuous stream of short and timely action publications. It could play a vital catalytic or facilitating role in the political process as a broker bringing together talented people, new ideas, political reserves, and specific opportunities—for example, through interstate party working teams or congressional action groups.

Third, an institute could develop political newsletters and publications directed specifically to the information needs of parties and citizen activists. It could encourage improved media coverage of politics through an affiliated Political News Service. An institute could also set up political data bank and information retrieval services, the continued non-availability of which remains one of the most scandalous examples of the Model-T approach to politics in the modern era of large political parties and hundred-billion-dollar government. In general, an Institute of Politics could direct public attention to the role of the media, the parties and educational and private institutions in educating Americans for informed citizen participation.

With a proper and adequate investment in these areas, the citizen politicians who shook the party system in 1972 can become effective practitioners of the healing and restorative art of politics. Once they have discovered and learned to use the power of their ideas and numbers they can literally work political miracles in making the parties and government truly responsive to the people. This is the as yet unfulfilled challenge and promise of the new citizen politics.

Index

ability to govern: criteria for nomination, appointment, 74–9, 208–19; failure to develop, 7–8, 183–207, 354; new party capabilities for, 112–13, 140–1, 148–51, 178–81, 207–16, 366–7; *see also* parties, governmental purpose of

Abzug, Bella S., 152

accountability: failure to develop, 6–7, 9, 63–7, 69–70, 96–7, 100–2, 127–8, 130–1, 138, 246–8, 307–8, 355–6, 366; new conception of, 140–1, 355, 373–4; party and other programs to promote, 46–7, 66, 74, 81, 84–6, 114–15, 141–3, 181–2, 278, 313, 356–7, 369–70, 373–4

Adamany, David, 363 and n., 364 and n.

Agnew, Spiro T., 238, 327, 331

Agranoff, Robert, 299 and n.

Agree, George, 136, 315–17

Ailes, Roger E., 280

Albert, Carl, 14, 62, 125, 135, 146

Alder, Thomas P., 16

Alexander, Herbert E., 61 n., 360 and n., 362 n.

Alexander, Holmes, 77 and n., 183

Allison, James N., Jr., 287

Alsop, Joseph, 28 and n.

alternative media, growth of, 265–6

American Association of Political Consultants, 262 n., 280–1, 292 and n., 294, 302, 313

American Broadcasting Company, 90, 253, 254

American Conservative Union, 220, 222, 223, 224

American Enterprise Institute for Public Policy Research, 206, 222

American Independent Party, 3, 50; and emerging Republican majority, 326; third-party prospects, 332–4, 340–2, 348–9; use of political consultants, 300; *see also* Wallace, George C.

American Medical Association Political Action Committee, 286, 370

American Political Science Association, 10 and n., 85, 140 n., 201, 203

American Telephone and Telegraph Company, 56, 107, 272

Americans for Democratic Action, 13, 26, 227, 228, 272

Andrews, John, 163

Armstrong, Anne L., 247

Ashbrook, John M., 222

Aspin, Leslie, 134

Associated Press, 256, 258

Auerbach, Carl, 67–8

Bagdikian, Ben H., 269 and n., 270 n.

Bailey, Deardourff & Bowen, 280, 289, 290–1, 293

Bailey, John M., 14

Barabba, Vincent, 289 n.

Barkan, Alexander E., 17, 296

Bass, Doris, 110

Bayh, Birch, 21, 335

Becker, John F., 281

Beer, Samuel H., 13, 108, 344 and n.

Belliveau, Severin, 164

Beichman, Arnold, 348

Bernstein, Marver H., 193–4, 194 n., 199 and n., 202 n.

Bickel, Alexander M., 51 and n.

Bipartisan Congressional Clearing House, 237, 238

blacks: cable television impact, 271; party role and programs for, 23, 26, 30, 32, 35, 36, 41, 50, 96, 98, 108, 111, 116–17, 167,

blacks (*continued*)
316–20, 322, 324, 325–31;
potential independent political
role, 3, 43, 108, 152, 154, 167,
172–3, 236–7, 301, 319–20,
323, 332, 343, 359; use of
political consultants in national
organizations, 300–1
Bliss, Ray C., 33, 64, 92–3, 95 *n.*,
98, 105, 106, 145, 162–5
passim
Bode, Kenneth A., 17, 20 *n.*, 41
Bond, Julian, 172–3
Boston *Globe*, 257
Brinkley, David, 251
Broder, David S., 57 and *n.*, 128–9,
129 *n.*, 191 and *n.*, 217 and *n.*,
354 and *n.*
Brookings Institution, 60, 70 *n.*,
193 and *n.*, 194 *n.*, 199, 202,
203, 206
Brown, Sam, 227–8, 228 *n.*, 230
and *n.*
Bruno, Jerry, 293
Brzezinski, Zbigniew, 347
Buchanan, Patrick J., 206
Buckley, James L., 223, 300
Buckley, William F., Jr., 223
Burch, Dean, 272
Burnham, Walter Dean, 314 and *n.*,
342–3, 342 *n.*
Burns, Arthur, 203
Burns, James MacGregor, 10 *n.*,
130 and *n.*
Butler, Paul, 101, 103, 107
Butz, Earl L., 196

Cabinet, 190, 192, 194, 196, 199,
205, 209, 213, 214
cable television: citizen and party
role in development of, 245,
272–3, 278–9; political consultants as brokers of, 307;
potential political impact, 48,
155, 171, 173, 180, 235, 245,
266–73, 278–9, 301, 312, 350,
357, 358
Cahill, William T., 39
Cahn, Jean C., 39
Califano, Joseph A., Jr., 93, 207
and *n.*
CALPLAN, 287–8

campaign finance: *see* political
finance
Campaign Systems, 290
candidates, upgrading recruit-
ment of, 74–9, 87, 129, 148–9,
169, 177, 187, 208–9, 211, 244–
5, 310, 350, 366, 379–80
Canham, Erwin D., 34 and *n.*
Carswell, G. Harrold, 196, 301
Caso, Ralph G., 171–2, 172 *n.*
Center for Political Reform, 26, 36
and *n.*, 41, 227
Center for Political Research: *see*
Government Research Service
Center for the Study of Responsive Law, 39
Chafee, John H., 163
Chavez, Gus, 67
Childs, Richard S., 158 and *n.*, 159
and *n.*
Chisholm, Shirley, 320
Christian Science Monitor, 256,
259
citizen activists, upgrading role and
capabilities of, 176–7, 239–
45, 350–2, 373, 380–1; *see also*
citizen participation, party and
other programs to promote
citizen groups: as party rival, 344–
5; developing the potential of,
239–45; importance to citizen
parties, 11–12, 219–20, 235–6,
239, 349–52; in Democratic
party coalition, 323; limited
success of, 217–18, 220–9; partisan imbalance in, 236–9, 323,
330–1; party modernization role,
3–5, 11, 26, 44, 49, 86–90, 129,
145, 171, 176–7, 200–1, 235–6,
239, 244–5, 312–13, 358–9, 370–
1, 377–9, 380–1, 388–9, 389–90;
reasons for ineffectiveness, 229–
36, 239, 355; role in cable television development, 272–3, 278–
9; use of political consultants,
284, 300–2, 312–13
citizen participation: goal, role in
party modernization, 3–12
passim, 22, 25–6, 31, 37, 39, 42–
3, 51–2, 94, 108–10, 154–62,
185–6, 191–2, 218–20, 232–4,
284, 349–52, 355, 357, 370, 373–

citizen participation (*continued*)
4; party and other programs to
promote, 22, 42–9, 74, 79–80,
83–91, 111, 112–14, 118–19,
141–2, 143–5, 151–2, 166–7, 173,
176–9, 181–2, 212–15, 239–45,
269, 273–9, 301–2, 309–10, 312–
13, 349–52, 366, 369–70, 373–4

citizen parties, goal, prospects in
party modernization, 5–12, 14,
42–3, 51–2, 74–5, 94, 110, 121–
3, 140, 155–7, 175, 185–6, 207–
8, 219–20, 239, 246–8, 273, 284,
309, 349–52, 373–4

Citizens' Research Foundation, 40–
1, 360, 361

Civic Service Incorporated, 286,
305

civil service, 187–92, 203–5, 216;
see also personnel development

Clay, Lucius D., 234

Clergy and Laity Concerned, 221

Columbia Broadcasting System,
251, 253, 254

Columbia Journalism Review, 263
and *n.*, 266–7

Commission on Party Structure and
Delegate Selection: *see*
McGovern-Fraser Commission

Committee on Convention Reforms,
report of, 33 and *n.*, 61–2

Committee for the Democratic
Process, 136, 294, 315

Committee on Political Education,
AFL-CIO, 28, 103, 118, 154,
296–8, 303, 370

Common Cause, 34, 40, 120, 220
and *n.*, 227, 229–30, 230 *n.*, 231,
233, 236, 245, 323

communications technology, use in
politics, 55–6, 81, 104, 105, 114,
133, 155, 173, 178, 180, 182,
213, 235, 241, 262, 282, 301,
350, 358

computers, use in politics, 41, 95–6,
97, 102, 134, 152, 154, 169,
173, 180, 235, 245, 262, 269, 271,
288–301 *passim*, 302–6, 312–13,
385, 363

Congress, 6, 73, 85, 120–52 *passim*,
154, 185, 188, 190, 192, 197,
202–3, 211, 212, 237, 270, 295,
301, 309, 322, 340, 356, 357;
see also congressional parties

Congress, members of, 31, 85, 87,
105, 120–52 *passim*, 156, 188,
202, 203, 208–9, 210, 228, 250,
278, 311, 340, 357; increasing
capabilities for party modernization, 148–52, 381–2

Congressional Action Fund, 120,
237, 244

congressional action groups, 45,
151–2

Congressional Black Caucus, 108,
152, 236–7, 301, 320, 323

congressional district party offices,
118, 143

congressional parties: closed nature
of, 120–39, 185; developments in,
132–9; party modernization
role, 45–6, 121–3; upgrading
capabilities of, 45, 80, 139–52,
381–2

Congressional Quarterly, 47, 90 *n.*,
94 *n.*, 123, 145, 259 and *n.*

Congressional Record, 47, 90, 123,
133, 147, 278

congressional and state party
caucuses, developing potential of,
45–6, 138–9, 140, 141–3, 144,
178, 381–2, 386–7

congressional and state party staffing, importance and role of, 7,
104, 125, 126–7, 134–5, 149–51,
168, 178, 211–12, 299

conservative movement: apparatus
and strengths, 221–4; strategy
and role for future Republican
majority, 32–3, 324–32, 349

Conservative party (N.Y.), 40, 73,
222–3, 300

Conway, Jack T., 230, 236

cooperative political action, unrealized potential for and steps
to promote, 117–18, 163–70,
172–5, 179–82, 230–1, 234, 239–
44, 367; *see also* party teams

COPE: *see* Committee on Political
Education

Costikyan, Edward N., 70

Cotton, Stephen, 359 and *n.*

Council of Republican Organizations, 220, 224

county party organizations, role and potential for, 6, 79, 103, 170–2, 175, 177, 178, 179, 191, 205, 350

Cowan, Geoffrey, 15, 16, 42

Crangle, Joseph F., Jr., 16, 63, 93

Crater, Flora, 109–10

Criswell, John, 64

Cronkite, Walter, 251

Curtis, Thomas B., 151 *n.*, 265

Daley, Richard J., 64

data banks: party and citizen guidelines on, 244–5, 309–10; use in politics, 137, 240–1, 244–5, 274, 293, 297–8, 304, 357

Datamatics, 290, 291

David, Paul T., 52 *n.*, 60 and *n.*, 69 and *n.*, 70 and *n.*, 71–2, 72 *n.*

David Hackett Associates, 300–1

Davis, Will D., 21

Dean, John, 98

Decision Making Information, 285, 286, 289 and *n.*, 290, 291, 293

Decision Technology, Inc., 299, 305

delegate selection procedures: Democratic party reform and evaluation, 14–22, 24, 27–8, 41, 56, 60–1, 71, 80, 170, 236–7, 323–4; party information service proposed, 87–8; Republican party consideration and prospects, 29–32, 35–7, 46; *see also* McGovern-Fraser Commission; Republican party reform movement

Delegates and Organizations Committee: *see* Republican party reform movement

Democratic Advisory Council, 99, 199, 200, 206

Democratic Caucus, House of Representatives, 135, 139, 141–3, 144

Democratic Congressional Campaign Committee, 136–9 *passim*, 293

Democratic Governors Association (caucus), 46, 163, 165, 205

Democratic National Chairman, 25, 26, 105; *see also* national chairmen

Democratic National Committee, 9 *n.*, 40, 73; functions and performance, 62, 92–110 *passim*, 162–3, 164, 165, 247, 293–300 *passim*, 303; role in Democratic party reform movement, 20, 22, 24, 25, 26, 29, 66, 226, 237, 350; upgrading role and capabilities, 43–5, 47, 79–82, 83, 84–6, 110–19, 181–2, 212–16, 243–4, 277–9, 309–10, 350

Democratic National Convention, 56, 58–9, 94, 99; closed nature of, 63–4; of 1968, 14, 16, 17, 28, 58, 60, 62, 64, 68, 80, 252; of 1972, 13, 14, 16, 20, 21, 22, 24, 28, 29, 41, 43, 44, 45, 50, 58, 62, 66–7, 95, 108, 236, 238, 334; role in Democratic party reform movement, 14, 20–1, 21 *n.*, 22, 24, 29, 80, 358; steps to modernize, 43–7, 66, 67–8, 74–91, 108, 111, 367

Democratic National Finance Committee, 93, 106–7

Democratic party: organized labor role in, 25–6, 28, 56, 103, 118, 154, 284, 295–8, 303, 315–18, 348–9, 370; prospects for renewed New Deal coalition, 238–9, 315–24, 331, 334, 351; support from citizen groups, 236–9; use of political consultants, 137–8, 168–9, 292–300, 306–8

Democratic party reform movement: effect on third-party prospects, 334, 341; contrasts with Republican reform movement, 30–3, 35–7, 41–3, 46, 66–7, 129, 236–9, 299–300, 351; evaluation, 8, 21–9, 36–7, 41–3, 44, 56, 60–1, 71, 80, 108, 129, 170, 299–300, 323–4, 351, 377; origins, 14–21; public interest movement role in, 37–42; *see also* McGovern-Fraser Commission; O'Hara Commission

Democratic Policy Council, 99, 100, 109, 112

Democratic Senatorial Campaign Committee, 136–7

Democratic Study Group, 122, 124,

Democratic Study Group
(*continued*)
   125, 126, 130–1, 136–9 *passim*,
   142, 148, 152, 168, 294, 295
Dent, Harry S., 197
DeVries, Walter, 252 *n.*, 305
Dewey, Thomas E., 54, 221, 324–5
Diamond, Edwin, 252 *n.*, 255
Dirksen, Everett M., 64, 132
DO Committee: *see* Republican
   party reform movement
Dobrovir, William A., 41, 154
Dodds, William, 297
Dole, Robert J., 98, 100, 101, 105,
   163, 196, 247
Donovan, William, 210 and *n.*
Draper, Theodore, 348
Drinan, Robert F., 301, 302
Drucker, Peter F., 183
Drummond, Roscoe, 345
Duscha, Julius, 258 and *n.*
Dutton, Frederick G., 332 and *n.*,
   339 and *n.*, 341 and *n.*, 351 *n.*

Edelman, Marion Wright, 39
Efron, Edith, 264 and *n.*
Eisenhower, Dwight D., 33, 54,
   92, 189, 194, 217, 221, 349
Electoral College, 59, 73, 77, 154,
   334, 340, 341
Etzioni, Amitai, 271 and *n.*
Evans, M. Stanton, 223–4
Everett, John R., 346–7, 347 *n.*

Fairlie, Henry, 346 and *n.*
Federal Communications Commis-
   sion, 263–5 *passim*, 267, 271–3
   passim, 278, 279
Fenn, Dan H., Jr., 194 and *n.*, 199
Fenton, John H., 160 *n.*, 161–2,
   162 *n.*, 176 *n.*
Field, Mervin D., 335
Finch, Robert, 200
Fingerhut, Vic, 368 and *n.*
Flanigan, Peter, 196
Flemming, Harry S., 195
Ford, Gerald R., 64, 100, 139
Ford Foundation, 70 *n.*, 213, 272,
   371
foundations, role in party policy-
   making, 205–6, 213, 274, 312–
   13, 370–1, 383

Fraser, Donald M., 15
Friendly, Fred W., 253 and *n.*

Gaby, Daniel M., 227
Galbraith, John Kenneth, 322–3
   and *n.*
Gardner, John W., 34, 120, 220 *n.*,
   229–30, 230 *n.*, 231, 236
Garth, David, 280, 293
Gechas, Olga, 107
General Counsel, party Office of,
   44, 86, 117, 207, 385
Ginn, Mrs. M. Stanley, 29–30, 36
Glaser, Vera, 108
Goldsmith, Lester, 137
Goldwater, Barry, 3, 33, 55, 57,
   58, 60, 217, 220, 221, 238, 291,
   324, 325, 326, 329, 334, 365
Good, Josephine L., 262 *n.*
Goodell, Charles E., 125
Goodwin, Richard N., 318–19,
   318 *n.*
government, party role in: *see*
   parties, governmental purpose of
Government Research Service, 145
governors, role and potential, 6,
   31, 46, 96, 132, 156, 164–6, 173,
   178, 179–81, 191, 202, 205, 208,
   209, 210, 228, 243, 308, 384–5
Greenfield, Jeff, 293
Gross, Bertram M., 347 and *n.*
Group Research, Inc., 231
Guggenheim, Charles, 280, 294

Haber, William, 23
Hacker, Andrew, 331 and *n.*
Haldeman, Robert, 196
Hall, Leonard W., 33
Halley, James W., 330
Harriman, Averell, 203
Harrington, Michael, 318 and *n.*
Harris, Fred R., 17, 95, 99, 293
Harris, Louis, 185, 255, 320, 328,
   337–9 *passim*, 337 *n.*, 348
Harris, Patricia Roberts, 17
Harsch, Joseph C., 251 and *n.*
Hart, Peter, 293
Hatcher, Richard G., 108
Hatfield, Mark O., 152, 332
Hays, F. Bradford, 97

Heard, Alexander, 105 *n.*, 337 *n.*, 362 *n.*, 364 and *n.*, 367–8, 368 *n.*
Hearnes, Warren E., 15, 22
Hemenway, Russell, 294–5
Hill, Herbert, 319
Hohenberg, John, 260 and *n.*
Holton, Linwood, 167, 320
Houtchens, Delton, 22
Huckshorn, Robert J., 134 *n.*, 169 and *n.*
Hughes, Harold E., 13–17 *passim*, 27, 229
Hughes Commission, 15–17, 42, 43
Humphrey, Hubert H., 14, 58, 104, 109, 217, 293, 326, 335, 362

Ickes, Harold, Jr., 15
Independents, 49, 57, 196, 231, 236, 245, 300, 328, 334; *see also* citizen participation
Indians, 26, 343, 371
interim national conventions, mandate and role in party modernization, 44, 45, 82, 214, 350, 367
International Association of Machinists, 138, 297
International Telephone & Telegraph Corporation, 67
interstate party organization, team concept of: *see* party teams
Iovino, Peter, 303

Jackson, Henry M., 323
Jackson, Jesse, 319–20
Javits, Jacob K., 36
Jennings, William, 128
Jensen, Richard, 283 *n.*
John, DeWitt, 259
Johnson, C. Montgomery, 35
Johnson, Haynes, 217 and *n.*, 354 and *n.*, 361 *n.*
Johnson, Lyndon Baines, 69, 92, 103, 104, 107, 125, 130 *n.*, 150, 191, 195, 217, 317, 320, 325, 326
Johnson, Nicholas, 16, 263
Johnson, William, 15
Joint Center for Political Studies, 300–1, 371
Jones, Ruth, 293
Jordan, Vernon, 317–18, 318 *n.*
Joseph, Geraldine M., 109

Kanter, Julian, 313

Kaufman, Arnold, 318
Kaufman, Herbert, 187 *n.*, 189
Keniston, Kenneth, 335–6 and *n.*
Kennedy, David M., 196
Kennedy, Edward M., 14, 15
Kennedy, John F., 55, 56, 68, 103, 104, 107, 144, 150, 193, 194 and *n.*, 198, 199, 201, 221, 332
Kennedy, Robert F., 3, 194, 228, 293, 321, 332, 362
Key, V. O., Jr., 160 and *n.*, 176 *n.*, 247 *n.*, 257 and *n.*, 314 *n.*
King, Martin Luther, Jr., 252
Kissinger, Henry A., 65
Klein, Alexander, 233–4, 234 *n.*
Klein, Herbert G., 67
Kleindienst, Richard G., 195
Knowland, William F., 33 and *n.*
Knowles, Robert P., 64
Kraft, John F., 294

labor: *see* organized labor
Laird, Melvin R., 65, 139, 206
Lane, Robert E., 343 and *n.*
Lankler, Alexander M., 335
Larson, Reed, 297
law, role in party modernization, 15–17, 109, 113, 241, 359, 372–3, 379, 385; *see also* public interest movement
Lawrence, William H., 253
Lazarus, Simon, 16, 21 *n.*, 38 *n.*, 80 *n.*
Leadership Conference on Civil Rights, 221, 237
League of Women Voters, 9, 159, 176, 371
Lewis, Flora, 36 and *n.*
liberal Democratic citizen groups, 226–9
Liberal party (N.Y.), 73
Lindsay, John V., 293, 323, 348
Lipscomb, Glenard P., 65
Lipset, Seymour Martin, 333–4, 334 *n.*, 346 and *n.*
Little McGovern-Fraser Commissions: *see* state reform commissions, Democratic party
local party organizations: *see* county party organizations; state parties
Lodge, Henry Cabot, 55

Long, Russell, 340
Lowenstein, Allard K., 238
Lowi, Theodore J., 190 and *n*.
Lubell, Samuel, 252 and *n*., 314
    and *n*., 320 and *n*., 324, 327–8,
    328 *n*., 332 and *n*., 335 and *n*.

Macy, John W., Jr., 195
Madeson, Marvin L., 226
Maguire, Richard, 97
Mailer, Norman, 51
Majority and Minority Leaders,
    House of Representatives, Senate,
    84, 123, 136, 146, 340
Malek, Fred, 198
Mann, Dean E., 193 and *n*., 199
    and *n*.
Mansfield, Mike, 296
Market Opinion Research Corpora-
    tion, 171, 289, 290–1, 293
Martin, Louis, 98
Martin, Winn, 292, 306
Marttila, John, 302
Matthews, Donald R., 70 *n*.
Mayo, Robert, 196
McCarthy, Eugene J., 3, 14–17
    passim, 60, 226, 228, 321, 332,
    338, 362
McCloskey, Paul N., Jr., 33–4, 225
McGinniss, Joe, 280
McGovern, George S., 3, 16–17,
    19, 28, 152, 228, 323
McGovern-Fraser Commission:
    evaluation, 17, 21–9, 36–7, 41–
    2, 46, 56, 60–1, 71, 80, 170, 226,
    236–9, 299–300, 323–4, 356,
    357–8, 374; guidelines and inter-
    pretation, 18–21, 41; origins,
    14–17; *see also* Democratic party
    reform movement
Meany, George, 28, 320–1
media: party and other efforts to
    upgrade capabilities and per-
    formance of, 85, 90–1, 99, 118–
    19, 147, 263–6, 273–9, 385–6;
    role in reporting politics, 26–7,
    56, 57–8, 61–2, 67–8, 102, 343,
    355, 357, 358–9, 361, 370
Megastates of America, The, 153
    n., 172 and *n*., 176 *n*.
Mexican Americans, 26, 50, 67, 96,
    111, 198, 221, 301, 320, 343

Miller, Clem, 126
Miller, J. Irwin, 302
Miller, William E., 64, 164, 165
Milliken, William G., 320
Mills, Wilbur D., 154, 323
minority groups: increasing partic-
    ipation in parties, 386; *see also*
    blacks; Indians; Mexican Ameri-
    cans; older Americans; women;
    youth
minority party staffing in Congress:
    see congressional and state party
    staffing
Miracode, 106, 216, 262
Mission 70's, 33, 106, 163, 244
Mitchell, John N., 196
Mixner, David, 26, 227
Moe, Richard, 164
Morning News, The, 257,
Morton, Rogers C. B., 29, 33, 98,
    163, 285, 287
Mott, Stewart, 41
Movement for a New Congress,
    237, 238, 244–5
Moyle, Jon, 164
multiparty system: opportunities
    for political consultants in, 306–
    7; prospects for, 332–42
Murphy, George L., 288
Murphy, Richard J., 68
Muskie, Edmund S., 58, 228, 335

Nader, Ralph, 39–40, 42, 48, 120,
    129, 154, 232, 236
Napolitan, Joseph, 138, 280, 281,
    282, 293
National Broadcasting Company,
    27, 165, 251, 253, 254
national chairmen: functions and
    performance, 6–7, 96, 100–1,
    105, 108, 110, 112, 114, 162–7,
    234; upgrading capabilities of,
    111, 115–19, 145–6, 174–5, 181–
    2, 214, 215, 386–7
National Committee for an Effec-
    tive Congress, 104, 120, 129,
    136, 232, 237, 294–5, 295 *n*.,
    315, 370
national committees: functions and
    performance, 6–7, 92–110, 137,
    162–7, 234, 250, 259, 306, 307,
    354–5; upgrading role and capa-

national committees (*continued*)
bilities, 43–5, 47–8, 79–83, 84–6,
110–19, 145–8, 181–2, 212–16,
243–4, 277–9, 306, 309–10, 367,
386–7
national convention delegates:
functions and importance, 57,
60–1, 69–70; upgrading role of,
74, 80, 82–4, 86–91, 382–3; *see
also* delegate selection procedures
national conventions: alternatives
to, 71–4; role in party modernization, 22, 111, 358; trends and
evaluation, 6–7, 50–71; upgrading capabilities and performance,
43–7, 66, 67–8, 74–81, 108, 111,
358, 367
National Governors' Conference,
164, 165
national institute of politics, programs and support for, 49, 210–
11, 313, 359–60, 367, 371
National Journal, 27 and n., 94 n.,
145, 204 and n., 231 and n.,
259, 261, 274
National Legislative Conference,
147, 166, 172
National Municipal League, 158,
371
National Republican Senatorial
Campaign Committee, 125, 128,
136
National Women's Political Caucus,
43, 108–9, 154, 236, 320, 323
National Youth Caucus, 236, 238
Nelson, Robert W., 17
Neustadt, Richard E., 192 and n.
New American Movement, 220
New Deal Democratic coalition:
conservative analysis of breakdown, 325–9 *passim;* prospects
for renewed Democratic coalition, 315–24, 331, 334; *see also*
Democratic party reform movement
New Democratic Coalition, 23 and
n., 170, 220, 226–7, 228, 233,
318–19
New Party, role and prospects as
third party, 36, 42, 50, 332–3,
334–5; *see also* third parties
new politics Democrats, role in

Democratic party coalition, 207,
315–16, 317, 318–19, 323, 341
New Republic, The, 360
New York Times, The, 247, 255–9
passim, 262, 274
Nimmo, Dan, 281 *n.,* 286
Niven, Paul, 184
Nixon, Richard M., 33, 34, 55, 64,
65, 66, 69, 99, 100, 103, 106,
150, 154, 183, 192, 195–200 *passim,* 204, 206, 207, 216, 217, 222,
228, 238, 305, 317, 319, 321, 326,
327, 329, 331, 335, 340–1, 348

O'Brien, James Cuff, 296, 297
O'Brien, Lawrence F., 17, 28, 69,
93, 96, 98, 99, 104, 105, 107,
108, 234, 282, 293, 321
O'Donnell, Gladys, 92–3
Office of Strategic Services, 210
O'Hara, James G., 17, 66 *n.*
O'Hara Commission: origins, 14–
17; work and evaluation, 17–18,
21–9, 41, 47, 56, 61, 66 and *n.,*
67–8, 71, 80, 129, 226, 323–4,
357–8; *see also* Democratic party
reform movement
older Americans, potential political
role of, 35, 96, 152, 343–4
open budget process, 112, 114–15,
369–70
open information policy and programs, role in promoting accountability, 24, 46–7, 66, 84, 85,
114–15, 141–3, 147, 356, 370
open party sessions, role in promoting accountability and participation, 24, 25, 47–8, 84–5, 112–15,
141–2, 149, 208–9, 309, 356,
369–70
opposition party: governmental
role of, 126–7, 130, 150, 151,
206–7, 211–12, 214, 215, 340;
staffing in Congress for, 134–5,
149–51, 211–12
organized labor: potential role in
Republican party, 46, 326–7;
role in Democratic party coalition, 28, 56, 103, 118, 154, 227,
284, 295–8, 303, 315–18, 348–9,
370; role in Democratic party
reform movement, 25–6, 28

Ostrogorski, Moisei, 250–1, 251 *n.*, 344 *n.*
O'Toole, Dennis T., 26
Otten, Alan L., 27 and *n.*, 298 and *n.*

Parkinson, Gaylord, 163, 317
Parma, Leon, 67 *n.*
participation: *see* citizen participation
Participation Systems, Inc., 299, 301, 305
parties: alternative futures for, 11–12, 235–6, 306–7, 314–52; closed nature of, 6–7, 36, 61–8, 69–71, 95–108, 120–39, 156–67, 174–5, 185, 234–5, 246–51, 283–4, 306–8, 365–6; competitive forms of political organization, 306–7, 309, 344–5; decline of, prospects for, 342–5; governmental purpose of, failure to develop and upgrading capabilities for, 7–8, 75–9, 112–13, 148–51, 178–216, 354; *see also* citizen parties; party reform movement
partisanship: constructive role for, 8–9, 126–7, 140, 150–1, 184, 187–92, 236; failure to develop, 130, 234–5, 368
party activists, role in party modernization, 43–9, 176–9, 387–8
party development programs, promoting and upgrading the finance of, 181–2, 368–71; *see also* Action Guide; recommendations
party enforcement and appeals procedures, role in promoting accountability, 85–6, 114–15, 143, 313, 356–7
party guest house and meeting facilities, 143, 144–5
party leadership: closed nature of, 6–7, 68–9, 70–1, 100–1, 125–32, 308; upgrading role and resources for, 115–19, 145–8, 174–5, 177, 179–81, 215, 358; *see also* personnel development
party modernization: *see* citizen parties; party reform movement
party policymaking: failure to develop, 6, 99–100, 138–9, 205–7; role of universities, foundations, think tanks, 205–7, 213, 274, 298–9, 371; upgrading party capabilities for, 112–14, 143–8, 151, 178, 211–15, 350, 389–90
party reform movement: *see* Democratic party reform movement; Republican party reform movement; public interest movement; citizen parties
party rules and procedures, role in promoting accountability, 66, 81, 84–6, 114–15, 141–2, 356–7
party teams, unrealized potential for, 8, 9, 117–18, 142, 147–8, 163–70, 172–5, 178, 179–82, 212–15, 350, 358, 367, 373–4; *see also* congressional action groups; cooperative political action; representative party commissions
patronage: *see* personnel development
Peabody, Endicott, 76 *n.*
Peirce, Neal R., 90 *n.*, 153 and *n.*, 172 and *n.*, 176 *n.*, 341
Pennoyer, Robert M., 34
people press, 85, 265–6
People's Party: *see* New Party
Peretz, Martin, 334
Perry, James M., 281 *n.*, 295 and *n.*
personnel development: citizen programs for, 242–3; failure to develop party role in, 100, 112, 134–5, 192–208, 200–1, 210; upgrading party capabilities for, 83–4, 88–9, 104, 113, 116, 117, 142, 144, 148–50, 178, 179–80, 208–16, 243–4, 351
Peterson, Arthur, 64
Peterson, Donald, 68
Peterson, Elly M., 300
Pfautch, Roy, 286, 305
Phillips, Kevin P., 33, 197 and *n.*, 222, 262 *n.*, 325–32, 340
Pincus, Walter, 360–1, 361 *n.*
Plunkitt, George Washington, 13 and *n.*, 183 and *n.*, 372–3, 373 *n.*
Podhoretz, Norman, 348
political coalitions: *see* parties, alternative futures for

political consultants: as rival of party organization, 306–8, 309, 344–5; Democratic party use of, 62, 102–3, 137–8, 292–300, 303, 306–8; independent citizen group use of, 241–2, 300–2; Republican party use of, 102–3, 137, 168–9, 284–9, 304–5, 306–8, 324; role in parties, 6, 62, 102–3, 137–8, 168–9, 171, 269, 280–313, 344, 345; upgrading role of, 313–15, 382

political consulting conglomerates, growth and political role of, 289–91, 306–8, 309, 310, 344

political finance: citizen groups lack of, 231–2; closed nature of, 6, 96–7, 99, 125–6, 127–9, 138, 234, 356, 365–6; Democratic party approach to, 103–4, 106–7, 136–8, 294–7, 354–5, 366; need for major new investment, 360–72; new techniques, approaches, 6, 9, 40, 41, 45, 46, 104, 112, 115, 179, 180–2, 215–16, 239, 240, 241–2, 244, 310, 340, 358, 369–71, 383–4; Republican party approach to, 102–3, 104, 105–6, 125–6, 135–8, 294, 366

political information: limited nature of, 26–7, 57–8, 97–8, 99, 101–2, 123–4, 127–8, 166–7, 231, 246–66, 273, 355, 356, 357, 359, 361; party and citizen programs to improve, 24, 47, 48–9, 67–8, 84–6, 89–91, 114–15, 117, 118–19, 141–3, 147, 177, 179, 180, 181–2, 216, 239–42, 263–6, 273–9, 311, 312–13, 357, 360, 366, 370, 371, 378–9, 389; potential cable television impact, 266–73; retrieval of, 106, 182, 216, 261–2, 274, 357, 370; *see also* cable television; political newsletters

political newsletters, need and role for, 45, 48–9, 97, 119, 177, 222, 241, 258, 262 and *n.*, 274–6, 357, 361

political reporting: *see* media; political information

political technology: party guidelines for, 309–10; promoting citizen participation in use of, 312–13; *see also* political consultants; polls; data banks; computers

politics: impact of youth on, 336–9; need for advanced training in, 201–3, 210–12, 242–3; need for strategy in, 354–74; rediscovery and redefinition of, 4–5, 12, 183–5, 371–4; real costs of, 360–7; upgrading the finance of, 367–71; *see also* citizen parties; computers

politics without parties, prospects for, 342–5, 351

polls: party guidelines for, 309–10; promoting citizen participation in use of, 312–13; use in politics, 56, 58, 59, 87, 105, 137, 152, 275–6, 288, 291, 297–8, 300, 302, 308, 363

Pomper, Gerald M., 10 *n.*, 59 and *n.*, 72 and *n.*

Potomac Associates, 302

Potter, Philip, 256 and *n.*

Prendergast, William, 65

President, nomination of: alternatives to convention system of, 71–4, 334–5; convention system and misplaced priorities in, 51–61, 68–9, 132, 174; new criteria and priorities for, 46–7, 74–9, 87, 208–9, 350, 379–80

President, Office of, 6, 42, 55, 66, 69, 74–9, 84, 96, 100, 101, 107, 110, 132, 144, 146, 149, 151, 154, 183, 185, 188, 191, 192, 193, 199, 202, 203, 207, 210, 214, 215, 216, 257, 308, 340, 347, 349, 373

Press Intelligence, Inc., 277

Prewitt, Marsha O'Bannon, 264

primaries, 8, 23, 41, 53–4, 56, 59–60, 71–2, 87, 158, 170

Pryor, David, 152

Public Affairs Analysts, 282

Public Broadcasting Service, 90, 211

Public Citizen, Inc., 232, 236

public interest movement: importance to parties and party modernization, 4, 38–43, 44, 86, 109, 117, 129, 154, 235–6, 241, 345, 359, 373; prospects for, 41–3, 185, 235–6, 345; role in Democratic party reform movement, 15–17, 23–4, 37, 43; upgrading media performance, 277–8
Putzell, Edwin J., Jr., 86 n.

Quayle, Oliver, III, 137, 294

Raab, Earl, 333–4, 334 n., 346 and n.
race issue, 316, 318, 324, 330
Radio-T.V. Reports, 277
Raskin, Marcus, 36, 42, 333, 335
Reagan, Ronald, 290, 365
Reasoner, Harry, 251
recommendations, approach of, 5, 10–12, 373–4; text of, 42–9, 74–91, 110–19, 139–52, 175–82, 207–16, 239–45, 273–9, 308–13; see also Action Guide
redistricting, 97, 117, 136, 153, 154, 179, 287, 300, 363–4, 373
Reese, Matthew, 138, 282, 294, 298
regional party capabilities, steps to promote, 17, 46, 79, 83, 116, 117–18, 163, 211, 214, 242–3, 276–7, 367
Reich, Charles A., 337 and n., 339
reporting process, role in promoting accountability, 66, 81, 84, 114–15, 141–2, 149, 215–16, 309–11, 356, 366, 369–70
representative party commissions, significance and use in party modernization, 22–5, 43–7, 77–9, 79–80, 80–1, 111, 112–14, 151–2, 181–2, 208, 212–15, 243–4, 309–10, 350–1, 373–4
Republican Citizens Committee, 220, 224, 229
Republican Conference, House of Representatives, 126, 127, 138, 139, 141–3
Republican Congressional Boosters Club, 135–6, 137

Republican Congressional Campaign Committee, 106, 125–6, 135–9 passim, 291
Republican Coordinating Committee, 64–5, 99, 100, 112, 200, 206
Republican Governors Association, 46, 64, 100, 163, 164–5, 164 n., 205
Republican moderate citizen groups, 32, 224–6
Republican National Chairman, 33, 105, 108, 164–6 passim, 234; see also national chairmen
Republican National Committee: functions and performance, 9 n., 40, 65, 92–110 passim, 162–3, 164–6, 197–8, 220 and n., 222, 225, 262, 284–91, 304–5; role in Republican party reform, 29, 30 and n., 31, 33 and n., 46; upgrading role and capabilities, 43–5, 46, 47, 79–82, 84–6, 110–19, 181–2, 212–16, 243–5, 277–9, 309–10, 350; see also national committees
Republican National Convention: 33, 94, 132, of 1964, 33, 55, 62, 221; of 1968, 29, 33, 60, 62, 64, 66; of 1972, 14, 32, 34, 36, 43, 44, 45, 46, 50, 62, 66–7, 108, 237; steps to modernize, 43–7, 74–91, 111, 367
Republican National Finance Committee, 105, 136
Republican party: majority coalition, prospects for, 32–7, 239, 324–32, 349, 351; support from citizen groups, 236–9, 323, 330–1; use of political consultants, 137, 168–9, 171, 284–94, 306–8; see also Republican party reform movement; conservative movement
Republican party reform movement: Delegates and Organization Committee, 29–37; evaluation and contrast with Democratic party reform movement, 30–2, 35–7, 41–3, 46, 66–7, 71, 129, 236–9, 299–300, 351; program to promote, 46–7

Republican Research Committee, House of Representatives, 126, 138, 148

Reston, James, 196–7, 197 *n.*, 239 and *n.*

Ripon Society, 34–5, 34 *n.*, 164 *n.*, 224–6, 237, 342 *n.*

Ridgeway, James, 42 and *n.*

Roberts, William E., 343

Rockefeller, Nelson A., 55, 65, 156, 165, 282, 290, 332, 362

Romney, George W., 58, 200, 290, 362

Rosenbloom, David Lee, 281 *n.*, 344 and *n.*

Ross, Donald R., 64

Rostow, Eugene V., 268 and *n.*

Roszak, Theodore, 336–7, 336 *n.*

Rothchild, John, 260 and *n.*

Rowe, James H., Jr., 298

Rumsfeld, Donald, 130

Rusher, William A., 221, 223, 324

Russell, Howard E., Jr., 197

Rustin, Bayard, 317

Scammon, Richard M., 318 and *n.*, 324, 327, 331, 335

Schlesinger, Arthur, Jr., 59–60, 60 *n.*

Schlesinger, Stephen, 207 and *n.*

Schrade, Paul, 227

Schwartz, Tony, 293

Schwengel, Fred, 150 *n.*, 164, 362 *n.*

Scott, Hugh, 196

Scranton, William W., 55, 57, 58

Scribner, Fred G., 31

Segal, Eli J., 15, 17, 21 *n.*, 80 *n.*

Segal, Phyllis N., 109 and *n.*

Seidman, Harold, 191–2, 192 *n.*

Shapiro, Samuel H., 14

Sherwood, Jack, 64

Shields, Mark, 293

Shirer, William L., 348

Shriver, R. Sargent, 228, 234

Shultz, George P., 196

Sloan Commission on Cable Communications, 266 *n.*, 272–3

Smith, Dick, 333

Smith, Howard K., 196, 251

Smith, Ralph Lee, 268 and *n.*

Smylie, Robert E., 164

Southern strategy, prospects for, 167, 316–17, 319, 325–32, 340–1

Speaker of House, modernization of, 84, 125, 146

Spencer-Roberts, 282, 286–91 *passim*, 293

Sperling, Godfrey, Jr., 183, 259, 261

Spock, Benjamin, 333

Squier, Robert, 138, 293, 294

Staebler, Neil, 103, 161 *n.*, 162 and *n.*

Stagg, Tom, 100

state parties, potential and programs for modernization, 6–7, 8, 45, 46, 47–8, 79, 83, 87–8, 96, 103, 104–5, 110–19, 143, 147–8, 153–82, 208, 211, 237, 244, 276, 277–8, 307, 308, 350, 351, 354, 367, 369, 373, 379, 384–5, 386–7; *see also* state reform commissions; McGovern-Fraser Commission, guidelines and interpretation

state party chairmen, role and potential of, 105, 160–1, 163–4, 166, 169, 174–5, 176, 178, 179–81, 384–5, 386–7; *see also* national party chairmen, upgrading role and capabilities of

state reform commissions, 176, 177, 178, 179; Democratic party, 17, 22–4, 26, 41, 44, 46, 129, 162–3, 170, 374; Republican party, 35, 46, 129

states, importance of, 153–7

Steinem, Gloria, 109

Stevens, Chandler Harrison, 301 and *n.*

Stewart, John G., 293, 300, 308 *n.*

strategy, role in party modernization, 9–12, 15–17, 43, 74, 229–30, 353–60

Strauss, Robert S., 93, 107, 321

Sundquist, James L., 322 and *n.*

supplemental party lines, use and prospects, 71, 72–4, 87, 307, 334, 340; *see also* third parties

Survey Research Center, University of Michigan, 218 *n.*, 321, 364–5

technocratic authoritarianism, prospects for, 345–9, 351–2
Teeter, Robert, 171
third parties, prospects for, 28, 42, 71, 72–4, 87, 235–6, 319, 321, 323, 332–42, 351–2; *see also* two-party system, defenses of
Tolchin, Martin and Susan, 70 *n.*, 200–1, 201 *n.*
Townes, Clarence L., Jr., 98
Treleaven, Harry W., Jr., 280, 287
two-party system: defenses of, 5–6, 73–4, 339–42, 348–9; prospects for, 5–12, 235–6, 306–7, 320, 324–5, 345, 339–42, 349, 351–2, 372–4; real costs of, 364 and *n.; see also* parties, alternative futures for

United Automobile Workers, 138, 162, 297
United Press International, 253, 256, 258
United Steelworkers of America, 137, 138, 297
universities, party support and policymaking role, 104, 205–6, 213, 274, 298–9, 312–13
Unruh, Jesse M., 168

Valenti, Jack, 92
Valentine, Sherman & Associates, 299
Van Buren, Martin, 54, 249
Vice President: misplaced priorities in nomination of, 68–9, 132; Office of, 146; upgrading, 74–9, 208–9, 350
Vidal, Gore, 42
Vietnam Moratorium, 220–1, 225, 226, 227, 230, 232, 252, 265, 323
Viguerie, Richard, 223, 301
voter registration, programs and techniques for, 23, 38, 40, 154, 177, 293, 297, 298, 371

Wallace, George C., 3, 28, 69, 154, 209, 228, 247, 300, 315, 319, 321, 326, 329, 332, 333–4, 335, 338, 340–1, 348, 349
Wallwork, James H., 35
Warner, William, 64
Warschaw, Mrs. Carmen, 93
Washington *Post,* 27, 255–8 *passim*
Wattenberg, Ben J., 318 and *n.,* 327
Wednesday Group, 122, 125, 126, 127, 237
Wexler, Anne L., 16
White, F. Clifton, 55 and *n.,* 68, 221, 222, 282, 300
White, Theodore H., 51, 58 and *n.*
Wicker, Tom, 321 and *n.,* 332 and *n.,* 368 and *n.*
Wilson, Robert C., 64, 67 *n.,* 135, 265
Wirthlin, Richard B., 285–6, 288
Witcover, Jules, 58 and *n.,* 99 and *n.,* 252 *n.,* 258 and *n.*
Witónski, Peter, 222
women: party role and programs for, 21, 23, 26, 30, 32, 35, 41, 43, 50, 96, 108–10, 116–17, 277, 331, 359, 390; potential independent political role, 108–10, 152, 154, 320, 332, 343, 359, 390
Wyly, Sam, 195

Yankelovich, Daniel, Inc., 337–9, 337 *n.*
Young Americans for Freedom, 221, 222, 224–5
Young Democrats, 99
Young Republican National Federation, 55, 98, 222
youth: Nader efforts to organize, 40; party role and programs for, 20, 21, 23, 26, 30, 31, 32, 35, 41, 50, 96, 98–9, 111, 116–17; political impact of, 320, 323, 331, 332, 335–9, 343, 351 *n.,* 390

JOHN S. SALOMA III was born in New York City. He received a B.S. from M.I.T. in 1956 and an M.A. and Ph.D. in political economy and government from Harvard. He is professor of political science at the University of Massachusetts (Boston), and is with the Kennedy Institute of Politics. Dr. Saloma has been a consultant to several congressional committees and is a member of the Advisory Council on European Affairs of the Department of State. He has participated in political campaigns, as director of research for Senator Edward Brooke in 1966 and as researcher and speechwriter for Governor William Scranton in 1964. He is a founding member and was the first president of the Ripon Society. In 1969 he was selected by the United States Junior Chamber of Commerce as one of America's ten outstanding young men. Dr. Saloma has written a political column for the Boston *Globe* and is the author of *Congress and the New Politics* (1969).

FREDERICK H. SONTAG is a graduate of Phillips Academy and Colby College. He is a public affairs, research and public relations consultant active in business, financial, labor, church and cause-group work. From 1951 to 1955 he was director of public relations for *Business Week* magazine. Mr. Sontag was Special Consultant to the secretaries of Labor and of Health, Education, and Welfare, and he specialized in trade, foreign and domestic economic policy, and communications during his association with former Congressman Thomas B. Curtis of Missouri. He has served in presidential, state and local campaigns of both major political parties. He lives with his wife in Montclair, New Jersey, and Seal Harbor, Maine.